CCRN Study Guide

LATEST All-In-One Adult CCRN Review + 500 Practice Questions with Detailed Answer Explanation for the AACN Adult Critical Care Registered Nurse Certification Exam (Contains 4 Full-Length Practice Tests)

CCRN Literary Press
© 2025-2026
Printed in USA

Disclaimer:

© Copyright 2025 by CCRN Literary Press All rights reserved.

All rights reserved. It is illegal to distribute, reproduce or transmit any part of this book by any means or forms. Every effort has been made by the author and editor to ensure correct information in this book. This book is prepared with extreme care to give the best to its readers. However, the author and editor hereby disclaim any liability to any part for any loss, or damage caused by errors or omission. Recording, photocopying or any other mechanical or electronic transmission of the book without prior permission of the publisher is not permitted, except in the case of critical reviews and certain other non-commercial uses permitted by copyright law.

Printed in the United States of America.

CCRN ® is a registered trademark. They hold no affiliation with this product. We are not affiliated with or endorsed by any official testing organization.

Contents

1 CLINICAL JUDGMENT

1.1 Cardiovascular:
- 1.1.1 Acute Coronary Syndrome:
- 1.1.2 Acute Peripheral Vascular Insufficiency:
- 1.1.3 Acute Pulmonary Edema:
- 1.1.4 Aortic Aneurysm:
- 1.1.5 Aortic Dissection:
- 1.1.6 Aortic Rupture:
- 1.1.7 Cardiac Surgery:
- 1.1.8 Cardiac Tamponade
- 1.1.9 Cardiac Trauma:
- 1.1.10 Cardiac/Vascular Catheterization: 12
- 1.1.11 Cardiogenic Shock:
- 1.1.12 Cardiomyopathies:
- 1.1.13 Dysrhythmias: 15
- 1.1.14 Heart Failure:
- 1.1.15 Hypertensive Crisis:
- 1.1.16 Myocardial Conduction System Abnormalities:
- 1.1.17 Papillary Muscle Rupture
- 1.1.18 Structural Heart Defects Overview:
- 1.1.19 TAVR Overview:

1.2 Respiratory:
- 1.2.1 Acute Pulmonary Embolus
- 1.2.2 ARDS:
- 1.2.3 Acute Respiratory Failure:
- 1.2.4 Acute Respiratory Infection:
- 1.2.5 Aspiration:
- 1.2.6 Chronic Conditions:
- 1.2.7 Mechanical Ventilation Weaning Failure:
- 1.2.8 Pleural Space Abnormalities:
- 1.2.9 Pulmonary Fibrosis:
- 1.2.10 Pulmonary Hypertension:
- 1.2.11 Status Asthmaticus:
- 1.2.12 Thoracic Surgery:
- 1.2.13 Thoracic Trauma:
- 1.2.14 Understanding TRALI: Causes and Impacts

1.3 Endocrine/Hematology/Gastrointestinal/Renal/Integumentary:
- 1.3.1 Endocrine:
- 1.3.2 Hematology And Immunology:
- 1.3.3 Gastrointestinal:
- 1.3.4 Renal And Genitourinary:
- 1.3.5 Integumentary:

1.4 Musculoskeletal/Neurological/Psychosocial:
- 1.4.1 Musculoskeletal:

- 1.4.2 Neurological:
- 1.4.3 Behavioral And Psychosocial:

1.5 Multisystem:
- 1.5.1 Acid-base Imbalance:
- 1.5.2 Bariatric Complications:
- 1.5.3 Comorbidity in Transplant Patients:
- 1.5.4 End-of-life Care:
- 1.5.5 Healthcare-associated Conditions:
- 1.5.6 Hypotension:
- 1.5.7 Life-threatening Maternal/fetal Complications
- 1.5.8 Understanding Multiple Organ Dysfunction Syndrome (MODS):
- 1.5.9 Multisystem Trauma:
- 1.5.10 Pain: Acute, Chronic:
- 1.5.11 Post-intensive Care Syndrome (PICS):
- 1.5.12 Sepsis:
- 1.5.13 Septic Shock:
- 1.5.14 Impact of Sensory Overload on Sleep Disruption:
- 1.5.15 Thermoregulation:
- 1.5.16 Toxic Ingestion/Inhalations:
- 1.5.17 Toxin/drug Exposure (including Allergies)

2 Ethical Practice in Professional Caring:
2.1 Advocacy/Moral Agency:
2.2 Caring Practices:
2.3 Response To Diversity:
2.4 Facilitation Of Learning:
2.5 Collaboration:
2.6 Systems Thinking:
2.7 Clinical Inquiry:

CCRN Practice Test 1
Answers with Explanation for Practice Test 1
CCRN Practice Test 2
Answers with Explanation for Practice Test 2
CCRN Practice Test 3
Answers with Explanation for Practice Test 3
CCRN Practice Test 4
Answers with Explanation for Practice Test 4

Key to Success: Do's to pass the exam with ease:

1. Study Smart:
To easily pass the CCRN exam, it is important to study smart. Instead of trying to memorize every single detail, focus on understanding the key concepts and information that are most likely to be tested on the exam. This will help you retain the information better and be more prepared for the questions that you will encounter. We give you the key concepts that is covered in the exam.

2. Set a Study Schedule:
Create a study schedule that works for you and allows you to dedicate enough time to each section of the exam. Consistency is key in retaining information and mastering the material.

3. Review Content Outline:
Familiarize yourself with the content outline provided by the organization to understand what topics will be covered on the exam. Focus on areas where you may need extra study time.

4. Practice, Practice, Practice: Take Practice Tests
One of the best ways to prepare for the CCRN exam is to take practice tests. This will not only familiarize you with the format of the exam but also help you gauge your level of readiness. Make sure to take multiple practice tests and review the questions you missed to further strengthen your knowledge.

5. Seek Support:
Reach out to peers, mentors, or online communities for support and guidance throughout your study process. Surround yourself with people who understand the challenges of preparing for the CCRN exam and can offer advice or encouragement.

6. Stay Positive:
Believe in yourself and your ability to pass the CCRN exam. Stay positive, focused, and determined to achieve your certification.

Why this book is your key to success in the CCRN Exam:

Stay Ahead with Updated Content:
This study guide is your go-to resource for the most current information and practice questions tailored for the CCRN Exam. With regular updates to match exam standards, you can be confident that you are well-prepared to excel.

Learn from the Best with Expert Guidance:
Written by experts who have conquered the CCRN Exam, this book offers priceless guidance and strategies for achieving success. Benefit from their experience and expertise to approach the exam with assurance.

Understand Deeper with Insightful Explanations:
Enhance your understanding of the material with detailed explanations accompanying each question. By exploring the reasoning behind the answers, you will improve your comprehension and be better equipped to handle challenging questions on exam day.

Get Familiar with Exam Format:
Practice with questions mirroring the actual CCRN Exam structure to build confidence and readiness for test day. Familiarize yourself with the exam format to set yourself up for success.

Sharpen Your Critical Thinking:
Engage with the questions, answers, and explanations in this book to boost your critical thinking skills and ability to analyze and respond effectively. Strengthen your cognitive skills and problem-solving abilities as you prepare for the CCRN Exam.

Study with Confidence in a Clear and Concise Manner:
This CCRN Prep simplifies complex concepts in a straightforward and easy-to-understand style, ensuring clarity without overwhelming you with technical jargon. Dive into the material knowing
 that this resource will help you grasp key concepts and excel on exam day

1 CLINICAL JUDGMENT

Clinical judgment is the process by which nurses come to understand the problems, issues, or concerns of patients; attend to relevant information; and respond in concerned and involved ways. It involves critical thinking, clinical reasoning, and decision-making skills that are essential for effective patient care. In critical care settings, where patients often present with complex and rapidly changing conditions, clinical judgment is crucial for identifying life-threatening situations promptly and accurately.

The process of clinical judgment in nursing begins with the collection of data through observation, assessment, and interaction with the patient. Nurses must then interpret this data to identify potential problems or abnormalities. This requires a deep understanding of pathophysiology, pharmacology, and the specific needs of critically ill patients.

Once potential issues are identified, nurses must prioritize them based on severity and urgency. This step involves weighing the risks and benefits of different interventions and considering the patient's values and preferences. Effective clinical judgment also requires collaboration with other healthcare professionals to ensure comprehensive care.

Finally, clinical judgment involves evaluating the outcomes of interventions to determine their effectiveness and make necessary adjustments. This ongoing process ensures that patient care is continually optimized.

In summary, clinical judgment is a dynamic and iterative process that integrates knowledge, experience, intuition, and evidence-based practice. It is fundamental to providing high-quality care in critical settings and is a key component assessed in the CCRN exam for critical care nurses.

1.1 Cardiovascular:

The cardiovascular system, also known as the circulatory system, is a complex network responsible for the transportation of blood throughout the body. It comprises the heart, blood vessels (arteries, veins, and capillaries), and blood. The primary function of this system is to deliver oxygen and essential nutrients to tissues while removing carbon dioxide and metabolic waste products.

The heart, a muscular organ located in the thoracic cavity, acts as a pump that ensures continuous blood flow through two main circuits: the systemic and pulmonary circuits. The systemic circuit carries oxygenated blood from the left side of the heart to all body tissues, while the pulmonary circuit transports deoxygenated blood from the right side of the heart to the lungs for oxygenation.

Blood vessels play a crucial role in this system. Arteries carry oxygen-rich blood away from the heart, whereas veins return deoxygenated blood to the heart. Capillaries, the smallest blood vessels, facilitate the exchange of gases, nutrients, and waste products between blood and tissues.

Regulation of cardiovascular function involves intricate mechanisms, including neural control via autonomic nervous system inputs and hormonal influences such as adrenaline and angiotensin. These mechanisms ensure adequate perfusion pressure and flow to meet varying metabolic demands.

Understanding cardiovascular physiology is paramount for critical care nurses, as it underpins clinical judgments related to managing conditions like acute coronary syndrome. Mastery of cardiovascular concepts enables nurses to assess hemodynamic status accurately, interpret diagnostic data effectively, and implement evidence-based interventions to optimize patient outcomes in critical care settings.

1.1.1 Acute Coronary Syndrome:

Acute Coronary Syndrome (ACS) is an umbrella term used to describe a range of conditions associated with sudden, reduced blood flow to the heart. It encompasses three major clinical entities: unstable angina, non-ST-segment elevation myocardial infarction (NSTEMI), and ST-segment elevation myocardial infarction (STEMI). ACS is primarily caused by the rupture of an atherosclerotic plaque in a coronary artery, leading to thrombus formation and subsequent myocardial ischemia.

The clinical presentation of ACS can vary, but it typically involves chest pain or discomfort that may radiate to the shoulders, neck, arms, or back. This pain is often described as pressure-like and may be accompanied by symptoms such as dyspnea, diaphoresis, nausea, or syncope. Prompt recognition and differentiation between the types of ACS are crucial for effective management.

Diagnostic evaluation includes electrocardiography (ECG), which helps distinguish between STEMI and NSTEMI/unstable angina. Cardiac biomarkers, such as troponins, are also essential in identifying myocardial injury. Management strategies for ACS involve both pharmacological and interventional approaches. Immediate treatment often includes antiplatelet agents, anticoagulants, beta-blockers, and statins. In cases of STEMI, reperfusion therapy through percutaneous coronary intervention (PCI) or thrombolytics is critical.

Understanding the pathophysiology, clinical manifestations, diagnostic criteria, and treatment protocols for ACS is vital for critical care nurses. Their role in early identification and initiation of appropriate interventions significantly impacts patient outcomes in acute coronary events.

1.1.1.1 NSTEMI:

NSTEMI, or Non-ST-Elevation Myocardial Infarction, is a type of acute coronary syndrome characterized by the partial blockage of a coronary artery, leading to reduced blood flow to the heart muscle. Unlike STEMI (ST-Elevation Myocardial Infarction), NSTEMI does not show ST-segment elevation on an electrocardiogram (ECG). However, it does result in elevated cardiac biomarkers such as troponins, indicating myocardial injury.

In NSTEMI, the obstruction is typically caused by a ruptured atherosclerotic plaque and subsequent thrombus formation. This partial blockage results in ischemia but does not lead to full-thickness myocardial necrosis, as seen in STEMI. Patients may present with symptoms such as chest pain or discomfort, which may radiate to the arm, neck, or jaw, along with dyspnea, diaphoresis, and nausea.

Diagnosis is confirmed through ECG changes that may include ST-segment depression or T-wave inversion, as well as elevated cardiac enzymes. Management of NSTEMI involves antiplatelet therapy (e.g., aspirin and P2Y12 inhibitors), anticoagulation (e.g., heparin), beta-blockers, statins, and potentially coronary angiography with revascularization if indicated by risk stratification.

Risk assessment tools like the TIMI (Thrombolysis In Myocardial Infarction) score help determine the need for invasive strategies. Early intervention can mitigate complications such as heart failure or arrhythmias. Understanding the pathophysiology and management of NSTEMI is crucial for critical care nurses to provide optimal patient care and improve outcomes.

1.1.1.2 STEMI:

ST-Elevation Myocardial Infarction (STEMI) is a severe form of acute coronary syndrome characterized by the complete blockage of a coronary artery, leading to significant myocardial necrosis. This condition is identified by the presence of ST-segment elevation on a 12-lead electrocardiogram (ECG), indicating acute transmural ischemia. STEMI requires immediate medical intervention to restore coronary blood flow and minimize cardiac muscle damage.

Pathophysiologically, STEMI occurs when atherosclerotic plaque within a coronary artery ruptures, triggering platelet aggregation and thrombus formation. This occlusion impedes oxygen delivery to the myocardium, resulting in ischemia and subsequent infarction if not promptly resolved. Clinically, patients may present with chest pain or discomfort, often described as pressure or tightness, radiating to the jaw, neck, back, or arms. Associated symptoms include dyspnea, diaphoresis, nausea, and syncope.

Management of STEMI focuses on rapid reperfusion therapy. Primary percutaneous coronary intervention (PCI) is preferred within 90 minutes of first medical contact. Alternatively, fibrinolytic therapy may be administered if PCI is unavailable within the recommended timeframe. Adjunctive treatments include antiplatelet agents (aspirin and P2Y12 inhibitors), anticoagulants (heparin), beta-blockers, ACE inhibitors, and statins to stabilize the patient and prevent further cardiac events.

Nurses play a crucial role in monitoring vital signs, administering medications, and providing patient education on lifestyle modifications post-STEMI to reduce the risk of recurrence. Understanding the pathophysiology and management of STEMI is essential for effective critical care delivery.

1.1.1.3 Unstable Angina:

Unstable angina is a clinical syndrome that falls under the umbrella of acute coronary syndrome (ACS), characterized by unexpected chest pain or discomfort that typically occurs at rest or with minimal exertion. Unlike stable angina, which follows a predictable pattern and is relieved by rest or nitroglycerin, unstable angina is more unpredictable and severe, often indicating a higher risk of myocardial infarction.

Pathophysiologically, unstable angina is primarily caused by the rupture of an atherosclerotic plaque in a coronary artery, leading to platelet aggregation and thrombus formation. This results in partial occlusion of the coronary artery, reducing blood flow to the myocardium. The key differentiator from myocardial infarction is that in unstable angina, the occlusion does not result in significant myocardial necrosis.

Clinically, patients may present with new-onset angina, angina at rest lasting more than 20 minutes, or an increase in severity or frequency of previously stable angina. The pain may radiate to the neck, jaw, shoulder, or arms and is often accompanied by shortness of breath, diaphoresis, nausea, or dizziness.

Diagnostic evaluation includes electrocardiograms (ECGs), which may show ST-segment depression or T-wave inversion but no definitive ST elevation. Cardiac biomarkers such as troponins remain normal, as there is no myocardial cell death.

Management involves antiplatelet therapy (aspirin and clopidogrel), anticoagulation (heparin), beta-blockers, nitrates for symptom relief, and potentially invasive procedures like angiography if symptoms persist or worsen. Early recognition and intervention are crucial to prevent progression to myocardial infarction.

1.1.2 Acute Peripheral Vascular Insufficiency:

Acute Peripheral Vascular Insufficiency (APVI) is a critical condition characterized by a sudden reduction or cessation of blood flow to the peripheral tissues, commonly affecting the limbs. This condition results from an acute obstruction of the peripheral arteries, which can be caused by embolism, thrombosis, or trauma, leading to compromised perfusion and potential tissue ischemia.

Clinically, APVI presents with the classic six Ps: pain, pallor, pulselessness, paresthesia, paralysis, and poikilothermia. Pain is often severe and sudden in onset. Pallor indicates reduced blood flow, while pulselessness is due to the absence of arterial circulation distal to the obstruction. Paresthesia and paralysis result from nerve ischemia, and poikilothermia reflects the limb's inability to regulate temperature due to impaired circulation.

Immediate recognition and intervention are crucial in APVI to prevent irreversible tissue damage and limb loss. Diagnosis typically involves clinical assessment supported by imaging modalities such as Doppler ultrasound or angiography to identify the location and cause of the obstruction.

Management strategies focus on promptly restoring perfusion. This may involve pharmacological interventions such as anticoagulants or thrombolytics, surgical procedures like embolectomy or bypass grafting, or endovascular techniques such as angioplasty. Post-intervention care includes monitoring for reperfusion injury and managing any underlying conditions contributing to vascular insufficiency.

For nurses preparing for the CCRN exam, understanding the pathophysiology, clinical presentation, diagnostic approaches, and management options for APVI is essential for effective patient care in critical settings.

1.1.2.1 Arterial/Venous Occlusion:

Arterial occlusion refers to the blockage of blood flow in an artery, which can result from a thrombus (blood clot), an embolus (traveling clot), or external compression. This condition leads to acute ischemia, where tissues beyond the occlusion are deprived of oxygen and nutrients. The classic symptoms include the six P's: pain, pallor, pulselessness, paresthesia, paralysis, and poikilothermia (inability to regulate temperature). Immediate intervention is critical to prevent tissue necrosis and potential loss of limb function. Diagnostic tools such as Doppler ultrasound or angiography are often employed to confirm the presence and location of the occlusion.

Venous occlusion, on the other hand, involves the blockage of blood flow in a vein, commonly due to thrombosis. Deep vein thrombosis (DVT) is a typical example where a clot forms in the deep veins of the legs. Symptoms may include swelling, pain, warmth, and redness in the affected limb. Unlike arterial occlusions, venous occlusions do not typically cause immediate ischemia but can lead to complications such as pulmonary embolism if the clot dislodges and travels to the lungs.

Management strategies for both arterial and venous occlusions focus on restoring circulation and preventing further clot formation. For arterial occlusions, treatments may include anticoagulants, thrombolytics, or surgical interventions like thrombectomy. Venous occlusions are generally managed with anticoagulation therapy to prevent clot propagation and reduce the risk of embolization. Understanding these conditions is crucial for critical care nurses to provide timely and effective patient care.

1.1.2.2 Carotid Artery Stenosis:

Carotid artery stenosis refers to the narrowing of the carotid arteries, which are major blood vessels in the neck that supply blood to the brain, neck, and face. This condition is primarily caused by atherosclerosis, where plaque—a mixture of fat, cholesterol, and other substances—builds up on the artery walls. As the plaque accumulates, it reduces the lumen of the artery, restricting blood flow to critical areas of the brain.

Clinically, carotid artery stenosis may be asymptomatic or present with symptoms such as transient ischemic attacks (TIAs) or strokes. TIAs are brief episodes of neurological dysfunction resulting from temporary cerebral ischemia and serve as warning signs for potential cerebrovascular accidents. Symptoms can include sudden weakness or numbness on one side of the body, difficulty speaking, vision problems, and dizziness.

Diagnosis typically involves imaging studies such as carotid ultrasound, magnetic resonance angiography (MRA), or computed tomography angiography (CTA) to assess the degree of stenosis. Management strategies depend on the severity of stenosis and symptomatology. For mild cases, medical management, including antiplatelet therapy and risk factor modification, is recommended. Severe cases may require surgical interventions like carotid endarterectomy or carotid artery stenting to restore adequate blood flow.

Understanding carotid artery stenosis is crucial for critical care nurses, as they play a pivotal role in monitoring patients for signs of cerebral ischemia and managing postoperative care following surgical interventions. This knowledge ensures timely intervention and optimal patient outcomes for those at risk of stroke due to carotid artery disease.

1.1.2.3 Endarterectomy:

Endarterectomy is a surgical procedure aimed at removing atherosclerotic plaque material, or blockage, from the lining of an artery that has been constricted by the buildup of deposits. This procedure is primarily performed to restore normal blood flow and prevent complications such as stroke or peripheral vascular disease. It is most commonly associated with the carotid arteries in the neck, which supply blood to the brain, but it can also be applied to other arteries in the body.

In detail, endarterectomy involves making an incision along the affected artery to access the site of occlusion. The surgeon carefully opens the artery and peels away the plaque from the arterial wall. This removal helps to widen the artery's lumen, thereby improving blood circulation. The artery is then sutured closed, often with a patch to enlarge it further and reduce the risk of re-narrowing (restenosis).

Nurses preparing for the CCRN exam should understand that endarterectomy is indicated for patients with significant arterial stenosis who are symptomatic or at high risk for vascular events. Postoperative care involves monitoring for potential complications such as bleeding, infection, or nerve injury. Neurological assessments are crucial, especially following carotid endarterectomy, to detect any signs of stroke. Understanding this procedure enables nurses to provide comprehensive care and education to patients undergoing endarterectomy, ensuring optimal recovery and management of their vascular health.

1.1.2.4 Fem-Pop Bypass:

A Femoral-Popliteal (Fem-Pop) Bypass is a surgical procedure designed to bypass diseased blood vessels above or below the knee. This procedure is commonly performed to treat peripheral artery disease (PAD), where plaque buildup causes narrowing or blockage of arteries, leading to reduced blood flow to the lower extremities. The goal of the Fem-Pop Bypass is to restore adequate blood circulation to prevent tissue damage or loss.

In this procedure, a graft is used to create a new pathway for blood flow around the blocked artery segment. The graft can be either an autologous vein, often the saphenous vein from the patient's leg, or a synthetic material like polytetrafluoroethylene (PTFE). The choice of graft depends on factors such as the patient's anatomy and the location of the blockage.

The surgery involves making incisions near the groin and at the knee or below, depending on where the bypass needs to occur. The surgeon then attaches one end of the graft to the femoral artery in the groin and the other end to the popliteal artery near or below the knee. This effectively reroutes blood flow around the obstructed area.

Post-surgery, patients require careful monitoring for signs of complications such as graft occlusion, infection, or bleeding. Long-term management includes lifestyle modifications, medications to prevent clotting, and regular follow-up to ensure graft patency. Understanding this procedure is crucial for critical care nurses managing patients with vascular insufficiencies, as it directly impacts patient outcomes and recovery trajectories.

1.1.3 Acute Pulmonary Edema:

Acute pulmonary edema is a critical condition characterized by the rapid accumulation of fluid in the alveoli and interstitial spaces of the lungs, leading to impaired gas exchange and respiratory distress. This condition often arises due to left ventricular dysfunction, where the heart fails to effectively pump blood, causing increased pressure in the pulmonary circulation. As a result, fluid leaks from the pulmonary capillaries into the alveolar spaces.

The pathophysiology involves an imbalance in Starling forces, where elevated hydrostatic pressure in the pulmonary capillaries overcomes oncotic pressure, facilitating fluid transudation into the lung parenchyma. Common causes include acute myocardial infarction, severe hypertension, valvular heart disease, and acute volume overload.

Clinically, patients with acute pulmonary edema present with sudden onset dyspnea, orthopnea, and paroxysmal nocturnal dyspnea. Physical examination may reveal tachypnea, hypoxemia, crackles on auscultation, and frothy sputum production. Chest X-ray findings typically show bilateral pulmonary infiltrates and cardiomegaly.

Management aims to reduce pulmonary congestion and improve oxygenation. Initial interventions include supplemental oxygen or non-invasive ventilation to enhance gas exchange. Pharmacologic treatment involves diuretics such as furosemide to reduce preload, vasodilators like nitroglycerin to decrease afterload, and inotropic agents if cardiac output is compromised.

Nurses must recognize the early signs of acute pulmonary edema and initiate prompt interventions to prevent further respiratory compromise. Understanding its pathophysiology and management strategies is crucial for effective patient care in critical settings.

1.1.4 Aortic Aneurysm:

An aortic aneurysm is a pathological dilation of the aorta, the largest artery in the body. It can occur in any segment of the aorta but is most commonly found in the abdominal or thoracic regions. This condition results from the weakening of the arterial wall, leading to a bulge or ballooning effect. Aortic aneurysms are classified into two main types: abdominal aortic aneurysms (AAA) and thoracic aortic aneurysms (TAA), based on their location.

The etiology of aortic aneurysms is multifactorial, with risk factors including hypertension, smoking, hyperlipidemia, connective tissue disorders such as Marfan syndrome, and age-related degeneration. The clinical presentation may vary; many patients remain asymptomatic until rupture occurs, which can lead to life-threatening hemorrhage. When symptomatic, patients may experience back or abdominal pain, a pulsatile abdominal mass, or signs of compression on adjacent structures.

Diagnosis is typically confirmed through imaging modalities such as ultrasound, computed tomography (CT) scan, or magnetic resonance imaging (MRI). Management strategies depend on the size and growth rate of the aneurysm and may include regular monitoring for smaller aneurysms or surgical intervention for larger ones. Surgical options include open repair or endovascular aneurysm repair (EVAR), which involves placing a stent graft within the vessel.

For critical care nurses preparing for the CCRN exam, understanding the pathophysiology, risk factors, clinical manifestations, diagnostic approaches, and management strategies of aortic aneurysms is crucial for providing optimal patient care and anticipating potential complications.

1.1.5 Aortic Dissection:

Aortic dissection is a critical condition characterized by a tear in the intimal layer of the aorta, leading to the creation of a false lumen between the intima and media layers. This condition can rapidly progress and result in life-threatening complications if not promptly diagnosed and managed. The dissection allows blood to flow between the layers of the aortic wall, causing the layers to separate. This can lead to compromised blood flow to vital organs, rupture, or even death.

Clinically, aortic dissection is classified into two types: Type A, which involves the ascending aorta and requires immediate surgical intervention, and Type B, which involves the descending aorta and may be managed medically unless complications arise. Symptoms often include sudden, severe chest or back pain described as tearing or ripping, hypertension, and signs of organ ischemia, depending on the dissection's location.

Diagnosis is typically confirmed through imaging modalities such as CT angiography, MRI, or transesophageal echocardiography (TEE), which provide detailed visualization of the aorta and any dissection present. Management strategies focus on controlling blood pressure to prevent further tearing and addressing any complications that arise. In Type A dissections, surgical repair is often necessary to replace or repair the affected section of the aorta.

Understanding the pathophysiology, clinical presentation, diagnostic approaches, and management strategies for aortic dissection is crucial for critical care nurses preparing for the CCRN exam, as they play an integral role in monitoring and caring for patients with this life-threatening condition.

1.1.6 Aortic Rupture:

Aortic rupture is a critical and life-threatening condition characterized by the tearing of the aorta, the largest artery in the body. This rupture can occur in either the thoracic or abdominal sections of the aorta and often results from trauma, aneurysm, or dissection. The integrity of the aorta is compromised, leading to massive internal bleeding and rapid hemodynamic instability.

In clinical practice, aortic rupture presents with a sudden onset of severe chest or abdominal pain, hypotension, and signs of shock due to blood loss. Patients may exhibit symptoms such as syncope, altered mental status, or even cardiac arrest. Immediate recognition and intervention are crucial for survival.

Diagnostic evaluation typically involves imaging modalities like CT angiography, which provides rapid and detailed visualization of the aorta to confirm the presence and extent of the rupture. Management strategies focus on stabilizing the patient hemodynamically while preparing for surgical repair. This may involve fluid resuscitation, blood transfusions, and pharmacological support to manage blood pressure.

Surgical intervention is often required, with options including open surgical repair or endovascular techniques such as thoracic endovascular aortic repair (TEVAR). The choice of procedure depends on the location and extent of the rupture, as well as the patient's stability.

Understanding the pathophysiology, prompt recognition of symptoms, and appropriate management strategies are essential for critical care nurses in optimizing outcomes for patients experiencing an aortic rupture. Proficiency in these areas is vital for success in the CCRN exam and practical application in critical care settings.

1.1.7 Cardiac Surgery:

Cardiac surgery involves surgical procedures performed on the heart or great vessels by cardiac surgeons. It is often necessary to treat complications of ischemic heart disease, correct congenital heart defects, or address valvular heart disease due to various causes, including endocarditis, rheumatic heart disease, and atherosclerosis. The most common types of cardiac surgery include coronary artery bypass grafting (CABG), valve repair or replacement, and heart transplantation.

In CABG, a healthy artery or vein from the body is connected, or grafted, to the blocked coronary artery. This allows the grafted artery to bypass the blocked portion of the coronary artery, restoring blood flow to the heart muscle. Valve repair or replacement involves fixing a damaged heart valve or replacing it with a prosthetic valve. Heart transplantation is reserved for patients with end-stage heart failure or severe coronary artery disease who do not respond to other medical treatments.

The perioperative management of cardiac surgery patients requires careful monitoring and support in an intensive care setting. Nurses play a crucial role in managing hemodynamic stability, ensuring effective ventilation and oxygenation, preventing infections, and providing postoperative care that includes pain management and early mobilization. Understanding the pathophysiology of cardiac diseases and the implications of surgical interventions is essential for critical care nurses preparing for the CCRN exam, as they are key players in optimizing patient outcomes post-cardiac surgery.

1.1.7.1 CABG:

Coronary Artery Bypass Grafting (CABG) is a surgical procedure utilized to treat coronary artery disease (CAD), which is characterized by the narrowing or blockage of coronary arteries due to atherosclerosis. This condition reduces blood flow to the heart muscle, potentially leading to angina, myocardial infarction, or other cardiac complications. The aim of CABG is to restore adequate blood flow by creating new pathways around the obstructed arteries.

In CABG, a surgeon harvests a healthy blood vessel from another part of the patient's body, typically the saphenous vein from the leg or the internal mammary artery from the chest. This graft is then attached above and below the blocked artery, allowing blood to bypass the obstruction and improve myocardial perfusion.

The procedure can be performed using traditional open-heart surgery with cardiopulmonary bypass or via off-pump techniques, where the heart continues beating. The choice of method depends on patient-specific factors and the surgeon's preference.

Post-operatively, patients require intensive monitoring in a critical care setting. Nurses must be vigilant for complications such as bleeding, infection, arrhythmias, and graft occlusion. Hemodynamic stability, pain management, and early mobilization are crucial aspects of post-CABG care.

Understanding the pathophysiology of CABG, surgical techniques, and post-operative management is essential for nurses preparing for the CCRN exam. Mastery of these concepts ensures optimal patient outcomes and enhances critical care proficiency in managing complex cardiac conditions.

1.1.7.2 Valve Replacement Or Repair:
Valve replacement or repair is a surgical procedure aimed at correcting malfunctioning heart valves, which are crucial for directing blood flow through the heart and into the rest of the body. This procedure is essential when valves become stenotic (narrowed) or regurgitant (leaky), leading to compromised cardiac function.

Valve repair involves reconstructive surgery to restore the valve's function and is often preferred due to its potential to preserve the patient's native valve and reduce the risk of infection or anticoagulation-related complications. Techniques may include patching holes, reshaping valve leaflets, or chordal transfer. Repair is typically more successful with mitral valves than with aortic valves.

Valve replacement, on the other hand, involves substituting the defective valve with either a mechanical or biological prosthesis. Mechanical valves are durable and require lifelong anticoagulation therapy to prevent thromboembolism, while biological valves, made from animal tissue, have a shorter lifespan but generally do not necessitate long-term anticoagulation.

Postoperative care for patients undergoing valve replacement or repair includes vigilant monitoring for complications such as bleeding, infection, thromboembolism, and heart failure. Nurses must be adept in hemodynamic assessment and management, ensuring optimal cardiac output and tissue perfusion. Understanding the nuances of each type of valve surgery is critical for providing comprehensive care and education to patients and their families, ultimately improving surgical outcomes and quality of life.

1.1.8 Cardiac Tamponade:
Cardiac tamponade is a critical condition characterized by the accumulation of fluid in the pericardial space, which exerts pressure on the heart, impairing its ability to function effectively. This fluid buildup can result from various causes, including trauma, pericarditis, malignancy, or post-surgical complications. The hallmark of cardiac tamponade is the restriction of ventricular filling during diastole, leading to decreased stroke volume and cardiac output.

Clinically, cardiac tamponade presents with Beck's triad: hypotension, jugular venous distension, and muffled heart sounds. Additionally, patients may exhibit pulsus paradoxus, which is a significant drop in systolic blood pressure during inspiration. Tachycardia and dyspnea are also common symptoms as the body attempts to compensate for reduced cardiac output.

Diagnosis typically involves echocardiography, which reveals pericardial effusion and signs of compromised cardiac function. Other diagnostic tools include chest X-ray and electrocardiogram (ECG), although these are less definitive.

Immediate management of cardiac tamponade focuses on stabilizing the patient hemodynamically. Pericardiocentesis, the aspiration of fluid from the pericardial sac, is often performed to relieve pressure on the heart. In some cases, surgical intervention may be necessary to address underlying causes or recurrent effusions.

Understanding the pathophysiology and clinical presentation of cardiac tamponade is crucial for critical care nurses preparing for the CCRN exam. Prompt recognition and intervention can significantly improve patient outcomes in this life-threatening condition.

1.1.9 Cardiac Trauma:
Cardiac trauma refers to any injury to the heart muscle, coronary arteries, or surrounding structures resulting from either blunt or penetrating trauma. It is a critical condition often seen in emergency and critical care settings. Blunt cardiac trauma commonly results from motor vehicle accidents, falls, or sports injuries and can lead to myocardial contusion, pericardial effusion, or cardiac rupture. Penetrating cardiac trauma, often caused by stab wounds or gunshot injuries, can result in direct damage to the heart chambers and may lead to life-threatening complications such as cardiac tamponade or massive hemorrhage.

The clinical presentation of cardiac trauma varies depending on the severity and type of injury. Symptoms may include chest pain, hypotension, tachycardia, or signs of shock. Diagnosis is typically achieved through a combination of physical examination, imaging studies such as echocardiography or CT scans, and sometimes exploratory surgery.

Management of cardiac trauma requires prompt assessment and stabilization of the patient. Initial treatment focuses on maintaining hemodynamic stability through fluid resuscitation and addressing life-threatening conditions like tamponade with pericardiocentesis. Surgical intervention may be necessary for repairing structural damage or controlling bleeding.

Understanding the mechanisms of injury, potential complications, and appropriate interventions is crucial for critical care nurses managing patients with cardiac trauma. Proficiency in recognizing early signs of deterioration and collaborating effectively with multidisciplinary teams is essential for optimizing patient outcomes in these high-stakes scenarios.

1.1.10 Cardiac/Vascular Catheterization:
Cardiac and vascular catheterization is a diagnostic and interventional procedure used to evaluate and treat cardiovascular conditions. This technique involves the insertion of a catheter, a thin flexible tube, into the vascular system, typically through the femoral or radial artery, to access the heart and surrounding vasculature. The procedure serves multiple purposes, including measuring intracardiac pressures, obtaining blood samples, and imaging the coronary arteries through angiography.

In cardiac catheterization, contrast dye is injected through the catheter to visualize the coronary arteries and identify blockages or abnormalities using X-ray imaging. This allows for the assessment of coronary artery disease, heart valve function, and congenital heart defects. Vascular catheterization also extends to peripheral vessels for evaluating conditions such as peripheral artery disease.

Interventional procedures performed during catheterization include angioplasty and stent placement to open narrowed or blocked arteries. These interventions are critical in restoring adequate blood flow and preventing myocardial infarction or stroke.

Nurses in critical care must be proficient in pre-procedural preparation, which includes obtaining informed consent and ensuring patient fasting. Post-procedure care involves monitoring for complications such as bleeding at the insertion site, arrhythmias, or contrast-induced nephropathy. Understanding hemodynamic data interpretation and recognizing signs of complications are essential skills for nurses involved in cardiac and vascular catheterization care.

This procedure remains a cornerstone in cardiology due to its diagnostic accuracy and therapeutic potential, requiring skilled nursing care to optimize patient outcomes.

1.1.11 Cardiogenic Shock:

Cardiogenic shock is a critical condition characterized by the heart's inability to pump sufficient blood to meet the body's needs, leading to inadequate tissue perfusion and oxygenation. This condition often results from severe myocardial infarction but can also be caused by other cardiac issues such as end-stage heart failure, cardiomyopathy, or valvular heart disease.

In cardiogenic shock, the primary problem is the reduced cardiac output due to impaired contractility of the heart muscle. The decreased cardiac output leads to hypotension, which in turn causes diminished coronary perfusion, further exacerbating myocardial dysfunction. Clinically, patients present with signs of systemic hypoperfusion, such as altered mental status, cold and clammy skin, oliguria, and metabolic acidosis. Additionally, pulmonary congestion may occur due to elevated left ventricular filling pressures.

Diagnosis is typically confirmed through clinical assessment and hemodynamic monitoring, often involving echocardiography and invasive measurements like pulmonary artery catheterization. Treatment focuses on restoring adequate cardiac output and tissue perfusion. This may involve pharmacological interventions such as inotropes (e.g., dobutamine) to enhance cardiac contractility and vasopressors (e.g., norepinephrine) to maintain blood pressure. Mechanical support devices, such as intra-aortic balloon pumps or ventricular assist devices, may be necessary in severe cases.

Early recognition and prompt management are crucial for improving outcomes in patients with cardiogenic shock. Understanding the pathophysiology and treatment modalities is essential for critical care nurses preparing for the CCRN exam to effectively manage this life-threatening condition.

1.1.12 Cardiomyopathies:

Cardiomyopathies are a group of diseases that affect the heart muscle, impairing its ability to pump blood effectively. They are classified into several types based on their pathophysiological characteristics: dilated, hypertrophic, restrictive, arrhythmogenic right ventricular cardiomyopathy (ARVC), and unclassified cardiomyopathies.

Dilated cardiomyopathy is characterized by the enlargement of the heart chambers and a decrease in systolic function, often leading to heart failure. Hypertrophic cardiomyopathy involves the thickening of the heart muscle, particularly the interventricular septum, which can obstruct blood flow and cause diastolic dysfunction. Restrictive cardiomyopathy results in rigid ventricular walls that impede ventricular filling during diastole, despite normal systolic function.

Arrhythmogenic right ventricular cardiomyopathy is marked by the replacement of myocardial tissue with fibrofatty tissue, predominantly affecting the right ventricle and leading to arrhythmias. Unclassified cardiomyopathies include conditions that do not fit neatly into other categories but still result in impaired cardiac function.

The etiology of cardiomyopathies can be genetic or acquired. Genetic factors play a significant role, especially in hypertrophic and arrhythmogenic right ventricular cardiomyopathies. Acquired causes include viral infections, alcoholism, and exposure to toxins or drugs.

Clinical manifestations vary but commonly include symptoms of heart failure, such as dyspnea, fatigue, and peripheral edema. Arrhythmias and thromboembolic events may also occur. Diagnosis typically involves echocardiography, MRI, genetic testing, and sometimes endomyocardial biopsy. Management strategies focus on alleviating symptoms, preventing complications, and addressing underlying causes where possible. Treatment may involve medications such as beta-blockers or ACE inhibitors, lifestyle modifications, implantable devices, or surgical interventions such as septal myectomy or heart transplantation in severe cases.

1.1.12.1 Dilated Cardiomyopathy (DCM):

Dilated Cardiomyopathy (DCM) is a cardiac disorder characterized by the enlargement and impaired contraction of the left ventricle or both ventricles, leading to systolic dysfunction. This condition results in a decreased ejection fraction, typically below 40%, and subsequent symptoms of heart failure. The ventricular dilation occurs due to the weakening of the myocardial fibers, which impairs the heart's ability to pump blood efficiently.

The etiology of DCM is multifactorial, encompassing genetic predispositions, viral infections (such as myocarditis), excessive alcohol consumption, exposure to toxins, and certain medications. It can also be idiopathic, where no specific cause is identified. Genetic mutations have been implicated in familial cases, often involving genes responsible for cytoskeletal proteins within cardiac muscle cells.

Clinically, patients with DCM may present with signs and symptoms of heart failure, including dyspnea on exertion, orthopnea, paroxysmal nocturnal dyspnea, fatigue, and peripheral edema. Auscultation may reveal an S3 gallop due to increased ventricular filling pressures. Diagnostic evaluation involves echocardiography to assess ventricular size and function, along with other imaging modalities like MRI if needed.

Management of DCM focuses on alleviating symptoms and preventing disease progression. This includes pharmacological interventions such as ACE inhibitors, beta-blockers, diuretics, and aldosterone antagonists. In advanced cases, device therapy, such as implantable cardioverter-defibrillators (ICDs) or cardiac resynchronization therapy (CRT), may be indicated. Ultimately, some patients may require heart transplantation.

Understanding DCM is crucial for critical care nurses, as they play a vital role in monitoring patient status and administering complex treatment regimens effectively.

1.1.12.2   Hypertrophic Cardiomyopathy (HCM):

Hypertrophic Cardiomyopathy (HCM) is a genetic cardiac disorder characterized by the thickening of the heart muscle, particularly affecting the interventricular septum and the left ventricular wall. This hypertrophy can lead to obstruction of blood flow, primarily during diastole, and may result in significant clinical manifestations such as dyspnea, angina, syncope, or sudden cardiac death. The thickened myocardium can also interfere with the heart's electrical system, potentially causing arrhythmias.

In HCM, the myocardial fibers are arranged in a disorganized pattern, known as myofiber disarray, which contributes to impaired cardiac function. This condition is often inherited in an autosomal dominant manner, with mutations in genes encoding sarcomeric proteins being the most common cause. Echocardiography is the primary diagnostic tool used to identify myocardial thickening and assess ventricular function. Magnetic resonance imaging (MRI) may also be employed for detailed anatomical visualization.

Management of HCM focuses on alleviating symptoms and preventing complications. Beta-blockers or calcium channel blockers are frequently prescribed to reduce myocardial oxygen demand and improve diastolic filling. In cases where medication is insufficient, surgical interventions such as septal myectomy or alcohol septal ablation may be considered to relieve outflow tract obstruction. Implantable cardioverter-defibrillators (ICDs) are recommended for patients at high risk of sudden cardiac death due to arrhythmias.

Understanding the pathophysiology of HCM and its treatment options is crucial for critical care nurses in providing comprehensive care and patient education, ensuring effective management and improved patient outcomes.

1.1.12.3   Idiopathic:

The term idiopathic is used in the medical field to describe a condition or disease whose cause is unknown or not well understood. In the context of cardiomyopathies, idiopathic cardiomyopathy refers to a type of heart muscle disease where the underlying etiology cannot be determined despite thorough investigation. This classification is crucial for critical care nurses, as it influences both the diagnostic approach and management strategies.

Idiopathic cardiomyopathy is often diagnosed after excluding other potential causes, such as coronary artery disease, hypertension, valvular heart disease, and congenital heart defects. It is important for critical care nurses to understand that idiopathic does not imply a lack of severity or impact. Patients with idiopathic cardiomyopathy may present with symptoms ranging from mild dyspnea and fatigue to severe heart failure and arrhythmias.

The management of idiopathic cardiomyopathy focuses on symptomatic relief and the prevention of complications. Nurses should be adept at monitoring cardiac function, administering medications like ACE inhibitors, beta-blockers, and diuretics, and providing education on lifestyle modifications that can help manage the condition. Regular follow-ups and echocardiographic evaluations are essential components of patient care.

In preparing for the CCRN exam, critical care nurses must be familiar with the diagnostic criteria, clinical manifestations, and treatment protocols associated with idiopathic cardiomyopathy. Understanding this concept is vital for delivering comprehensive care and optimizing patient outcomes in a critical care setting.

1.1.12.4   Restrictive Cardiomyopathy:

Restrictive cardiomyopathy is a form of heart muscle disease characterized by the rigidity of the ventricular walls, which leads to impaired ventricular filling during diastole. Unlike other types of cardiomyopathy, the ventricles in restrictive cardiomyopathy maintain normal size and systolic function but exhibit decreased compliance, resulting in elevated filling pressures. This condition is often associated with fibrosis or infiltration of the myocardium by abnormal substances such as amyloid proteins, sarcoid granulomas, or iron deposits (as seen in hemochromatosis).

Clinically, patients with restrictive cardiomyopathy present with symptoms of heart failure, primarily related to diastolic dysfunction. These symptoms may include exertional dyspnea, fatigue, and peripheral edema. Jugular venous distension and ascites are also common due to systemic venous congestion. Diagnostic evaluation typically involves echocardiography, which reveals normal ventricular wall thickness and chamber size but impaired diastolic filling. Cardiac MRI and endomyocardial biopsy may be employed to identify specific infiltrative processes.

Management of restrictive cardiomyopathy focuses on symptom relief and treatment of the underlying cause, if identifiable. Diuretics are used to manage fluid overload, while beta-blockers and calcium channel blockers may aid in controlling heart rate and improving diastolic filling time. In cases where an underlying infiltrative disorder is diagnosed, targeted therapies such as chemotherapy for amyloidosis or phlebotomy for hemochromatosis may be indicated.

Understanding the pathophysiology and management of restrictive cardiomyopathy is crucial for critical care nurses preparing for the CCRN exam, as it directly impacts patient outcomes in a critical care setting.

1.1.13 Dysrhythmias:

Dysrhythmias, also known as arrhythmias, are abnormal heart rhythms resulting from irregularities in the heart's electrical conduction system. These disturbances can affect the heart rate, rhythm, or both, leading to either tachycardia (an abnormally fast heart rate) or bradycardia (an abnormally slow heart rate). Dysrhythmias can originate from various parts of the heart, including the atria, ventricles, or the atrioventricular node.

The etiology of dysrhythmias is multifactorial and may include electrolyte imbalances, ischemic heart disease, structural heart defects, or the influence of certain medications. Clinical manifestations vary widely depending on the type and severity of the dysrhythmia. Patients may experience palpitations, dizziness, syncope, chest pain, or even asymptomatic presentations detected only through electrocardiogram (ECG) monitoring.

For critical care nurses preparing for the CCRN exam, understanding dysrhythmias is crucial, as they often require prompt identification and intervention. Management strategies include pharmacological treatments such as antiarrhythmic drugs or beta-blockers, electrical interventions like cardioversion or defibrillation, and invasive procedures such as catheter ablation. Nurses must also be adept at interpreting ECGs to identify specific dysrhythmias, such as atrial fibrillation, ventricular tachycardia, or complete heart block.

In summary, dysrhythmias encompass a wide spectrum of cardiac rhythm disorders that necessitate comprehensive assessment and management in critical care settings. Proficiency in recognizing and treating these conditions is essential for ensuring optimal patient outcomes in those with compromised cardiac function.

1.1.14 Heart Failure:

Heart failure, also known as congestive heart failure (CHF), is a chronic, progressive condition in which the heart muscle is unable to pump sufficiently to maintain blood flow that meets the body's needs for oxygen and nutrients. It can result from structural or functional cardiac disorders that impair the heart's ability to fill with or eject blood efficiently.

In heart failure, the heart's diminished capacity leads to a backlog of blood in the veins, causing fluid accumulation in the lungs and other tissues. This fluid retention results in symptoms such as shortness of breath, fatigue, swollen legs, and a rapid heartbeat. Heart failure can be classified into systolic dysfunction, where the heart muscle cannot contract vigorously, and diastolic dysfunction, where the heart has difficulty relaxing and filling with blood.

The etiology of heart failure includes coronary artery disease, hypertension, myocardial infarction, valvular heart disease, and cardiomyopathy. Risk factors such as diabetes, obesity, smoking, and a sedentary lifestyle significantly contribute to its development.

Management of heart failure involves pharmacological interventions such as ACE inhibitors, beta-blockers, diuretics, and aldosterone antagonists to alleviate symptoms and improve survival. Non-pharmacological strategies include lifestyle modifications like dietary changes, exercise regimens, and fluid restriction. Advanced cases may require device implantation or surgical interventions such as ventricular assist devices or transplantation.

For critical care nurses preparing for the CCRN exam, understanding the pathophysiology, clinical manifestations, and management strategies of heart failure is essential for providing optimal patient care and improving outcomes.

1.1.15 Hypertensive Crisis:

A hypertensive crisis is a severe and sudden increase in blood pressure that can lead to acute end-organ damage. It is classified into two categories: hypertensive urgency and hypertensive emergency. Hypertensive urgency involves elevated blood pressure levels (typically above 180/120 mmHg) without acute organ damage, necessitating prompt but non-emergent intervention. In contrast, a hypertensive emergency presents with similarly elevated blood pressure but with evidence of acute target organ damage, such as encephalopathy, myocardial infarction, pulmonary edema, or renal impairment, requiring immediate medical intervention to prevent morbidity and mortality.

The pathophysiology of a hypertensive crisis involves abrupt increases in systemic vascular resistance due to excessive vasoconstriction, often triggered by factors such as medication non-compliance, autonomic dysregulation, or underlying conditions like pheochromocytoma or renovascular disease. Clinical manifestations vary based on the affected organs and may include severe headache, visual disturbances, chest pain, dyspnea, or neurological deficits.

Management strategies differ between urgency and emergency cases. In hypertensive emergencies, rapid but controlled reduction of blood pressure using intravenous antihypertensives such as nitroprusside, labetalol, or nicardipine is crucial to mitigate organ damage. Conversely, hypertensive urgencies can be managed with oral antihypertensives and close outpatient follow-up.

Understanding the distinction between hypertensive urgency and emergency is vital for critical care nurses to ensure timely and appropriate treatment interventions, thereby optimizing patient outcomes in high-pressure scenarios.

1.1.16 Myocardial Conduction System Abnormalities:

Myocardial conduction system abnormalities refer to disorders that affect the electrical conduction pathways of the heart, leading to irregular heart rhythms or arrhythmias. The myocardial conduction system is responsible for the initiation and propagation of electrical impulses that coordinate the contraction of the heart chambers. It includes structures such as the sinoatrial (SA) node, atrioventricular (AV) node, bundle of His, bundle branches, and Purkinje fibers.

Abnormalities in this system can arise from various factors, including ischemia, fibrosis, electrolyte imbalances, or congenital defects. These disturbances can manifest as bradyarrhythmias or tachyarrhythmias. Bradyarrhythmias occur when there is a delay or blockage in impulse conduction, often seen in conditions like sick sinus syndrome or AV block. Tachyarrhythmias result from increased automaticity or re-entry circuits and include atrial fibrillation, ventricular tachycardia, and supraventricular tachycardia.

The clinical presentation of conduction abnormalities can range from asymptomatic to life-threatening events such as syncope or cardiac arrest. Diagnosis typically involves electrocardiography (ECG) to identify characteristic patterns associated with specific arrhythmias. Management strategies depend on the underlying cause and may include pharmacological interventions like antiarrhythmic drugs, electrical therapies such as pacemakers or defibrillators, and lifestyle modifications.

Understanding these abnormalities is crucial for critical care nurses, as they play a vital role in monitoring cardiac rhythms, recognizing early signs of deterioration, and implementing timely interventions to prevent adverse outcomes.

1.1.16.1 Prolonged QT Interval:

A prolonged QT interval is a cardiac conduction abnormality characterized by an extended duration of the QT segment on an electrocardiogram (ECG). The QT interval represents the time taken for ventricular depolarization and repolarization, essentially reflecting the electrical recovery phase of the heart. Normally, the QT interval varies with heart rate but is considered prolonged if it exceeds 450 milliseconds in men and 460 milliseconds in women when corrected for heart rate (QTc).

Clinically, a prolonged QT interval is significant because it predisposes patients to a type of ventricular tachycardia known as Torsades de Pointes, which can lead to sudden cardiac death. Causes of a prolonged QT interval can be congenital, such as Long QT Syndrome, or acquired due to factors like electrolyte imbalances (hypokalemia, hypomagnesemia), medications (antiarrhythmics, certain antibiotics), or other conditions (myocardial ischemia).

In critical care settings, recognizing a prolonged QT interval is crucial for preventing life-threatening arrhythmias. Nurses should be adept at identifying this condition on ECGs and understanding its potential causes and implications. Management involves addressing underlying causes, discontinuing offending drugs, correcting electrolyte imbalances, and, in some cases, administering magnesium sulfate or using temporary pacing.

Critical care nurses must remain vigilant in monitoring patients at risk for prolonged QT intervals and collaborate with interdisciplinary teams to implement appropriate interventions swiftly. Understanding this cardiac conduction abnormality is essential for ensuring patient safety and optimizing outcomes in critical care environments.

1.1.16.2 Wolff-Parkinson-White Syndrome:

Wolff-Parkinson-White (WPW) syndrome is a type of pre-excitation syndrome characterized by an abnormal electrical conduction pathway between the atria and ventricles of the heart, known as the accessory pathway or bundle of Kent. This condition can lead to episodes of tachycardia due to the bypassing of normal atrioventricular (AV) node conduction, resulting in a rapid heartbeat.

In WPW syndrome, the presence of this accessory pathway allows electrical impulses to travel from the atria to the ventricles more quickly than through the AV node. This can lead to a phenomenon called reentrant tachycardia, where impulses continuously circulate between the atria and ventricles, causing rapid heart rates. On an electrocardiogram (ECG), WPW is often identified by a short PR interval, a delta wave (a slurred upstroke in the QRS complex), and a widened QRS complex.

Clinically, patients with WPW may experience palpitations, dizziness, syncope, or, in some cases, sudden cardiac arrest. The management of WPW involves controlling arrhythmias through medications such as antiarrhythmics or procedures like catheter ablation to destroy the accessory pathway. In acute settings, vagal maneuvers or adenosine may be used to terminate supraventricular tachycardias associated with WPW.

Understanding WPW syndrome is crucial for critical care nurses, as it enables them to recognize symptoms promptly and participate effectively in managing acute episodes, ensuring patient safety and optimal outcomes in critical care environments.

1.1.17 Papillary Muscle Rupture:

Papillary muscle rupture is a catastrophic complication often associated with acute myocardial infarction (AMI), particularly involving the inferior wall of the left ventricle. This condition arises when the papillary muscles, which anchor the mitral valve leaflets via chordae tendineae, undergo necrosis and rupture due to ischemic damage. The rupture leads to acute mitral regurgitation, characterized by the backward flow of blood from the left ventricle into the left atrium during systole.

Clinically, papillary muscle rupture presents with a sudden onset of severe dyspnea, pulmonary edema, and cardiogenic shock due to abrupt hemodynamic instability. Auscultation may reveal a new, loud systolic murmur at the apex, often radiating to the axilla. Diagnosis is typically confirmed through echocardiography, which demonstrates flail mitral valve leaflets and severe mitral regurgitation.

Management of papillary muscle rupture requires urgent surgical intervention. Mitral valve repair or replacement is necessary to restore valve function and stabilize hemodynamics. Preoperative stabilization may include the use of inotropes, vasodilators, and intra-aortic balloon pump support to reduce afterload and improve cardiac output.

Understanding papillary muscle rupture is crucial for critical care nurses, as it involves rapid recognition and intervention to prevent mortality. Nurses must be vigilant in monitoring patients post-AMI for signs of mechanical complications and collaborate closely with multidisciplinary teams to ensure timely surgical management.

1.1.18 Structural Heart Defects Overview:

Structural heart defects encompass a range of abnormalities in the heart's anatomy, which can be either congenital (present at birth) or acquired later in life. Congenital heart defects (CHDs) are the most common type of birth defect and can include conditions such as atrial septal defects, ventricular septal defects, and patent ductus arteriosus. These defects result from improper development of the heart during fetal growth and can lead to issues such as abnormal blood flow patterns, increased cardiac workload, and potential heart failure.

Acquired structural heart defects develop after birth due to factors such as infections, rheumatic fever, or degenerative changes. Valvular heart disease is a significant category within acquired structural defects and involves the malfunctioning of one or more of the heart's valves (aortic, mitral, tricuspid, or pulmonary). This can manifest as stenosis (narrowing of the valve opening) or regurgitation (leakage of blood backward through the valve), leading to compromised cardiac efficiency and symptoms such as dyspnea, fatigue, and palpitations.

Critical care nurses must be adept at recognizing the signs and symptoms associated with these defects and understanding diagnostic procedures such as echocardiography or cardiac catheterization. Management may involve medical therapy to control symptoms or surgical interventions such as valve repair or replacement. A comprehensive understanding of these conditions is crucial for optimizing patient outcomes and providing high-quality care in critical settings.

1.1.19 TAVR Overview:

Transcatheter Aortic Valve Replacement (TAVR) is a minimally invasive surgical procedure used to replace a diseased aortic valve in patients with severe aortic stenosis. Aortic stenosis involves the narrowing of the aortic valve opening, which restricts blood flow from the heart to the rest of the body and can lead to heart failure if untreated. TAVR offers an alternative to traditional open-heart surgery, particularly for patients who are at high or intermediate risk for surgical complications.

The procedure involves inserting a catheter through a small incision, often in the femoral artery in the groin, and guiding it to the heart. Once positioned, a new valve made from animal tissue is expanded and anchored within the existing valve. This restores normal blood flow and alleviates symptoms such as shortness of breath, chest pain, and fatigue.

Critical care nurses should be aware of potential complications associated with TAVR, including vascular injury, bleeding, stroke, and heart block requiring pacemaker insertion. Post-procedure care involves monitoring for signs of infection, ensuring hemodynamic stability, and assessing for arrhythmias or changes in neurological status.

Understanding TAVR is crucial for critical care nurses, as they play a vital role in pre-procedural assessment, intraoperative support, and post-procedural recovery. They must be adept at recognizing complications early and providing comprehensive care to optimize patient outcomes following this life-saving intervention.

1.2 Respiratory:

The respiratory system is a complex network responsible for gas exchange, providing oxygen to the bloodstream and removing carbon dioxide from the body. This system comprises the upper and lower airways, lungs, and respiratory muscles. The primary function of the respiratory system is to maintain homeostasis through effective ventilation and perfusion.

In critical care settings, understanding the nuances of respiratory physiology is crucial. Ventilation refers to the movement of air in and out of the lungs, while perfusion involves blood flow through the pulmonary capillaries. Effective gas exchange depends on optimal ventilation-perfusion matching. Disruptions in this balance can lead to conditions such as hypoxemia or hypercapnia.

Critical care nurses must be adept at recognizing signs of respiratory distress, which may include tachypnea, dyspnea, or altered mental status. Advanced skills in interpreting arterial blood gases (ABGs) are essential for assessing a patient's respiratory status. ABG analysis provides insights into pH balance, partial pressures of oxygen (PaO_2) and carbon dioxide ($PaCO_2$), and bicarbonate levels.

Mechanical ventilation is often employed in critical care to support patients with compromised respiratory function. Nurses must understand various ventilator modes and settings to optimize patient outcomes while minimizing potential complications such as barotrauma or ventilator-associated pneumonia.

In summary, proficiency in respiratory care within critical settings requires an intricate understanding of anatomy, physiology, pathophysiology, and advanced monitoring techniques to ensure effective patient management and care delivery.

1.2.1 Acute Pulmonary Embolus:

An acute pulmonary embolus (PE) is a sudden blockage in one of the pulmonary arteries in the lungs, usually caused by a blood clot that has traveled from the deep veins of the legs or other parts of the body. This condition is critical and potentially life-threatening, requiring immediate medical attention.

Pathophysiologically, an embolus obstructs blood flow in the pulmonary vasculature, leading to increased pulmonary vascular resistance and impaired gas exchange. This results in hypoxemia and can place strain on the right side of the heart, potentially leading to right ventricular failure if not promptly addressed.

Clinically, patients with an acute PE may present with sudden onset dyspnea, chest pain that may be pleuritic in nature, tachypnea, tachycardia, and, in severe cases, syncope or hemodynamic instability. A physical examination might reveal signs such as hypoxemia and elevated jugular venous pressure.

Diagnostic evaluation typically includes imaging studies such as CT pulmonary angiography, which is considered the gold standard for diagnosing PE. D-dimer testing can be useful in ruling out PE in low-risk patients. Management involves anticoagulation therapy to prevent further clot formation and reduce mortality. In cases of massive PE with hemodynamic compromise, thrombolytic therapy or surgical intervention may be necessary.

Understanding acute pulmonary embolus is crucial for nursing care, as prompt recognition and treatment are vital to improving patient outcomes and reducing mortality associated with this condition.

1.2.2 ARDS:

Acute Respiratory Distress Syndrome (ARDS) is a severe, life-threatening condition characterized by sudden and progressive pulmonary edema, refractory hypoxemia, and decreased lung compliance. It results from direct or indirect injury to the alveolar-capillary membrane, leading to increased permeability and fluid accumulation in the alveoli. This impairs gas exchange and results in severe hypoxemia that is unresponsive to supplemental oxygen.

The pathophysiology of ARDS involves an inflammatory response that damages the capillary endothelium and alveolar epithelium. This damage increases vascular permeability, allowing protein-rich fluid to leak into the alveolar spaces. The resultant edema reduces lung compliance and functional residual capacity, leading to ventilation-perfusion mismatch and shunting.

Clinically, ARDS presents with the rapid onset of dyspnea, tachypnea, and hypoxemia following a precipitating event such as sepsis, trauma, pneumonia, or aspiration. Diagnostic criteria include acute onset within one week of a known clinical insult or new/worsening respiratory symptoms, bilateral opacities on chest imaging not fully explained by effusions, lobar or lung collapse, or nodules, and respiratory failure not fully explained by cardiac failure or fluid overload.

Management of ARDS focuses on supportive care with mechanical ventilation using low tidal volumes and high PEEP to prevent further lung injury. Prone positioning may improve oxygenation in severe cases. Addressing the underlying cause is crucial for recovery. Understanding the pathophysiology and management strategies of ARDS is essential for critical care nurses preparing for the CCRN exam.

1.2.3 Acute Respiratory Failure:

Acute Respiratory Failure (ARF) is a critical condition characterized by the inability of the respiratory system to maintain adequate gas exchange, resulting in insufficient oxygenation or carbon dioxide elimination. This condition is defined by arterial blood gas measurements showing a PaO2 of less than 60 mmHg (hypoxemia) or a PaCO2 of greater than 50 mmHg (hypercapnia), with accompanying respiratory acidosis.

There are two primary types of ARF: hypoxemic and hypercapnic. Hypoxemic respiratory failure occurs when there is inadequate exchange of oxygen between the alveoli and the blood, often due to conditions such as pneumonia, pulmonary edema, or acute respiratory distress syndrome (ARDS). Hypercapnic respiratory failure results from inadequate ventilation, leading to elevated carbon dioxide levels; it is often associated with diseases such as chronic obstructive pulmonary disease (COPD), asthma, or neuromuscular disorders.

The pathophysiology of ARF involves a mismatch between ventilation and perfusion, diffusion impairment, or shunt physiology. Clinically, patients may present with symptoms such as dyspnea, tachypnea, cyanosis, confusion, and altered mental status. Diagnostic evaluation includes arterial blood gas analysis, chest radiography, and pulse oximetry.

Management of ARF focuses on addressing the underlying cause while supporting the patient's respiratory function. Interventions may include supplemental oxygen, mechanical ventilation, bronchodilators, corticosteroids, and antibiotics if an infection is present. Early recognition and prompt treatment are crucial to preventing complications and improving patient outcomes in acute respiratory failure.

1.2.4 Acute Respiratory Infection:

Acute Respiratory Infection (ARI) is a condition characterized by the sudden onset of infection in the respiratory tract, which can affect both the upper and lower airways. It is a significant concern in critical care due to its potential to rapidly progress to severe respiratory distress or failure. ARIs are typically caused by viral pathogens such as influenza, rhinovirus, and respiratory syncytial virus; however, bacterial infections like Streptococcus pneumoniae can also be culprits.

The clinical presentation of ARI varies but often includes symptoms such as cough, fever, sore throat, nasal congestion, and difficulty breathing. In severe cases, especially when involving the lower respiratory tract, patients may experience hypoxemia and require supplemental oxygen or mechanical ventilation.

Diagnosis is primarily clinical, supported by laboratory tests such as PCR assays for viral identification or cultures for bacterial infections. Imaging studies, such as chest X-rays or CT scans, can help assess the extent of lung involvement.

Management of ARI focuses on supportive care, including hydration, antipyretics for fever control, and oxygen therapy. Antiviral medications may be indicated for specific viral infections like influenza, while antibiotics are reserved for confirmed or strongly suspected bacterial infections.

Prevention strategies include vaccination (e.g., influenza vaccine), hand hygiene, and minimizing exposure to infected individuals. Understanding the pathophysiology and management of ARI is crucial for critical care nurses to effectively monitor and treat patients while preventing complications.

1.2.4.1 Pneumonia:

Pneumonia is an acute respiratory infection that affects the alveoli, the small air sacs in the lungs, leading to inflammation and fluid accumulation. It can be caused by a variety of pathogens, including bacteria, viruses, fungi, and parasites. The most common bacterial cause is Streptococcus pneumoniae. Viral pneumonia can be caused by influenza, respiratory syncytial virus (RSV), and SARS-CoV-2, among others.

Clinically, pneumonia presents with symptoms such as cough, fever, chills, dyspnea, and pleuritic chest pain. Patients may also exhibit tachypnea, hypoxemia, and crackles upon auscultation. Diagnosis typically involves a combination of clinical assessment, chest X-ray findings showing infiltrates or consolidation, and laboratory tests such as sputum cultures and blood tests for inflammatory markers.

Management of pneumonia depends on the causative agent and the severity of the disease. Antibiotic therapy is the cornerstone for bacterial pneumonia, with empirical treatment often initiated before pathogen-specific results are available. Antiviral medications may be used for viral pneumonia if indicated. Supportive care includes oxygen therapy to maintain adequate oxygen saturation and hydration to ensure proper mucociliary clearance.

In critically ill patients or those with underlying health conditions, pneumonia can lead to complications such as sepsis, acute respiratory distress syndrome (ARDS), and multi-organ failure. Preventive measures include vaccination against pneumococcal bacteria and the influenza virus, hand hygiene, smoking cessation, and addressing risk factors such as chronic lung diseases. Understanding these aspects is crucial for critical care nurses preparing for the CCRN exam.

1.2.5 Aspiration:

Aspiration refers to the inhalation of foreign material, such as food, liquid, or gastric contents, into the respiratory tract. This can lead to serious complications, including aspiration pneumonia, acute respiratory distress syndrome (ARDS), and even death. Aspiration is particularly concerning in critically ill patients who may have compromised swallowing reflexes or altered consciousness.

In the context of critical care, understanding the risk factors for aspiration is crucial. These factors include neurological impairments (such as stroke or traumatic brain injury), sedation or anesthesia, mechanical ventilation, and conditions that affect swallowing mechanisms, such as esophageal disorders. Patients with a decreased level of consciousness are at heightened risk due to impaired protective airway reflexes.

Preventative strategies are essential for managing aspiration risk. These strategies include elevating the head of the bed to 30-45 degrees during feeding and for at least 30 minutes afterward, ensuring proper cuff inflation in intubated patients to prevent the leakage of secretions into the lower airways, and using swallow assessments to identify dysphagia early.

In cases where aspiration is suspected, immediate intervention is required. This may involve suctioning the airway to remove aspirated material and administering supplemental oxygen. Antibiotic therapy may be initiated if aspiration pneumonia develops. Continuous monitoring and reassessment are critical for effectively managing potential complications.

Understanding the pathophysiology of aspiration and implementing evidence-based preventative measures are key components for critical care nurses preparing for the CCRN exam. Mastery of these concepts ensures optimal patient outcomes in high-risk scenarios.

1.2.6 Chronic Conditions:

Chronic conditions are long-term health issues that persist for an extended period, often for the remainder of an individual's life. These conditions typically develop slowly and can be managed but are not usually curable. In the context of critical care nursing, understanding chronic conditions is crucial, as they often complicate acute episodes and significantly impact patient outcomes.

Chronic conditions encompass a wide range of diseases, including diabetes mellitus, heart disease, chronic obstructive pulmonary disease (COPD), arthritis, and hypertension. These illnesses require ongoing medical attention and can limit daily activities. They are often characterized by periods of exacerbation and remission, demanding vigilant monitoring and management.

For critical care nurses, the complexity of managing patients with chronic conditions lies in balancing acute needs with the management of underlying chronic diseases. This involves a comprehensive approach that includes medication management, lifestyle modifications, patient education, and coordination of care among multiple healthcare providers.

Furthermore, chronic conditions often lead to multi-system complications, necessitating a holistic understanding of how these diseases interact with one another and affect overall health. The presence of chronic conditions can alter the presentation of acute symptoms, influence treatment options, and affect recovery trajectories.

In preparing for the CCRN exam, it is essential to grasp the pathophysiology, common interventions, and evidence-based practices related to chronic conditions. This knowledge enables nurses to deliver high-quality care that improves patient outcomes and enhances the quality of life for those living with these persistent health challenges.

1.2.6.1 Understanding Chronic Obstructive Pulmonary Disease (COPD):

Chronic Obstructive Pulmonary Disease (COPD) is a progressive respiratory disorder characterized by persistent airflow limitation, primarily caused by emphysema and chronic bronchitis. This condition is largely attributed to long-term exposure to irritating gases or particulate matter, most commonly from cigarette smoke. COPD is marked by an inflammatory response in the lungs, leading to structural changes, narrowing of the airways, destruction of lung parenchyma, and loss of elastic recoil.

Clinically, COPD presents with symptoms such as chronic cough, sputum production, dyspnea on exertion, and frequent respiratory infections. As the disease progresses, patients may experience exacerbations, which are acute episodes of worsening symptoms that can significantly impact quality of life and may require hospitalization.

The diagnosis of COPD is confirmed through spirometry, which demonstrates a reduced FEV1/FVC ratio post-bronchodilator administration. Management strategies for COPD include smoking cessation, pharmacotherapy with bronchodilators and corticosteroids, pulmonary rehabilitation, and supplemental oxygen therapy for those with severe hypoxemia. Vaccinations against influenza and pneumococcus are also recommended to prevent respiratory infections.

In the context of critical care, nurses must be adept at recognizing signs of respiratory distress and managing acute exacerbations. This includes administering medications, monitoring arterial blood gases, providing ventilatory support if necessary, and educating patients on self-management strategies to prevent future exacerbations. Understanding the pathophysiology and management of COPD is crucial for critical care nurses to effectively care for this patient population.

1.2.6.2   Asthma:

Asthma is a chronic inflammatory disorder of the airways characterized by reversible airflow obstruction and bronchospasm. It involves complex interactions between airway inflammation, intermittent airflow obstruction, and bronchial hyperresponsiveness. The hallmark symptoms include wheezing, coughing, chest tightness, and shortness of breath, which can vary in frequency and severity among individuals.

In asthma, triggers such as allergens, respiratory infections, exercise, cold air, and stress can exacerbate symptoms by initiating an inflammatory response. This response involves the activation of mast cells, eosinophils, T lymphocytes, macrophages, neutrophils, and epithelial cells within the airways. The release of mediators like histamines and leukotrienes leads to bronchoconstriction, increased mucus production, and airway edema.

Diagnosis typically involves a detailed patient history and pulmonary function tests (PFTs), such as spirometry, which measures the forced expiratory volume in one second (FEV1) and its ratio to forced vital capacity (FVC). A significant improvement in FEV1 following bronchodilator administration supports the diagnosis.

Management focuses on reducing exposure to triggers and controlling symptoms through pharmacological interventions. Inhaled corticosteroids are the cornerstone of long-term control therapy due to their efficacy in reducing inflammation. Short-acting beta-agonists (SABAs) provide quick relief during acute exacerbations by relaxing bronchial smooth muscles.

Asthma education is crucial for patients to understand self-management strategies, including proper inhaler techniques and recognizing early signs of exacerbations. Effective management aims to minimize symptoms, prevent exacerbations, maintain normal activity levels, and achieve optimal lung function.

1.2.6.3   Bronchitis:

Bronchitis is an inflammation of the bronchial tubes, which are the air passages that extend from the trachea into the lungs. This condition results in swelling and irritation of these airways, leading to the production of mucus. There are two main types of bronchitis: acute and chronic. Acute bronchitis often develops from respiratory infections such as colds or the flu and is characterized by a cough that may produce mucus, chest discomfort, fatigue, shortness of breath, and sometimes fever. It typically resolves within a few weeks.

Chronic bronchitis, on the other hand, is a long-term condition that falls under the umbrella of Chronic Obstructive Pulmonary Disease (COPD). It is defined by a productive cough that lasts for at least three months in two consecutive years. The primary cause of chronic bronchitis is long-term exposure to irritants such as tobacco smoke, air pollution, dust, or chemical fumes. This exposure leads to persistent inflammation and thickening of the bronchial walls, excessive mucus production, and decreased airflow.

In chronic bronchitis, patients often experience frequent respiratory infections and exacerbations that can lead to further lung damage. Management includes smoking cessation, bronchodilators, corticosteroids to reduce inflammation, pulmonary rehabilitation, and oxygen therapy in advanced stages. Understanding the pathophysiology of bronchitis is crucial for critical care nurses to effectively assess respiratory function, implement appropriate interventions, and educate patients on lifestyle modifications to manage symptoms and prevent complications.

1.2.6.4   Emphysema:

Emphysema is a chronic, progressive lung condition that falls under the broader category of chronic obstructive pulmonary disease (COPD). It is characterized by the destruction and enlargement of the air spaces distal to the terminal bronchioles, resulting in decreased respiratory function and breathlessness. The primary pathological change in emphysema is the irreversible damage to the alveoli, which are the tiny air sacs in the lungs where gas exchange occurs. This damage leads to a loss of elastic recoil, causing air trapping and hyperinflation of the lungs.

The most common cause of emphysema is long-term exposure to airborne irritants, with cigarette smoking being the predominant risk factor. Other contributing factors include exposure to occupational dust and chemicals, air pollution, and a rare genetic disorder known as alpha-1 antitrypsin deficiency.

Clinically, patients with emphysema often present with a history of progressive dyspnea, chronic cough, and wheezing. Physical examination may reveal signs such as barrel chest, the use of accessory muscles for breathing, and decreased breath sounds upon auscultation. Diagnostic evaluation typically includes pulmonary function tests that show reduced forced expiratory volume (FEV1) and increased total lung capacity (TLC).

Management of emphysema focuses on symptom relief and slowing disease progression. This includes smoking cessation, bronchodilator therapy, corticosteroids, pulmonary rehabilitation, and supplemental oxygen therapy for advanced cases. Understanding the pathophysiology and management strategies for emphysema is crucial for critical care nurses in providing comprehensive care to patients with this debilitating condition.

1.2.7 Mechanical Ventilation Weaning Failure:

Failure to wean from mechanical ventilation occurs when a patient is unable to sustain spontaneous breathing after attempts to discontinue ventilatory support. This condition can arise due to various factors, including respiratory muscle weakness, inadequate oxygenation, or underlying medical conditions that impede respiratory function. Successful weaning requires the patient to maintain adequate ventilation and oxygenation without mechanical assistance.

In critical care settings, the process of weaning involves gradually reducing ventilatory support while closely monitoring the patient's respiratory status. Factors contributing to failure include neuromuscular disorders, persistent lung disease, cardiac insufficiency, and metabolic imbalances. Additionally, psychological factors such as anxiety or lack of motivation can hinder the weaning process.

Assessment for readiness to wean involves evaluating parameters such as the patient's respiratory rate, tidal volume, arterial blood gases, and overall clinical stability. Protocols like spontaneous breathing trials (SBT) are employed to test the patient's capability to breathe independently. During these trials, patients are observed for signs of distress, such as tachypnea, hypoxemia, or hemodynamic instability.

Management of failure to wean necessitates identifying and addressing reversible causes. Interventions may include optimizing nutritional support, treating infections, adjusting medications that affect respiratory drive, or employing non-invasive ventilation strategies as a bridge during the weaning process.

Understanding the multifactorial nature of weaning failure is crucial for critical care nurses in developing individualized care plans that enhance the likelihood of successful liberation from mechanical ventilation.

1.2.8 Pleural Space Abnormalities:

Pleural space abnormalities refer to pathological conditions affecting the pleural cavity, the thin fluid-filled space between the two pulmonary pleurae (visceral and parietal) of each lung. These abnormalities often result from an imbalance in the production and absorption of pleural fluid or from pathological processes affecting the pleura.

One common pleural space abnormality is a pleural effusion, which is the accumulation of excess fluid in the pleural space. This can be caused by various conditions, such as heart failure, pneumonia, malignancies, or pulmonary embolism. Pleural effusions can be classified as transudative, resulting from systemic factors like increased hydrostatic pressure or decreased oncotic pressure, or exudative, due to local factors such as inflammation or malignancy.

Another significant abnormality is pneumothorax, which occurs when air enters the pleural space, leading to lung collapse. This can happen spontaneously or as a result of trauma or medical procedures. Tension pneumothorax is a life-threatening condition in which air trapped in the pleural space increases pressure on thoracic structures, requiring immediate intervention.

Hemothorax involves the accumulation of blood in the pleural cavity, often due to trauma or surgical complications. Chylothorax is characterized by the accumulation of lymphatic fluid, usually resulting from thoracic duct disruption.

Understanding these abnormalities is crucial for critical care nurses, as they require prompt identification and management to prevent respiratory compromise and ensure optimal patient outcomes. Management strategies may include thoracentesis, chest tube placement, or surgical interventions, depending on the underlying cause and severity.

1.2.8.1 Pneumothorax:

Pneumothorax is a critical condition characterized by the presence of air in the pleural space, which is the area between the visceral and parietal pleura of the lungs. This accumulation of air leads to a partial or complete collapse of the lung on the affected side due to increased intrapleural pressure, disrupting the normal negative pressure required for lung expansion during inspiration.

There are several types of pneumothorax, including spontaneous, traumatic, and tension pneumothorax. Spontaneous pneumothorax can be classified as primary, occurring without underlying lung disease—often in tall, young males—or secondary, which is associated with pre-existing pulmonary conditions such as chronic obstructive pulmonary disease (COPD) or cystic fibrosis. Traumatic pneumothorax results from blunt or penetrating chest injuries, while tension pneumothorax is a life-threatening variant in which trapped air progressively accumulates, causing mediastinal shift and compromised venous return to the heart.

Clinically, patients may present with sudden onset of chest pain and dyspnea. Physical examination may reveal decreased breath sounds and hyperresonance on percussion over the affected side. Diagnosis is confirmed through imaging, typically a chest X-ray that shows a visceral pleural line with an absence of vascular markings beyond this line.

Management depends on severity; small pneumothoraces may resolve spontaneously, while larger ones require interventions such as needle decompression or chest tube insertion to evacuate air and re-expand the lung. Prompt recognition and treatment are crucial to prevent complications such as respiratory distress or cardiovascular instability.

1.2.8.2 Hemothorax:

Hemothorax is a pleural space abnormality characterized by the accumulation of blood in the pleural cavity, the space between the visceral and parietal pleura surrounding the lungs. This condition often results from traumatic injury to the chest, such as rib fractures or penetrating wounds, but it can also arise from non-traumatic causes like malignancy, anticoagulation therapy, or complications from thoracic surgery.

Clinically, hemothorax presents with symptoms such as chest pain, dyspnea (shortness of breath), tachypnea (rapid breathing), and reduced breath sounds on the affected side. The accumulation of blood in the pleural space can lead to lung compression and impaired respiratory function. On physical examination, there may be dullness to percussion over the affected area due to the presence of fluid.

Diagnostic evaluation typically involves imaging studies such as a chest X-ray, which may reveal pleural effusion or mediastinal shift in large hemothoraces. A CT scan can provide more detailed visualization of the extent and source of bleeding. Thoracentesis or thoracostomy (chest tube insertion) is both diagnostic and therapeutic, allowing for the drainage of blood and assessment of its nature.

Management of hemothorax focuses on stabilizing the patient and addressing the source of bleeding. Initial treatment involves volume resuscitation and oxygen support. Surgical intervention may be necessary for ongoing hemorrhage or if there is significant retained clotting. Prompt recognition and management are crucial to preventing complications such as fibrothorax or infection. Understanding these aspects is essential for critical care nurses in effectively managing patients with hemothorax.

1.2.8.3 Empyema:

Empyema is a condition characterized by the accumulation of pus in the pleural space, which is the area between the lung and the chest wall. This occurs due to an infection that leads to the collection of purulent material in this normally fluid-filled space, often as a complication of pneumonia, thoracic surgery, or trauma. The presence of pus indicates a bacterial infection, with common causative organisms including Streptococcus pneumoniae, Staphylococcus aureus, and Haemophilus influenzae.

In the context of critical care nursing, understanding empyema is crucial due to its potential to cause significant respiratory distress and systemic infection. Clinically, patients with empyema may present with symptoms such as fever, chest pain, cough, dyspnea, and malaise. On physical examination, decreased breath sounds and dullness on percussion over the affected area may be noted.

Diagnosis typically involves imaging studies such as chest X-rays or CT scans to visualize fluid collections. Thoracentesis can be performed to obtain pleural fluid for analysis, confirming the presence of pus and identifying the causative organism through culture.

Management of empyema involves antibiotic therapy tailored to the identified pathogen and drainage of the pleural space. This can be achieved through procedures such as thoracostomy (chest tube insertion) or more invasive surgical interventions like video-assisted thoracoscopic surgery (VATS) if necessary.

For critical care nurses preparing for the CCRN exam, it is essential to recognize the signs and symptoms of empyema promptly and understand its management strategies to effectively care for affected patients.

1.2.8.4 Pleural Effusions:

Pleural effusions refer to the abnormal accumulation of fluid in the pleural space, the thin cavity between the visceral and parietal pleurae surrounding the lungs. This condition can significantly affect respiratory function, leading to symptoms such as dyspnea, chest pain, and cough. Pleural effusions are categorized as transudative or exudative based on the protein content and other characteristics of the fluid.

Transudative effusions are typically caused by systemic factors that alter hydrostatic or oncotic pressure, such as heart failure or cirrhosis. These effusions have low protein content and are generally less inflammatory. In contrast, exudative effusions result from local factors that increase capillary permeability or decrease lymphatic drainage, often due to infections like pneumonia, malignancies, or pulmonary embolism. Exudative fluids have higher protein content and may contain cells indicative of inflammation or infection.

The diagnosis of pleural effusion involves clinical assessment, imaging studies such as chest X-rays or ultrasounds, and thoracentesis for fluid analysis. Light's criteria are commonly used to differentiate between transudative and exudative effusions based on fluid protein and lactate dehydrogenase levels compared to serum values.

Management depends on the underlying cause but may include therapeutic thoracentesis to relieve symptoms, treating the primary disease process, or surgical interventions in recurrent cases. Understanding the pathophysiology and management of pleural effusions is crucial for critical care nurses to provide effective patient care and optimize outcomes for affected individuals.

1.2.9 Pulmonary Fibrosis:

Pulmonary fibrosis is a progressive and chronic lung disease characterized by the thickening and scarring (fibrosis) of lung tissue, primarily affecting the interstitium, which is the tissue and space surrounding the air sacs of the lungs. This scarring disrupts the normal architecture of the lungs, leading to a decline in respiratory function as it impairs gas exchange. Patients often present with symptoms such as a persistent dry cough, shortness of breath, fatigue, and unexplained weight loss. On auscultation, fine crackles or Velcro-like sounds may be heard.

The etiology of pulmonary fibrosis can be idiopathic, known as Idiopathic Pulmonary Fibrosis (IPF), or secondary to other conditions such as connective tissue diseases, environmental exposures, certain medications, or radiation therapy. Idiopathic Pulmonary Fibrosis is the most common type and typically affects individuals over 50 years of age.

The diagnosis of pulmonary fibrosis involves a combination of clinical evaluation, pulmonary function tests showing a restrictive pattern, imaging studies like high-resolution computed tomography (HRCT) scans revealing reticular opacities and honeycombing patterns, and sometimes lung biopsy for a definitive diagnosis.

Management focuses on slowing disease progression and alleviating symptoms. Antifibrotic agents such as nintedanib and pirfenidone are used to manage IPF. Supplemental oxygen therapy and pulmonary rehabilitation may also be beneficial. In advanced cases, lung transplantation might be considered.

Understanding pulmonary fibrosis is crucial for critical care nurses, as they play a pivotal role in monitoring disease progression, managing symptoms, and providing holistic care to improve patients' quality of life.

1.2.10 Pulmonary Hypertension:

Pulmonary Hypertension (PH) is a complex and progressive condition characterized by elevated blood pressure within the pulmonary arteries, which are responsible for transporting blood from the heart to the lungs. In PH, the increased pressure results from the narrowing or obstruction of these vessels, leading to increased resistance against which the right ventricle must pump. Over time, this can lead to right ventricular hypertrophy and eventually to right-sided heart failure.

The pathophysiology of PH involves endothelial dysfunction, vasoconstriction, vascular remodeling, and thrombosis in situ. These processes contribute to the increased pulmonary vascular resistance. PH is classified into five groups based on underlying causes: Group 1 (pulmonary arterial hypertension), Group 2 (due to left heart disease), Group 3 (due to lung diseases or hypoxia), Group 4 (chronic thromboembolic pulmonary hypertension), and Group 5 (PH with unclear multifactorial mechanisms).

Clinically, patients may present with symptoms such as dyspnea on exertion, fatigue, chest pain, syncope, and peripheral edema. Diagnosis typically involves echocardiography followed by right heart catheterization for confirmation and hemodynamic assessment.

Management of PH is multifaceted, aiming to address underlying causes and alleviate symptoms. Treatment options include diuretics, oxygen therapy, anticoagulation, and targeted pharmacotherapy, such as endothelin receptor antagonists, phosphodiesterase-5 inhibitors, and prostacyclin analogs. In advanced cases, surgical interventions such as atrial septostomy or lung transplantation may be considered.

For CCRN exam preparation, understanding the classification, pathophysiology, clinical manifestations, diagnostic approaches, and management strategies of PH is crucial for critical care nurses.

1.2.11 Status Asthmaticus:

Status Asthmaticus is a severe, life-threatening asthma exacerbation that does not respond to standard treatments, such as inhaled bronchodilators and corticosteroids. It is characterized by prolonged respiratory distress and requires immediate medical intervention to prevent respiratory failure or arrest. This condition represents the extreme end of the asthma severity spectrum and necessitates intensive care management.

In patients with Status Asthmaticus, airway inflammation, bronchospasm, and mucus plugging lead to significant airflow obstruction. Clinically, it manifests as severe dyspnea, wheezing, chest tightness, and hypoxemia. As the condition progresses, patients may exhibit signs of respiratory fatigue, altered mental status due to hypercapnia or hypoxia, and paradoxical breathing patterns.

Management in a critical care setting involves aggressive pharmacologic therapy and supportive measures. High-dose inhaled beta-agonists and systemic corticosteroids are administered to reduce bronchospasm and inflammation. Intravenous magnesium sulfate may be used for its bronchodilatory effects. In refractory cases, non-invasive ventilation or mechanical ventilation may be required to maintain adequate oxygenation and ventilation.

Continuous monitoring of vital signs, arterial blood gases, and pulmonary function is essential to assess treatment efficacy and detect early signs of deterioration. Critical care nurses must be vigilant in recognizing the progression of symptoms and collaborating with the healthcare team to adjust therapeutic interventions promptly.

Understanding Status Asthmaticus is crucial for critical care nurses, as it involves rapid assessment skills, knowledge of advanced therapeutic modalities, and proficiency in managing complex respiratory emergencies.

1.2.12 Thoracic Surgery:

Thoracic surgery involves surgical interventions within the chest cavity, encompassing procedures on the lungs, esophagus, trachea, chest wall, diaphragm, and mediastinum. It is a critical component of care for patients with conditions such as lung cancer, esophageal cancer, emphysema, and other complex thoracic pathologies. Thoracic surgeons perform both open surgeries and minimally invasive techniques, such as video-assisted thoracoscopic surgery (VATS) and robotic-assisted thoracic surgery (RATS), which offer reduced recovery times and less postoperative pain compared to traditional methods.

For critical care nurses preparing for the CCRN exam, it is essential to understand the preoperative and postoperative management of patients undergoing thoracic surgery. Preoperatively, nurses must ensure thorough patient assessments, including pulmonary function tests and imaging studies, to evaluate surgical risks. Postoperatively, vigilant monitoring is crucial for detecting complications such as pneumothorax, hemothorax, and respiratory distress. Pain management is paramount; thus, nurses must be adept at administering analgesics and employing adjunctive therapies like epidural analgesia.

Moreover, nurses should be proficient in managing chest tubes, which are often placed to drain air or fluid from the pleural space post-surgery. Understanding the principles of chest tube care—such as maintaining patency, preventing infection, and monitoring output—is vital. Additionally, promoting early ambulation and pulmonary rehabilitation exercises can significantly enhance recovery by improving lung function and reducing the risk of atelectasis or pneumonia. Mastery of these aspects is crucial for optimizing patient outcomes in thoracic surgery cases.

1.2.13 Thoracic Trauma:

Thoracic trauma refers to any injury to the chest area, which encompasses the thoracic cavity, rib cage, lungs, heart, and major blood vessels. It is a critical condition that demands immediate attention due to its potential to impair respiratory and cardiovascular function. Thoracic injuries can be classified as either blunt or penetrating. Blunt trauma typically results from impacts such as motor vehicle accidents or falls, leading to rib fractures, pulmonary contusions, or cardiac tamponade. Penetrating trauma involves objects like bullets or knives breaching the chest wall, potentially causing pneumothorax, hemothorax, or damage to vital organs.

In the context of critical care nursing, it is essential to assess and manage thoracic trauma promptly. The initial evaluation includes ensuring airway patency, breathing adequacy, and circulatory stability (the ABCs). Diagnostic tools such as chest X-rays, CT scans, and ultrasounds are integral for identifying the extent of the injury. Treatment strategies may involve chest tube insertion for pneumothorax or hemothorax, surgical intervention for severe cases like cardiac tamponade or major vessel injury, and supportive care, including oxygen therapy and pain management.

Understanding the pathophysiology of thoracic trauma is crucial for predicting complications such as tension pneumothorax or acute respiratory distress syndrome (ARDS). Critical care nurses must be adept at recognizing signs of deterioration and coordinating multidisciplinary interventions to optimize patient outcomes in these life-threatening scenarios.

1.2.13.1 Fractured Rib:

A fractured rib, commonly referred to as a rib fracture, is a break or crack in one of the bones of the rib cage. This condition is typically caused by direct trauma to the chest, such as from a fall, motor vehicle accident, or sports injury. It can also result from repetitive stress or severe coughing in individuals with underlying health conditions that weaken bone integrity.

Clinically, a fractured rib presents with sharp, localized pain that exacerbates with deep breathing, coughing, or movement of the torso. Patients may also experience tenderness when the affected area is palpated. In some cases, crepitus—a grating sensation felt during palpation—may be present due to bone fragments rubbing against each other.

The primary concern with rib fractures in critical care settings is the potential for complications such as pneumothorax (air in the pleural space), hemothorax (blood in the pleural space), or flail chest—where multiple adjacent ribs are fractured in multiple places, leading to paradoxical chest wall movement and impaired ventilation.

Management of rib fractures focuses on pain control to facilitate adequate ventilation and prevent atelectasis or pneumonia. Analgesic options include oral medications, intercostal nerve blocks, or epidural analgesia. Encouraging deep breathing exercises and using incentive spirometry are essential components of care to maintain lung expansion and prevent pulmonary complications.

Nurses must closely monitor patients for signs of respiratory distress and ensure effective pain management strategies are employed to promote optimal recovery and prevent further morbidity associated with rib fractures.

1.2.13.2 Lung Contusion:

Lung contusion is a form of blunt thoracic trauma characterized by injury to the lung parenchyma without laceration. It results from a direct impact or rapid deceleration, causing alveolar-capillary damage and hemorrhage into the lung tissue. This injury leads to pulmonary edema and impaired gas exchange, often manifesting as hypoxemia and respiratory distress.

Clinically, lung contusions are diagnosed through imaging studies, with chest X-rays and CT scans revealing patchy infiltrates or ground-glass opacities that may not appear immediately post-trauma but develop over 24 to 48 hours. The severity of a lung contusion is directly related to the extent of the trauma and can range from mild to severe, potentially leading to acute respiratory distress syndrome (ARDS).

Management of lung contusion is primarily supportive. It involves ensuring adequate oxygenation and ventilation while minimizing further lung injury. This may require supplemental oxygen, non-invasive ventilation, or mechanical ventilation in severe cases. Fluid management is crucial; excessive fluid administration can exacerbate pulmonary edema, whereas conservative fluid strategies help limit this risk.

Monitoring for complications such as pneumonia or ARDS is essential. Prophylactic antibiotics are not routinely recommended unless there is evidence of infection. Pain control is vital to enable effective coughing and deep breathing exercises, thereby reducing the risk of atelectasis.

In summary, understanding the pathophysiology and management principles of lung contusion is critical for nurses preparing for the CCRN exam, as it underscores the importance of early recognition and appropriate intervention in thoracic trauma care.

1.2.13.3 Tracheal Perforation:

Tracheal perforation refers to a breach or tear in the tracheal wall, which can lead to significant respiratory compromise and requires prompt medical attention. It can occur due to various causes, including traumatic injury, iatrogenic factors (such as intubation or surgical procedures), infections, or malignancy. The condition is characterized by air leakage into surrounding tissues, potentially leading to subcutaneous emphysema, pneumomediastinum, or pneumothorax.

Clinically, patients with tracheal perforation may present with symptoms such as dyspnea, cough, hemoptysis, and voice changes. Physical examination may reveal subcutaneous emphysema, particularly in the neck or chest region. The diagnosis is often confirmed through imaging studies like chest X-ray or CT scan, which can show air outside the trachea or in the mediastinum.

Management of tracheal perforation depends on the size and cause of the tear. Small perforations may be managed conservatively with close observation and supportive care, including oxygen therapy and antibiotics if infection is suspected. Larger or symptomatic perforations may require surgical intervention to repair the defect.

In critical care settings, maintaining airway patency and ensuring adequate ventilation are paramount. Nursing staff must monitor for signs of respiratory distress and be prepared to assist in advanced airway management if necessary. Understanding the pathophysiology and management strategies for tracheal perforation is essential for providing comprehensive care to affected patients and minimizing potential complications.

1.2.14 Understanding TRALI: Causes and Impacts

Transfusion-related Acute Lung Injury (TRALI) is a serious and potentially life-threatening condition characterized by acute respiratory distress following a blood transfusion. It is one of the leading causes of transfusion-related mortality. TRALI typically occurs within 1 to 6 hours after the transfusion of blood products, including red blood cells, platelets, plasma, or whole blood. The pathophysiology of TRALI involves an immune-mediated reaction in which donor antibodies react with recipient leukocytes, leading to the activation and sequestration of neutrophils in the pulmonary vasculature. This results in increased capillary permeability and the development of non-cardiogenic pulmonary edema.

Clinically, TRALI presents with a sudden onset of dyspnea, hypoxemia, bilateral pulmonary infiltrates on chest X-ray, and fever, without evidence of circulatory overload or cardiac failure. It is crucial to differentiate TRALI from Transfusion-associated Circulatory Overload (TACO), as both conditions present with respiratory distress but have different management strategies.

The management of TRALI primarily involves supportive care, including oxygen therapy and mechanical ventilation if necessary. There is no specific pharmacological treatment for TRALI; thus, prevention through careful donor selection and minimizing unnecessary transfusions is key. Awareness and prompt recognition by healthcare providers are essential to mitigate the impact of TRALI on patient outcomes. Understanding the etiology, clinical presentation, and management strategies for TRALI is critical for nurses preparing for the Critical Care Certification (CCRN) exam.

1.3 Endocrine/Hematology/Gastrointestinal/Renal/Integumentary:

The integration of the endocrine, hematologic, gastrointestinal, renal, and integumentary systems is critical for maintaining homeostasis and responding to acute changes in critically ill patients.

The endocrine system comprises glands that release hormones directly into the bloodstream to regulate metabolism, growth, and physiological responses. Key glands include the pituitary, thyroid, adrenal glands, and pancreas. In critical care, understanding hormone imbalances, such as adrenal insufficiency or thyroid storm, is vital for effective patient management.

Hematology focuses on blood and its components, including disorders such as anemia, coagulopathies, and thrombocytopenia. Critical care nurses must be adept at interpreting laboratory results and managing complications like disseminated intravascular coagulation (DIC).

The gastrointestinal system encompasses organs involved in digestion and nutrient absorption. Critical conditions may include gastrointestinal bleeding or hepatic failure. Nurses should be proficient in assessing bowel sounds, managing nutritional support, and recognizing signs of liver dysfunction.

Renal function is essential for waste excretion and maintaining fluid and electrolyte balance. Acute kidney injury (AKI) is a common issue in critical care settings. Understanding renal replacement therapies and electrolyte management is crucial for patient stability.

The integumentary system includes the skin and its appendages, serving as a barrier against infection. In critical care, the prevention of pressure ulcers and the management of wounds or burns are key responsibilities.

Proficiency in these systems enables critical care nurses to provide comprehensive care tailored to the complex needs of critically ill patients.

1.3.1 Endocrine:

The endocrine system is a network of glands that produce and secrete hormones, which are chemical messengers that regulate numerous bodily functions. These functions include metabolism, growth and development, tissue function, sexual function, reproduction, sleep, and mood, among others. The primary glands of the endocrine system include the hypothalamus, pituitary gland, thyroid gland, parathyroid glands, adrenal glands, pancreas, ovaries in females, and testes in males.

In critical care settings, understanding the endocrine system is crucial due to its role in maintaining homeostasis. Hormonal imbalances can lead to significant clinical conditions requiring immediate intervention. For instance, adrenal insufficiency can result in life-threatening hypotension and electrolyte imbalances due to inadequate production of cortisol. Similarly, thyroid storm and myxedema coma represent extreme states of thyroid hormone imbalance with severe implications for cardiovascular and neurological status.

The pancreas plays a vital role in glucose metabolism through the secretion of insulin and glucagon. Dysregulation can lead to diabetic emergencies such as diabetic ketoacidosis (DKA) or hyperosmolar hyperglycemic state (HHS), both of which require vigilant monitoring and management in critical care environments.

Endocrine emergencies also include pheochromocytoma crisis and hypercalcemic crisis. These conditions necessitate a comprehensive understanding of pathophysiology and prompt therapeutic strategies to prevent morbidity and mortality.

Critical care nurses must be adept at recognizing signs of endocrine dysfunction and implementing appropriate interventions to stabilize patients while collaborating with multidisciplinary teams for optimal outcomes in critical care settings.

1.3.1.1 Adrenal Insufficiency:

Adrenal insufficiency is a condition characterized by inadequate production of hormones by the adrenal glands, primarily cortisol and, in some cases, aldosterone. This deficiency can result from primary adrenal failure (Addison's disease) or secondary causes due to pituitary gland dysfunction. In critical care settings, understanding adrenal insufficiency is vital, as it can lead to life-threatening complications if not promptly identified and managed.

Primary adrenal insufficiency occurs when the adrenal glands are directly damaged, often due to autoimmune destruction, infections, or hemorrhage. It results in a decrease in both glucocorticoids and mineralocorticoids. Secondary adrenal insufficiency arises from insufficient adrenocorticotropic hormone (ACTH) production by the pituitary gland, often due to abrupt cessation of exogenous steroids or pituitary disorders, leading primarily to glucocorticoid deficiency.

Clinically, patients may present with nonspecific symptoms such as fatigue, weight loss, hypotension, and hyperpigmentation in primary cases. Electrolyte imbalances, such as hyponatremia and hyperkalemia, are common due to aldosterone deficiency. In acute scenarios, known as an adrenal crisis, patients can experience severe hypotension, shock, and electrolyte disturbances, requiring immediate intervention with intravenous fluids and glucocorticoids.

Diagnosis involves measuring serum cortisol levels and conducting ACTH stimulation tests. Treatment focuses on hormone replacement therapy using hydrocortisone or fludrocortisone while addressing the underlying cause. Critical care nurses must be adept at recognizing signs of adrenal insufficiency and managing acute crises to prevent morbidity and mortality associated with this endocrine disorder.

1.3.1.2 Diabetes Insipidus (DI):

Diabetes Insipidus (DI) is a disorder characterized by an imbalance in the body's water regulation, leading to excessive thirst and the excretion of large volumes of dilute urine. Unlike diabetes mellitus, DI is not related to blood sugar levels but rather involves the hormone vasopressin, also known as antidiuretic hormone (ADH), which is responsible for regulating water balance in the body.

There are two primary forms of DI: central and nephrogenic. Central DI occurs due to insufficient production or release of ADH from the pituitary gland, often resulting from head injury, surgery, infection, or genetic factors. Nephrogenic DI arises when the kidneys fail to respond properly to ADH, which can be due to genetic mutations, certain medications like lithium, or chronic kidney disorders.

Clinically, patients with DI present with polyuria (excessive urination) and polydipsia (excessive thirst). Diagnostic evaluation includes a water deprivation test to assess the kidneys' ability to concentrate urine and measuring plasma and urine osmolality. Additionally, desmopressin stimulation tests help differentiate between central and nephrogenic DI.

Management of DI focuses on addressing the underlying cause and restoring fluid balance. Central DI is often treated with desmopressin acetate, a synthetic ADH analog. In contrast, nephrogenic DI may require dietary modifications, thiazide diuretics, or non-steroidal anti-inflammatory drugs (NSAIDs) to reduce urine output.

Understanding DI is crucial for critical care nurses as they monitor fluid balance and implement appropriate interventions to prevent complications such as dehydration and electrolyte imbalances.

1.3.1.3 Diabetes Mellitus: Types 1 & 2

Diabetes Mellitus is a chronic endocrine disorder characterized by hyperglycemia due to impaired insulin secretion, insulin action, or both. Type 1 Diabetes Mellitus (T1DM) is an autoimmune condition in which the immune system attacks and destroys insulin-producing beta cells in the pancreas, leading to absolute insulin deficiency. It typically presents in childhood or adolescence but can occur at any age. Patients with T1DM require lifelong exogenous insulin therapy for survival.

Type 2 Diabetes Mellitus (T2DM) is primarily associated with insulin resistance and relative insulin deficiency. It is more common in adults and is often linked to obesity, a sedentary lifestyle, and genetic predisposition. In T2DM, the body's cells become less responsive to insulin, leading to increased blood glucose levels. Initially, the pancreas compensates by producing more insulin; however, over time, this compensatory mechanism fails.

Management of diabetes involves maintaining blood glucose levels within a target range to prevent acute complications such as diabetic ketoacidosis in T1DM and hyperosmolar hyperglycemic state in T2DM. Long-term management aims to prevent microvascular (retinopathy, nephropathy, neuropathy) and macrovascular (cardiovascular disease) complications through lifestyle modifications, pharmacotherapy, and regular monitoring of blood glucose levels and HbA1c.

Nurses play a critical role in educating patients about self-management strategies, recognizing signs of hypo- and hyperglycemia, and understanding the importance of adherence to treatment regimens. Their expertise ensures optimal patient outcomes through vigilant monitoring and timely intervention.

1.3.1.4 Diabetic Ketoacidosis (DKA):

Diabetic Ketoacidosis (DKA) is a serious acute complication of diabetes, primarily seen in individuals with type 1 diabetes, though it can also occur in type 2 diabetes under certain circumstances. DKA arises from a profound deficiency of insulin, leading to hyperglycemia, ketosis, and metabolic acidosis. The pathophysiology involves the body's inability to utilize glucose for energy due to insufficient insulin, prompting lipolysis and subsequent ketone production by the liver. This results in an accumulation of ketones in the blood, causing a decrease in blood pH.

Clinically, DKA is characterized by elevated blood glucose levels (typically >250 mg/dL), an arterial pH of less than 7.3, and serum bicarbonate levels below 18 mEq/L. Patients often present with polyuria, polydipsia, dehydration, tachycardia, Kussmaul respirations (deep, labored breathing), abdominal pain, and altered mental status.

Management of DKA involves prompt fluid resuscitation to address dehydration and electrolyte imbalances, particularly potassium. Insulin therapy is initiated to reduce hyperglycemia and suppress ketogenesis. Monitoring of electrolytes is crucial, as insulin therapy can cause shifts leading to hypokalemia. Additionally, addressing any precipitating factors, such as infection or non-compliance with insulin therapy, is essential.

For critical care nurses preparing for the CCRN exam, understanding DKA's pathophysiology, clinical presentation, and management strategies is vital for effective patient care and successful examination performance.

1.3.1.5 Hyperglycemia:

Hyperglycemia is a condition characterized by an excessive amount of glucose circulating in the blood plasma. It is typically defined as blood glucose levels exceeding 180 mg/dL. In critically ill patients, hyperglycemia can occur due to stress-induced insulin resistance, increased hepatic glucose production, or exogenous glucose administration. While it is a common finding in patients with diabetes mellitus, it can also occur in non-diabetic individuals under stress or illness.

In critical care settings, hyperglycemia is associated with increased morbidity and mortality. It impairs immune function, increases the risk of infection, and can lead to osmotic diuresis, resulting in dehydration and electrolyte imbalances. Uncontrolled hyperglycemia can progress to diabetic ketoacidosis (DKA) or hyperosmolar hyperglycemic state (HHS), both of which require immediate medical intervention.

The management of hyperglycemia involves careful monitoring of blood glucose levels and the use of insulin therapy to maintain target glucose ranges, typically between 140-180 mg/dL for critically ill patients. Continuous insulin infusions may be necessary for tight glycemic control in intensive care units. It is crucial to identify and address underlying causes such as sepsis, steroid use, or enteral/parenteral nutrition.

Nurses play a vital role in managing hyperglycemia by performing regular blood glucose monitoring, administering insulin as prescribed, and educating patients on lifestyle modifications to prevent future episodes. Understanding the pathophysiology and management strategies for hyperglycemia is essential for optimizing patient outcomes in critical care environments.

1.3.1.6 Hyperosmolar Hyperglycemic State (HHS):

Hyperosmolar Hyperglycemic State (HHS) is a serious, life-threatening complication of diabetes mellitus, predominantly occurring in individuals with type 2 diabetes. It is characterized by extremely high blood glucose levels, profound dehydration, and an absence of significant ketoacidosis, which differentiates it from diabetic ketoacidosis (DKA). HHS typically presents with blood glucose levels exceeding 600 mg/dL, plasma osmolality above 320 mOsm/kg, and severe dehydration due to osmotic diuresis.

The pathophysiology of HHS involves a relative insulin deficiency that reduces glucose utilization by peripheral tissues while hepatic glucose production remains unopposed. This leads to marked hyperglycemia, causing osmotic diuresis and subsequent dehydration. Dehydration exacerbates hyperglycemia by impairing renal function, which further elevates serum glucose levels. Electrolyte imbalances, particularly hyponatremia and hypokalemia, are common due to fluid shifts and renal losses.

Clinically, patients may present with altered mental status ranging from confusion to coma, extreme thirst, dry mucous membranes, tachycardia, hypotension, and polyuria. The absence of significant ketone production is attributed to the presence of some circulating insulin, which inhibits lipolysis.

Management of HHS focuses on aggressive fluid resuscitation to restore intravascular volume and improve renal perfusion. Insulin therapy is administered to gradually lower blood glucose levels. Electrolyte imbalances should be corrected cautiously to prevent complications such as cerebral edema. Early recognition and prompt treatment are crucial in reducing morbidity and mortality associated with HHS.

1.3.1.7 Hyperthyroidism:

Hyperthyroidism is a condition characterized by the excessive production of thyroid hormones, namely thyroxine (T4) and triiodothyronine (T3), by the thyroid gland. This overproduction leads to an acceleration of the body's metabolism, manifesting in various systemic symptoms. The most common cause of hyperthyroidism is Graves' disease, an autoimmune disorder in which antibodies stimulate the thyroid gland to produce more hormones. Other causes include toxic multinodular goiter and thyroiditis.

Clinically, hyperthyroidism presents with symptoms such as weight loss despite an increased appetite, tachycardia, palpitations, heat intolerance, sweating, tremors, and nervousness. Patients may also experience fatigue, muscle weakness, and changes in menstrual patterns. In severe cases, a life-threatening condition known as thyroid storm can occur, characterized by fever, delirium, and cardiovascular collapse.

Diagnosis involves clinical evaluation and laboratory tests showing elevated levels of free T4 and T3, with suppressed thyroid-stimulating hormone (TSH). Imaging studies, such as radioactive iodine uptake tests, can help identify the underlying cause.

Management of hyperthyroidism includes antithyroid medications, such as methimazole or propylthiouracil, to reduce hormone synthesis. Beta-blockers may be prescribed to alleviate cardiovascular symptoms. Radioactive iodine therapy is another option that targets thyroid tissue to reduce hormone production. In certain cases, surgical intervention may be necessary.

Understanding the pathophysiology and management of hyperthyroidism is crucial for critical care nurses to provide optimal patient care and education. Monitoring for complications and ensuring adherence to treatment regimens are key responsibilities in effectively managing this endocrine disorder.

1.3.1.8 Hypoglycemia (acute):

Hypoglycemia, defined as an abnormally low blood glucose level, is a critical condition that requires immediate attention in acute care settings. It is typically characterized by blood glucose levels falling below 70 mg/dL, although symptoms can vary based on individual thresholds and the rate of decline. Acute hypoglycemia can result from several factors, including excessive insulin administration, inadequate food intake, increased physical activity without appropriate dietary adjustments, or alcohol consumption.

Clinically, acute hypoglycemia presents with neuroglycopenic and autonomic symptoms. Neuroglycopenic symptoms arise due to insufficient glucose supply to the brain and include confusion, dizziness, headache, seizures, and even loss of consciousness. Autonomic symptoms result from the activation of the sympathetic nervous system and may include sweating, palpitations, tremors, anxiety, and hunger.

The management of acute hypoglycemia involves prompt recognition and treatment to prevent neurological damage. The primary intervention is the administration of rapid-acting carbohydrates, such as glucose tablets or juice, if the patient is conscious and able to swallow. In cases where oral intake is not possible or practical, intravenous administration of 50% dextrose or intramuscular glucagon may be necessary.

Critical care nurses must be adept at recognizing the early signs of hypoglycemia and implementing treatment protocols swiftly to mitigate potential complications. Continuous monitoring of blood glucose levels in at-risk patients is essential for preventing recurrent episodes. Education on identifying symptoms and understanding causes can empower patients to manage their condition effectively outside the hospital setting.

1.3.1.9 Hypothyroidism:

Hypothyroidism is a condition characterized by an underactive thyroid gland, which results in insufficient production of thyroid hormones, primarily thyroxine (T4) and triiodothyronine (T3). These hormones are crucial for regulating metabolism, and their deficiency can lead to a variety of systemic effects. In critical care settings, understanding hypothyroidism is essential due to its potential impact on cardiovascular function, metabolism, and overall patient stability.

Clinically, hypothyroidism may present with fatigue, weight gain, cold intolerance, bradycardia, dry skin, and constipation. In severe cases, myxedema coma can occur, characterized by hypothermia, altered mental status, and cardiovascular collapse. This is a life-threatening emergency that requires immediate intervention.

The pathophysiology involves either primary dysfunction of the thyroid gland itself or secondary causes, such as pituitary or hypothalamic disorders. Primary hypothyroidism is often due to autoimmune thyroiditis (Hashimoto's disease), iodine deficiency, or iatrogenic causes like thyroidectomy or radiation therapy.

Diagnosis involves measuring serum levels of Thyroid-Stimulating Hormone (TSH) and free T4. Elevated TSH with low T4 confirms primary hypothyroidism. Treatment typically involves hormone replacement therapy with levothyroxine, which must be carefully titrated based on regular monitoring of TSH levels to avoid over-replacement and subsequent hyperthyroidism.

For critical care nurses preparing for the CCRN exam, it is vital to recognize symptoms early and understand management strategies to prevent complications associated with this endocrine disorder.

1.3.1.10 SIADH Overview and Management:

SIADH is a condition characterized by the excessive release of antidiuretic hormone (ADH) from the posterior pituitary gland or other sources, leading to water retention and dilutional hyponatremia. This inappropriate secretion results in the kidneys reabsorbing more water than necessary, causing a decrease in serum osmolality and sodium levels. It is often associated with various conditions, including central nervous system disorders, malignancies (particularly small cell lung cancer), pulmonary diseases, and certain medications.

In SIADH, despite low plasma osmolality, ADH continues to be secreted, causing the kidneys to retain water. This fluid retention leads to an increase in total body water without a corresponding increase in sodium, resulting in hyponatremia.

Patients may present with symptoms ranging from mild (nausea, headache) to severe (confusion, seizures, coma), depending on the rapidity and severity of sodium depletion.

Diagnosis involves confirming low plasma osmolality alongside inappropriate urine osmolality and high urine sodium concentration. It is crucial to rule out other causes of hyponatremia, such as adrenal insufficiency or hypothyroidism.

Management focuses on treating the underlying cause and correcting the hyponatremia. Fluid restriction is the cornerstone treatment for mild cases. In severe cases or when rapid correction is necessary, hypertonic saline may be used cautiously. Medications like vasopressin receptor antagonists can also be considered for chronic cases. Monitoring for potential complications, such as osmotic demyelination syndrome, during treatment is essential for patient safety.

1.3.2 Hematology And Immunology:

Hematology is the branch of medicine that focuses on the study of blood, blood-forming organs, and blood diseases. It encompasses an understanding of the components of blood, such as red blood cells, white blood cells, platelets, hemoglobin, plasma, and bone marrow. Critical care nurses must be adept at recognizing and managing hematological disorders like anemia, clotting disorders, leukemia, and lymphoma. These conditions can significantly impact a patient's oxygen delivery, coagulation status, and immune response.

Immunology involves the study of the immune system, which is crucial for protecting the body against pathogens. It includes both innate immunity (the body's first line of defense) and adaptive immunity (which develops as a response to exposure to specific antigens). In critical care settings, nurses must understand how immunological responses can affect patient outcomes, particularly in conditions like sepsis, autoimmune disorders, and hypersensitivity reactions.

In critical care environments, hematology and immunology are intertwined. For instance, an understanding of immunohematology is essential for safe blood transfusions. Nurses must also be vigilant for signs of transfusion reactions or complications related to immunosuppression in patients undergoing treatments like chemotherapy or organ transplantation.

Proficiency in these areas enables critical care nurses to anticipate complications, implement appropriate interventions swiftly, and collaborate effectively with multidisciplinary teams to optimize patient care outcomes. Recognizing subtle changes in laboratory values or clinical presentations can be crucial in preventing adverse events and ensuring timely therapeutic measures.

1.3.2.1 Anemia:

Anemia is a hematological condition characterized by a deficiency in the number or quality of red blood cells (RBCs) or hemoglobin, leading to impaired oxygen transport to tissues. This condition can result from various etiologies, including decreased RBC production, increased RBC destruction, or blood loss. In critical care settings, understanding the pathophysiology of anemia is essential for effective management and intervention.

The primary function of hemoglobin within RBCs is to bind and transport oxygen from the lungs to peripheral tissues. Anemia can lead to hypoxia, which may exacerbate underlying conditions in critically ill patients. Symptoms often include fatigue, pallor, tachycardia, and shortness of breath. In severe cases, it can precipitate cardiac failure or exacerbate existing cardiovascular conditions.

Anemia is classified based on mean corpuscular volume (MCV) into microcytic, normocytic, and macrocytic types. Common causes include iron deficiency (microcytic), chronic disease (normocytic), and vitamin B12 or folate deficiency (macrocytic). In critical care, acute blood loss anemia is frequently encountered due to surgical procedures or trauma.

Diagnostic evaluation involves a complete blood count (CBC), reticulocyte count, and peripheral blood smear analysis. Treatment strategies are etiology-specific and may involve nutritional supplementation, erythropoiesis-stimulating agents, or transfusion therapy. In critically ill patients, transfusion thresholds are carefully determined to balance the risks of anemia against potential transfusion complications.

For CCRN candidates, a thorough understanding of the pathophysiology of anemia, diagnostic approaches, and management principles is vital for optimizing patient outcomes in critical care environments.

1.3.2.2 Coagulopathies:

Coagulopathies refer to a group of disorders that affect the blood's ability to coagulate or form clots. These disorders can lead to excessive bleeding or, conversely, an increased risk of thrombosis. In critical care settings, understanding coagulopathies is essential, as they can complicate patient management and outcomes.

Coagulopathies can be congenital or acquired. Congenital coagulopathies include conditions such as Hemophilia A and B, which are caused by deficiencies in clotting factors VIII and IX, respectively. Von Willebrand disease is another inherited disorder characterized by a deficiency or dysfunction of von Willebrand factor, which is crucial for platelet adhesion.

Acquired coagulopathies are more common in critical care and can result from various conditions, such as liver disease, vitamin K deficiency, disseminated intravascular coagulation (DIC), or the use of anticoagulant medications like warfarin or heparin. Liver disease impairs the synthesis of clotting factors, while DIC involves widespread activation of the clotting cascade, leading to both thrombosis and bleeding due to factor consumption.

The diagnosis of coagulopathies typically involves laboratory tests such as Prothrombin Time (PT), Activated Partial Thromboplastin Time (aPTT), platelet count, fibrinogen levels, and specific factor assays. Management depends on the underlying cause and may include replacement therapy with clotting factors or fresh frozen plasma, administration of vitamin K, or reversal agents for anticoagulants.

In critical care environments, prompt recognition and treatment of coagulopathies are vital to prevent severe complications such as hemorrhage or thromboembolism.

1.3.2.2.1 ITP (Immune Thrombocytopenic Purpura):

Immune Thrombocytopenic Purpura (ITP) is an autoimmune disorder characterized by a low platelet count, which can lead to easy or excessive bruising and bleeding. This condition occurs when the immune system mistakenly attacks and destroys platelets, which are essential for normal blood clotting. In ITP, the body produces antibodies against its own platelets, leading to their premature destruction primarily in the spleen.

The clinical presentation of ITP can vary widely, ranging from asymptomatic cases to severe bleeding episodes. Common symptoms include petechiae (small red or purple spots on the skin), purpura (larger areas of bleeding into the skin), epistaxis (nosebleeds), and prolonged bleeding from cuts. In severe cases, patients may experience gastrointestinal bleeding or intracranial hemorrhage.

The diagnosis of ITP is primarily one of exclusion, as there is no specific test for the condition. It involves a thorough patient history, physical examination, and laboratory tests to rule out other causes of thrombocytopenia. A complete blood count typically reveals isolated thrombocytopenia with normal white blood cell and red blood cell counts.

Management of ITP depends on the severity of the condition and may include observation for mild cases, corticosteroids to suppress the immune response, intravenous immunoglobulin (IVIG) for rapid platelet increase, and splenectomy in refractory cases. Newer treatments, such as thrombopoietin receptor agonists, are also available for chronic ITP. Understanding the pathophysiology and management strategies of ITP is crucial for critical care nurses in providing optimal patient care and preparing for the CCRN exam.

1.3.2.2.2 DIC (Disseminated Intravascular Coagulation):

Disseminated Intravascular Coagulation (DIC) is a complex and severe condition characterized by the systemic activation of blood coagulation, leading to the generation of fibrin clots and the subsequent consumption of clotting factors and platelets. This paradoxical situation results in both thrombotic and bleeding complications. DIC can arise as a complication of various conditions, including sepsis, trauma, malignancy, obstetric complications, and severe transfusion reactions.

In DIC, the initial trigger is often an excessive release of procoagulant factors into the circulation, such as tissue factor, which activates the coagulation cascade. This widespread activation leads to the formation of microthrombi throughout the microvasculature. As clotting factors and platelets are consumed faster than they can be produced, the patient becomes susceptible to bleeding. The fibrinolytic system may also become activated, further exacerbating bleeding tendencies.

Clinically, DIC presents with a spectrum of symptoms ranging from subtle laboratory abnormalities to severe hemorrhage or organ dysfunction due to microvascular thrombosis. Laboratory findings typically reveal thrombocytopenia, prolonged prothrombin time (PT), activated partial thromboplastin time (aPTT), elevated D-dimer levels, and reduced fibrinogen levels.

Management of DIC involves treating the underlying cause while providing supportive care. This may include the transfusion of blood products such as platelets or fresh frozen plasma to manage bleeding, along with anticoagulants in cases where thrombosis predominates. Careful monitoring and a multidisciplinary approach are essential for optimizing patient outcomes in this critical condition.

1.3.2.2.3 HIT (Heparin-Induced Thrombocytopenia):

Heparin-Induced Thrombocytopenia (HIT) is a serious immune-mediated adverse reaction to heparin therapy, characterized by a significant drop in platelet count and an increased risk of thrombosis. It occurs when the immune system forms antibodies against complexes of heparin and platelet factor 4 (PF4). These antibodies activate platelets, leading to their aggregation and consumption, resulting in thrombocytopenia. Despite the reduction in platelets, HIT is paradoxically associated with thrombotic complications rather than bleeding.

HIT typically manifests 5 to 10 days after the initiation of heparin therapy. Clinically, it is suspected when there is a decrease in platelet count of more than 50% from baseline or below 150,000/μL. The risk of thrombosis in HIT is high, affecting both the venous and arterial systems, which can lead to life-threatening conditions such as deep vein thrombosis, pulmonary embolism, myocardial infarction, or stroke.

Diagnosis involves clinical criteria and laboratory testing for HIT antibodies. The 4Ts score (Thrombocytopenia, Timing of platelet count fall, Thrombosis or other sequelae, and oTher causes of thrombocytopenia) is often used as a pre-test probability tool. Confirmatory tests include immunoassays and functional assays, such as the serotonin release assay.

Management of HIT requires immediate cessation of all heparin products and initiation of alternative anticoagulation with non-heparin agents such as argatroban or fondaparinux. Early recognition and treatment are crucial to prevent complications associated with this condition. Understanding HIT's pathophysiology and management is essential for critical care nurses preparing for the CCRN exam.

1.3.2.3 Immune Deficiencies:

Immune deficiencies refer to disorders in which the immune system's ability to fight infectious diseases and cancer is compromised or entirely absent. These deficiencies can be classified into two main categories: primary (congenital) and secondary (acquired). Primary immune deficiencies are typically genetic and present at birth, affecting components such as B cells, T cells, or phagocytes. Examples include Severe Combined Immunodeficiency (SCID) and X-linked Agammaglobulinemia.

Secondary immune deficiencies occur due to external factors such as infections, malnutrition, aging, or medical treatments. Human Immunodeficiency Virus (HIV) leading to Acquired Immunodeficiency Syndrome (AIDS) is a prominent example. Other causes include chemotherapy, radiation therapy, and immunosuppressive drugs used in organ transplantation.

Clinically, patients with immune deficiencies present with recurrent infections, unusual pathogens, or infections that respond poorly to standard treatments. They may also experience autoimmune disorders or an increased incidence of malignancies due to impaired immune surveillance.

Diagnosis involves a thorough clinical evaluation, family history assessment, and laboratory tests such as immunoglobulin levels, lymphocyte counts, and specific antibody responses. Genetic testing may be required for a definitive diagnosis of primary deficiencies.

Management strategies focus on preventing infections through prophylactic antibiotics and immunizations with non-live vaccines. Immunoglobulin replacement therapy is critical for certain conditions. In severe cases, such as SCID, hematopoietic stem cell transplantation can be curative.

Understanding immune deficiencies is crucial for critical care nurses to provide optimal care and anticipate complications in affected patients.

1.3.2.4 Leukopenia:

Leukopenia is a medical condition characterized by a decrease in the number of white blood cells (WBCs) in the blood, specifically below the normal range of 4,000 to 11,000 WBCs per microliter. This reduction can compromise the body's ability to fight infections, making patients more susceptible to illnesses. Leukopenia can be caused by a variety of factors, including bone marrow disorders, autoimmune diseases, severe infections, certain medications (such as chemotherapy or immunosuppressants), and nutritional deficiencies (such as vitamin B12 or folate deficiency).

In critical care settings, leukopenia is particularly concerning, as it may indicate an underlying condition that requires immediate attention. It can also be a side effect of treatments that are common in these environments, such as radiation therapy or chemotherapy for cancer patients. Care nurses should be vigilant in monitoring patients with leukopenia for signs of infection, which may include fever, chills, and other systemic symptoms.

Management of leukopenia involves addressing the underlying cause. For instance, if it is medication-induced, altering the drug regimen might be necessary. In cases related to nutritional deficiencies, supplementation may be required. Additionally, protective isolation measures may be implemented to minimize the risk of infection.

Understanding leukopenia is crucial for care nurses preparing for the CCRN exam, as they need to recognize its implications for patient care and management strategies effectively. This knowledge ensures comprehensive patient assessment and contributes to improved clinical outcomes in critical care environments.

1.3.2.5 Oncologic Complications:

Oncologic complications refer to the acute and chronic medical issues that arise as a direct or indirect consequence of cancer or its treatment. These complications can significantly impact patient outcomes and quality of life, necessitating prompt recognition and management by critical care nurses.

Common oncologic complications include febrile neutropenia, tumor lysis syndrome, spinal cord compression, hypercalcemia of malignancy, and superior vena cava syndrome. Febrile neutropenia occurs when a patient with cancer develops a fever in the context of neutropenia, often due to chemotherapy, leading to an increased risk of infections. Tumor lysis syndrome is a potentially life-threatening condition caused by the rapid breakdown of malignant cells, resulting in metabolic abnormalities such as hyperkalemia, hyperphosphatemia, hypocalcemia, and hyperuricemia.

Spinal cord compression is an oncologic emergency in which tumor growth leads to pressure on the spinal cord, causing neurological deficits if not promptly treated. Hypercalcemia of malignancy is characterized by elevated calcium levels in the blood due to bone metastases or paraneoplastic syndromes, leading to symptoms such as confusion, nausea, and cardiac arrhythmias. Superior vena cava syndrome results from the obstruction of blood flow through the superior vena cava by a tumor or thrombosis, causing facial swelling and respiratory distress.

Critical care nurses must be adept at identifying these complications early and initiating appropriate interventions. This includes administering medications such as antibiotics for febrile neutropenia or bisphosphonates for hypercalcemia and coordinating with oncology teams for advanced treatments like radiation therapy for spinal cord compression. Effective management of oncologic complications is crucial in improving patient prognosis and maintaining quality of life during cancer treatment.

1.3.2.5.1 Tumor Lysis Syndrome:

Tumor Lysis Syndrome (TLS) is a potentially life-threatening oncologic emergency that occurs when a large number of neoplastic cells are rapidly destroyed, releasing their intracellular contents into the bloodstream. This phenomenon is most commonly associated with the treatment of hematologic malignancies, such as acute leukemias and high-grade lymphomas, particularly following the initiation of chemotherapy or radiation therapy.

The rapid release of cellular components leads to metabolic abnormalities, including hyperuricemia, hyperkalemia, hyperphosphatemia, and hypocalcemia. These electrolyte imbalances can result in acute renal failure, cardiac arrhythmias, seizures, and even sudden death if not promptly identified and managed. Care nurses must be vigilant in monitoring patients at risk for TLS, especially during the initial phases of cancer treatment.

Preventive measures include aggressive hydration to maintain high urine output and the use of medications such as allopurinol or rasburicase to mitigate hyperuricemia. Early recognition of laboratory changes is crucial; therefore, frequent monitoring of electrolytes and renal function is essential for at-risk patients.

Management of TLS involves correcting electrolyte imbalances, ensuring adequate hydration, and possibly using renal replacement therapy in severe cases. Understanding the pathophysiology and clinical manifestations of TLS enables care nurses to implement timely interventions, minimizing complications and improving patient outcomes. Mastery of these concepts is critical for those preparing for the Critical Care Certification (CCRN) exam, as it underscores the importance of anticipatory guidance and prompt response in critical care settings.

1.3.2.5.2 Pericardial Effusion:

Pericardial effusion is the accumulation of excess fluid in the pericardial cavity, the space between the heart and the surrounding sac known as the pericardium. Normally, this space contains a small amount of lubricating fluid, typically 15-50 mL, which facilitates smooth cardiac movements. However, in pathological states such as malignancies, infections, or inflammatory conditions, fluid can accumulate excessively.

In oncologic patients, pericardial effusion may arise due to direct tumor invasion, metastatic spread to the pericardium, or as a paraneoplastic phenomenon. This effusion can lead to increased intrapericardial pressure, potentially causing cardiac tamponade—a life-threatening condition characterized by impaired ventricular filling and reduced cardiac output.

Clinically, patients with pericardial effusion may present with symptoms such as dyspnea, chest pain, orthopnea, or a sensation of fullness in the chest. Physical examination may reveal muffled heart sounds and jugular venous distension. Diagnostic evaluation typically involves echocardiography to assess fluid volume and hemodynamic impact.

Management strategies depend on the underlying cause and severity. In cases of tamponade or significant hemodynamic compromise, urgent pericardiocentesis—needle drainage of the effusion—is warranted. In recurrent or malignant effusions, additional interventions such as pericardial window surgery or sclerotherapy may be considered.

Understanding the pathophysiology and management of pericardial effusion is crucial for critical care nurses to facilitate timely recognition and intervention, optimizing patient outcomes in oncologic settings.

1.3.2.6 Thrombocytopenia:

Thrombocytopenia is a hematological condition characterized by an abnormally low platelet count in the blood, typically defined as fewer than 150,000 platelets per microliter. Platelets, or thrombocytes, are crucial for normal blood clotting and maintaining hemostasis. When platelet levels drop significantly, patients are at increased risk for bleeding complications, which can range from minor bruising to severe hemorrhages.

The etiology of thrombocytopenia is diverse and can be categorized into three primary mechanisms: decreased platelet production, increased platelet destruction, and sequestration. Decreased production may result from bone marrow disorders such as aplastic anemia or leukemia. Increased destruction is often immune-mediated, as seen in immune thrombocytopenic purpura (ITP) or as a result of medications and infections. Sequestration occurs when platelets are trapped in an enlarged spleen.

Clinical manifestations of thrombocytopenia vary depending on severity but often include petechiae, purpura, mucosal bleeding, and prolonged bleeding times. Diagnosis typically involves a complete blood count (CBC) and a peripheral blood smear to assess platelet morphology and rule out pseudothrombocytopenia.

Management strategies focus on addressing the underlying cause and may include corticosteroids or immunoglobulins for immune-mediated cases, splenectomy for splenic sequestration, or transfusions in critical scenarios. Nurses must monitor patients closely for signs of bleeding and educate them about the potential risks associated with low platelet counts. Understanding the pathophysiology and management of thrombocytopenia is essential for nurses preparing for the CCRN exam, as it directly impacts patient care in critical settings.

1.3.2.7 Transfusion Reactions:

Transfusion reactions are adverse responses that occur when a patient's immune system reacts to transfused blood products. These reactions can range from mild to life-threatening and are classified into several types: acute hemolytic, febrile non-hemolytic, allergic, anaphylactic, transfusion-related acute lung injury (TRALI), and delayed hemolytic reactions.

Acute hemolytic reactions result from ABO incompatibility and lead to the destruction of donor red blood cells by the recipient's antibodies. Symptoms include fever, chills, back pain, hemoglobinuria, and, in severe cases, disseminated intravascular coagulation or renal failure.

Febrile non-hemolytic reactions are characterized by fever and chills without hemolysis, often due to leukocyte antibodies. They are typically benign but can be uncomfortable for the patient.

Allergic reactions present with urticaria and itching, caused by sensitivity to plasma proteins. Anaphylactic reactions are severe, presenting with hypotension, respiratory distress, and shock due to IgA deficiency or other allergens in the blood product.

TRALI is a serious condition characterized by acute respiratory distress following transfusion, attributed to donor antibodies reacting with recipient leukocytes in the lungs. It requires immediate intervention.

Delayed hemolytic reactions occur days to weeks post-transfusion as antibodies develop against minor antigens on transfused red cells. Symptoms may be subtle but can include unexplained anemia or jaundice.

Recognizing and managing transfusion reactions promptly is crucial for patient safety. Interventions include stopping the transfusion immediately, maintaining venous access with normal saline, monitoring vital signs, and providing supportive care as needed.

1.3.3 Gastrointestinal:

The gastrointestinal (GI) system, also known as the digestive system, is a complex network of organs and glands responsible for the digestion and absorption of nutrients, as well as the excretion of waste products. It extends from the mouth to the anus and includes the oral cavity, esophagus, stomach, small intestine, large intestine, rectum, and anus. Accessory organs such as the liver, pancreas, and gallbladder play crucial roles in digestion by producing enzymes and bile that aid in breaking down food.

In critical care settings, understanding the gastrointestinal system is essential due to its involvement in various life-threatening conditions. Disorders such as gastrointestinal bleeding, pancreatitis, bowel obstructions, and liver failure can significantly impact patient outcomes. Nurses must be adept at assessing GI function through clinical signs such as abdominal pain, distension, bowel sounds, and changes in stool patterns. Diagnostic tests such as endoscopy, imaging studies, and laboratory evaluations are often utilized to identify underlying issues.

Management of GI problems in critical care involves stabilizing hemodynamics, ensuring adequate nutrition through enteral or parenteral feeding when necessary, and addressing specific pathologies with medications or surgical interventions. Monitoring for complications such as infection or electrolyte imbalances is crucial. Additionally, understanding the implications of stress-related mucosal disease and implementing prophylactic measures to prevent gastrointestinal bleeding in critically ill patients is vital.

In summary, proficiency in gastrointestinal assessment and intervention is a key component of critical care nursing practice, ensuring optimal patient management and recovery outcomes.

1.3.3.1 Abdominal Compartment Syndrome:

Abdominal Compartment Syndrome (ACS) is a critical condition characterized by increased intra-abdominal pressure (IAP) that leads to significant organ dysfunction. It occurs when the pressure within the abdominal cavity exceeds 20 mmHg, coupled with new organ dysfunction or failure. This condition can arise from various causes, such as trauma, intra-abdominal hemorrhage, massive fluid resuscitation, or bowel obstruction.

The pathophysiology of ACS involves the restriction of blood flow to vital organs due to elevated IAP, which compromises perfusion and can lead to ischemia. The increased pressure affects multiple systems: it impairs respiratory function by elevating the diaphragm, decreases renal perfusion, leading to oliguria or anuria, and can cause cardiovascular instability due to decreased venous return and cardiac output.

Clinically, patients may present with tense abdominal distension, decreased urine output, hypotension, and respiratory distress. Diagnosis is confirmed by measuring intra-abdominal pressure using a bladder catheter technique.

Management of ACS requires prompt intervention to reduce IAP and mitigate organ dysfunction. Initial strategies include optimizing fluid balance, using diuretics or vasopressors judiciously, and ensuring adequate ventilation. Surgical decompression through laparotomy may be necessary in severe cases to relieve pressure and restore organ function.

Understanding ACS is crucial for critical care nurses, as timely recognition and intervention can significantly impact patient outcomes. Nurses play a vital role in monitoring at-risk patients, assessing for early signs of ACS, and collaborating with the multidisciplinary team for effective management.

1.3.3.2 Acute Abdominal Trauma:

Acute abdominal trauma refers to any injury to the abdomen that necessitates immediate medical attention due to its potential to cause significant morbidity or mortality. These injuries can be classified into two main types: blunt and penetrating trauma. Blunt trauma, often resulting from motor vehicle accidents or falls, involves non-penetrative forces that may cause damage to internal organs without an open wound. Penetrating trauma, on the other hand, involves objects such as knives or bullets that breach the abdominal wall, directly injuring internal structures.

In critical care settings, the primary concern with acute abdominal trauma is identifying life-threatening conditions such as hemorrhage or organ perforation. The liver and spleen are commonly affected in blunt trauma, while penetrating injuries frequently involve the intestines. Key signs and symptoms include abdominal pain, distension, tenderness, and signs of shock, such as hypotension and tachycardia.

Diagnostic evaluation typically involves imaging studies like ultrasound (FAST exam) or CT scans to assess internal damage. Laboratory tests may reveal anemia or elevated white blood cell counts, which are indicative of bleeding or infection.

Management involves stabilizing the patient using the ABCs (Airway, Breathing, Circulation), controlling hemorrhage, and preventing infection. Surgical intervention may be required for the definitive repair of damaged organs. Early recognition and prompt management are critical in improving outcomes for patients with acute abdominal trauma in a critical care environment.

1.3.3.3 Acute GI Hemorrhage:

Acute gastrointestinal (GI) hemorrhage refers to a sudden onset of bleeding within the gastrointestinal tract, which can manifest as either upper GI bleeding (UGIB) or lower GI bleeding (LGIB). UGIB typically originates from the esophagus, stomach, or duodenum, while LGIB arises from the jejunum, ileum, colon, or rectum. This condition is a critical emergency that requires prompt assessment and intervention due to the risk of significant morbidity and mortality.

The clinical presentation of acute GI hemorrhage includes hematemesis (vomiting blood), melena (black, tarry stools), and hematochezia (passage of fresh blood per rectum). Hemodynamic instability may occur, characterized by hypotension, tachycardia, and signs of shock if substantial blood loss has occurred.

Etiologies for UGIB include peptic ulcers, esophageal varices, Mallory-Weiss tears, and gastritis. For LGIB, common causes are diverticulosis, colorectal cancer, inflammatory bowel disease, and hemorrhoids. Diagnostic evaluation involves endoscopy for UGIB and colonoscopy for LGIB to identify the source and cause of bleeding.

Management strategies focus on stabilizing the patient through fluid resuscitation and blood transfusions as needed. Pharmacologic interventions may include proton pump inhibitors for ulcer-related bleeding or octreotide for variceal bleeding. Endoscopic therapies, such as band ligation or sclerotherapy, can be employed to control active bleeding. Surgical intervention may be necessary if conservative measures fail.

Understanding the pathophysiology and management of acute GI hemorrhage is essential for critical care nurses in providing effective care and improving patient outcomes.

1.3.3.4 Bowel Infarction, Obstruction, Perforation:

Bowel infarction, obstruction, and perforation are critical gastrointestinal conditions that require immediate attention in a critical care setting. Bowel infarction occurs when there is a loss of blood supply to the intestines, leading to tissue death. This can result from mesenteric artery occlusion due to embolism, thrombosis, or low-flow states. Clinically, it presents with severe abdominal pain, often disproportionate to physical findings, and may progress to peritonitis and sepsis if not promptly treated.

Bowel obstruction is a mechanical or functional blockage of the intestines that prevents the normal transit of contents. Causes include adhesions, hernias, tumors, or strictures. Symptoms include abdominal pain, distension, vomiting, and constipation. Physical examination may reveal high-pitched bowel sounds initially, which can diminish as the obstruction persists.

Bowel perforation is a life-threatening condition characterized by a hole in the wall of the gastrointestinal tract. It can result from various causes, including peptic ulcer disease, diverticulitis, or trauma. Perforation leads to the leakage of intestinal contents into the peritoneal cavity, causing peritonitis and potential sepsis. Clinical signs include sudden severe abdominal pain, rigidity, and rebound tenderness.

Management of these conditions involves rapid assessment and intervention. For infarction and perforation, surgical intervention is often required. Obstruction may be managed conservatively with nasogastric decompression and fluid resuscitation unless strangulation or complete obstruction necessitates surgery. Understanding these conditions is crucial for critical care nurses in providing timely and effective patient care.

1.3.3.4.1 Mesenteric Ischemia:

Mesenteric ischemia is a serious condition characterized by insufficient blood flow to the small intestine, leading to tissue damage and potential necrosis. This condition can be acute or chronic, with acute mesenteric ischemia being a medical emergency due to the rapid onset of symptoms and the potential for bowel infarction. The primary causes of mesenteric ischemia include arterial embolism, thrombosis, non-occlusive mesenteric ischemia (NOMI), and venous thrombosis.

In acute cases, arterial embolism is the most common cause, often originating from cardiac sources such as atrial fibrillation. Thrombosis typically occurs in patients with atherosclerosis. NOMI is associated with low-flow states, such as heart failure or shock, while venous thrombosis can result from hypercoagulable conditions.

Clinically, mesenteric ischemia presents with severe abdominal pain that is disproportionate to physical findings, as well as nausea, vomiting, and possibly bloody stools. Diagnosis involves a high clinical suspicion and may include imaging studies like CT angiography to assess blood flow in the mesenteric vessels.

Management of mesenteric ischemia requires prompt intervention to restore blood flow and may include surgical revascularization or endovascular techniques such as angioplasty. In some cases, bowel resection may be necessary if necrosis has occurred. Supportive care includes fluid resuscitation and addressing underlying causes such as arrhythmias or heart failure.

Understanding the pathophysiology and prompt recognition of symptoms are critical for critical care nurses managing patients at risk for or diagnosed with mesenteric ischemia. Early diagnosis and treatment are essential to prevent irreversible bowel damage and improve patient outcomes.

1.3.3.4.2 Adhesions:

Adhesions are fibrous bands that form between tissues and organs, often as a result of surgery, inflammation, or injury. These bands can cause tissues and organs to stick together abnormally, which can lead to complications such as bowel obstruction. In the context of the gastrointestinal tract, adhesions are a common cause of small bowel obstruction. They occur when scar tissue forms after abdominal or pelvic surgery, leading to a mechanical blockage of the intestines.

The formation of adhesions is part of the body's natural healing process. When tissue is damaged, the body responds by forming fibrous connective tissue to repair the area. However, this process can sometimes go awry, resulting in excessive scar tissue that binds organs together. This can restrict normal movement and function, particularly in the intestines, where mobility is crucial for peristalsis.

Clinically, adhesions may be asymptomatic or cause significant symptoms such as abdominal pain, bloating, nausea, vomiting, and constipation. Diagnosis is often challenging since adhesions are not visible on standard imaging studies like X-rays or CT scans. Instead, diagnosis may rely on clinical history and the exclusion of other causes.

Treatment for symptomatic adhesions may involve conservative management with bowel rest and nasogastric decompression. In persistent or severe cases, surgical intervention may be necessary to release the adhesions (adhesiolysis). However, surgery carries the risk of forming new adhesions, making prevention strategies during initial surgeries critical to minimizing adhesion formation.

1.3.3.5   GI Surgeries:

Gastrointestinal (GI) surgeries encompass a range of operative procedures aimed at addressing diseases and disorders affecting the digestive tract, which includes the esophagus, stomach, small intestine, large intestine (colon), rectum, liver, gallbladder, and pancreas. These surgeries are pivotal in managing conditions such as cancer, inflammatory bowel disease (IBD), gallstones, hernias, and gastrointestinal bleeding.

GI surgeries can be categorized into open and minimally invasive procedures. Open surgeries involve larger incisions and direct visualization of the organs, whereas minimally invasive techniques, such as laparoscopic or robotic-assisted surgeries, utilize smaller incisions and specialized instruments for enhanced precision and reduced recovery times.

Common GI surgeries include appendectomy (removal of the appendix), cholecystectomy (gallbladder removal), colectomy (removal of part or all of the colon), and gastric bypass (for obesity management). Surgeons may also perform resections to remove tumors or diseased tissue and anastomosis to reconnect healthy sections of the GI tract.

Preoperative assessment is crucial for identifying potential complications such as infections or nutritional deficiencies. Postoperative care focuses on pain management, monitoring for signs of infection or leaks at surgical sites, and ensuring proper nutritional support. Understanding the physiological impacts of these surgeries is essential for critical care nurses to provide comprehensive care and facilitate patient recovery. Mastery of these concepts is vital for CCRN certification candidates to effectively manage patients undergoing GI surgeries in a critical care setting.

1.3.3.5.1   Whipple Procedure:

The Whipple procedure, also known as pancreaticoduodenectomy, is a complex surgical operation primarily performed to treat pancreatic cancer located in the head of the pancreas. This procedure may also be indicated for other conditions such as chronic pancreatitis, benign pancreatic tumors, or trauma. The Whipple procedure involves the resection of several structures: the head of the pancreas, the duodenum, a portion of the bile duct, the gallbladder, and sometimes part of the stomach. Following resection, reconstruction is necessary to restore continuity to the digestive tract. This is typically achieved by anastomosing the remaining pancreas, bile duct, and stomach to different segments of the small intestine.

Critical care nurses must understand that patients undergoing a Whipple procedure are at high risk for postoperative complications such as delayed gastric emptying, pancreatic fistula, hemorrhage, and infections. Comprehensive preoperative assessment and meticulous postoperative management are crucial. Monitoring involves maintaining fluid and electrolyte balance, managing pain effectively, and preventing infection through stringent aseptic techniques.

Nutritional support is vital due to altered gastrointestinal anatomy; therefore, enteral feeding may be initiated early post-surgery. Nurses should also be adept at recognizing signs of complications such as sepsis or anastomotic leaks and responding promptly.

Understanding the complexity of the Whipple procedure equips critical care nurses with the knowledge necessary to provide optimal care for patients undergoing this life-altering surgery and ensures they are well-prepared for related questions on the CCRN exam.

1.3.3.5.2   Esophagectomy:

An esophagectomy is a surgical procedure that involves the removal of all or part of the esophagus, the muscular tube connecting the throat to the stomach. This operation is primarily indicated for patients with esophageal cancer, but it may also be performed for severe cases of benign esophageal disease, such as achalasia or strictures that do not respond to other treatments.

The procedure can be approached in several ways, including open surgery, minimally invasive surgery, or a combination of both. The choice of technique depends on various factors, such as the location and stage of the tumor and the patient's overall health. Commonly, the stomach is pulled up into the chest or neck to replace the resected portion of the esophagus, creating a new conduit for food passage.

Postoperative care for patients who have undergone an esophagectomy is critical and involves close monitoring in an intensive care setting. Care nurses must be vigilant for potential complications such as anastomotic leaks, respiratory issues, infections, and nutritional deficiencies. Pain management and early mobilization are essential components of recovery.

Nutritional support is crucial, as patients may experience difficulty swallowing initially and may require enteral feeding through a jejunostomy tube until oral intake can be safely resumed. Long-term follow-up includes monitoring for recurrence of disease, managing any swallowing difficulties, and addressing nutritional needs.

Understanding the complexities of esophagectomy and its postoperative management is vital for care nurses preparing for the CCRN exam, as it underscores their role in providing comprehensive care to critically ill surgical patients.

1.3.3.5.3 Resections:

Resections refer to surgical procedures that involve the removal of a part of an organ or tissue, typically due to disease, injury, or cancer. In the context of gastrointestinal (GI) surgeries, resections are commonly performed on organs such as the stomach, intestines, liver, and pancreas. The primary goal of a resection is to excise diseased tissue while preserving as much healthy tissue as possible to maintain organ function.

In GI surgeries, resections can be categorized based on the organ involved. For instance, a gastrectomy involves the partial or total removal of the stomach, often indicated for gastric cancer or severe ulcers. Similarly, a colectomy entails the resection of part or all of the colon and is frequently performed for colorectal cancer or inflammatory bowel disease.

The complexity and extent of a resection depend on various factors, including the location and size of the diseased area, the patient's overall health, and potential complications. Surgeons may employ open surgery or minimally invasive techniques such as laparoscopy to perform resections. Minimally invasive approaches often result in reduced recovery times and a lower risk of infection.

Post-operative care for patients who have undergone resections is crucial. It includes monitoring for complications such as bleeding, infection, or anastomotic leakage. Nutritional support and gradual reintroduction of diet are essential components of recovery. Understanding resection procedures and post-operative management is vital for critical care nurses to provide optimal patient care and support recovery effectively.

1.3.3.6 Hepatic Failure/coma:

Hepatic failure, also known as liver failure, is a life-threatening condition characterized by the inability of the liver to perform its essential metabolic, synthetic, and detoxification functions. This condition can be acute or chronic. Acute hepatic failure develops rapidly, often within days or weeks, and is typically caused by viral hepatitis, drug-induced liver injury (such as acetaminophen overdose), or toxins. Chronic hepatic failure progresses over months to years, commonly due to cirrhosis from chronic alcohol abuse or chronic viral hepatitis.

One of the critical complications of hepatic failure is hepatic encephalopathy, which can progress to hepatic coma. Hepatic encephalopathy results from the accumulation of neurotoxic substances, such as ammonia, that are normally detoxified by the liver. These substances affect brain function, leading to a spectrum of neurological symptoms ranging from mild confusion and altered mental status to deep coma.

In severe cases, patients may present with jaundice, coagulopathy, ascites, and renal impairment (hepatorenal syndrome). The diagnosis of hepatic failure involves clinical assessment supported by laboratory tests that show elevated liver enzymes, bilirubin levels, and prolonged prothrombin time. Imaging studies and liver biopsy may be used for further evaluation.

Management focuses on treating the underlying cause, supporting liver function, and preventing complications. In cases of acute liver failure or advanced chronic liver disease unresponsive to medical therapy, liver transplantation may be necessary. Critical care nurses play a vital role in monitoring for signs of deterioration and managing complications associated with hepatic failure and coma.

1.3.3.6.1 Portal Hypertension:

Portal hypertension is a pathological increase in blood pressure within the portal venous system, which comprises the portal vein and its branches. This condition typically arises from an obstruction in blood flow through the liver, most commonly due to cirrhosis; however, it can also result from other liver diseases or conditions affecting the hepatic vasculature.

Increased resistance to portal blood flow leads to elevated pressure, causing significant clinical manifestations. One of the primary consequences is the development of collateral circulation, where blood is diverted to lower-pressure systemic veins, leading to varices. These varices commonly occur in the esophagus and stomach and are prone to rupture, posing a risk of life-threatening hemorrhage.

Ascites, another common complication, results from increased hydrostatic pressure that forces fluid into the peritoneal cavity. Additionally, splenomegaly may occur due to congestion in the splenic vein, a tributary of the portal system.

Management of portal hypertension focuses on addressing its underlying cause and mitigating complications. Pharmacologic interventions include non-selective beta-blockers, such as propranolol, to reduce portal pressure by decreasing cardiac output and splanchnic vasodilation. Endoscopic procedures, such as band ligation or sclerotherapy, are employed to manage variceal bleeding. In refractory cases, a transjugular intrahepatic portosystemic shunt (TIPS) may be considered to create a pathway for blood flow that bypasses the liver, thus reducing portal pressure.

Understanding portal hypertension is crucial for critical care nurses, as they play an essential role in monitoring and managing patients at risk for complications associated with this condition.

1.3.3.6.2 Cirrhosis:

Cirrhosis is a chronic, progressive liver disease characterized by the replacement of healthy liver tissue with fibrotic scar tissue, leading to impaired liver function. This irreversible condition results from prolonged liver damage due to various causes, including chronic alcohol abuse, hepatitis B and C infections, nonalcoholic fatty liver disease, and autoimmune disorders. As the disease progresses, the liver's ability to perform essential functions, such as detoxification, protein synthesis, and the production of biochemicals necessary for digestion, diminishes.

In cirrhosis, the normal architecture of the liver is disrupted by nodules surrounded by fibrous bands. This distortion affects blood flow through the liver and can lead to portal hypertension—a condition in which increased pressure in the portal venous system causes complications like variceal bleeding, ascites (accumulation of fluid in the abdominal cavity), and hepatic encephalopathy (a decline in brain function due to toxin accumulation).

Clinical manifestations of cirrhosis include jaundice (yellowing of the skin and eyes), fatigue, weakness, easy bruising or bleeding, and pruritus (itching). Advanced stages may present with complications such as hepatorenal syndrome or hepatocellular carcinoma.

Management focuses on treating underlying causes, preventing further liver damage, and addressing complications. Lifestyle modifications, such as abstaining from alcohol and maintaining a balanced diet, are crucial. Pharmacological interventions may include diuretics for ascites and beta-blockers for portal hypertension. In severe cases, liver transplantation remains the definitive treatment. Understanding cirrhosis is vital for critical care nurses in managing patients effectively and improving outcomes.

1.3.3.6.3 Esophageal Varices:

Esophageal varices are dilated submucosal veins in the lower third of the esophagus, primarily resulting from portal hypertension, a common complication of cirrhosis. When the liver becomes scarred, blood flow through it is obstructed, leading to increased pressure in the portal venous system. This pressure causes blood to be diverted through smaller veins, including those in the esophagus, which become distended and fragile.

In patients with hepatic failure or advanced liver disease, esophageal varices pose a significant risk due to their propensity to rupture and cause massive upper gastrointestinal bleeding. Such bleeding is a life-threatening emergency that requires immediate medical intervention. Clinical manifestations of ruptured varices include hematemesis (vomiting blood), melena (black, tarry stools), and signs of hypovolemic shock, such as hypotension and tachycardia.

Diagnosis is typically confirmed via endoscopy, which allows for direct visualization of the varices and assessment of their size and risk of bleeding. Management strategies focus on preventing bleeding and stabilizing the patient if bleeding occurs. Non-selective beta-blockers, such as propranolol, are commonly used to reduce portal pressure prophylactically. In cases of acute bleeding, endoscopic interventions like band ligation or sclerotherapy are employed to control hemorrhage.

Understanding esophageal varices is crucial for critical care nurses, as early recognition and prompt management can significantly impact patient outcomes in those with hepatic complications. Monitoring for signs of bleeding and maintaining hemodynamic stability are key responsibilities in caring for these patients.

1.3.3.6.4 Fulminant Hepatitis:

Fulminant hepatitis is a severe and rapidly progressing form of liver failure characterized by the sudden loss of hepatic function in a patient without pre-existing liver disease. It typically occurs within eight weeks of the initial symptoms of liver dysfunction, such as jaundice. The condition is marked by encephalopathy, coagulopathy, and often progresses to multi-organ failure. The most common causes include viral infections, particularly hepatitis A, B, and E, drug-induced liver injury (notably from acetaminophen overdose), autoimmune hepatitis, and exposure to toxins.

Pathophysiologically, fulminant hepatitis results from massive hepatocyte necrosis, leading to a significant reduction in liver mass and function. This impairment affects the liver's ability to detoxify substances, synthesize proteins, and regulate blood coagulation. The resultant accumulation of toxic substances, such as ammonia, contributes to cerebral edema and hepatic encephalopathy.

Clinically, patients present with symptoms ranging from nausea, vomiting, and abdominal pain to confusion, altered mental status, and coma. Laboratory findings typically reveal elevated liver enzymes, prolonged prothrombin time (PT), elevated bilirubin levels, and low albumin. Imaging may show a shrunken liver due to necrosis.

Management of fulminant hepatitis involves supportive care in an intensive care unit setting. This includes monitoring for complications such as cerebral edema and infections, managing coagulopathy with vitamin K or fresh frozen plasma, and considering liver transplantation as definitive treatment if no spontaneous recovery occurs. Early diagnosis and prompt intervention are critical to improving outcomes in patients with this life-threatening condition.

1.3.3.6.5 Biliary Atresia:

Biliary atresia is a rare, life-threatening congenital condition characterized by the absence or obstruction of bile ducts, which are responsible for transporting bile from the liver to the gallbladder and small intestine. This obstruction leads to bile accumulation in the liver, causing progressive liver damage and eventual hepatic failure if untreated. The condition typically presents in newborns within the first few weeks of life, often marked by jaundice, dark urine, pale stools, and hepatomegaly.

The etiology of biliary atresia remains unclear, but it is believed to result from an inflammatory process that occurs either in utero or shortly after birth. Diagnosis is critical and involves a combination of laboratory tests, imaging studies such as ultrasound and hepatobiliary scintigraphy, and liver biopsy to assess the extent of liver damage and rule out other causes of neonatal cholestasis.

The primary treatment for biliary atresia is surgical intervention through a procedure known as the Kasai portoenterostomy. This surgery involves connecting a segment of the intestine directly to the liver to allow bile drainage. While the Kasai procedure can restore some bile flow and delay liver damage, many patients eventually require liver transplantation due to progressive cirrhosis.

Early diagnosis and timely surgical intervention are crucial for improving outcomes. Nurses caring for these patients must be vigilant in monitoring for signs of liver dysfunction, providing postoperative care, and supporting families through this challenging diagnosis. Understanding the pathophysiology and management strategies of biliary atresia is essential for critical care nurses preparing for the CCRN exam.

1.3.3.6.6 Drug-induced:

Drug-induced hepatic failure and coma refer to liver dysfunction and altered mental status resulting from the adverse effects of medications. This condition occurs when drugs cause hepatotoxicity, leading to liver cell damage, impaired liver function, and subsequent hepatic encephalopathy. The pathophysiology involves direct hepatocellular injury or idiosyncratic reactions, which can provoke inflammation, necrosis, or cholestasis in the liver.

Common culprits include acetaminophen, which, in overdose, causes massive necrosis due to toxic metabolite accumulation, and antibiotics like isoniazid or amoxicillin-clavulanate, which may trigger idiosyncratic reactions. Nonsteroidal anti-inflammatory drugs (NSAIDs), anticonvulsants, and certain herbal supplements are also implicated.

Clinically, drug-induced hepatic failure presents with jaundice, coagulopathy, elevated liver enzymes (AST, ALT), and hyperbilirubinemia. The progression to hepatic coma is marked by confusion, asterixis (flapping tremor), and eventually stupor or coma due to the accumulation of neurotoxic substances like ammonia.

Management involves the immediate cessation of the offending drug and supportive care. In cases of acetaminophen toxicity, the administration of N-acetylcysteine is crucial. Monitoring for complications such as cerebral edema or renal failure is essential. Liver transplantation may be considered in severe cases where medical therapy fails to restore liver function.

Understanding the pharmacokinetics and potential hepatotoxic profiles of medications is vital for critical care nurses to prevent and recognize early signs of drug-induced hepatic failure and to initiate timely interventions to mitigate adverse outcomes.

Malnutrition And Malabsorption:

Malnutrition refers to a condition in which the body does not receive adequate nutrients to maintain optimal health, either due to insufficient intake, increased nutritional requirements, or improper nutrient utilization. It can manifest as undernutrition, characterized by a deficiency of calories or essential nutrients, or overnutrition, which involves excessive nutrient intake leading to obesity and related disorders.

Malabsorption, on the other hand, is a disorder in which the small intestine fails to absorb nutrients efficiently from ingested food. This can result from various conditions such as celiac disease, Crohn's disease, chronic pancreatitis, or surgical resections of the intestine. Malabsorption can lead to deficiencies in vitamins (such as B12, A, D, E, and K), minerals (like iron and calcium), proteins, and fats.

In critical care settings, malnutrition and malabsorption can significantly impact patient outcomes by impairing immune function, delaying wound healing, and increasing susceptibility to infections. It is crucial for nursing staff to assess patients' nutritional status through clinical evaluation and laboratory tests. Identifying signs such as unintended weight loss, muscle wasting, or specific nutrient deficiencies is vital.

Management includes addressing the underlying cause of malabsorption and ensuring adequate nutritional support. This may involve dietary modifications, supplementation of deficient nutrients, or, in severe cases, parenteral nutrition. Continuous monitoring and collaboration with dietitians are essential to formulate individualized care plans that optimize nutritional status and improve recovery in critically ill patients.

Pancreatitis:

Pancreatitis is an inflammatory condition of the pancreas, a vital organ responsible for producing digestive enzymes and hormones, such as insulin. It can manifest in two forms: acute and chronic. Acute pancreatitis is characterized by sudden inflammation, often resulting from gallstones or excessive alcohol consumption, whereas chronic pancreatitis involves prolonged inflammation that leads to permanent damage, frequently associated with long-term alcohol abuse or genetic factors.

In acute pancreatitis, the premature activation of pancreatic enzymes causes autodigestion, leading to inflammation and potential systemic complications, such as acute respiratory distress syndrome (ARDS) or renal failure. Clinically, patients present with severe abdominal pain radiating to the back, nausea, vomiting, and elevated serum amylase and lipase levels. Management focuses on supportive care, including fluid resuscitation, pain management, and nutritional support. In severe cases, interventions may include endoscopic retrograde cholangiopancreatography (ERCP) for gallstone removal or surgical debridement of necrotic tissue.

Chronic pancreatitis results in irreversible damage characterized by fibrosis and calcification, leading to exocrine and endocrine insufficiency. Patients may experience persistent pain, malabsorption, steatorrhea, and diabetes mellitus. Management aims to control pain, provide enzyme replacement therapy, implement lifestyle modifications such as alcohol cessation, and address nutritional deficiencies.

Understanding the pathophysiology and management strategies for pancreatitis is crucial for critical care nurses to effectively monitor and support patients through acute episodes and manage long-term complications associated with chronic disease.

1.3.4 Renal And Genitourinary:

The renal and genitourinary systems encompass the kidneys, ureters, bladder, urethra, and associated structures responsible for the production, storage, and elimination of urine. These systems play a critical role in maintaining homeostasis by regulating fluid balance, electrolytes, acid-base balance, and blood pressure. The kidneys filter blood to remove waste products and excess substances, forming urine that travels through the ureters to be stored in the bladder until excretion via the urethra.

In critical care settings, understanding renal function is crucial due to its impact on overall patient health. Acute kidney injury (AKI) is a common condition characterized by a sudden decrease in kidney function, leading to an accumulation of waste products and fluid imbalances. Causes of AKI include prerenal factors such as decreased perfusion, intrinsic renal damage from nephrotoxins or ischemia, and postrenal obstructions.

Chronic kidney disease (CKD) involves the progressive loss of renal function over time. It requires monitoring of the glomerular filtration rate (GFR) and management of complications such as hypertension and anemia.

Genitourinary disorders in critical care may involve urinary tract infections (UTIs), nephrolithiasis (kidney stones), or bladder dysfunctions. Nurses must be proficient in assessing signs of infection, managing catheter-related issues, and understanding pharmacological interventions that affect renal function.

Proficiency in interpreting laboratory values such as serum creatinine, blood urea nitrogen (BUN), and electrolyte levels is essential for the effective management of renal and genitourinary conditions in critically ill patients. Understanding the complexities of these systems aids in delivering comprehensive care and optimizing patient outcomes.

1.3.4.1 Acute Genitourinary Trauma:

Acute genitourinary trauma refers to sudden injuries affecting the urinary system, including the kidneys, ureters, bladder, urethra, and reproductive organs. These injuries can result from blunt or penetrating trauma, often occurring in motor vehicle accidents, falls, sports injuries, or assaults. The severity of genitourinary trauma varies, ranging from minor contusions to life-threatening hemorrhages.

In evaluating acute genitourinary trauma, a systematic approach is crucial. The initial assessment involves ensuring hemodynamic stability and identifying any associated life-threatening injuries. Hematuria, or blood in the urine, is a common indicator of genitourinary injury; however, its absence does not rule out significant trauma. Imaging studies, such as computed tomography (CT) scans, are essential for diagnosing renal injuries and assessing the extent of damage.

Management of acute genitourinary trauma depends on the injury's location and severity. Renal injuries may require conservative management with observation and bed rest or surgical intervention if there is significant hemorrhage or urinary extravasation. Bladder injuries often necessitate catheterization and surgical repair if there is perforation. Urethral injuries demand careful evaluation to avoid complications such as stricture formation.

Preventing complications, such as infection and preserving renal function, are priorities in managing these injuries. Multidisciplinary collaboration among urologists, radiologists, and trauma surgeons is often necessary to optimize patient outcomes. Understanding the pathophysiology and treatment options for acute genitourinary trauma is vital for critical care nurses preparing for the CCRN exam, ensuring they can provide comprehensive care to affected patients.

1.3.4.2 Acute Kidney Injury (AKI):

Acute Kidney Injury (AKI) is a sudden and often reversible decline in renal function, characterized by an abrupt increase in serum creatinine levels and/or a decrease in urine output. This condition can develop over hours to days and is commonly categorized into three stages based on the severity of kidney impairment. AKI is frequently seen in critically ill patients and can result from various causes, including prerenal, intrinsic, and postrenal factors.

Prerenal AKI occurs due to inadequate perfusion of the kidneys, often caused by hypovolemia, decreased cardiac output, or systemic vasodilation. Intrinsic AKI results from direct damage to the renal parenchyma, which may be due to acute tubular necrosis (ATN), glomerulonephritis, or interstitial nephritis. Postrenal AKI arises from obstruction of urine flow, which can occur at any point along the urinary tract.

The diagnosis of AKI involves monitoring changes in serum creatinine levels and urine output, as well as identifying potential underlying causes through patient history, physical examination, and diagnostic imaging. Early recognition and management are crucial to prevent progression to chronic kidney disease (CKD) or end-stage renal disease (ESRD).

Management strategies focus on addressing the underlying cause, optimizing hemodynamic status, ensuring adequate fluid balance, and avoiding nephrotoxic agents. In severe cases, renal replacement therapy (RRT) may be necessary to temporarily support kidney function. Understanding the pathophysiology and management of AKI is essential for critical care nurses to effectively care for patients at risk of or suffering from this condition.

1.3.4.3 Chronic Kidney Disease (CKD):

Chronic Kidney Disease (CKD) is a progressive condition characterized by the gradual loss of kidney function over time. It is defined by a decreased glomerular filtration rate (GFR) of less than 60 mL/min/1.73 m² for three months or more, irrespective of the cause. CKD can also be identified through markers of kidney damage, such as albuminuria, abnormalities in urine sediment, or structural abnormalities detected through imaging.

The pathophysiology of CKD involves damage to the nephrons, which are the functional units of the kidneys. This damage can result from a variety of underlying conditions, such as diabetes mellitus, hypertension, glomerulonephritis, and polycystic kidney disease. As nephron damage progresses, compensatory mechanisms initially maintain renal function but eventually lead to further nephron injury and fibrosis.

Patients with CKD may remain asymptomatic until significant nephron loss occurs. Symptoms can include fatigue, edema, hypertension, and electrolyte imbalances as the disease advances. Additionally, CKD increases the risk of cardiovascular disease and other complications due to disrupted homeostasis.

Management focuses on slowing disease progression and addressing underlying causes. This includes optimizing blood pressure control, managing blood glucose levels in diabetic patients, and using medications such as ACE inhibitors or ARBs to reduce proteinuria. Dietary modifications and lifestyle changes are also essential components of care.

Early detection and intervention are crucial to delaying progression to end-stage renal disease (ESRD), where renal replacement therapy or transplantation becomes necessary. Regular monitoring of kidney function and adherence to treatment plans are vital for improving patient outcomes in CKD.

1.3.4.4 Infections:

Infections are the invasion and multiplication of microorganisms such as bacteria, viruses, fungi, or parasites that are not normally present within the body. An infection can cause disease and provoke an inflammatory response in the host. In critical care settings, infections pose significant risks due to the vulnerability of patients who often have compromised immune systems or invasive devices that breach natural barriers.

The pathophysiology of infections involves a complex interaction between the pathogen and the host's immune system. The clinical manifestations of infections can vary widely depending on the organism involved and the site of infection. Common signs include fever, chills, fatigue, and localized symptoms such as cough or dysuria. In severe cases, infections can lead to systemic inflammatory response syndrome (SIRS), sepsis, and septic shock, which require immediate medical intervention.

In critical care environments, healthcare-associated infections (HAIs) are of particular concern. These include ventilator-associated pneumonia (VAP), catheter-associated urinary tract infections (CAUTIs), and central line-associated bloodstream infections (CLABSIs). Preventive measures such as hand hygiene, aseptic techniques, and antimicrobial stewardship are crucial in reducing the incidence of HAIs.

Understanding the principles of antibiotic therapy is essential for managing infections in critically ill patients. This includes knowledge of antibiotic spectra, mechanisms of action, resistance patterns, and potential side effects. Prompt identification and treatment of infections are vital to improving patient outcomes in critical care settings. As future critical care nurses, recognizing the early signs of infection and implementing appropriate interventions is paramount to providing high-quality patient care.

1.3.4.4.1 Kidney:

The kidneys are vital, bean-shaped organs located in the retroperitoneal space on either side of the vertebral column. Their primary function is to filter blood, removing waste products and excess substances, which are excreted as urine. Each kidney contains approximately one million nephrons, the functional units responsible for urine formation. Nephrons consist of a glomerulus and a tubular component, where filtration, reabsorption, and secretion occur.

In critical care settings, understanding renal physiology is crucial due to the kidneys' role in maintaining homeostasis. They regulate fluid and electrolyte balance, acid-base equilibrium, and blood pressure through the renin-angiotensin-aldosterone system. Additionally, the kidneys produce erythropoietin, which stimulates red blood cell production in response to hypoxia.

Acute kidney injury (AKI) and chronic kidney disease (CKD) are common complications in critically ill patients. AKI is characterized by a sudden decline in renal function, leading to the accumulation of nitrogenous wastes and dysregulation of electrolytes. It may result from prerenal, intrinsic renal, or postrenal causes. CKD involves a gradual loss of kidney function over time and may progress to end-stage renal disease (ESRD), necessitating dialysis or transplantation.

Critical care nurses must monitor renal function through serum creatinine levels, glomerular filtration rate (GFR), and urine output. Early recognition and intervention are pivotal in managing renal complications to prevent further deterioration and optimize patient outcomes in critical care environments.

1.3.4.4.2 Urosepsis:

Urosepsis is a severe and potentially life-threatening condition that arises from an infection in the urinary tract, which spreads into the bloodstream, leading to systemic inflammatory response syndrome (SIRS) and sepsis. It is a critical concern in critical care settings due to its rapid progression and high mortality rate if not promptly recognized and treated.

The pathophysiology of urosepsis involves the invasion of pathogens, commonly Escherichia coli, into the urinary tract, leading to an infection that can ascend to the kidneys, causing pyelonephritis. If the body's immune response fails to localize the infection, bacteria can enter the bloodstream, triggering widespread inflammation and potentially leading to septic shock.

Clinical manifestations of urosepsis include fever or hypothermia, tachycardia, tachypnea, altered mental status, and hypotension. Laboratory findings often reveal leukocytosis or leukopenia, elevated lactate levels, and positive blood cultures for uropathogens.

Management of urosepsis requires the prompt initiation of broad-spectrum intravenous antibiotics tailored to culture results once available. Hemodynamic support with intravenous fluids and vasopressors may be necessary to maintain adequate tissue perfusion. Source control through interventions such as the drainage of abscesses or removal of obstructing calculi is crucial.

Early recognition and intervention are vital in improving outcomes for patients with urosepsis. Critical care nurses play a key role in monitoring for signs of deterioration and ensuring the timely implementation of sepsis protocols. Understanding the complexities of urosepsis equips nurses with the knowledge necessary to provide effective patient care and improve survival rates in critically ill patients.

1.3.4.5 Life-threatening Electrolyte Imbalances:

Life-threatening electrolyte imbalances occur when there are significant deviations in the concentrations of essential electrolytes in the body, which can disrupt cellular function and lead to critical health issues. Key electrolytes include sodium, potassium, calcium, magnesium, chloride, bicarbonate, and phosphate. These electrolytes play vital roles in maintaining fluid balance, nerve conduction, muscle function, and acid-base homeostasis.

A common life-threatening imbalance is hyperkalemia, an elevated potassium level that can cause cardiac arrhythmias and muscle weakness. Hypokalemia, or low potassium levels, can lead to muscle cramps and potentially life-threatening cardiac dysrhythmias. Hyponatremia (low sodium) can result in cerebral edema and neurological dysfunction, while hypernatremia (high sodium) may cause dehydration and neurological impairment.

Hypocalcemia (low calcium) can trigger tetany and seizures due to increased neuromuscular excitability. Conversely, hypercalcemia may lead to decreased neuromuscular activity, renal stones, and cardiac arrest. Magnesium imbalances also pose risks; hypomagnesemia can cause neuromuscular irritability and arrhythmias, whereas hypermagnesemia might result in respiratory depression and hypotension.

Chloride imbalances are often linked with sodium disturbances and acid-base disorders. Bicarbonate imbalances directly affect the body's pH level, influencing metabolic acidosis or alkalosis. Phosphate disturbances can impact bone metabolism and energy production.

Critical care nurses must promptly recognize the signs of these imbalances through vigilant monitoring of laboratory values and clinical symptoms to initiate timely interventions that restore electrolyte balance and prevent life-threatening complications.

1.3.5 Integumentary:

The integumentary system is the body's largest organ system, comprising the skin, hair, nails, and associated glands. It serves as a protective barrier against environmental hazards, regulates temperature, and provides sensory information. The skin, the most significant component, consists of three primary layers: the epidermis, dermis, and hypodermis.

The epidermis is the outermost layer, primarily composed of keratinized stratified squamous epithelium. It provides a waterproof barrier and contributes to our skin tone. The dermis lies beneath the epidermis and contains tough connective tissue, hair follicles, and sweat glands. It is responsible for the skin's structural integrity and elasticity due to its collagen and elastin fibers. The hypodermis, or subcutaneous layer, is made up of fat and connective tissue that insulates the body and absorbs shock.

The integumentary system plays a critical role in homeostasis by regulating body temperature through sweating and the vasodilation or vasoconstriction of blood vessels. It also synthesizes vitamin D when exposed to sunlight, which is essential for calcium absorption.

In critical care settings, understanding the integumentary system is vital for assessing patients' overall health status. Nurses must be adept at identifying signs of pressure ulcers, infections, or other skin integrity issues that could complicate recovery. Proper management includes regular skin assessments, maintaining adequate nutrition and hydration, and implementing preventive measures to protect against potential damage. This knowledge is crucial for ensuring optimal patient outcomes in critical care environments.

1.3.5.1 Cellulitis:

Cellulitis is an acute, spreading bacterial infection of the dermis and subcutaneous tissues. It is commonly caused by Streptococcus pyogenes or Staphylococcus aureus, including methicillin-resistant strains (MRSA). The condition typically manifests as an area of redness, swelling, warmth, and pain on the skin, often with poorly defined borders. Systemic symptoms such as fever, chills, and malaise may accompany the local manifestations.

In critical care settings, prompt recognition and treatment of cellulitis are essential to prevent complications such as abscess formation, necrotizing fasciitis, or sepsis. Diagnosis is primarily clinical, supported by patient history and physical examination findings. Blood cultures and imaging may be warranted in severe cases to rule out deeper infections or systemic involvement.

Management involves antimicrobial therapy targeting the most likely pathogens; empirical treatment often includes beta-lactams or clindamycin for typical cases, while MRSA coverage may require vancomycin or linezolid. Elevation of the affected limb and analgesics can help alleviate symptoms. Monitoring for signs of clinical improvement or deterioration is crucial.

Nurses play a pivotal role in the management of cellulitis by assessing skin integrity, administering medications, educating patients about proper skin care and hygiene, and recognizing early signs of complications. Understanding the pathophysiology and therapeutic approaches to cellulitis equips critical care nurses to effectively contribute to patient outcomes and support multidisciplinary teams in managing this common yet potentially serious condition.

1.3.5.2 IV Infiltration:

Intravenous (IV) infiltration occurs when a non-vesicant fluid or medication inadvertently leaks into the surrounding tissue outside the vein. This may happen due to improper catheter placement, dislodgement, or vein rupture. The hallmarks of IV infiltration include localized swelling, pallor, and coolness at the infusion site, often accompanied by discomfort or pain.

Infiltration can lead to complications such as tissue damage, compartment syndrome, and infection if not promptly identified and managed. It is crucial for critical care nurses to frequently assess IV sites for signs of infiltration. Key indicators include a slowed or stopped infusion rate, resistance during flushing, and changes in skin texture or temperature around the catheter site.

Management of IV infiltration involves the immediate cessation of the infusion and the removal of the cannula. Elevating the affected limb can help reduce swelling. The application of warm or cold compresses may be recommended based on the type of infiltrated solution and clinical guidelines. Monitoring for further complications is essential, especially if large volumes were infiltrated.

Preventive measures include proper catheter selection, securement techniques, and regular site assessment. Educating patients about symptoms to report can also aid in early detection. Understanding IV infiltration is vital for CCRN candidates, as it ensures prompt intervention and minimizes patient harm, aligning with best practices in critical care nursing.

1.3.5.3 Necrotizing Fasciitis:

Necrotizing fasciitis is a rare but severe bacterial infection characterized by the rapid destruction of soft tissue, including the fascia, which is the connective tissue surrounding muscles, nerves, fat, and blood vessels. This condition is often referred to as flesh-eating disease due to its aggressive nature. It typically arises from a minor cut or injury that allows bacteria to enter the body, most commonly Group A Streptococcus, though other bacteria can also be involved.

The pathophysiology of necrotizing fasciitis involves the release of toxins by bacteria that lead to tissue necrosis. The disease progresses quickly, often within hours, and can result in systemic toxicity. Early symptoms may include the sudden onset of intense pain at the site of infection, swelling, erythema, and fever. As the condition advances, skin discoloration, blisters, and subcutaneous emphysema may develop.

Diagnosis is primarily clinical but can be supported by imaging studies such as MRI or CT scans that show fascial thickening and gas formation. Laboratory findings may reveal leukocytosis and elevated inflammatory markers. Immediate surgical debridement is critical for removing necrotic tissue and controlling the spread of infection. Broad-spectrum intravenous antibiotics are administered to target potential pathogens.

Prompt recognition and treatment are crucial to improving outcomes in patients with necrotizing fasciitis. Delayed intervention can lead to severe complications such as sepsis, organ failure, or death. Therefore, critical care nurses must maintain a high index of suspicion when assessing patients with rapidly progressing soft tissue infections.

1.3.5.4 Pressure Injury:

A pressure injury, also known as a pressure ulcer or bedsore, is localized damage to the skin and underlying tissue, typically occurring over a bony prominence, resulting from prolonged pressure or pressure in combination with shear. These injuries are a significant concern in critical care settings due to patients' immobility and compromised health status.

The pathophysiology of pressure injuries involves sustained mechanical loading that exceeds capillary closing pressure, leading to ischemia, tissue anoxia, and eventually necrosis. Risk factors include immobility, malnutrition, moisture, advanced age, and impaired sensory perception. Pressure injuries are classified into stages based on their severity:

- Stage 1: Non-blanchable erythema of intact skin.
- Stage 2: Partial-thickness loss of skin with exposed dermis.
- Stage 3: Full-thickness loss of skin, where adipose tissue is visible.
- Stage 4: Full-thickness skin and tissue loss with exposed fascia, muscle, tendon, ligament, cartilage, or bone.

Unstageable pressure injuries occur when the extent of tissue damage cannot be determined due to slough or eschar covering the wound bed. Deep tissue pressure injuries present as persistent non-blanchable deep red, maroon, or purple discoloration.

Prevention is paramount and includes regular repositioning, the use of support surfaces like specialized mattresses or cushions, maintaining skin hygiene, ensuring adequate nutrition and hydration, and educating healthcare staff on early identification and management strategies. Effective management requires a multidisciplinary approach focusing on relieving pressure, optimizing the wound environment, and addressing underlying risk factors.

1.3.5.5 Wounds:

Wounds are disruptions in the normal integrity of the skin and underlying tissues, resulting from various forms of trauma or pathological processes. They can be classified based on their etiology, depth, and healing process. Acute wounds, such as surgical incisions or lacerations, typically follow a predictable healing trajectory, while chronic wounds, like pressure ulcers or diabetic foot ulcers, persist due to underlying pathophysiological factors.

The wound healing process involves several phases: hemostasis, inflammation, proliferation, and remodeling. Hemostasis occurs immediately post-injury, with vasoconstriction and clot formation to stop bleeding. The inflammatory phase follows, characterized by the recruitment of immune cells to prevent infection and clear debris. During proliferation, new tissue forms as fibroblasts synthesize collagen, and angiogenesis restores blood supply. Finally, remodeling strengthens the tissue through collagen maturation and reorganization.

Critical care nurses must assess wounds meticulously to determine their type, size, depth, exudate level, and signs of infection. This evaluation informs the selection of appropriate wound care interventions. Key considerations include maintaining a moist wound environment to facilitate healing, managing exudate with suitable dressings, and preventing infection through aseptic techniques.

In critical care settings, nurses must also consider systemic factors affecting wound healing, such as nutrition, perfusion, and comorbidities like diabetes or immunosuppression. Understanding these aspects ensures comprehensive management strategies that promote optimal healing outcomes for patients with wounds.

1.3.5.5.1 Infectious:

Infectious wounds are those that have been contaminated by pathogenic microorganisms, leading to an infection. These infections can arise from various sources, including bacteria, viruses, fungi, or parasites. The presence of these microorganisms in a wound can impede the natural healing process and may result in increased tissue damage, delayed healing, and systemic complications if not properly managed.

The pathophysiology of infectious wounds involves the invasion and multiplication of pathogens within the wound bed. This triggers an immune response characterized by inflammation, which is marked by redness, swelling, heat, pain, and sometimes loss of function. The body's immune system attempts to eradicate the invading pathogens through the recruitment of white blood cells and the release of inflammatory mediators.

Clinically, infectious wounds may present with purulent drainage, foul odor, increased pain, and erythema extending beyond the wound margins. Systemic signs, such as fever and leukocytosis, may also be evident in more severe cases. Diagnosing an infectious wound typically involves clinical evaluation and may require laboratory tests, such as wound cultures, to identify the specific pathogen responsible.

Management of infectious wounds includes thorough wound cleaning and debridement to remove necrotic tissue and reduce microbial load. Antimicrobial therapy is often necessary and should be guided by culture results when possible. Additionally, optimizing patient factors, such as nutrition and glycemic control, is crucial in supporting wound healing. Effective management requires a multidisciplinary approach involving nurses, physicians, and other healthcare professionals to ensure comprehensive care and promote optimal outcomes for patients with infectious wounds.

1.3.5.5.2 Surgical Wounds:

Surgical wounds are incisions or cuts made intentionally by a surgeon during a procedure to access the body's internal structures. These wounds are typically clean and controlled, contrasting with traumatic wounds that occur accidentally. The primary goal of surgical wound management is to promote optimal healing while minimizing the risk of infection and complications.

Surgical wounds are classified based on their level of contamination: clean, clean-contaminated, contaminated, and dirty-infected. Clean wounds are made under sterile conditions without involving inflamed or infected tissue, while clean-contaminated wounds may involve entry into the respiratory, gastrointestinal, or genitourinary tracts under controlled conditions. Contaminated wounds show evidence of inflammation or gross spillage from the gastrointestinal tract, and dirty-infected wounds involve pre-existing infection.

Care for surgical wounds involves maintaining a sterile environment during dressing changes, assessing for signs of infection such as redness, swelling, heat, pain, and purulent discharge, and ensuring adequate nutritional support for healing. Nurses must also monitor for dehiscence (wound reopening) and evisceration (protrusion of internal organs through the wound), which require immediate medical attention.

Sutures, staples, or adhesive strips are commonly used to close surgical wounds. The choice of closure method depends on the location and type of surgery performed. Healing occurs in phases: hemostasis, inflammation, proliferation, and maturation. During these phases, nurses play a critical role in educating patients about proper wound care techniques at home to ensure successful recovery and prevent complications. Understanding these aspects is crucial for critical care nurses preparing for the CCRN exam.

1.3.5.5.3 Trauma:

Trauma refers to a physical injury or wound caused by an external force, which can be either accidental or intentional. It is a critical condition that requires immediate assessment and intervention to prevent further complications or mortality. In the context of critical care, trauma encompasses a wide range of injuries, including blunt force trauma, penetrating injuries, burns, and fractures. The severity of trauma is often assessed using the Injury Severity Score (ISS), which helps determine the extent of multiple traumas.

For nurses preparing for the CCRN exam, understanding trauma involves recognizing the mechanisms of injury and their implications for patient management. Blunt trauma, often resulting from motor vehicle accidents or falls, can lead to internal bleeding and organ damage without visible external signs. Penetrating trauma, such as stab wounds or gunshot injuries, requires rapid identification of entry and exit points to assess potential damage to underlying structures.

The initial management of trauma involves following the Advanced Trauma Life Support (ATLS) protocol, which prioritizes airway management, breathing support, circulation stabilization, disability evaluation (neurological status), and exposure/environmental control. This systematic approach ensures that life-threatening conditions are addressed promptly.

Nurses must also be adept at monitoring vital signs, recognizing signs of shock or hypovolemia, and administering appropriate interventions such as fluid resuscitation or blood transfusions. Understanding the pathophysiology of trauma and its systemic effects is crucial for effective critical care nursing practice. Additionally, nurses should be familiar with post-trauma care, including pain management, infection prevention, and rehabilitation planning to optimize patient outcomes.

1.4 Musculoskeletal/Neurological/Psychosocial:

The musculoskeletal, neurological, and psychosocial systems are integral components of human physiology and psychology that play crucial roles in maintaining overall health and function. In the context of critical care nursing, understanding these systems is essential for assessing and managing patients with complex health issues.

The musculoskeletal system comprises bones, muscles, tendons, ligaments, and cartilage. It provides structural support, facilitates movement, and protects vital organs. In critical care settings, nurses must be adept at identifying musculoskeletal injuries or disorders, such as fractures, compartment syndrome, or rhabdomyolysis, which may arise from trauma or prolonged immobility.

The neurological system encompasses the central and peripheral nervous systems. It controls body functions by transmitting signals between different parts of the body. Critical care nurses must be proficient in conducting neurological assessments to detect changes in consciousness, motor function, or sensory perception. Conditions such as traumatic brain injury, stroke, or seizures require prompt intervention to prevent further deterioration.

The psychosocial aspect involves the interplay between psychological factors and the social environment impacting a patient's mental health and well-being. Critical care nurses should recognize signs of anxiety, depression, or delirium in patients and provide appropriate interventions. Understanding family dynamics and providing emotional support are also vital for holistic patient care.

In summary, mastery of the musculoskeletal, neurological, and psychosocial domains enables critical care nurses to deliver comprehensive care that addresses both the physiological and psychological needs of critically ill patients.

1.4.1 Musculoskeletal:

The musculoskeletal system is a complex network comprising bones, muscles, tendons, ligaments, and connective tissues that provide structural support, stability, and movement to the human body. This system plays a crucial role in maintaining posture, enabling locomotion, and safeguarding vital organs. In the context of critical care nursing, understanding the intricacies of this system is essential for assessing and managing patients who may experience trauma, degenerative conditions, or systemic diseases affecting musculoskeletal integrity.

Bones serve as the framework of the body, supporting soft tissues and protecting organs. They also act as levers for muscle action and are pivotal in hematopoiesis and mineral storage. Muscles facilitate movement through contraction and relaxation, while tendons connect muscles to bones, transmitting the forces necessary for motion. Ligaments stabilize joints by linking bones together.

In critical care settings, nurses must be adept at recognizing signs of musculoskeletal compromise, such as fractures, dislocations, compartment syndrome, and rhabdomyolysis. These conditions can arise from direct trauma or as a secondary effect of systemic issues like electrolyte imbalances or prolonged immobility. Effective assessment involves evaluating the range of motion, strength, pain levels, and neurovascular status.

Interventions may include immobilization techniques, pain management strategies, and collaboration with multidisciplinary teams for rehabilitation. Nurses also play a key role in preventing complications such as pressure ulcers or deep vein thrombosis in immobilized patients. Comprehensive knowledge of the musculoskeletal system allows critical care nurses to deliver holistic care that enhances patient outcomes in acute settings.

1.4.1.1 Compartment Syndrome:

Compartment syndrome is a serious condition that occurs when there is increased pressure within a closed muscle compartment, leading to a decrease in blood flow and subsequent tissue ischemia. This condition can result from trauma, such as fractures or crush injuries, or from non-traumatic causes like tight bandaging or prolonged limb compression. The affected compartment, surrounded by inelastic fascia, cannot expand to accommodate swelling or bleeding, causing pressure to build up.

Clinically, compartment syndrome presents with the "6 Ps": pain out of proportion to the injury, paresthesia (tingling sensation), pallor (paleness), paralysis (loss of function), pulselessness (absence of pulse), and poikilothermia (inability to regulate temperature). Pain is often the earliest and most significant symptom, especially pain that intensifies with passive stretching of the muscles within the compartment.

Diagnosis is primarily clinical but can be confirmed by measuring intracompartmental pressures using a needle manometer. Pressures exceeding 30 mmHg typically indicate the need for intervention. The definitive treatment for compartment syndrome is surgical fasciotomy, which involves cutting open the fascia to relieve pressure and restore perfusion to the affected tissues.

Delayed treatment can lead to irreversible muscle and nerve damage, resulting in functional impairment or limb loss. Therefore, early recognition and prompt intervention are crucial. Nurses preparing for the CCRN exam should understand the pathophysiology, clinical presentation, diagnostic criteria, and management strategies for compartment syndrome to ensure optimal patient outcomes in critical care settings.

1.4.1.2 Fractures:

A fracture is a medical condition characterized by a break in the continuity of the bone. This can occur due to high-force impact, stress, or as a result of certain medical conditions that weaken the bones, such as osteoporosis or bone cancer. Fractures are classified based on the pattern of the break, whether the skin is intact (closed fracture) or broken (open fracture), as well as the location and severity of the injury.

In critical care settings, understanding fractures is essential for effective patient management. The primary types of fractures include transverse, oblique, spiral, comminuted, and greenstick fractures. Transverse fractures feature a horizontal break across the bone, while oblique fractures have an angled pattern. Spiral fractures result from a twisting force, creating a helical break. Comminuted fractures involve the bone shattering into multiple pieces, and greenstick fractures, which are more common in children, occur when the bone bends and cracks on one side.

The diagnosis of fractures typically involves a clinical examination and imaging studies, such as X-rays, CT scans, or MRIs, to determine the extent and specific type of fracture. Treatment varies based on the fracture type and may include immobilization with casts or splints, traction, or surgical intervention to realign and stabilize the bone fragments using pins, plates, or screws.

Proper management aims to restore normal function by ensuring adequate healing through immobilization and rehabilitation exercises while preventing complications such as infection in open fractures or impaired blood supply leading to avascular necrosis.

1.4.1.2.1 Femur:

The femur, commonly known as the thigh bone, is the longest and strongest bone in the human body, playing a critical role in supporting the weight of the body and enabling locomotion. It extends from the hip joint to the knee joint, forming a key component of the lower limb skeletal structure. The proximal end of the femur articulates with the acetabulum of the pelvis, creating the hip joint, while its distal end connects with the tibia and patella at the knee joint.

Anatomically, the femur consists of several parts: the head, neck, greater and lesser trochanters, shaft, and condyles. The head of the femur fits into the acetabulum to facilitate a wide range of hip movements. The neck connects the head to the shaft and is a common site for fractures, especially in elderly individuals due to osteoporosis or trauma. The greater and lesser trochanters serve as attachment sites for muscles that aid in hip and thigh movement.

Femoral fractures can be classified based on their location: proximal (including neck and intertrochanteric), shaft (diaphyseal), and distal (supracondylar). These fractures often result from high-energy trauma or falls and require prompt medical attention due to potential complications such as significant blood loss or fat embolism syndrome. Treatment may involve surgical intervention, such as internal fixation or arthroplasty, depending on the type of fracture and patient factors.

Understanding femoral anatomy and fracture management is crucial for critical care nurses in providing comprehensive care to patients with musculoskeletal injuries, ensuring optimal recovery outcomes.

1.4.1.2.2 Pelvic Fractures:

Pelvic fractures refer to breaks in the bony structure of the pelvis, which is a complex ring-like formation comprising the sacrum, coccyx, and paired hip bones. These fractures can range from minor, stable injuries to severe, life-threatening disruptions of the pelvic ring. Pelvic fractures are often caused by high-energy trauma, such as motor vehicle accidents or falls from significant heights; however, they can also occur in low-energy incidents in osteoporotic patients.

The classification of pelvic fractures is typically based on the mechanism of injury and stability. They are categorized as stable, where there is no disruption of the pelvic ring, or unstable, where the integrity of the ring is compromised. Unstable fractures often involve significant hemorrhage due to the disruption of major blood vessels and can be associated with damage to internal organs such as the bladder and intestines.

Management of pelvic fractures involves initial stabilization, often using a pelvic binder to reduce bleeding and stabilize the fracture. Advanced imaging techniques, like CT scans, are used for accurate diagnosis and assessment of associated injuries. Surgical intervention may be necessary for unstable fractures to restore pelvic stability and function.

In critical care settings, nurses must monitor for signs of hemodynamic instability, manage pain effectively, and assess for complications such as thromboembolism or infection. Understanding the anatomy and potential complications associated with pelvic fractures is essential for providing comprehensive care to affected patients and optimizing their recovery outcomes.

1.4.1.3 Functional Issues:

Functional issues in critical care refer to the challenges related to a patient's ability to perform activities of daily living (ADLs) and maintain independence due to their critical illness or injury. These issues are crucial in assessing a patient's overall health status and recovery trajectory. In the context of critical care nursing, functional issues encompass a wide range of physical, cognitive, and psychological impairments that may arise from conditions such as prolonged immobility, neurological deficits, or severe systemic illnesses.

A comprehensive assessment of functional issues involves evaluating the patient's baseline functional status before admission, current level of functioning, and potential for rehabilitation. This includes examining mobility, self-care abilities, communication skills, and cognitive functions. Nurses play a vital role in identifying these issues early by using standardized assessment tools like the Barthel Index or the Functional Independence Measure (FIM).

Addressing functional issues requires a multidisciplinary approach involving physical therapy, occupational therapy, speech therapy, and psychological support. Interventions may include mobilization exercises, cognitive rehabilitation, adaptive equipment for ADLs, and emotional support to enhance coping mechanisms. The goal is to prevent further decline, promote recovery, and facilitate a safe transition from critical care to less intensive settings.

Understanding functional issues is essential for critical care nurses, as it directly impacts patient outcomes and quality of life post-discharge. By effectively managing these issues, nurses contribute significantly to optimizing patient recovery and enhancing long-term functionality.

1.4.1.3.1 Immobility:

Immobility refers to the inability of a patient to move freely and independently, which can result from a variety of conditions such as prolonged bed rest, paralysis, severe illness, or injury. In critical care settings, immobility is a significant concern, as it can lead to numerous complications affecting multiple body systems.

Prolonged immobility can result in musculoskeletal deconditioning, leading to muscle atrophy and joint contractures. This may severely impact a patient's functional ability and prolong recovery time. The cardiovascular system is also affected; immobility can cause orthostatic hypotension and increase the risk of venous thromboembolism due to venous stasis. Additionally, respiratory complications such as atelectasis and pneumonia are common due to reduced lung expansion and impaired clearance of secretions.

The integumentary system is vulnerable to pressure injuries from sustained pressure on bony prominences, resulting in reduced blood flow and tissue ischemia. Gastrointestinal issues like constipation can arise from decreased peristalsis, while urinary stasis increases the risk of urinary tract infections and renal calculi.

Psychologically, immobility can lead to feelings of isolation, anxiety, and depression due to reduced social interaction and loss of independence. It is crucial for critical care nurses to implement strategies such as regular repositioning, passive or active range-of-motion exercises, and early mobilization protocols to mitigate these risks. Understanding the multifaceted impacts of immobility enables nurses to provide comprehensive care that promotes recovery and enhances the quality of life for critically ill patients.

1.4.1.3.2 Falls:

Falls in the critical care setting refer to unintentional descents to the floor or ground, which can occur with or without injury. They are a significant concern due to the potential for serious complications, including fractures, head injuries, and increased morbidity. In critical care units, patients are often at heightened risk for falls due to factors such as altered mental status, medication effects (e.g., sedatives, diuretics), and physical weakness resulting from acute illness.

Preventing falls in critically ill patients involves a multifaceted approach. First, thorough risk assessment is essential; this includes evaluating patient history, current medications, and physical abilities. Implementing individualized care plans based on these assessments can significantly reduce fall risk. Environmental modifications, such as ensuring adequate lighting, removing obstacles, and using non-slip mats, are practical measures that enhance safety.

Nursing interventions play a crucial role in fall prevention. Regularly orienting patients to their surroundings and ensuring call bells are within reach empowers patients to seek assistance when needed. Moreover, using assistive devices like bed alarms and ensuring proper footwear can further mitigate risks. Continuous education and training of healthcare staff on fall prevention strategies are vital to maintaining a culture of safety.

In summary, falls in the critical care setting require vigilant assessment and proactive management strategies to prevent adverse outcomes. Care nurses must remain attentive to the unique needs of critically ill patients to effectively minimize fall risks and ensure optimal patient safety.

1.4.1.3.3 Gait Disorders:

Gait disorders encompass a range of abnormalities in the manner or pattern of walking, which can significantly impact a patient's mobility and quality of life. These disorders often arise from neurological, muscular, skeletal, or sensory impairments and are commonly observed in critical care settings due to underlying acute or chronic conditions.

In the context of neurological causes, gait disorders may result from stroke, Parkinson's disease, multiple sclerosis, or peripheral neuropathy. Each condition presents distinct gait characteristics; for instance, Parkinsonian gait is marked by shuffling steps and reduced arm swing, while ataxic gait, often seen in cerebellar dysfunction, involves unsteady and staggering movements.

Musculoskeletal issues such as arthritis or joint deformities can also lead to gait disturbances by causing pain or limiting joint range of motion. Additionally, muscle weakness from conditions like myopathy or prolonged immobility in critical care can contribute to altered gait patterns.

Sensory deficits, including those affecting vision or proprioception, disrupt normal gait by impairing balance and spatial orientation. This can lead to compensatory mechanisms that further alter walking patterns.

For nurses preparing for the CCRN exam, it is crucial to understand the underlying etiology of gait disorders to provide appropriate interventions. Assessment should include a thorough history and physical examination focusing on neuromuscular function and coordination. Management strategies may involve physical therapy, assistive devices, pharmacological treatments for underlying conditions, and multidisciplinary team involvement to optimize patient outcomes.

1.4.1.4 Osteomyelitis:

Osteomyelitis is a severe infection of the bone, typically caused by bacteria, most commonly Staphylococcus aureus. This condition can be acute or chronic and often results from an extension of a nearby infection, direct contamination during trauma or surgery, or hematogenous spread from a distant site. In critical care settings, recognizing osteomyelitis is crucial due to its potential to cause significant morbidity.

The pathophysiology involves bacteria invading the bone tissue, leading to inflammation, increased vascular permeability, and subsequent edema. This inflammatory process can compromise blood supply, resulting in bone necrosis and the formation of sequestra (dead bone segments). The body attempts to wall off the infection by forming new bone (involucrum), but this can complicate the eradication of the infection.

Clinically, patients may present with localized bone pain, tenderness, swelling, fever, and erythema over the affected area. Chronic osteomyelitis may present with draining sinus tracts. Diagnosis is confirmed through imaging studies such as MRI or bone scans and microbiological cultures obtained from blood or biopsy.

Management involves both medical and surgical approaches. Empirical antibiotic therapy should be initiated promptly and later tailored based on culture results. Surgical intervention may be necessary to debride necrotic tissue and drain abscesses. Long-term antibiotic therapy is often required to ensure the complete eradication of the infection.

Understanding the complex nature of osteomyelitis is essential for critical care nurses to provide effective patient management and improve outcomes for those afflicted with this challenging condition.

1.4.1.5 Rhabdomyolysis:

Rhabdomyolysis is a serious medical condition characterized by the rapid breakdown of skeletal muscle tissue, leading to the release of intracellular contents, including myoglobin, into the bloodstream. This process can result in significant complications, primarily acute kidney injury (AKI), due to the nephrotoxic effects of myoglobin. The etiology of rhabdomyolysis is diverse, encompassing traumatic causes such as crush injuries and prolonged immobilization, as well as non-traumatic factors like intense physical exertion, drug use (e.g., statins, cocaine), infections, and metabolic disorders.

Clinically, rhabdomyolysis presents with symptoms ranging from muscle pain and weakness to tea-colored urine due to myoglobinuria. Laboratory findings typically reveal elevated levels of creatine kinase (CK), often exceeding five times the normal upper limit, which serves as a key diagnostic marker. Additionally, electrolyte imbalances such as hyperkalemia and hypocalcemia may occur due to the release of cellular contents.

Management of rhabdomyolysis focuses on early recognition and aggressive fluid resuscitation to prevent renal damage. Intravenous fluids help maintain adequate urine output and dilute nephrotoxic agents. Monitoring and correcting electrolyte abnormalities are crucial to prevent cardiac arrhythmias and other systemic complications. In severe cases, dialysis may be required if renal failure ensues.

Understanding the pathophysiology, risk factors, and management strategies for rhabdomyolysis is essential for critical care nurses. Prompt intervention can significantly reduce morbidity and improve patient outcomes in this potentially life-threatening condition.

1.4.2 Neurological:

The neurological component of critical care nursing involves the assessment, monitoring, and management of patients with acute neurological conditions. It encompasses a thorough understanding of the anatomy and physiology of the nervous system, including the central nervous system (CNS), which comprises the brain and spinal cord, and the peripheral nervous system (PNS). Critical care nurses must be adept at recognizing and responding to neurological emergencies such as stroke, traumatic brain injury, seizures, and increased intracranial pressure.

A comprehensive neurological assessment is vital in critical care settings. This includes evaluating the patient's level of consciousness using tools like the Glasgow Coma Scale, assessing pupil size and reactivity, monitoring motor and sensory function, and observing for any signs of neurological deterioration. Nurses must also be familiar with diagnostic procedures such as CT scans, MRIs, EEGs, and lumbar punctures.

The management of neurological patients involves maintaining adequate cerebral perfusion and oxygenation, controlling seizures, managing pain, and preventing complications such as deep vein thrombosis or infections. Critical care nurses play a crucial role in implementing interventions like positioning strategies to reduce intracranial pressure, administering medications such as antiepileptics or osmotic diuretics, and coordinating multidisciplinary care.

Continuous education on advances in neurocritical care is essential for nurses to provide evidence-based interventions. Understanding the pathophysiology behind neurological disorders enables nurses to deliver holistic care aimed at optimizing patient outcomes in this complex field of critical care nursing.

1.4.2.1 Acute Spinal Cord Injury:

Acute Spinal Cord Injury (SCI) refers to sudden trauma to the spinal cord, resulting in temporary or permanent changes in its function. It is a critical condition that requires immediate medical attention and can lead to severe neurological deficits. The injury may occur due to motor vehicle accidents, falls, sports injuries, or acts of violence, and it often results in partial or complete loss of motor control and sensation below the level of the injury.

The pathophysiology of acute SCI involves primary and secondary injury mechanisms. The primary injury is the initial mechanical disruption of axons and blood vessels. Secondary injury processes include ischemia, inflammation, edema, and excitotoxicity, which exacerbate neural damage over time.

Clinically, acute SCI is classified based on the level of injury (cervical, thoracic, lumbar) and completeness (complete vs. incomplete). Complete injuries result in total loss of sensory and motor function below the injury site, while incomplete injuries retain some degree of function.

Management focuses on stabilizing the spine to prevent further damage, maintaining adequate perfusion to the spinal cord, and minimizing secondary injury through pharmacological interventions like high-dose methylprednisolone (though its use is controversial). Surgical intervention may be required to decompress the spinal cord or stabilize fractures.

Rehabilitation plays a crucial role in recovery by maximizing functional outcomes and improving quality of life. Care nurses must monitor for complications such as autonomic dysreflexia, pressure ulcers, and respiratory issues while supporting patients' physical and emotional needs during rehabilitation.

1.4.2.2 Brain Death:

Brain death is a clinical and legal determination of death based on the irreversible cessation of all brain activity, including that of the brainstem. It is distinct from other states such as coma or vegetative state, where some brain functions may persist. Brain death is equivalent to death because the brain is responsible for integrating the bodily functions necessary for life.

The diagnosis of brain death requires a comprehensive evaluation to ensure that the condition is not due to reversible causes such as hypothermia, drug intoxication, or metabolic disturbances. The assessment typically involves a series of clinical tests to confirm the absence of cerebral and brainstem activity. These tests include checking for unresponsiveness, lack of brainstem reflexes (such as pupillary response to light, corneal reflex, and gag reflex), and apnea testing to confirm the inability to breathe independently when removed from mechanical ventilation.

In some cases, ancillary tests such as electroencephalography (EEG) or cerebral blood flow studies may be used to provide additional confirmation of brain death. These tests demonstrate the absence of electrical activity in the brain or a lack of blood flow to the brain, respectively.

Understanding brain death is critical for critical care nurses, as they play a vital role in monitoring patients for signs consistent with this diagnosis and supporting families through the process. It is essential for nurses to be knowledgeable about institutional protocols and legal requirements surrounding the declaration of brain death to ensure ethical and accurate practice.

1.4.2.3 Delirium:

Delirium is an acute, fluctuating change in mental status characterized by disturbances in attention, awareness, and cognition. It is a serious condition commonly encountered in critical care settings and requires prompt recognition and management. Delirium manifests as confusion, disorganized thinking, a reduced ability to focus, sustain, or shift attention, and perceptual disturbances. It is often accompanied by altered levels of consciousness, ranging from hyperactive (agitation) to hypoactive (lethargy) states.

The pathophysiology of delirium is complex and multifactorial, involving neurotransmitter imbalances, inflammation, and impaired cerebral metabolism. Risk factors include advanced age, pre-existing cognitive impairment, severe illness, infection, medication effects (especially anticholinergics and sedatives), metabolic disturbances, and sensory deprivation.

Diagnosis is primarily clinical and relies on tools such as the Confusion Assessment Method for the Intensive Care Unit (CAM-ICU) or the Intensive Care Delirium Screening Checklist (ICDSC). These tools help differentiate delirium from other neuropsychiatric conditions, such as dementia or depression.

Management focuses on identifying and treating the underlying cause while minimizing risk factors. Non-pharmacological strategies are first-line interventions and include reorientation techniques, ensuring adequate hydration and nutrition, optimizing sleep-wake cycles, and providing sensory aids. Pharmacological treatment may be considered for severe cases or when non-pharmacological measures fail. Antipsychotics, such as haloperidol, can be used cautiously but require careful monitoring due to potential side effects.

Understanding the presentation and management of delirium is crucial for critical care nurses to improve patient outcomes and reduce morbidity associated with this condition.

1.4.2.3.1 Hyperactive Delirium:

Hyperactive delirium is a subtype of delirium characterized by heightened arousal, increased motor activity, and restlessness. This condition often presents with symptoms such as agitation, combativeness, hallucinations, and rapid speech. Patients may exhibit an exaggerated response to stimuli and may be difficult to manage due to their unpredictable behavior. Hyperactive delirium is frequently observed in critical care settings and can be triggered by various factors, including metabolic imbalances, infections, medications, or withdrawal from substances.

Clinically, hyperactive delirium poses significant challenges in patient management due to the potential for self-harm or harm to others. It is crucial for nurses to differentiate hyperactive delirium from other psychiatric disorders to ensure appropriate interventions. Assessment tools like the Confusion Assessment Method for the Intensive Care Unit (CAM-ICU) can aid in accurate diagnosis.

Management strategies primarily focus on addressing underlying causes, ensuring patient safety, and minimizing environmental stressors. Pharmacological interventions may include the use of antipsychotics or benzodiazepines; however, these should be used judiciously due to potential side effects. Non-pharmacological approaches, such as reorientation techniques, maintaining a calm environment, and involving family members in care, can be beneficial.

Understanding hyperactive delirium is vital for critical care nurses, as it significantly impacts patient outcomes. Early recognition and intervention are key components in the management of this condition, emphasizing the importance of comprehensive training and awareness among healthcare professionals preparing for the CCRN exam.

1.4.2.3.2 Hypoactive Delirium:

Hypoactive delirium is a subtype of delirium characterized by reduced motor activity, lethargy, and decreased responsiveness. Unlike hyperactive delirium, which presents with agitation and restlessness, hypoactive delirium often goes unnoticed due to its subtle presentation. It is crucial for nurses to recognize this condition, as it can significantly impact patient outcomes if left untreated.

Patients with hypoactive delirium may appear withdrawn or apathetic, often being mistaken for having depression or fatigue. They may exhibit slowed speech, diminished alertness, and a lack of spontaneous movement. This form of delirium is particularly common in older adults and critically ill patients, making vigilant assessment essential in the critical care setting.

The pathophysiology of hypoactive delirium involves complex interactions between neurotransmitter imbalances, inflammation, and changes in cerebral perfusion. Acetylcholine deficiency and dopamine excess are considered key contributors. Risk factors include advanced age, pre-existing cognitive impairment, severe illness, and certain medications, such as sedatives or anticholinergics.

Assessment tools like the Confusion Assessment Method for the Intensive Care Unit (CAM-ICU) can aid in identifying hypoactive delirium by evaluating attention, orientation, and cognitive function. Management involves addressing underlying causes, optimizing the patient's environment to promote orientation (e.g., ensuring adequate lighting and noise control), and ensuring proper hydration and nutrition. Pharmacologic interventions may include the cautious use of antipsychotics if non-pharmacologic measures are insufficient.

Understanding hypoactive delirium is vital for nurses preparing for the CCRN exam, as it underscores the importance of comprehensive patient assessment and multidisciplinary management strategies in critical care settings.

1.4.2.3.3 Mixed Delirium:

Mixed delirium is a subtype of delirium characterized by fluctuating symptoms that exhibit both hyperactive and hypoactive features. In this condition, patients may alternate between states of heightened arousal, agitation, or restlessness (hyperactive delirium) and periods of lethargy, decreased responsiveness, or apathy (hypoactive delirium). This fluctuation can occur over hours or days, making it challenging to diagnose and manage.

The pathophysiology of mixed delirium involves complex interactions between neurotransmitter imbalances, inflammation, and metabolic disturbances. Factors such as severe illness, medication effects, or withdrawal, particularly in critical care settings, can precipitate mixed delirium. The clinical presentation is often variable; patients may appear confused and disoriented at one moment, then become withdrawn and unresponsive shortly after.

Assessment tools like the Confusion Assessment Method for the Intensive Care Unit (CAM-ICU) are essential for identifying mixed delirium. These tools help differentiate it from other cognitive disorders by focusing on acute onset and fluctuating course, inattention, disorganized thinking, and altered levels of consciousness.

Management of mixed delirium involves addressing underlying causes, optimizing the patient's environment to reduce stressors, and ensuring safety. Pharmacological interventions may be necessary but should be used cautiously due to the risk of exacerbating symptoms. Non-pharmacological strategies such as reorientation techniques, sleep hygiene improvement, and family involvement play a crucial role in managing this condition.

Understanding the complexity of mixed delirium is vital for critical care nurses to provide effective care and improve patient outcomes in the intensive care setting.

1.4.2.4 Dementia:

Dementia is a clinical syndrome characterized by a progressive decline in cognitive function that is severe enough to interfere with daily life and independent functioning. It encompasses a range of symptoms affecting memory, thinking, orientation, comprehension, calculation, learning capacity, language, and judgment. The decline in cognitive abilities is often accompanied by deterioration in emotional control, social behavior, and motivation.

Pathophysiologically, dementia results from damage to brain cells that impairs their ability to communicate with one another. This damage can be caused by various diseases and conditions, the most common of which is Alzheimer's disease. Other causes include vascular dementia, Lewy body dementia, frontotemporal dementia, and mixed dementia. Each type has distinct pathologies but often shares overlapping symptoms.

Clinically, patients with dementia may present with forgetfulness, confusion about time or place, difficulty with complex tasks or problem-solving, language disturbances such as aphasia, and changes in personality or behavior. As the condition progresses, these symptoms intensify and can lead to complete dependency on caregivers for basic activities of daily living.

Diagnosis involves a comprehensive assessment, including medical history, physical examination, neurological evaluations, cognitive testing, and sometimes neuroimaging to rule out other causes of cognitive impairment. Management focuses on symptomatic relief and supportive care. Pharmacological treatments, such as cholinesterase inhibitors and memantine, can help manage symptoms but do not cure the disease. Non-pharmacological interventions aim to improve quality of life through cognitive therapies and environmental modifications.

Understanding the multifaceted nature of dementia is crucial for critical care nurses to provide effective patient-centered care and support families navigating this challenging condition.

1.4.2.5 Encephalopathy:

Encephalopathy is a broad term that refers to any diffuse disease of the brain that alters its function or structure. It is characterized by an altered mental state, which can range from mild confusion to deep coma. The etiology of encephalopathy is diverse, encompassing metabolic, toxic, infectious, and structural causes. Common types include hepatic encephalopathy, resulting from liver failure; uremic encephalopathy, due to renal failure; and Wernicke's encephalopathy, associated with thiamine deficiency.

Clinically, patients with encephalopathy may present with cognitive dysfunction, memory impairment, personality changes, or motor abnormalities such as tremors or myoclonus. Diagnosis is primarily clinical but is often supported by laboratory tests and neuroimaging to identify underlying causes. Electroencephalography (EEG) may show generalized slowing of brain activity.

Management of encephalopathy focuses on identifying and treating the underlying cause. For instance, in hepatic encephalopathy, lactulose is used to reduce ammonia levels. In cases of toxic encephalopathy, removing the offending agent is crucial. Supportive care includes ensuring adequate oxygenation, hydration, and nutrition.

Prognosis varies depending on the etiology and severity of the condition. Acute forms may be reversible with prompt treatment, while chronic forms might lead to permanent neurological deficits. Understanding the pathophysiology and management strategies for different types of encephalopathy is essential for critical care nurses in providing optimal patient care and improving outcomes for affected individuals.

1.4.2.6 Hemorrhage:

Hemorrhage refers to the escape of blood from a ruptured blood vessel, which can occur either internally or externally. It is a critical condition that requires immediate medical attention due to the potential for rapid deterioration and life-threatening consequences. Hemorrhage can be classified based on the source of bleeding: arterial, venous, or capillary, with arterial hemorrhage being the most severe due to the high pressure and rapid blood loss involved.

Clinically, hemorrhage is categorized into four classes based on the volume of blood loss and the corresponding physiological responses. Class I involves up to 15% blood volume loss with minimal symptoms. Class II involves a 15-30% loss, leading to tachycardia, tachypnea, and decreased urine output. Class III involves a 30-40% loss, resulting in hypotension, confusion, and significant tachycardia. Class IV exceeds 40% blood loss, causing profound shock and potential organ failure.

The management of hemorrhage focuses on controlling bleeding and restoring circulatory volume. Initial interventions include applying direct pressure to external bleeding sites, elevating affected limbs, and utilizing tourniquets if necessary. Intravenous fluid resuscitation is crucial for maintaining hemodynamic stability, often followed by blood transfusions to replenish lost red blood cells and clotting factors.

In critical care settings, rapid identification and intervention are paramount. Advanced techniques such as endoscopic procedures, angiographic embolization, or surgical intervention may be required to control internal hemorrhages. Understanding the pathophysiology and appropriate management strategies for hemorrhage is essential for critical care nurses to effectively respond to this potentially fatal condition.

1.4.2.6.1 Intracranial Hemorrhage (ICH):

Intracranial Hemorrhage (ICH) refers to bleeding within the skull, which can occur in various compartments, such as the brain tissue itself (intracerebral), between the brain and its protective coverings (subarachnoid or subdural), or within the ventricles (intraventricular). ICH is a critical condition requiring immediate medical attention due to its potential to increase intracranial pressure, leading to brain tissue damage, herniation, and potentially death.

In the context of critical care nursing, understanding ICH involves recognizing its causes, which include hypertension, trauma, aneurysm rupture, complications from anticoagulation therapy, and certain vascular malformations. Clinical manifestations often include a sudden headache, nausea, vomiting, altered consciousness, focal neurological deficits, and seizures. Rapid assessment and intervention are crucial.

Diagnosis typically involves neuroimaging techniques such as CT scans or MRIs to determine the location and extent of the bleeding. Management strategies focus on stabilizing the patient's condition by controlling blood pressure, managing intracranial pressure through medications like mannitol or hypertonic saline, and performing surgical interventions when necessary. Surgical options may include hematoma evacuation or decompressive craniectomy.

Nurses play a vital role in monitoring neurological status using tools like the Glasgow Coma Scale, ensuring airway patency, maintaining hemodynamic stability, and providing supportive care. Critical care nurses must also educate families about prognosis and potential outcomes while coordinating with multidisciplinary teams for comprehensive patient management. Understanding these aspects is essential for effective care delivery in patients with ICH.

1.4.2.6.2 Intraventricular Hemorrhage (IVH):
Intraventricular Hemorrhage (IVH) is a type of bleeding that occurs within the brain's ventricular system, where cerebrospinal fluid is produced and circulates. It is most commonly seen in premature infants due to the fragility of the germinal matrix but can also occur in adults, often as a result of trauma or ruptured aneurysms. In neonates, IVH is graded on a scale from I to IV, with Grade I being mild and confined to the germinal matrix, and Grade IV involving extensive bleeding into the brain tissue itself.

The pathophysiology of IVH involves the rupture of delicate blood vessels within the germinal matrix or subependymal region, which then allows blood to enter the ventricles. This can lead to increased intracranial pressure, hydrocephalus, and subsequent damage to brain tissue due to impaired cerebrospinal fluid circulation and pressure effects.

Clinically, IVH may present with signs of neurological deterioration, such as altered consciousness, seizures, bulging fontanelles in infants, or changes in vital signs. Diagnosis is typically confirmed through neuroimaging techniques like cranial ultrasound in neonates or CT/MRI scans in older patients.

Management of IVH focuses on stabilizing the patient's condition, controlling intracranial pressure, and preventing further complications. This may include supportive care measures such as mechanical ventilation and the administration of medications like diuretics or anticonvulsants. In severe cases, surgical intervention might be necessary to relieve pressure or address hydrocephalus.

Understanding IVH is crucial for critical care nurses, as they play a vital role in monitoring neurological status and implementing timely interventions to optimize patient outcomes.

1.4.2.6.3 Subarachnoid Hemorrhage: Traumatic vs. Aneurysmal
A subarachnoid hemorrhage (SAH) refers to bleeding into the subarachnoid space, the area between the arachnoid membrane and the pia mater surrounding the brain. This condition can be categorized as either traumatic or aneurysmal. Traumatic SAH results from head injury, where physical trauma causes blood vessels to rupture. Aneurysmal SAH occurs due to the rupture of a cerebral aneurysm, which is a weakened area in the wall of a blood vessel in the brain that balloons and fills with blood.

In the case of an aneurysmal SAH, the rupture leads to a sudden increase in intracranial pressure, causing a severe headache often described as a thunderclap headache, along with neck stiffness, photophobia, and altered consciousness. Neurological deficits may occur depending on the location and severity of the bleed. The risk factors for aneurysmal SAH include hypertension, smoking, excessive alcohol consumption, and genetic predispositions.

Diagnosis is typically confirmed through computed tomography (CT) scanning or lumbar puncture if the CT is inconclusive. Management requires the prompt stabilization of vital signs, securing the airway and breathing, controlling blood pressure, and preventing rebleeding. Surgical interventions such as clipping or endovascular coiling are employed to secure the aneurysm.

For critical care nurses preparing for the CCRN exam, understanding both types of SAH is essential. Recognizing early symptoms and providing immediate care can significantly impact patient outcomes. Knowledge of postoperative care, monitoring for complications like vasospasm or hydrocephalus, and implementing evidence-based interventions are crucial components in effectively managing patients with SAH.

1.4.2.7 Increased Intracranial Pressure:
Increased intracranial pressure (ICP) refers to the elevation of pressure within the skull, which houses the brain, blood, and cerebrospinal fluid (CSF). Under normal conditions, ICP ranges from 5 to 15 mmHg in adults. When ICP rises beyond this range, it can compromise cerebral perfusion and lead to brain injury. The Monroe-Kellie doctrine explains that the cranial cavity is a fixed volume; thus, an increase in one component (brain tissue, blood, or CSF) necessitates a compensatory decrease in another to maintain equilibrium.

Causes of increased ICP include traumatic brain injury, intracerebral hemorrhage, tumors, hydrocephalus, and cerebral edema. Clinically, increased ICP manifests as headache, vomiting without nausea, altered mental status, and papilledema. Cushing's triad—hypertension with widened pulse pressure, bradycardia, and irregular respirations—is a late sign indicative of brainstem compression.

Management strategies aim to reduce ICP while ensuring adequate cerebral perfusion. Interventions include elevating the head of the bed to 30 degrees to promote venous drainage, controlling fever to reduce metabolic demand, administering osmotic diuretics like mannitol or hypertonic saline to draw fluid out of brain tissue, and ensuring normocapnia through controlled ventilation. In severe cases, surgical interventions such as decompressive craniectomy may be necessary.

Understanding the pathophysiology and management of increased ICP is crucial for critical care nurses to prevent secondary brain injury and optimize patient outcomes in neurocritical care settings.

1.4.2.7.1 Hydrocephalus:
Hydrocephalus is a neurological condition characterized by an abnormal accumulation of cerebrospinal fluid (CSF) within the ventricles of the brain, leading to increased intracranial pressure. This condition can result from either overproduction of CSF, obstruction of its flow, or impaired absorption. The excess fluid causes the ventricles to enlarge, which can compress and damage brain tissue.

In adults, symptoms of hydrocephalus may include headaches, nausea, vomiting, blurred vision, balance problems, and cognitive impairments. In infants and young children, it often presents with an unusually large head size, bulging fontanelles, irritability, and developmental delays due to the skull's ability to expand.

There are two main types of hydrocephalus: communicating and non-communicating. Communicating hydrocephalus occurs when CSF flow is blocked after it exits the ventricles but remains open within the subarachnoid space. Non-communicating hydrocephalus, also known as obstructive hydrocephalus, results from a blockage within the ventricular system itself.

Diagnosis typically involves neuroimaging techniques such as MRI or CT scans to visualize ventricular enlargement and identify potential causes. Treatment often requires surgical intervention to divert the excess fluid. The most common procedure is the insertion of a shunt system that redirects CSF from the ventricles to another part of the body where it can be absorbed. Alternatively, endoscopic third ventriculostomy (ETV) may be performed to create a pathway for fluid drainage.

Understanding hydrocephalus is crucial for critical care nurses, as timely recognition and management are vital in preventing neurological deterioration and optimizing patient outcomes.

1.4.2.8   Neurologic Infectious Disease:

Neurologic infectious diseases encompass a range of conditions caused by infectious agents such as bacteria, viruses, fungi, and parasites that affect the central nervous system (CNS), including the brain and spinal cord. These infections can lead to significant morbidity and mortality if not promptly diagnosed and treated. Common neurologic infectious diseases include meningitis, encephalitis, brain abscesses, and neurosyphilis.

Meningitis is characterized by inflammation of the protective membranes covering the brain and spinal cord, known as the meninges. It can be bacterial or viral in origin, with bacterial meningitis being more severe and requiring immediate medical intervention. Encephalitis involves inflammation of the brain tissue itself, often caused by viral infections such as the herpes simplex virus or arboviruses like the West Nile virus.

Brain abscesses are localized infections within the brain tissue that can result from direct infection, spread from nearby structures, or hematogenous dissemination from distant sites. Neurosyphilis is a late-stage manifestation of syphilis infection affecting the CNS, leading to various neurological symptoms.

Diagnosis of neurologic infectious diseases typically involves neuroimaging studies like MRI or CT scans, cerebrospinal fluid analysis via lumbar puncture, and serological tests to identify specific pathogens. Treatment varies depending on the causative agent but may include antimicrobial therapy, supportive care, and management of complications such as increased intracranial pressure.

Understanding the pathophysiology, clinical presentation, diagnostic approaches, and management strategies for these conditions is crucial for critical care nurses to provide effective patient care and improve outcomes for those affected by neurologic infectious diseases.

1.4.2.8.1   Viral:

Viral infections, within the context of neurologic infectious diseases, refer to conditions where viruses invade and affect the central nervous system (CNS), leading to various degrees of neurological impairment. These infections can manifest as meningitis, encephalitis, or myelitis, depending on which part of the CNS is affected. Common viral pathogens include Herpes Simplex Virus (HSV), Varicella-Zoster Virus (VZV), enteroviruses, West Nile Virus, and Cytomegalovirus (CMV).

In viral meningitis, the protective membranes covering the brain and spinal cord become inflamed. Symptoms often include headache, fever, neck stiffness, and photophobia. Viral encephalitis involves inflammation of the brain tissue itself, leading to altered mental status, seizures, and focal neurological deficits. Myelitis affects the spinal cord and can result in motor and sensory deficits.

The pathophysiology involves viral entry through hematogenous spread or neural pathways, followed by replication within CNS cells. This triggers an inflammatory response that contributes to neuronal damage. Diagnosis typically involves cerebrospinal fluid (CSF) analysis through lumbar puncture, revealing elevated white blood cell counts with a lymphocytic predominance, normal glucose levels, and elevated protein levels. Polymerase chain reaction (PCR) testing can identify specific viral DNA or RNA.

Management primarily focuses on supportive care and antiviral therapies when available. For instance, acyclovir is used for HSV encephalitis. Early recognition and intervention are crucial in minimizing long-term neurological sequelae. Care nurses must be vigilant in monitoring neurological status and managing complications such as increased intracranial pressure or seizures to optimize patient outcomes.

1.4.2.8.2   Bacterial:

Bacterial infections in the neurologic context refer to the invasion and multiplication of pathogenic bacteria within the central nervous system (CNS), leading to conditions such as bacterial meningitis, brain abscesses, and spinal infections. Bacterial meningitis, one of the most critical forms, is an acute inflammation of the protective membranes covering the brain and spinal cord, known as the meninges. It is primarily caused by Neisseria meningitidis, Streptococcus pneumoniae, and Haemophilus influenzae type b (Hib). These pathogens can breach the blood-brain barrier through hematogenous spread or direct extension from adjacent infected sites.

Clinical manifestations often include fever, headache, neck stiffness, altered mental status, and photophobia. Rapid diagnosis is crucial and typically involves a lumbar puncture to obtain cerebrospinal fluid (CSF) for analysis. CSF findings in bacterial meningitis usually reveal an elevated white blood cell count (predominantly neutrophils), decreased glucose concentration, and increased protein levels.

Treatment mandates the prompt initiation of empiric broad-spectrum intravenous antibiotics, tailored based on age, immune status, and local resistance patterns. Commonly used antibiotics include ceftriaxone or cefotaxime combined with vancomycin. In specific cases, adjunctive corticosteroids may be administered to reduce inflammatory complications.

Critical care nurses must monitor for complications such as increased intracranial pressure, seizures, and septic shock. Preventative measures include vaccination against common causative organisms and prophylactic antibiotics for close contacts of patients with certain types of bacterial meningitis. Understanding the pathophysiology, clinical presentation, diagnostic approach, and management strategies is essential for nurses to effectively care for patients with bacterial neurologic infections.

1.4.2.8.3 Fungal:

Fungal infections of the central nervous system (CNS) are critical conditions that require prompt diagnosis and management, particularly in immunocompromised patients. These infections are primarily caused by opportunistic fungi such as Cryptococcus neoformans, Aspergillus species, and Candida species. Cryptococcal meningitis is the most common fungal CNS infection, often affecting individuals with HIV/AIDS. It presents with symptoms such as headache, fever, neck stiffness, and altered mental status. Diagnosis typically involves cerebrospinal fluid (CSF) analysis, which shows elevated opening pressure, lymphocytic pleocytosis, low glucose levels, and a positive cryptococcal antigen test.

Aspergillus infections can lead to cerebral aspergillosis, characterized by brain abscesses or infarcts due to angioinvasion by the fungus. Patients may present with focal neurological deficits or seizures. Imaging studies, such as MRI or CT scans, often reveal ring-enhancing lesions in the brain.

Candida species can cause meningitis or brain abscesses, particularly in patients with prolonged neutropenia or those who have undergone neurosurgical procedures. Diagnosis is confirmed through CSF culture or histopathological examination of brain tissue.

Management of fungal CNS infections involves antifungal therapy tailored to the specific pathogen. Amphotericin B and flucytosine are commonly used for cryptococcal meningitis, while voriconazole is preferred for invasive aspergillosis. Surgical intervention may be necessary for abscess drainage.

Critical care nurses must remain vigilant for signs of neurologic deterioration in patients at risk for fungal CNS infections and collaborate closely with infectious disease specialists to optimize treatment outcomes.

1.4.2.9 Neuromuscular Disorders:

Neuromuscular disorders encompass a broad range of conditions that impair the functioning of muscles, nerves, or the neuromuscular junctions where nerves and muscles meet. These disorders can result from genetic mutations, autoimmune reactions, infections, or other underlying health issues. Common examples include amyotrophic lateral sclerosis (ALS), myasthenia gravis, muscular dystrophies, and Guillain-Barré syndrome.

In these conditions, patients may experience muscle weakness, fatigue, spasms, or paralysis. The pathophysiology often involves disruption in the transmission of signals between the nervous system and muscles. For instance, in myasthenia gravis, antibodies attack acetylcholine receptors at the neuromuscular junction, leading to muscle weakness. In contrast, ALS involves the degeneration of motor neurons in the brain and spinal cord.

Diagnosis typically involves clinical evaluation, electromyography (EMG), nerve conduction studies, and sometimes genetic testing or muscle biopsy. Treatment strategies vary depending on the specific disorder but may include immunosuppressive therapies for autoimmune conditions, physical therapy to maintain muscle function, and symptomatic management to enhance quality of life.

Critical care nurses must be adept at recognizing signs of respiratory compromise and autonomic instability in these patients. Understanding the specific neuromuscular disorder is crucial for tailoring interventions such as respiratory support or nutritional management. Continuous monitoring and a multidisciplinary approach are essential to address complications and optimize patient outcomes in critical care settings.

1.4.2.9.1 Muscular Dystrophy:

Muscular Dystrophy (MD) is a group of genetic disorders characterized by progressive muscle weakness and degeneration. These disorders are caused by mutations in genes responsible for the structure and function of muscle fibers. The most common type, Duchenne Muscular Dystrophy (DMD), primarily affects boys and is linked to an X-linked recessive gene mutation. Other types include Becker, Myotonic, Limb-Girdle, and Facioscapulohumeral muscular dystrophies, each with distinct genetic causes and clinical manifestations.

In MD, the absence or deficiency of dystrophin, a protein critical for muscle integrity, leads to muscle fiber damage and eventual replacement by adipose and fibrotic tissue. This process results in the progressive loss of muscle strength and function. Clinical symptoms typically begin in childhood for Duchenne MD, with affected individuals experiencing difficulty in ambulation, frequent falls, and delayed motor skills. As the disease progresses, complications such as cardiomyopathy, respiratory failure, and scoliosis may develop.

Diagnosis involves a combination of clinical evaluation, genetic testing, electromyography (EMG), and muscle biopsy. Elevated serum creatine kinase (CK) levels are indicative of muscle damage. Management focuses on multidisciplinary care to optimize quality of life and includes physical therapy, corticosteroids to slow progression, cardiac care, respiratory support, and surgical interventions when necessary.

Understanding the pathophysiology of Muscular Dystrophy is crucial for critical care nurses to provide comprehensive care and anticipate potential complications in affected patients.

1.4.2.9.2 Cerebral Palsy (CP):

Cerebral Palsy (CP) is a group of permanent movement disorders that appear in early childhood, primarily affecting muscle tone, posture, and motor function. It is caused by damage to the developing brain, either during pregnancy, childbirth, or shortly after birth. CP is characterized by a variety of symptoms, including spasticity, which involves stiff or rigid muscles; dyskinesia, marked by involuntary movements; and ataxia, which affects balance and coordination.

The severity of CP varies significantly among individuals, ranging from slight clumsiness to severe impairments that necessitate lifelong care. It is crucial for critical care nurses to understand that CP is a non-progressive disorder, meaning the brain injury does not worsen over time, although the physical manifestations can change as the child grows.

Management of CP requires a multidisciplinary approach involving physiotherapy to improve mobility and strength, occupational therapy for daily living skills, and speech therapy for communication challenges. Medications such as muscle relaxants may be prescribed to manage spasticity. Surgical interventions might be necessary to correct anatomical abnormalities or reduce muscle tightness.

Critical care nurses should be adept at recognizing complications associated with CP, such as seizures, feeding difficulties, and respiratory issues. They play an essential role in coordinating care and providing education to families about managing symptoms and improving quality of life. Understanding the impact of CP on both patients and their families is critical in delivering compassionate and effective care in the critical care setting.

1.4.2.9.3 Guillain-Barré Syndrome (GBS):

Guillain-Barré Syndrome (GBS) is an acute, rapidly progressing neuromuscular disorder characterized by ascending symmetrical weakness and areflexia. It is an autoimmune condition in which the body's immune system mistakenly attacks the peripheral nerves, leading to demyelination and, in some cases, axonal damage. The exact cause of GBS is unknown, but it often follows a respiratory or gastrointestinal infection.

Clinically, GBS presents with initial symptoms of tingling and weakness that begin in the lower extremities and can progress to paralysis. This ascending paralysis may advance to involve the upper limbs and, in severe cases, the respiratory muscles, necessitating mechanical ventilation. Autonomic dysfunction is also common, manifesting as fluctuations in blood pressure, cardiac arrhythmias, and bladder dysfunction.

Diagnosis is primarily clinical but is supported by cerebrospinal fluid analysis, which shows albuminocytologic dissociation (elevated protein with a normal cell count), and nerve conduction studies indicating demyelination. Early recognition is crucial for management and prognosis.

Treatment focuses on supportive care and specific therapies to reduce immune-mediated damage. Intravenous immunoglobulin (IVIG) and plasmapheresis are the mainstays of treatment, both of which are effective in hastening recovery when initiated early. Rehabilitation plays a critical role in recovery, addressing muscle strength and functional abilities.

The prognosis of GBS varies; most patients recover fully with appropriate treatment, although some may experience residual weakness or fatigue. Nurses play a vital role in monitoring respiratory function, managing autonomic instability, and providing comprehensive supportive care throughout the recovery process.

1.4.2.9.4 Myasthenia:

Myasthenia gravis is an autoimmune neuromuscular disorder characterized by weakness and rapid fatigue of the voluntary muscles. This condition results from a breakdown in the normal communication between nerves and muscles. In myasthenia gravis, antibodies block, alter, or destroy the acetylcholine receptors at the neuromuscular junction, preventing muscle contraction.

Clinically, myasthenia gravis presents with fluctuating muscle weakness that worsens with activity and improves with rest. The most commonly affected muscles are those controlling eye and eyelid movement, facial expression, chewing, talking, and swallowing. Ptosis (drooping of one or both eyelids) and diplopia (double vision) are often initial symptoms. As the disease progresses, it can also affect the muscles involved in breathing and limb movements.

Diagnosis is typically confirmed through clinical examination, serological tests for acetylcholine receptor antibodies, and electrophysiological studies such as repetitive nerve stimulation or single-fiber electromyography. The Tensilon test, which uses edrophonium chloride to temporarily improve muscle strength, can also support the diagnosis.

Management of myasthenia gravis involves symptomatic treatment with acetylcholinesterase inhibitors like pyridostigmine to enhance neuromuscular transmission. Immunosuppressive therapies, such as corticosteroids or other agents like azathioprine, may be employed to reduce antibody production. Thymectomy is considered in certain cases due to its potential to induce remission or reduce medication dependence.

Critical care nurses must monitor patients for myasthenic crisis—a life-threatening exacerbation requiring respiratory support—and differentiate it from cholinergic crisis due to overmedication. Understanding these aspects is crucial for effective management and patient safety in a critical care setting.

1.4.2.10 Neurosurgery:

Neurosurgery is a specialized branch of surgery focused on the diagnosis, treatment, and rehabilitation of disorders affecting the nervous system, which includes the brain, spinal cord, peripheral nerves, and cerebrovascular system. It encompasses both elective and emergency surgical interventions to address conditions such as traumatic brain injuries, spinal cord injuries, aneurysms, tumors, and congenital anomalies.

Critical care nurses working with neurosurgical patients must have a deep understanding of the complex anatomy and physiology of the nervous system. They play a vital role in preoperative and postoperative care, ensuring that patients are closely monitored for neurological changes that may indicate complications, such as increased intracranial pressure or cerebral edema. This requires proficiency in neuro-assessment techniques, including the Glasgow Coma Scale and cranial nerve evaluations.

In addition to monitoring vital signs and neurological status, critical care nurses must manage advanced technologies often used in neurosurgery, such as intracranial pressure monitors and external ventricular drains. They are responsible for maintaining sterile conditions to prevent infections, such as meningitis, and providing meticulous wound care.

Pain management is another critical aspect of nursing care in neurosurgery. Nurses must balance effective analgesia with the need to perform frequent neurological assessments. Furthermore, they provide education to patients and their families about the surgical procedure, recovery expectations, and potential long-term outcomes.

Overall, neurosurgery demands a multidisciplinary approach in which critical care nurses are integral to optimizing patient outcomes through vigilant monitoring, expert intervention, and compassionate support.

1.4.2.10.1 Craniotomy:

A craniotomy is a surgical procedure that involves the removal of a portion of the skull, known as a bone flap, to access the brain for various medical interventions. This procedure is performed by neurosurgeons and is often indicated for conditions such as brain tumors, aneurysms, traumatic brain injury, or to relieve elevated intracranial pressure. Once the underlying issue is addressed, the bone flap is typically replaced and secured with plates and screws.

During a craniotomy, the patient is usually under general anesthesia. The surgeon makes an incision in the scalp and uses specialized instruments to carefully remove the bone flap. The dura mater, the protective membrane covering the brain, is then opened to allow access to the targeted area. Advanced imaging techniques, such as MRI or CT scans, are often used preoperatively to guide the surgical approach.

In critical care settings, nurses must monitor patients post-craniotomy for potential complications such as infection, bleeding, cerebral edema, or seizures. Close observation of neurological status through frequent assessments of consciousness level, pupil response, and motor function is crucial. Pain management and ensuring proper head positioning to optimize venous drainage are also important aspects of postoperative care.

Understanding the intricacies of craniotomy procedures enables critical care nurses to provide comprehensive care and anticipate potential complications effectively. Mastery of these concepts is essential for those preparing for the CCRN exam, as it ensures that they are equipped to manage complex neurosurgical cases in critical care environments.

1.4.2.10.2 Burr Holes:

Burr holes are small, circular openings drilled into the skull using a specialized surgical instrument known as a burr. This procedure is typically performed by neurosurgeons and is an essential technique in neurosurgery for both diagnostic and therapeutic purposes. The primary function of burr holes is to provide access to the intracranial space, allowing for the drainage of fluids or the insertion of monitoring devices.

In critical care settings, burr holes are often utilized to relieve intracranial pressure caused by conditions such as subdural hematomas, epidural hematomas, or other forms of brain hemorrhage. By allowing blood or fluid to escape, burr holes can prevent further brain injury and reduce the risk of severe neurological deficits.

The procedure involves the precise localization of the site where the burr hole will be made, often guided by imaging techniques such as CT or MRI scans. Once the site is determined, a sterile environment is maintained, and local anesthesia or general anesthesia is administered depending on the patient's condition. The neurosurgeon then uses a high-speed drill to create the opening in the skull.

Post-procedure care is crucial for patients who have undergone burr hole surgery. Nurses must monitor neurological status closely, manage pain effectively, and observe for any signs of infection or complications such as re-accumulation of fluid. Understanding the indications, procedure, and post-operative care associated with burr holes is vital for nurses preparing for the CCRN exam, ensuring they can provide competent care in critical situations.

1.4.2.11 Seizure Disorders:

Seizure disorders, also known as epilepsy, are a group of neurological conditions characterized by recurrent, unprovoked seizures. Seizures result from abnormal electrical discharges in the brain, leading to sudden changes in behavior, sensation, or consciousness. The manifestations of seizures can vary widely, ranging from brief lapses in attention or muscle jerks to severe and prolonged convulsions.

In critical care settings, understanding the pathophysiology and management of seizure disorders is crucial for nurses. Seizures can be classified into focal (partial) and generalized types. Focal seizures originate in a specific area of the brain and may or may not impair consciousness. Generalized seizures involve both hemispheres of the brain and typically result in a loss of consciousness.

Critical care nurses must be adept at recognizing seizure activity promptly to prevent complications such as hypoxia, injury, or status epilepticus—a medical emergency characterized by prolonged or repeated seizures without recovery between episodes. Management includes ensuring patient safety by protecting the airway, preventing aspiration, and administering appropriate pharmacological interventions, such as benzodiazepines or antiepileptic drugs.

Additionally, nurses should be familiar with potential triggers for seizures, which may include electrolyte imbalances, infections, or medication non-compliance. Continuous monitoring and assessment are vital for effectively managing and mitigating risks. Understanding the complex nature of seizure disorders enables critical care nurses to provide comprehensive care, ensuring optimal patient outcomes and safety during acute episodes.

1.4.2.12 Space-occupying Lesions:

Space-occupying lesions (SOLs) refer to abnormal growths or masses within the cranial cavity that can exert pressure on surrounding brain structures. These lesions can be neoplastic, such as primary brain tumors or metastatic deposits, or non-neoplastic, including abscesses, hematomas, cysts, and vascular malformations. The presence of an SOL can lead to increased intracranial pressure (ICP), which may cause headaches, nausea, vomiting, altered mental status, and focal neurological deficits, depending on the lesion's location and size.

The pathophysiology of SOLs involves the displacement of brain tissue and cerebrospinal fluid (CSF), potentially leading to herniation syndromes if left untreated. Herniation refers to the movement of brain structures from their normal compartments due to pressure gradients, which can result in life-threatening conditions such as uncal herniation or tonsillar herniation.

Diagnosis typically involves neuroimaging techniques like computed tomography (CT) scans or magnetic resonance imaging (MRI) to identify the lesion's characteristics and effects on surrounding tissues. Treatment strategies depend on the type of lesion and may include surgical resection, stereotactic radiosurgery, chemotherapy, or corticosteroids to reduce edema.

Critical care nurses must closely monitor patients with SOLs for signs of neurological deterioration and manage ICP through interventions such as head elevation, maintaining normothermia, and administering osmotic diuretics when indicated. Understanding the implications of space-occupying lesions is crucial for providing comprehensive care and optimizing patient outcomes in critical care settings.

1.4.2.12.1 Brain Tumors:

Brain tumors are abnormal growths of cells within the brain or central spinal canal. They can be classified as primary or secondary, with primary tumors originating in the brain and secondary (metastatic) tumors spreading from other parts of the body. Brain tumors can be further categorized into benign (non-cancerous) and malignant (cancerous) based on their growth behavior and potential to invade surrounding tissues.

The clinical presentation of brain tumors varies depending on their size, location, and rate of growth. Common symptoms include headaches, seizures, cognitive or personality changes, and focal neurological deficits such as weakness or sensory disturbances. The increased intracranial pressure caused by a growing tumor can lead to nausea, vomiting, and altered consciousness.

Diagnosis typically involves neuroimaging techniques such as MRI or CT scans to visualize the tumor. A biopsy may be performed to determine the histological type and grade, which guides treatment decisions. Treatment options include surgical resection, radiation therapy, and chemotherapy. The choice of treatment depends on factors such as the tumor's type, location, size, and the patient's overall health.

For critical care nurses preparing for the CCRN exam, understanding the pathophysiology of brain tumors is crucial. Nurses play a key role in monitoring neurological status, managing symptoms, providing postoperative care, and supporting patients and families through the treatment process. Comprehensive knowledge of brain tumors enables nurses to deliver effective care and improve patient outcomes in critical care settings.

1.4.2.13 Stroke:

A stroke, also known as a cerebrovascular accident (CVA), occurs when the blood supply to part of the brain is interrupted or reduced, depriving brain tissue of oxygen and nutrients. Within minutes, brain cells begin to die, making it a medical emergency that requires prompt intervention to minimize brain damage and potential complications. Strokes are broadly classified into two main types: ischemic and hemorrhagic.

Ischemic strokes account for approximately 87% of all cases and are caused by the obstruction of a blood vessel supplying the brain, often due to a clot. This obstruction can occur through thrombosis, where a clot forms within a cerebral artery, or through embolism, where a clot forms elsewhere in the body and travels to the brain. Hemorrhagic strokes result from the rupture of a weakened blood vessel, leading to bleeding within or around the brain. Common causes of hemorrhagic strokes include hypertension and aneurysms.

Clinical manifestations of a stroke depend on the affected brain region but commonly include sudden numbness or weakness in the face, arm, or leg, especially on one side of the body; confusion; trouble speaking or understanding speech; visual disturbances; dizziness; loss of balance or coordination; and a severe headache with no known cause.

Early recognition and management are crucial in stroke care. The acronym FAST (Face drooping, Arm weakness, Speech difficulties, Time to call emergency services) is widely used for public education. Treatment strategies may involve thrombolytic therapy for ischemic strokes or surgical interventions for hemorrhagic strokes. Rehabilitation is essential for recovery and includes physical therapy, occupational therapy, and speech therapy to regain lost functions.

1.4.2.13.1 Hemorrhagic Stroke:

A hemorrhagic stroke occurs when a weakened blood vessel ruptures and bleeds into the surrounding brain tissue, leading to increased intracranial pressure and subsequent brain damage. This type of stroke is less common than ischemic strokes but tends to be more severe, often resulting in higher morbidity and mortality rates. Hemorrhagic strokes are classified into two main types: intracerebral hemorrhage (ICH) and subarachnoid hemorrhage (SAH).

Intracerebral hemorrhage involves bleeding directly into the brain tissue, usually caused by hypertension, arteriovenous malformations, or head trauma. It leads to localized pressure effects and tissue destruction, which can result in neurological deficits depending on the location of the bleed.

Subarachnoid hemorrhage occurs when there is bleeding into the subarachnoid space, often due to a ruptured cerebral aneurysm. This type of hemorrhage can cause a sudden onset of severe headache, neck stiffness, and photophobia, along with a rapid decline in consciousness levels.

Management of hemorrhagic stroke focuses on stabilizing the patient, controlling blood pressure, and preventing further bleeding. Surgical interventions may be necessary to relieve pressure or repair vascular abnormalities. Critical care nurses play a vital role in monitoring neurological status, managing complications such as vasospasm or rebleeding, and providing supportive care to optimize recovery outcomes.

Understanding the pathophysiology and management strategies for hemorrhagic strokes is crucial for critical care nurses preparing for the CCRN exam, as it enables them to deliver evidence-based care and improve patient outcomes in critical care settings.

1.4.2.13.2 Ischemic (embolic):

Ischemic stroke, specifically the embolic type, occurs when a blood clot or debris forms elsewhere in the body and travels through the bloodstream to lodge in a cerebral artery, obstructing blood flow to part of the brain. This blockage leads to ischemia, which is an inadequate blood supply resulting in insufficient oxygen and nutrients reaching brain tissue, causing cellular death and neurological deficits.

Embolic strokes are commonly associated with cardiovascular conditions such as atrial fibrillation, myocardial infarction, or heart valve disease. These conditions promote clot formation within the heart chambers. Once dislodged, these emboli can travel via the carotid arteries or the vertebrobasilar system to the brain, causing a sudden onset of symptoms such as unilateral weakness, aphasia, or visual disturbances.

In critical care settings, rapid identification and management are crucial. Nurses must be adept at recognizing early signs of an embolic stroke using tools like the National Institutes of Health Stroke Scale (NIHSS). Immediate interventions include administering thrombolytics, such as tissue plasminogen activator (tPA), if within the therapeutic window, typically 3 to 4.5 hours from symptom onset. For patients outside this window or with contraindications to tPA, mechanical thrombectomy may be considered.

Preventive strategies focus on anticoagulation therapy for at-risk patients and addressing modifiable risk factors such as hypertension and hyperlipidemia. Critical care nurses play an essential role in patient education regarding medication adherence and lifestyle modifications to reduce the risk of recurrent strokes. Understanding these principles is vital for effective management and improving patient outcomes in ischemic embolic strokes.

1.4.2.13.3 TIA (Transient Ischemic Attack):

A Transient Ischemic Attack (TIA), often referred to as a mini-stroke, is a temporary period of neurological dysfunction resulting from an interruption of blood supply to a part of the brain. Unlike a full-blown stroke, the symptoms of a TIA typically resolve within 24 hours, often within minutes to a few hours, without causing permanent damage. TIAs serve as critical warning signs for potential future strokes and necessitate immediate medical evaluation.

The pathophysiology of TIA involves a transient reduction in cerebral blood flow, usually due to embolism or thrombotic occlusion that resolves spontaneously. Risk factors include hypertension, diabetes mellitus, hyperlipidemia, smoking, and atrial fibrillation. Clinically, TIAs present with a sudden onset of neurological deficits such as unilateral weakness or numbness, dysarthria, aphasia, vision disturbances, or ataxia.

Diagnosis is primarily clinical but may be supported by imaging studies like MRI or CT scans to rule out infarction. Carotid ultrasonography and echocardiography may be used to identify potential sources of emboli. Management of TIA focuses on secondary prevention to reduce the risk of subsequent strokes. This includes lifestyle modifications and pharmacological interventions such as antiplatelet agents (e.g., aspirin), anticoagulants for atrial fibrillation, statins for lipid control, and antihypertensive therapy.

Understanding the implications of TIA is crucial for critical care nurses, as they play an essential role in patient education about risk factor modification and adherence to preventive strategies to mitigate the risk of future cerebrovascular events.

1.4.2.14 Types of Traumatic Brain Injury:

Traumatic Brain Injury (TBI): Epidural, Subdural, Concussion

Traumatic Brain Injury (TBI) refers to damage to the brain resulting from an external mechanical force. TBIs can be classified into several types, including epidural hematoma, subdural hematoma, and concussion, each with distinct pathophysiological characteristics.

An epidural hematoma occurs when blood accumulates between the dura mater and the skull, often due to a tear in the middle meningeal artery following a skull fracture. This type of TBI is characterized by a lucid interval followed by rapid deterioration as the hematoma expands, increasing intracranial pressure. Prompt surgical intervention is typically required to evacuate the hematoma and prevent neurological compromise.

A subdural hematoma involves bleeding between the dura mater and the arachnoid membrane, generally resulting from the tearing of bridging veins due to acceleration-deceleration injuries. Subdural hematomas can be acute, subacute, or chronic based on the onset of symptoms. Acute subdural hematomas are particularly dangerous due to the rapid accumulation of blood, necessitating immediate surgical intervention.

Concussion is a mild form of TBI caused by a blow or jolt to the head that disrupts normal brain function. Symptoms may include headache, confusion, dizziness, and temporary loss of consciousness. While concussions are often self-limiting and resolve with rest and a gradual return to activity, repeated concussions can lead to cumulative neurological damage.

Understanding these variations in TBI is crucial for critical care nurses to ensure timely diagnosis, appropriate management, and optimal patient outcomes in individuals suffering from traumatic brain injuries.

1.4.3 Behavioral And Psychosocial:

Behavioral and psychosocial aspects in critical care nursing involve understanding and addressing the mental, emotional, and social factors that influence a patient's health and recovery. This domain emphasizes the importance of recognizing the psychological impact of critical illness on patients and their families, as well as the behavioral responses that may arise during treatment.

Critical care nurses must be adept at identifying signs of anxiety, depression, delirium, and other psychological conditions that can affect patient outcomes. They should be skilled in assessing a patient's mental status and providing appropriate interventions to support mental health. This includes implementing strategies to reduce stress, such as creating a calm environment, offering reassurance, and using therapeutic communication techniques.

Additionally, understanding the psychosocial dynamics involves acknowledging the role of family and social support systems in patient care. Nurses should facilitate effective communication between patients, families, and healthcare teams to ensure comprehensive care planning. They must also be sensitive to cultural, spiritual, and personal values that may influence a patient's experience and coping mechanisms.

Incorporating behavioral and psychosocial considerations into care plans can significantly improve patient outcomes by promoting holistic healing. This requires critical care nurses to possess strong interpersonal skills and empathy, enabling them to build trusting relationships with patients and their families. By addressing these dimensions of care, nurses contribute to a supportive environment that fosters recovery and enhances the quality of life for critically ill patients.

1.4.3.1 Abuse/Neglect:

Abuse and neglect are critical concepts in the realm of behavioral and psychosocial issues, particularly relevant to critical care nursing. Abuse refers to the intentional infliction of harm or injury on another individual, which can manifest in various forms, including physical, emotional, sexual, or financial. Neglect, on the other hand, involves the failure to provide necessary care, resulting in harm or risk of harm. Both abuse and neglect can have profound impacts on a patient's physical and psychological well-being.

In the context of critical care, nurses must be vigilant in recognizing signs of abuse or neglect. Physical indicators may include unexplained injuries, bruises, burns, or fractures. Emotional signs might involve anxiety, depression, withdrawal, or fearfulness around certain individuals. Neglect may present as malnutrition, poor hygiene, untreated medical conditions, or inadequate supervision.

Critical care nurses play a pivotal role in identifying and addressing these issues. They must conduct thorough assessments, maintain detailed documentation of findings, and communicate effectively with interdisciplinary teams. Understanding legal obligations is essential; nurses are mandated reporters who must report suspected abuse or neglect to the appropriate authorities.

Interventions should focus on ensuring patient safety and providing holistic care that addresses both physical and psychological needs. This may involve coordinating with social services for protective interventions or counseling support. Continuous education and training are crucial for nurses to stay informed about best practices in identifying and managing cases of abuse and neglect within the critical care setting.

1.4.3.2 Aggression:

Aggression in the critical care setting refers to a range of behaviors or actions that are hostile, injurious, or destructive. It can manifest physically, verbally, or emotionally and is often a response to stress, fear, or frustration experienced by patients. In critically ill patients, aggression can be triggered by factors such as pain, delirium, hypoxia, metabolic imbalances, or the side effects of medications. It is crucial for nurses to recognize and manage aggression effectively to ensure patient safety and promote a therapeutic environment.

Understanding the underlying causes of aggression is essential for effective management. Delirium, a common condition in intensive care units (ICUs), often leads to confusion and agitation, contributing to aggressive behavior. Additionally, withdrawal from substances like alcohol or drugs can precipitate aggression in patients with dependency issues. Identifying these triggers allows for targeted interventions.

Effective strategies for managing aggression include de-escalation techniques, environmental modifications, and pharmacological interventions when necessary. De-escalation involves maintaining a calm demeanor, using clear communication, and establishing trust with the patient. Modifying the environment may involve reducing noise levels and providing adequate lighting to decrease sensory overload. Pharmacological approaches should be employed judiciously and tailored to the individual's needs.

Nurses play a pivotal role in identifying early signs of aggression and implementing appropriate interventions. Continuous assessment and collaboration with the healthcare team are vital in managing aggressive behaviors and ensuring optimal patient outcomes in critical care settings.

1.4.3.3 Agitation:

Agitation in the critical care setting refers to a state of restlessness, increased motor activity, and emotional distress that can manifest in patients who are unable to remain calm or cooperative. It is a common occurrence in intensive care units (ICUs) and can be attributed to various factors, such as pain, delirium, hypoxia, metabolic imbalances, or withdrawal from substances like alcohol or sedatives.

In critically ill patients, agitation poses significant challenges, as it may lead to self-harm or interference with essential medical devices, such as endotracheal tubes or intravenous lines. Therefore, understanding the underlying causes is crucial for effective management. Agitation can be assessed using validated scales, such as the Richmond Agitation-Sedation Scale (RASS) or the Sedation-Agitation Scale (SAS), which help in determining the severity and guiding treatment strategies.

The management of agitation involves a multifaceted approach. Non-pharmacological interventions should be prioritized, including reorientation, ensuring comfort, and minimizing environmental stressors, such as noise and excessive light. Pharmacological treatments may be necessary for severe cases and include medications such as benzodiazepines, antipsychotics, or dexmedetomidine, tailored to the individual patient's needs and underlying conditions.

Continuous monitoring and reassessment are essential to adjust interventions appropriately and avoid potential complications from over-sedation. Effective communication with the healthcare team and family members is also vital to ensure a comprehensive approach to care. By addressing agitation promptly and appropriately, care nurses can significantly improve patient outcomes and safety in the critical care environment.

1.4.3.4 Anxiety:

Anxiety in the critical care setting refers to an emotional state characterized by feelings of tension, worried thoughts, and physical changes such as increased blood pressure and heart rate. It is a common psychological response among critically ill patients due to the stressors associated with their medical condition, unfamiliar environment, and uncertainty about outcomes.

For nurses preparing for the CCRN exam, it is essential to recognize that anxiety can manifest in various forms, including acute anxiety episodes and chronic anxiety disorders. The physiological symptoms of anxiety may include tachycardia, hypertension, hyperventilation, and diaphoresis. Psychologically, patients may exhibit restlessness, apprehension, or difficulty concentrating.

Understanding the etiology of anxiety is crucial for effective management. Factors contributing to anxiety in critically ill patients may include pain, sleep deprivation, sensory overload from medical equipment, and a lack of communication with healthcare providers. Additionally, personal factors such as previous mental health history or coping mechanisms can influence the severity of anxiety experienced.

Management strategies for anxiety involve both pharmacological and non-pharmacological interventions. Pharmacological options may include anxiolytics or sedatives prescribed by the healthcare team. Non-pharmacological approaches encompass creating a calming environment, ensuring effective communication, providing emotional support, and involving family members in care when appropriate.

Nurses must be adept at assessing anxiety levels using validated tools and tailoring interventions to individual patient needs. By addressing anxiety proactively, nurses can improve patient outcomes and enhance the overall experience within the critical care environment.

1.4.3.5 Suicidal Ideation And/or Behaviors:

Suicidal ideation refers to the contemplation or consideration of ending one's own life. It can range from fleeting thoughts to detailed planning. Suicidal behaviors, on the other hand, include actions taken toward self-harm with the intent of ending one's life, which may or may not result in injury or death. In the critical care setting, it is vital for nurses to recognize and assess these symptoms promptly to prevent potential harm.

Understanding the underlying causes is essential for effective intervention. Suicidal ideation and behaviors often stem from a complex interplay of psychological, biological, and environmental factors. Mental health disorders such as depression, anxiety, bipolar disorder, and schizophrenia are common contributors. Additionally, substance abuse, traumatic experiences, chronic pain, and significant life stressors can exacerbate these tendencies.

Assessment tools like the Columbia-Suicide Severity Rating Scale (C-SSRS) are instrumental in evaluating risk levels. Nurses should be trained to conduct thorough assessments that include direct questioning about suicidal thoughts and plans while maintaining a non-judgmental and empathetic approach.

Intervention strategies involve ensuring immediate safety by removing potential means of self-harm and engaging mental health professionals for further evaluation and treatment. Creating a supportive environment where patients feel heard and understood is crucial. Long-term management may include psychotherapy, medication management, and developing coping strategies to address underlying issues.

In summary, recognizing suicidal ideation and behaviors is critical in critical care settings. Prompt assessment and intervention can significantly reduce the risk of self-harm and improve patient outcomes.

1.4.3.6 Depression:

Depression is a prevalent and serious mood disorder characterized by persistent feelings of sadness, hopelessness, and a lack of interest or pleasure in activities once enjoyed. It can significantly impair daily functioning and quality of life. In the context of critical care, depression may arise as a primary condition or as a secondary response to the stressors associated with acute illness, prolonged hospitalization, or chronic health conditions.

Biologically, depression is linked to imbalances in neurotransmitters such as serotonin, norepinephrine, and dopamine. These chemical messengers play crucial roles in regulating mood, sleep, appetite, and energy levels. The etiology of depression is multifactorial, involving genetic predispositions, environmental stressors, and psychological factors.

Clinically, patients may present with a range of symptoms, including fatigue, changes in appetite or weight, sleep disturbances, difficulty concentrating, feelings of worthlessness or excessive guilt, and recurrent thoughts of death or suicide. In critical care settings, recognizing depression is vital, as it can affect recovery outcomes, adherence to treatment plans, and overall patient well-being.

Assessment tools like the Patient Health Questionnaire (PHQ-9) are useful for screening depression in hospitalized patients. Interventions may include pharmacotherapy with antidepressants such as selective serotonin reuptake inhibitors (SSRIs), psychotherapy approaches like cognitive-behavioral therapy (CBT), and supportive measures that address psychosocial needs.

Nurses play a pivotal role in identifying signs of depression early, providing compassionate care, and coordinating with multidisciplinary teams to implement comprehensive management strategies tailored to individual patient needs.

1.4.3.7 Medical Non-adherence:

Medical non-adherence refers to the failure of patients to follow prescribed medical regimens, which can include medication schedules, dietary restrictions, or lifestyle modifications. This phenomenon is a significant concern in healthcare, as it can lead to suboptimal treatment outcomes, increased morbidity, and higher healthcare costs. Non-adherence can be intentional or unintentional. Intentional non-adherence occurs when patients make a conscious decision not to follow the treatment plan due to factors such as perceived side effects, lack of perceived benefit, or financial constraints. Unintentional non-adherence may result from forgetfulness, misunderstanding instructions, or physical limitations.

For critical care nurses preparing for the CCRN exam, understanding the multifaceted nature of medical non-adherence is crucial. It requires recognizing the psychological and social factors that influence patient behavior. Psychological factors may include depression or anxiety, which can impair motivation and cognitive function. Social factors might involve inadequate support systems or cultural beliefs that conflict with medical advice.

Critical care nurses play a pivotal role in addressing medical non-adherence by fostering open communication with patients and their families, providing clear and concise instructions, and developing individualized care plans that consider the patient's unique circumstances. Additionally, employing motivational interviewing techniques can help uncover underlying barriers to adherence and empower patients to take an active role in their healthcare decisions. By addressing these issues proactively, nurses can enhance patient engagement and improve health outcomes.

1.4.3.8 PTSD:

Post-Traumatic Stress Disorder (PTSD) is a psychiatric condition that may occur in individuals who have experienced or witnessed a traumatic event, such as natural disasters, serious accidents, terrorist acts, war/combat, or violent personal assaults. In critical care settings, nurses may encounter patients with PTSD due to trauma-related hospitalizations or pre-existing conditions exacerbated by acute medical events.

The pathophysiology of PTSD involves alterations in brain function and structure, particularly in the amygdala, hippocampus, and prefrontal cortex. These changes affect how the brain processes stress and fear responses. Neurotransmitter imbalances, including serotonin and norepinephrine, also play a role.

Clinically, PTSD is characterized by four main symptom clusters: intrusive memories (e.g., flashbacks, nightmares), avoidance behaviors (e.g., avoiding reminders of the trauma), negative alterations in cognition and mood (e.g., feelings of detachment or negative beliefs about oneself), and hyperarousal symptoms (e.g., irritability, hypervigilance). These symptoms must persist for more than one month and significantly impair social or occupational functioning to meet diagnostic criteria.

For critical care nurses, understanding PTSD is crucial for providing holistic care. This includes recognizing symptoms that may affect patient cooperation with treatment plans and employing strategies to minimize triggers in the clinical environment. Interventions may involve collaborating with mental health professionals for comprehensive management, including psychotherapy (such as Cognitive Behavioral Therapy) and pharmacotherapy (such as SSRIs). Empathy and effective communication are key in supporting patients with PTSD through their recovery journey.

1.4.3.9 Risk-taking Behavior:

Risk-taking behavior refers to actions that expose individuals to potential harm or danger, yet are pursued for perceived benefits or rewards. In the context of critical care nursing, understanding risk-taking behavior is crucial, as it can significantly impact patient outcomes, particularly in high-stress environments where quick decision-making is essential.

Patients in critical care settings may engage in risk-taking behaviors due to a variety of factors, including psychological distress, substance abuse, or underlying psychiatric conditions. These behaviors can manifest as non-adherence to medical advice, refusal of treatment, or engagement in activities that exacerbate their medical condition. For example, a patient with severe respiratory issues might continue smoking despite medical advice to quit, thereby increasing their risk of complications.

Critical care nurses must be adept at identifying and addressing these behaviors by employing therapeutic communication techniques and fostering a supportive environment. This involves assessing the underlying motivations for such behaviors and collaborating with interdisciplinary teams to provide holistic care. Nurses should also be aware of the role of environmental factors, such as family dynamics and socio-economic status, which may influence a patient's propensity for risk-taking.

In preparing for the CCRN exam, nurses should focus on developing skills to effectively manage patients exhibiting risk-taking behaviors. This includes understanding the psychological underpinnings of these actions and implementing evidence-based interventions to mitigate risks while promoting patient safety and adherence to treatment plans.

1.4.3.10 Substance Use Disorders:

Substance Use Disorders (SUDs) refer to a complex condition characterized by the uncontrolled use of substances despite harmful consequences. These disorders encompass a range of substances, including alcohol, prescription medications, and illicit drugs. SUDs are defined by the American Psychiatric Association in the Diagnostic and Statistical Manual of Mental Disorders (DSM-5) as a pattern of symptoms resulting from the use of a substance that an individual continues to take despite experiencing problems as a result.

The hallmark of SUDs is the compulsive nature of substance use, which can lead to significant impairment or distress. This includes increased tolerance, withdrawal symptoms, and a persistent desire or unsuccessful efforts to cut down or control substance use. The disorder is often chronic and relapsing in nature, necessitating comprehensive treatment approaches that may include behavioral therapies, medication-assisted treatment, and support groups.

In critical care settings, nurses must be adept at recognizing signs of SUDs, which can complicate medical management and recovery. Patients with SUDs may present with acute intoxication, withdrawal syndromes, or complications such as infections or organ damage related to substance use. A thorough understanding of these disorders enables critical care nurses to provide holistic care that addresses both the physiological and psychological needs of patients. This includes monitoring for withdrawal symptoms, managing pain effectively without exacerbating addiction issues, and coordinating with interdisciplinary teams for comprehensive treatment planning.

1.4.3.10.1 Withdrawal:

Withdrawal refers to the physiological and psychological symptoms that occur when a person who has developed a dependence on a substance reduces or ceases its intake. This condition is a critical aspect of substance use disorders and is characterized by a range of symptoms that vary depending on the substance involved. For nurses in critical care, understanding withdrawal is crucial for providing effective patient care, especially in a setting where patients may present with severe withdrawal symptoms.

The pathophysiology of withdrawal involves the body's adaptation to the presence of a substance. Over time, the body becomes reliant on the substance to maintain normal function. When the substance is abruptly reduced or stopped, the body struggles to regain homeostasis, leading to withdrawal symptoms. These symptoms can be mild, such as anxiety and irritability, or severe, such as seizures and delirium tremens in alcohol withdrawal.

Management of withdrawal requires careful assessment and monitoring. Nurses must be adept at recognizing early signs of withdrawal to initiate appropriate interventions promptly. Treatment often includes supportive care and pharmacological interventions tailored to the specific substance involved. For instance, benzodiazepines are commonly used in the management of alcohol withdrawal due to their efficacy in reducing central nervous system excitability.

In summary, withdrawal is a complex physiological response that necessitates comprehensive nursing care. Understanding its mechanisms and manifestations enables nurses to mitigate risks and enhance patient outcomes during the detoxification process.

1.4.3.10.2 Chronic Substance Dependence:

Chronic alcohol or drug dependence, often referred to as substance use disorder (SUD), is a complex condition characterized by an individual's compulsive use of substances despite adverse consequences. This disorder involves a physical and psychological reliance on alcohol or drugs, leading to significant impairment in daily functioning and health.

From a clinical perspective, chronic dependence is marked by the development of tolerance—where increased amounts of the substance are needed to achieve the same effect—and withdrawal symptoms when use is reduced or stopped. These physiological changes are accompanied by behavioral patterns that include a persistent desire or unsuccessful efforts to cut down on substance use, as well as significant time spent obtaining, using, or recovering from the substance's effects.

In critical care settings, nurses must be adept at recognizing signs of chronic dependence, which may include frequent hospital admissions for related complications such as liver disease, cardiovascular issues, or infections. The management of patients with chronic alcohol or drug dependence requires a comprehensive approach that includes medical stabilization, management of withdrawal symptoms, and addressing co-occurring psychiatric disorders.

Furthermore, critical care nurses play a crucial role in facilitating referrals for long-term treatment programs and supporting harm-reduction strategies. Understanding the pathophysiology of addiction and its impact on various organ systems is essential for providing holistic care and improving patient outcomes. Therefore, continuous education on substance use disorders is vital for critical care nurses preparing for the CCRN exam.

1.5 Multisystem:

The term 'multisystem' in critical care refers to conditions or diseases that affect multiple organ systems simultaneously. In critical care settings, multisystem involvement is often a hallmark of severe illness and can result from conditions such as sepsis, trauma, or multi-organ dysfunction syndrome (MODS). Understanding multisystem issues is crucial for critical care nurses, as it requires comprehensive assessment and management strategies to stabilize the patient.

Multisystem conditions demand an integrative approach to patient care. Nurses must be adept at identifying early signs of deterioration across various organ systems, including the respiratory, cardiovascular, renal, hepatic, and neurologic systems. For instance, in sepsis, the systemic inflammatory response can lead to widespread endothelial damage, resulting in hypotension (cardiovascular), acute respiratory distress syndrome (ARDS) (respiratory), acute kidney injury (renal), and altered mental status (neurologic).

Effective management of multisystem involvement requires continuous monitoring and rapid intervention. Nurses should prioritize interventions that support hemodynamic stability, such as fluid resuscitation and vasoactive medications. Additionally, maintaining adequate oxygenation and ventilation is essential in preventing further organ compromise.

Collaboration with the multidisciplinary team is vital to address the complex needs of patients with multisystem involvement. This includes coordinating with physicians for timely diagnostic evaluations and therapeutic interventions, consulting with pharmacists for medication management, and working with dietitians to ensure nutritional support.

In summary, multisystem conditions in critical care necessitate a holistic approach to patient management, emphasizing vigilant monitoring, prompt intervention, and collaborative practice to optimize patient outcomes.

1.5.1 Acid-base Imbalance:

Acid-base imbalance refers to the disruption of the normal pH level in the blood, which is typically maintained within a narrow range of 7.35 to 7.45. This balance is crucial for optimal cellular function and is regulated by the kidneys, lungs, and buffer systems in the body. An imbalance can manifest as either acidosis or alkalosis, depending on whether there is an excess of hydrogen ions (H^+) or bicarbonate ions (HCO_3^-).

Acidosis occurs when the blood pH drops below 7.35, indicating an excess of acid or a loss of base. It can be classified into metabolic acidosis, where there is a decrease in bicarbonate concentration due to conditions such as renal failure or diabetic ketoacidosis, and respiratory acidosis, which results from elevated carbon dioxide (CO_2) levels due to hypoventilation.

Conversely, alkalosis arises when the blood pH exceeds 7.45, suggesting a loss of acid or an accumulation of base. Metabolic alkalosis can occur due to excessive vomiting or diuretic use, leading to increased bicarbonate levels, while respiratory alkalosis is caused by hyperventilation, resulting in reduced CO_2 levels.

Understanding acid-base imbalances is critical for critical care nurses, as they often encounter patients with these conditions. Accurate assessment involves arterial blood gas (ABG) analysis and identifying underlying causes to guide appropriate interventions, such as mechanical ventilation adjustments or electrolyte replacement therapy. Mastery of this knowledge ensures effective management and stabilization of patients with complex multisystem disorders.

1.5.2 Bariatric Complications:

Bariatric complications refer to the adverse events and medical issues that can arise following bariatric surgery, which is performed to aid in significant weight loss for individuals with obesity. These complications can be immediate or delayed and may affect multiple systems within the body, making them a critical area of focus for care nurses preparing for the CCRN exam.

Immediate postoperative complications include anastomotic leaks, which occur at the surgical connection between the stomach and intestines, potentially leading to peritonitis or sepsis. Hemorrhage is another immediate risk, requiring vigilant monitoring for signs of internal bleeding, such as hypotension and tachycardia.

Delayed complications often involve nutritional deficiencies due to altered absorption processes. Deficiencies in vitamins such as B12, iron, calcium, and vitamin D are common and can lead to anemia, osteoporosis, or neurological issues. Dumping syndrome is another frequent complication characterized by rapid gastric emptying, causing symptoms like nausea, diarrhea, and hypoglycemia.

Additionally, care nurses should be aware of the risk of gallstones due to rapid weight loss and small bowel obstruction from internal hernias or adhesions. Psychological effects also warrant attention, as patients may experience changes in mood or eating behaviors post-surgery.

Understanding these complications is crucial for critical care nurses, as early recognition and intervention can significantly improve patient outcomes. Comprehensive patient education on dietary compliance and regular follow-up care are essential components in managing bariatric patients effectively.

1.5.3 Comorbidity in Transplant Patients:

Comorbidity in patients with a transplant history refers to the presence of one or more additional medical conditions that co-occur with the primary condition for which the transplant was performed. These comorbidities can significantly affect the management and outcomes of transplant recipients. In critical care, understanding these comorbidities is essential for optimizing patient care and improving long-term survival.

Patients with a transplant history are often on immunosuppressive therapy to prevent organ rejection, which increases their susceptibility to infections and other complications. Common comorbidities include hypertension, diabetes mellitus, renal dysfunction, cardiovascular diseases, and osteoporosis. These conditions can be pre-existing or may develop as a consequence of the transplant and its associated treatments.

Hypertension is prevalent due to the nephrotoxic effects of certain immunosuppressants, such as calcineurin inhibitors. Diabetes mellitus may arise from steroid use or as a side effect of immunosuppressive drugs. Renal dysfunction can occur due to pre-existing kidney issues or as a result of nephrotoxic medications. Cardiovascular diseases are often exacerbated by the metabolic effects of immunosuppressants and pre-existing risk factors.

Management involves regular monitoring and tailored treatment strategies to address these comorbidities without compromising graft function. Care nurses must be vigilant in recognizing signs of complications, ensuring adherence to medication regimens, and coordinating multidisciplinary care. Understanding the interplay between comorbidities and transplant history is crucial for providing comprehensive care and enhancing patient outcomes in critical care settings.

1.5.4 End-of-life Care:

End-of-life care encompasses the support and medical care provided during the time surrounding death. This type of care is crucial in ensuring that patients experience a dignified and comfortable transition. It involves managing physical symptoms, addressing psychological, social, and spiritual needs, and providing support to families. In critical care settings, nurses play a pivotal role in delivering end-of-life care, which requires a compassionate approach and effective communication skills.

The primary goal of end-of-life care is to alleviate suffering and improve the quality of life for patients who are nearing death. This involves meticulous management of symptoms such as pain, dyspnea, nausea, and anxiety. Nurses must be adept at assessing these symptoms and implementing appropriate interventions. Additionally, they must recognize when to transition from curative treatment to palliative measures that focus on comfort.

Communication is a cornerstone of effective end-of-life care. Nurses should facilitate open discussions with patients and families about prognosis, treatment preferences, and advance directives. This ensures that care aligns with the patients' wishes and values.

Furthermore, end-of-life care includes providing emotional support to both patients and their families. This might involve counseling services or simply being present to listen and offer reassurance. Nurses should also be aware of cultural differences in end-of-life practices and respect these in their care delivery.

In summary, end-of-life care requires a holistic approach that addresses the comprehensive needs of patients and their families during this critical time.

1.5.5 Healthcare-associated Conditions:

Healthcare-associated conditions (HACs) are medical conditions or complications that occur as a result of receiving treatment in a healthcare setting, such as hospitals or long-term care facilities. These conditions are not present at the time of admission and typically arise during the course of treatment. HACs can include infections, injuries, or other adverse events that are preventable with proper care and adherence to evidence-based protocols.

The most common types of healthcare-associated conditions include healthcare-associated infections (HAIs), such as catheter-associated urinary tract infections (CAUTIs), central line-associated bloodstream infections (CLABSIs), surgical site infections (SSIs), and ventilator-associated pneumonia (VAP). Other HACs encompass pressure ulcers, falls resulting in injury, and adverse drug events.

Preventing HACs is crucial for improving patient outcomes and reducing healthcare costs. Strategies to mitigate these conditions involve implementing rigorous infection control practices, such as hand hygiene and sterilization procedures, utilizing checklists for invasive procedures, and ensuring appropriate staffing levels. Additionally, fostering a culture of safety and continuous quality improvement within healthcare facilities is essential.

For critical care nurses preparing for the CCRN exam, understanding HACs is vital. It involves recognizing risk factors, identifying early signs and symptoms, implementing preventative measures, and participating in multidisciplinary efforts to enhance patient safety. Mastery of these concepts not only aids in passing the certification exam but also contributes to delivering high-quality patient care in critical settings.

1.5.5.1 VAE:

Ventilator-Associated Events (VAE) represent a spectrum of conditions that occur in patients who are on mechanical ventilation. These events can lead to increased morbidity, prolonged hospital stays, and higher healthcare costs. VAE is a broader term encompassing three specific conditions: Ventilator-Associated Condition (VAC), Infection-related Ventilator-Associated Complication (IVAC), and Possible Ventilator-Associated Pneumonia (PVAP).

VAEs are identified through a systematic surveillance approach focusing on objective criteria such as changes in oxygenation and the use of antimicrobial agents, rather than relying solely on clinical diagnosis. This method aims to standardize the identification process across healthcare settings.

A VAC is characterized by a sustained increase in the daily minimum positive end-expiratory pressure (PEEP) or fraction of inspired oxygen (FiO2) after a period of stability or improvement, indicating potential lung injury or dysfunction. IVAC occurs when there is evidence of infection, such as fever or leukocytosis, alongside a VAC. PVAP is suspected when additional indicators of pneumonia are present, such as purulent respiratory secretions or positive cultures.

The prevention of VAE involves adherence to ventilator care bundles, which include strategies like maintaining head-of-bed elevation, daily sedation vacations, and early mobilization. Understanding the nuances of VAE is crucial for critical care nurses to implement effective preventive measures and improve patient outcomes. Mastery of this knowledge is essential for CCRN exam preparation and reflects competency in managing complex ventilated patients.

1.5.5.2 CAUTI Overview:

Catheter-Associated Urinary Tract Infection (CAUTI) is a significant healthcare-associated infection that occurs in patients who have a urinary catheter in place. A CAUTI is defined as a urinary tract infection in which an indwelling catheter has been in use for more than two days on the date of the event, with day one being the day of device placement.

The presence of a urinary catheter can introduce bacteria into the urinary tract, leading to infection. This risk increases with prolonged catheterization. Common causative organisms include Escherichia coli, Klebsiella pneumoniae, and Pseudomonas aeruginosa. Symptoms may include fever, suprapubic tenderness, or costovertebral angle pain or tenderness. However, in critically ill patients, symptoms may be atypical or masked by other conditions.

Preventing CAUTI involves adhering to strict aseptic techniques during catheter insertion and maintenance. Indications for catheter use should be critically assessed to minimize unnecessary catheterization. Regular assessment for early removal is crucial, and the use of alternatives such as external catheters or intermittent catheterization should be considered.

Infection control measures include proper hand hygiene, maintaining a closed drainage system, ensuring unobstructed urine flow, and securing the catheter to prevent urethral trauma. Education of healthcare personnel on best practices is essential to reduce the incidence of CAUTI.

Understanding the pathophysiology of CAUTI and prevention strategies is vital for critical care nurses preparing for the CCRN exam, as it highlights their role in minimizing healthcare-associated infections and improving patient outcomes.

1.5.5.3 CLABSI:

Central Line-Associated Bloodstream Infection (CLABSI) is a serious healthcare-associated condition that occurs when bacteria or viruses enter the bloodstream through a central venous catheter (CVC). A CVC is a tube placed into a large vein, often in the neck, chest, or groin, to deliver medications, fluids, or collect blood samples. CLABSIs are significant because they can lead to severe complications, including sepsis, prolonged hospital stays, increased healthcare costs, and even mortality.

The pathogenesis of CLABSI involves microbial colonization of the catheter, either at the insertion site or along the catheter's lumen. Risk factors contributing to CLABSI include prolonged catheterization, improper hand hygiene, inadequate aseptic technique during insertion and maintenance, and the immunocompromised states of patients.

Prevention strategies are crucial in reducing the incidence of CLABSI and include adherence to evidence-based guidelines, such as the use of maximal sterile barrier precautions during catheter insertion, chlorhexidine skin antisepsis, and daily review of line necessity with prompt removal of unnecessary catheters. Additionally, the education and training of healthcare personnel on infection control practices play a vital role in prevention efforts.

For nurses preparing for the CCRN exam, understanding CLABSI is essential not only for patient safety but also for demonstrating proficiency in critical care nursing. Nurses must be adept at recognizing the signs of infection early, implementing preventive measures effectively, and collaborating with multidisciplinary teams to ensure optimal patient outcomes.

1.5.6 Hypotension:

Hypotension, defined as abnormally low blood pressure, occurs when the systolic blood pressure falls below 90 mmHg or the diastolic pressure drops below 60 mmHg. In critical care settings, hypotension is a significant concern, as it can lead to inadequate perfusion of vital organs, potentially causing organ dysfunction or failure.

The etiology of hypotension is multifaceted, encompassing conditions such as hypovolemia due to hemorrhage or dehydration, cardiogenic shock from myocardial infarction, and distributive shock seen in sepsis or anaphylaxis. Additionally, certain medications, such as antihypertensives or diuretics, can precipitate hypotensive episodes.

Clinically, patients with hypotension may present with symptoms ranging from dizziness and syncope to altered mental status and oliguria. In severe cases, signs of shock, such as cool, clammy skin and tachycardia, may be evident.

Management of hypotension requires prompt identification and treatment of the underlying cause. Initial interventions often include fluid resuscitation with crystalloids to restore intravascular volume. In cases where fluid administration is insufficient, vasopressors, such as norepinephrine, may be employed to maintain hemodynamic stability. Monitoring central venous pressure and cardiac output can guide therapeutic decisions.

For critical care nurses preparing for the CCRN exam, understanding the pathophysiology, clinical manifestations, and management strategies for hypotension is crucial. Mastery of these concepts ensures proficient patient care and enhances outcomes in critically ill populations.

1.5.6.1 Influenza:

Influenza, commonly known as the flu, is an acute viral infection caused by the influenza virus, primarily affecting the respiratory tract. It is characterized by the sudden onset of symptoms such as fever, chills, cough, sore throat, muscle aches, fatigue, and headaches. Influenza viruses are classified into types A, B, and C, with types A and B being responsible for seasonal epidemics. Type A influenza is further categorized into subtypes based on two surface proteins: hemagglutinin (H) and neuraminidase (N), leading to variations such as H1N1 and H3N2.

The virus spreads through respiratory droplets when an infected person coughs or sneezes. It can also be transmitted by touching surfaces contaminated with the virus and then touching the face. Influenza has a high mutation rate, resulting in antigenic drift and shift, which necessitates annual updates of the influenza vaccine to provide effective protection.

In critical care settings, influenza can lead to severe complications such as pneumonia, acute respiratory distress syndrome (ARDS), multi-organ failure, and exacerbation of chronic medical conditions. High-risk groups include young children, elderly individuals, pregnant women, and those with underlying health issues like asthma or heart disease.

Management involves antiviral medications such as oseltamivir or zanamivir, supportive care to relieve symptoms, and preventive measures including vaccination and infection control practices. Understanding influenza's pathophysiology and transmission dynamics is crucial for critical care nurses in managing patients effectively and preventing outbreaks within healthcare facilities.

1.5.6.1.1 Pandemic Or Epidemic:

A pandemic refers to an outbreak of a disease that occurs on a global scale, affecting a large number of people across multiple countries or continents. In contrast, an epidemic is confined to a particular region or community, where the disease spreads rapidly among individuals. Both terms describe the widespread occurrence of infectious diseases, but their scope and impact differ significantly.

In the context of influenza, pandemics are caused by new strains of the virus to which the population has little to no immunity, leading to more severe consequences. Historically, influenza pandemics have resulted in high morbidity and mortality rates, necessitating global public health responses. An example is the H1N1 influenza pandemic in 2009, which required coordinated international efforts for vaccination and containment.

Epidemics, while more localized, can still pose significant challenges to healthcare systems. They require prompt identification and intervention strategies to prevent further spread. For instance, seasonal influenza often results in epidemics during colder months when transmission rates increase.

Understanding the distinction between pandemics and epidemics is crucial for critical care nurses preparing for the CCRN exam. It involves recognizing patterns of disease spread, implementing appropriate infection control measures, and participating in public health initiatives. Nurses play a vital role in managing patient care during such outbreaks by providing education on prevention strategies, administering vaccinations, and supporting affected individuals through evidence-based practices. Mastery of these concepts ensures that nurses are well-prepared to respond effectively during both pandemics and epidemics.

1.5.6.2 Multi-drug Resistant Organisms:

Multi-drug Resistant Organisms (MDROs) are pathogens that have developed resistance to multiple antimicrobial agents, making them challenging to treat. This resistance arises from genetic mutations and the acquisition of resistance genes, often facilitated by the overuse or misuse of antibiotics in healthcare and agriculture. MDROs include bacteria such as Methicillin-resistant Staphylococcus aureus (MRSA), Vancomycin-resistant Enterococci (VRE), and multidrug-resistant Gram-negative bacilli like Pseudomonas aeruginosa and Acinetobacter baumannii.

The presence of MDROs in critical care settings poses significant challenges, as these organisms can lead to severe infections with limited treatment options. They are associated with increased morbidity, mortality, and healthcare costs. Transmission occurs primarily through direct contact with contaminated surfaces or person-to-person spread, particularly in environments where infection control practices are inadequate.

Preventing the spread of MDROs requires stringent adherence to infection control measures, including hand hygiene, the use of personal protective equipment (PPE), and environmental cleaning. Surveillance and antimicrobial stewardship programs are crucial for monitoring resistance patterns and guiding appropriate antibiotic use. Critical care nurses play a vital role in implementing these strategies by educating patients and families about infection prevention and ensuring compliance with established protocols.

Understanding MDROs is essential for critical care nurses as they manage patients at high risk for these infections. Proficiency in identifying signs of infection, understanding laboratory results, and collaborating with multidisciplinary teams is imperative for effective patient management and the containment of these resistant organisms.

1.5.6.2.1 MRSA:

Methicillin-resistant Staphylococcus aureus (MRSA) is a type of staphylococcus bacteria that has developed resistance to methicillin and other beta-lactam antibiotics, including penicillins and cephalosporins. This resistance makes MRSA infections particularly challenging to treat and poses a significant concern in healthcare settings, especially in critical care environments where patients are more vulnerable.

MRSA colonization occurs when the bacteria are present on the skin or in the nose without causing disease. However, when MRSA breaches the skin or mucosal barriers, it can lead to various infections ranging from mild skin conditions to severe systemic infections, such as pneumonia, bloodstream infections, or surgical site infections.

Transmission primarily occurs via direct contact with an infected wound or the contaminated hands of healthcare providers. Consequently, adherence to stringent infection control practices, including hand hygiene, the use of personal protective equipment, and environmental cleaning, is crucial to preventing its spread.

In critical care settings, early identification and isolation of patients with MRSA are vital to controlling outbreaks. Treatment typically involves the use of non-beta-lactam antibiotics, such as vancomycin or linezolid. However, antibiotic stewardship is essential to prevent further development of resistance.

Understanding MRSA's pathophysiology and implementing effective infection control measures are pivotal for nurses preparing for the CCRN exam. They must be adept at recognizing signs of infection, implementing isolation protocols, and educating patients and families about prevention strategies to minimize the risk of MRSA transmission.

1.5.6.2.2 VRE (Vancomycin-Resistant Enterococcus):

Vancomycin-Resistant Enterococcus (VRE) refers to strains of Enterococcus bacteria that have developed resistance to vancomycin, an antibiotic commonly used to treat serious infections. Enterococci are part of the normal flora of the human gastrointestinal tract but can cause severe infections, particularly in individuals with weakened immune systems, such as those in critical care settings. VRE is a significant concern in healthcare environments due to its ability to spread easily and its resistance to standard antibiotic treatments.

The mechanism of resistance in VRE involves the alteration of the target site for vancomycin on the bacterial cell wall, usually through the acquisition of specific genes (e.g., vanA or vanB), which leads to a reduced binding affinity of the antibiotic. This resistance not only complicates treatment options but also necessitates stringent infection control measures to prevent transmission among patients.

Nurses must be vigilant in identifying potential sources and signs of VRE infections, which can include urinary tract infections, bacteremia, and wound infections. Standard precautions such as hand hygiene, the use of personal protective equipment (PPE), and environmental cleaning are critical components of controlling the spread of VRE within healthcare facilities. Additionally, nurses should be aware of alternative treatment options that may include linezolid or daptomycin, depending on the infection site and patient-specific factors.

Understanding the implications of VRE is crucial for nurses preparing for the CCRN exam, as it underscores the importance of infection prevention strategies and effective patient management in critical care environments.

1.5.6.2.3 CRE (Carbapenem-resistant Enterobacteriaceae):

CRE refers to a group of Gram-negative bacteria from the Enterobacteriaceae family that have developed resistance to carbapenem antibiotics, which are often considered the last line of defense for treating severe bacterial infections. This resistance poses significant challenges in clinical settings due to limited therapeutic options and the potential for rapid spread within healthcare facilities.

Enterobacteriaceae, including Klebsiella pneumoniae and Escherichia coli, are typically part of the normal gut flora but can become pathogenic when they acquire resistance mechanisms. The primary mechanism of resistance in CRE is the production of carbapenemase enzymes, such as KPC (Klebsiella pneumoniae carbapenemase), NDM (New Delhi metallo-beta-lactamase), and OXA-48-like enzymes, which hydrolyze carbapenems and render them ineffective.

Infections caused by CRE can include urinary tract infections, bloodstream infections, wound infections, and pneumonia. These infections are associated with high morbidity and mortality rates due to limited treatment options and the potential for complications. The management of CRE infections requires a multidisciplinary approach involving infection control measures, antimicrobial stewardship, and sometimes the use of novel or combination antibiotic therapies.

Preventive strategies in healthcare settings include strict adherence to hand hygiene protocols, contact precautions for infected or colonized patients, active surveillance cultures, and environmental cleaning. Understanding the epidemiology of CRE and implementing robust infection prevention measures are crucial for controlling its spread and ensuring patient safety in critical care environments. As a critical care nurse, staying informed about CRE is essential for effective patient management and for contributing to infection control efforts.

1.5.7 Life-threatening Maternal/fetal Complications:

Life-threatening maternal and fetal complications encompass a range of critical conditions that pose significant risks to the health and lives of both the mother and fetus during pregnancy, labor, or postpartum. These complications require immediate recognition and intervention by healthcare professionals to ensure optimal outcomes.

One such complication is preeclampsia, characterized by hypertension and proteinuria, which can progress to eclampsia, involving seizures. This condition can result in severe consequences such as organ dysfunction, placental abruption, and fetal growth restriction. Another critical condition is placenta previa, where the placenta partially or completely covers the cervix, risking severe hemorrhage during delivery.

Placental abruption, the premature separation of the placenta from the uterine wall, poses a threat to fetal oxygenation and maternal hemodynamic stability. Uterine rupture, though rare, can occur in women with previous uterine surgeries and may lead to catastrophic hemorrhage and fetal distress.

Amniotic fluid embolism is a rare but life-threatening condition in which amniotic fluid enters the maternal circulation, causing cardiovascular collapse and coagulopathy. Additionally, HELLP syndrome—a variant of preeclampsia—presents with hemolysis, elevated liver enzymes, and low platelet count, necessitating prompt delivery for maternal stabilization.

Nurses must be vigilant in monitoring for signs of these complications, understanding their pathophysiology, and collaborating with multidisciplinary teams for timely interventions. Effective management includes close monitoring of vital signs, laboratory assessments, and readiness for emergency delivery if indicated. Understanding these complications is crucial for ensuring maternal and fetal safety in critical care settings.

1.5.7.1 Eclampsia:

Eclampsia is a severe and life-threatening complication of pregnancy characterized by the onset of seizures in a woman with pre-existing preeclampsia. It typically occurs after the 20th week of gestation, during labor, or postpartum. The pathophysiology involves endothelial dysfunction, leading to cerebral edema and vasospasm, which contribute to seizure activity. Eclampsia is distinguished from other seizure disorders by its association with hypertension and proteinuria.

Clinically, eclampsia presents with tonic-clonic seizures, which may be preceded by headaches, visual disturbances, or altered mental status. These seizures pose significant risks to both maternal and fetal health, potentially leading to placental abruption, preterm birth, or fetal distress.

Management of eclampsia requires immediate stabilization of the patient. The primary treatment is magnesium sulfate, which acts as an anticonvulsant and helps prevent further seizures. Antihypertensive therapy may be necessary to control severe hypertension; however, care must be taken to avoid rapid blood pressure reductions that could compromise uteroplacental perfusion.

Prompt delivery is often indicated once the mother is stabilized, particularly if the gestational age is viable or if there are signs of fetal compromise. Multidisciplinary management involving obstetricians, critical care specialists, and neonatologists is crucial for optimizing outcomes.

Understanding the pathophysiology and clinical management of eclampsia is essential for critical care nurses preparing for the CCRN exam, as it underscores the importance of timely intervention in life-threatening maternal-fetal complications.

1.5.7.2 HELLP Syndrome:

HELLP syndrome is a severe form of preeclampsia characterized by hemolysis, elevated liver enzymes, and low platelet count. It is a life-threatening obstetric complication that typically occurs in the third trimester but can appear earlier or postpartum. The pathophysiology involves endothelial dysfunction, leading to microangiopathic hemolytic anemia, hepatic dysfunction, and thrombocytopenia.

Nurses must recognize the clinical manifestations of HELLP syndrome, which include right upper quadrant or epigastric pain, nausea, vomiting, malaise, and headache. These symptoms can easily be mistaken for other conditions, underscoring the need for heightened vigilance and prompt diagnostic evaluation. Laboratory findings critical for diagnosis include elevated lactate dehydrogenase (LDH), elevated liver transaminases (AST/ALT), and a platelet count below 100,000/mm^3.

Management of HELLP syndrome requires a multidisciplinary approach with immediate hospitalization. The primary treatment is the delivery of the fetus, especially if the gestational age is beyond 34 weeks or if maternal or fetal status is compromised. Prior to delivery, stabilization of the mother with antihypertensives and corticosteroids to enhance fetal lung maturity may be necessary. In cases of severe thrombocytopenia, platelet transfusion may be required.

HELLP syndrome poses significant risks, including disseminated intravascular coagulation (DIC), placental abruption, renal failure, pulmonary edema, and maternal mortality. Therefore, early recognition and intervention are paramount. Nurses play a crucial role in monitoring maternal and fetal well-being and coordinating care to optimize outcomes for both mother and child.

1.5.7.3 Postpartum Hemorrhage:

Postpartum hemorrhage (PPH) is defined as excessive bleeding following the birth of a baby, typically quantified as a blood loss of more than 500 mL after vaginal delivery or more than 1000 mL after cesarean section. It is a critical obstetric emergency and one of the leading causes of maternal morbidity and mortality worldwide. PPH can occur within the first 24 hours postpartum, known as primary PPH, or between 24 hours and 12 weeks postpartum, referred to as secondary PPH.

The etiology of PPH is commonly summarized by the Four T's: Tone, Trauma, Tissue, and Thrombin. Uterine atony, or the failure of the uterus to contract effectively, accounts for the majority of cases and is related to 'Tone.' Trauma may include lacerations or uterine rupture. Retained placental tissue can prevent adequate uterine contraction. Coagulation disorders ('Thrombin') can exacerbate bleeding.

Prompt recognition and management are crucial in PPH. Initial interventions focus on uterine massage to stimulate contraction and medications such as oxytocin to enhance uterine tone. If these measures are ineffective, additional pharmacologic agents like methylergometrine or carboprost may be administered. Surgical interventions may be necessary in severe cases, including uterine artery ligation or hysterectomy.

Nurses must be adept at monitoring vital signs and estimating blood loss accurately while providing emotional support to the patient and family. Understanding the pathophysiology, rapid assessment, and timely intervention are essential components in managing postpartum hemorrhage effectively.

1.5.7.4 Amniotic Embolism:

Amniotic embolism, also known as amniotic fluid embolism (AFE), is a rare but catastrophic obstetric emergency characterized by the sudden entry of amniotic fluid, fetal cells, hair, or other debris into the maternal circulation. This event triggers an intense anaphylactoid reaction, leading to acute respiratory distress, cardiovascular collapse, and disseminated intravascular coagulation (DIC). It typically occurs during labor, delivery, or in the immediate postpartum period.

The pathophysiology of amniotic embolism involves a breach of the uteroplacental barrier, allowing amniotic components to enter the maternal circulation. This incites a cascade of inflammatory and immunological responses. Clinically, AFE presents with the abrupt onset of hypotension, hypoxia, and coagulopathy. The patient may experience dyspnea, cyanosis, seizures, or cardiac arrest. Diagnosis is primarily clinical due to its rapid progression and lack of specific diagnostic tests.

Management is supportive and focuses on stabilizing the patient. Immediate interventions include securing the airway with oxygen supplementation or mechanical ventilation, providing aggressive hemodynamic support with fluids and vasopressors, and correcting coagulopathy with blood products. Multidisciplinary collaboration is crucial for optimizing outcomes.

Despite advances in critical care management, amniotic embolism remains associated with high maternal morbidity and mortality. Early recognition and prompt intervention are vital for improving survival rates. Nurses play a critical role in monitoring for early signs of distress and initiating emergency protocols to mitigate adverse outcomes in affected patients.

1.5.8 Understanding Multiple Organ Dysfunction Syndrome (MODS):

Multiple Organ Dysfunction Syndrome (MODS) is a progressive condition characterized by the failure of two or more organ systems in an acutely ill patient, where homeostasis cannot be maintained without medical intervention. MODS is often the end result of a dysregulated inflammatory response to a severe insult, such as infection (sepsis), trauma, or pancreatitis. It is crucial for critical care nurses to understand the pathophysiology and clinical manifestations of MODS in order to manage and support affected patients effectively.

The pathogenesis of MODS involves complex interactions between pro-inflammatory and anti-inflammatory mediators, leading to widespread endothelial damage, increased vascular permeability, and impaired tissue perfusion. This cascade results in cellular hypoxia and subsequent organ dysfunction. The organs most commonly affected include the lungs (Acute Respiratory Distress Syndrome - ARDS), kidneys (acute kidney injury), liver (hepatic dysfunction), cardiovascular system (myocardial depression), and central nervous system (encephalopathy).

Clinically, MODS presents with a spectrum of symptoms depending on the organs involved. For instance, respiratory failure may manifest as dyspnea and hypoxemia, whereas renal failure may present as oliguria and elevated creatinine levels. Management focuses on early recognition, supportive care for failing organs, and treating the underlying cause. Interventions may include mechanical ventilation, renal replacement therapy, hemodynamic support with fluids and vasopressors, and antibiotics for infections.

Understanding MODS is essential for critical care nurses to anticipate complications, implement timely interventions, and improve patient outcomes in the intensive care setting.

1.5.9 Multisystem Trauma:

Multisystem trauma refers to injuries that affect multiple organ systems within the body, typically resulting from high-impact events such as motor vehicle collisions, falls from significant heights, or violent assaults. It is a critical condition that requires immediate and comprehensive medical intervention due to the complexity and severity of the injuries involved.

In multisystem trauma, patients often present with a combination of injuries that may include head trauma, thoracic injuries, abdominal damage, musculoskeletal fractures, and soft tissue wounds. The primary concern in managing these patients is to rapidly identify life-threatening injuries and prioritize treatment based on the principles of Advanced Trauma Life Support (ATLS). This approach emphasizes the ABCDEs: Airway maintenance with cervical spine protection, Breathing and ventilation assessment, Circulation with hemorrhage control, Disability evaluation (neurological status), and Exposure/environmental control.

Nurses play a crucial role in the initial stabilization and ongoing management of multisystem trauma patients. They must be adept at recognizing signs of shock, monitoring vital signs, administering fluids and medications, and preparing patients for diagnostic imaging or surgical interventions. Effective communication with the multidisciplinary team is essential to ensure timely interventions and optimize patient outcomes.

Understanding the pathophysiology of trauma-related injuries and maintaining proficiency in trauma care protocols are vital for nurses preparing for the CCRN exam. Mastery of these concepts ensures they can provide high-quality care to critically injured patients while contributing to improved survival rates and recovery outcomes in the context of multisystem trauma.

1.5.10 Pain: Acute, Chronic:

Acute pain is a sudden onset of discomfort typically linked to a specific injury or illness, serving as a protective mechanism that signals harm to the body. It is characterized by its short duration, often resolving as the underlying cause heals. Acute pain can be sharp and severe, prompting immediate attention and treatment. Examples include post-surgical pain, fractures, and burns. Management typically involves analgesics and addressing the root cause to facilitate healing.

Chronic pain, in contrast, persists beyond the usual course of an acute illness or the healing of an injury, lasting for months or even years. It may arise from conditions such as arthritis, fibromyalgia, or neuropathy and is often more complex due to its multifactorial nature, which involves biological, psychological, and social components. Chronic pain does not serve a protective function and can lead to significant physical and emotional distress, impacting quality of life.

In critical care settings, accurate assessment and differentiation between acute and chronic pain are crucial for effective management. Nurses must employ comprehensive pain assessment tools to evaluate the intensity, duration, location, and characteristics of pain. Treatment strategies should be individualized, considering both pharmacological options, such as NSAIDs and opioids for acute pain, and multimodal approaches, including physical therapy, cognitive-behavioral therapy, and interventional procedures for chronic pain.

Understanding the nuances between acute and chronic pain is essential for critical care nurses to provide holistic care that addresses both immediate relief and long-term management strategies.

1.5.11   Post-intensive Care Syndrome (PICS):

Post-Intensive Care Syndrome (PICS) is a collection of physical, cognitive, and psychological impairments that persist after a patient has been discharged from the intensive care unit (ICU). It affects not only the patients but also their families, who may experience similar symptoms known as PICS-Family (PICS-F). PICS can manifest in various ways, including muscle weakness, fatigue, and decreased mobility due to prolonged bed rest and critical illness. Cognitive impairments may include memory loss, attention deficits, and difficulties with executive functions. Psychological issues such as anxiety, depression, and post-traumatic stress disorder (PTSD) are also common.

The pathophysiology of PICS is multifactorial. Factors contributing to its development include prolonged mechanical ventilation, sedation practices, delirium during the ICU stay, and the severity of the underlying illness. The ICU environment itself, characterized by sensory overload and sleep disturbances, can exacerbate these issues.

Management of PICS involves a multidisciplinary approach focusing on early mobilization during the ICU stay, minimizing sedation, and implementing strategies to prevent delirium. Post-discharge rehabilitation programs are essential for addressing physical and cognitive deficits. Psychological support is crucial for both patients and their families to manage emotional challenges.

Understanding PICS is vital for critical care nurses, as they play a key role in identifying at-risk patients and implementing preventative measures. By recognizing the signs early and coordinating appropriate interventions, nurses can significantly improve long-term outcomes for ICU survivors.

1.5.12   Sepsis:

Sepsis is a life-threatening condition that arises when the body's response to infection causes widespread inflammation, leading to tissue damage, organ failure, and potentially death. It occurs when chemicals released into the bloodstream to fight an infection trigger inflammatory responses throughout the body. This inflammation can result in a cascade of changes that damage multiple organ systems, causing them to fail.

In the context of critical care, early identification and prompt management of sepsis are crucial. Sepsis progresses through stages: sepsis, severe sepsis, and septic shock. Sepsis is characterized by a confirmed or suspected infection and evidence of systemic inflammatory response syndrome (SIRS), which includes symptoms such as fever, increased heart rate, increased respiratory rate, and an abnormal white blood cell count. Severe sepsis involves organ dysfunction, hypoperfusion, or hypotension. Septic shock is defined as severe sepsis with persistent hypotension despite adequate fluid resuscitation.

Management of sepsis involves the rapid administration of intravenous fluids to maintain blood pressure and perfusion, broad-spectrum antibiotics to combat the underlying infection, and supportive care for organ dysfunction. Monitoring and reassessment are vital in guiding ongoing treatment decisions. The Surviving Sepsis Campaign guidelines provide evidence-based recommendations for managing sepsis effectively.

Understanding the pathophysiology of sepsis and its clinical manifestations enables critical care nurses to swiftly identify at-risk patients and initiate appropriate interventions. Continuous education on updated guidelines and protocols is essential for optimizing patient outcomes in cases of sepsis.

1.5.13   Septic Shock:

Septic shock is a severe and potentially fatal condition characterized by a significant drop in blood pressure resulting from an overwhelming systemic infection. It represents the most advanced stage of sepsis, where the body's response to infection leads to widespread inflammation, resulting in tissue damage, organ dysfunction, and ultimately, circulatory and metabolic abnormalities. The hallmark of septic shock is persistent hypotension that requires vasopressor support despite adequate fluid resuscitation.

Pathophysiologically, septic shock arises when pathogens, typically bacteria, release endotoxins or exotoxins into the bloodstream, triggering an exaggerated immune response. This response involves the release of pro-inflammatory cytokines such as TNF-alpha and interleukins, leading to vasodilation, increased capillary permeability, and impaired cellular oxygen utilization. Consequently, patients experience profound hypotension, tachycardia, altered mental status, oliguria, and metabolic acidosis.

Management of septic shock demands prompt recognition and intervention. Initial treatment focuses on aggressive fluid resuscitation with crystalloids to restore intravascular volume. Concurrently, broad-spectrum antibiotics should be administered within the first hour of diagnosis to target the underlying infection. If hypotension persists despite adequate fluid therapy, vasopressors like norepinephrine are initiated to maintain mean arterial pressure (MAP) above 65 mmHg. Additional supportive measures include corticosteroids for refractory shock and source control interventions such as drainage or debridement.

Understanding the pathogenesis and management strategies for septic shock is crucial for critical care nurses preparing for the CCRN exam to ensure optimal patient outcomes in clinical practice.

1.5.13.1 Distributive:

Distributive shock is a type of circulatory shock characterized by an abnormal distribution of blood flow in the smallest blood vessels, resulting in an inadequate supply of blood to the body's tissues and organs. This condition often leads to a mismatch between oxygen delivery and consumption, ultimately causing cellular dysfunction and organ failure if not promptly addressed. The most common forms of distributive shock include septic shock, anaphylactic shock, and neurogenic shock.

In septic shock, the body's response to infection leads to widespread inflammation, causing vasodilation and increased capillary permeability. This results in decreased systemic vascular resistance and hypotension despite adequate cardiac output. Anaphylactic shock, triggered by severe allergic reactions, involves massive histamine release that causes similar vasodilatory effects, along with bronchoconstriction and increased vascular permeability. Neurogenic shock occurs due to the loss of sympathetic tone following spinal cord injury or central nervous system damage, leading to unopposed parasympathetic activity and subsequent vasodilation.

Management of distributive shock focuses on identifying and treating the underlying cause while supporting hemodynamics. This often involves fluid resuscitation to restore intravascular volume, vasopressors to counteract vasodilation, and specific treatments such as antibiotics for sepsis or epinephrine for anaphylaxis. Continuous monitoring of hemodynamic parameters and organ function is crucial in guiding therapy and ensuring optimal outcomes for patients experiencing distributive shock. Understanding these mechanisms is essential for critical care nurses preparing for the CCRN exam, as it enables them to provide effective care in acute settings.

1.5.13.1.1 Anaphylactic:

Anaphylactic shock is a severe, life-threatening systemic hypersensitivity reaction characterized by the rapid onset of airway, breathing, and circulatory problems. It is a type of distributive shock, where widespread vasodilation leads to decreased peripheral vascular resistance and subsequent hypotension. Anaphylaxis occurs when an individual who has been sensitized to an allergen is re-exposed to it, triggering a massive release of mediators such as histamines, leukotrienes, and cytokines from mast cells and basophils.

Clinically, anaphylaxis presents with symptoms ranging from mild skin reactions, such as urticaria and angioedema, to more severe manifestations, including bronchospasm, laryngeal edema, and cardiovascular collapse. The rapid identification and management of anaphylactic shock are critical to prevent morbidity and mortality. The first-line treatment involves the immediate administration of intramuscular epinephrine, which acts by causing vasoconstriction, bronchodilation, and inhibition of further mediator release. Adjunctive treatments may include oxygen supplementation, intravenous fluids to counteract hypotension, antihistamines for symptomatic relief of cutaneous manifestations, and corticosteroids to prevent biphasic reactions.

Nurses must be adept at recognizing the early signs of anaphylaxis and initiating prompt treatment. They should also be knowledgeable about potential allergens in the clinical setting and educate patients on avoiding known triggers. Understanding the pathophysiology of anaphylactic shock enables nurses to anticipate complications and provide comprehensive care during acute episodes.

1.5.13.1.2 Neurogenic Shock:

Neurogenic shock is a type of distributive shock that results from the loss of sympathetic tone due to a disruption in the autonomic pathways within the central nervous system, typically following an injury to the spinal cord. This condition is characterized by a triad of hypotension, bradycardia, and peripheral vasodilation. Unlike other forms of shock, where tachycardia serves as a compensatory mechanism, neurogenic shock presents with bradycardia due to unopposed parasympathetic activity.

The pathophysiology involves an interruption of sympathetic outflow, leading to a decrease in systemic vascular resistance (SVR) and resultant hypotension. The loss of sympathetic tone causes blood vessels to dilate, reducing venous return to the heart and subsequently decreasing cardiac output. The hallmark features include warm, dry skin due to peripheral vasodilation and an inability to regulate body temperature.

Management of neurogenic shock focuses on stabilizing hemodynamics. Fluid resuscitation is initiated cautiously to restore intravascular volume. Vasopressors such as norepinephrine are often required to counteract vasodilation and support blood pressure. Atropine may be administered to address significant bradycardia.

It is crucial for nurses to monitor patients closely for signs of worsening perfusion and to maintain spinal precautions to prevent further neurological damage. Understanding the unique presentation and management strategies for neurogenic shock is essential for effective patient care in critical settings, ensuring prompt recognition and intervention to mitigate complications associated with this type of distributive shock.

1.5.13.2 Hypovolemic Shock:

Hypovolemic shock is a critical condition that occurs when there is a significant loss of blood or body fluids, leading to inadequate perfusion and oxygenation of tissues. This state results from a decrease in intravascular volume, which can be caused by acute hemorrhage, severe dehydration, or fluid shifts due to burns or pancreatitis. The reduction in circulating volume diminishes venous return to the heart, thereby decreasing cardiac output and impairing tissue perfusion.

In hypovolemic shock, the body initiates compensatory mechanisms to maintain perfusion. These include tachycardia to increase cardiac output, vasoconstriction to preserve blood flow to vital organs, and activation of the renin-angiotensin-aldosterone system to retain sodium and water. Despite these efforts, if the underlying cause is not addressed promptly, cellular metabolism shifts from aerobic to anaerobic pathways, leading to lactic acidosis and eventual organ dysfunction.

Clinically, patients may present with hypotension, tachycardia, cool and clammy skin, decreased urine output, and altered mental status. Laboratory findings may reveal elevated lactate levels and hemoconcentration. Management involves the rapid identification of the source of volume loss and prompt restoration of intravascular volume with crystalloids or blood products as appropriate.

Critical care nurses must be adept at recognizing the early signs of hypovolemic shock and initiating interventions swiftly to prevent progression to irreversible damage. Understanding the pathophysiology and treatment protocols is crucial for optimizing patient outcomes in critical care settings.

1.5.14 Impact of Sensory Overload on Sleep Disruption:

Sleep disruption in critical care settings is a common issue that can significantly impact patient recovery and overall well-being. It refers to interruptions in the normal sleep cycle, which can be caused by various factors such as noise, light, medical interventions, and the psychological stress of being in an intensive care environment. Sensory overload occurs when patients are exposed to excessive stimuli, leading to increased stress and impaired sleep quality.

In critical care units, patients are often subjected to continuous monitoring, frequent alarms, bright lights, and constant activity from healthcare personnel. These environmental factors contribute to fragmented sleep patterns, reducing the duration of restorative deep sleep stages. Additionally, medical interventions such as medication administration, vital sign checks, and diagnostic procedures further disrupt sleep continuity.

The consequences of sleep disruption in critically ill patients include impaired cognitive function, a weakened immune response, increased pain perception, and delayed healing processes. Addressing sensory overload is crucial in minimizing these adverse effects. Strategies such as reducing noise levels, dimming lights during nighttime hours, and clustering care activities to allow uninterrupted rest periods can improve sleep quality.

Nurses play a pivotal role in managing sleep disruption by advocating for environmental modifications and implementing individualized care plans that prioritize patient comfort. Understanding the impact of sensory overload on sleep is essential for critical care nurses to enhance patient outcomes and promote a healing environment within intensive care units.

1.5.15 Thermoregulation:

Thermoregulation is the physiological process that allows the human body to maintain its core internal temperature within a narrow, optimal range, despite fluctuations in the external environment. This homeostatic mechanism is crucial for normal cellular function and overall metabolic processes. The hypothalamus acts as the body's thermostat, integrating signals from peripheral and central thermoreceptors to initiate appropriate responses to temperature changes.

In critical care settings, understanding thermoregulation is vital due to its impact on patient outcomes. Both hypothermia and hyperthermia can be detrimental, affecting enzyme activity, cardiac function, and cerebral metabolism. In critically ill patients, thermoregulatory responses may be impaired due to factors such as sepsis, neurological injury, or the effects of medications.

Nurses play a pivotal role in monitoring and managing thermoregulation in critical care. This includes accurately assessing body temperature using various methods, such as rectal, esophageal, or bladder thermometry, which are more reliable in unstable patients. Interventions may involve external warming or cooling techniques, such as heated blankets or cooling devices, ensuring adequate hydration to facilitate heat dissipation or retention, and adjusting environmental conditions.

Awareness of the patient's baseline temperature and the prompt recognition of deviations can guide interventions to prevent complications such as shivering-induced metabolic demands or fever-associated increases in oxygen consumption. Effective management of thermoregulation is integral to optimizing patient stability and recovery in the critical care environment.

1.5.16 Toxic Ingestion/Inhalations:

Toxic ingestion and inhalation refer to the harmful intake of substances through swallowing or breathing, which can lead to significant physiological disturbances. These exposures can occur accidentally or intentionally and encompass a wide range of substances, including pharmaceuticals, chemicals, gases, and biological toxins. When these substances enter the body, they can interfere with normal cellular functions, leading to symptoms that range from mild irritation to severe systemic toxicity.

Ingestion involves the oral intake of toxins, which are then absorbed through the gastrointestinal tract. Common agents include medications (such as acetaminophen or opioids), household chemicals (like bleach or antifreeze), and plants (such as belladonna). Inhalation exposure occurs when toxic substances are breathed in, affecting the respiratory system and potentially leading to systemic effects. Examples include carbon monoxide, chlorine gas, and volatile solvents.

The clinical presentation of toxic ingestion or inhalation varies depending on the substance involved, the dose, and the time elapsed since exposure. Symptoms can include nausea, vomiting, respiratory distress, altered mental status, seizures, and cardiovascular instability. Rapid identification and management are crucial to prevent morbidity and mortality.

Management strategies involve supportive care, decontamination procedures (such as activated charcoal for certain ingestions), specific antidotes when available (e.g., naloxone for opioid overdose), and symptomatic treatment. Critical care nurses must be adept at recognizing signs of toxicity, initiating appropriate interventions, and collaborating with toxicology experts to optimize patient outcomes.

1.5.16.1   Drug/alcohol Overdose:

A drug or alcohol overdose occurs when an individual consumes a toxic amount of a substance, overwhelming the body's ability to metabolize and eliminate it, which can lead to potentially life-threatening symptoms. In critical care settings, nurses must be adept at recognizing and managing overdoses to mitigate adverse outcomes.

An overdose can result from various substances, including prescription medications, illicit drugs, or alcohol. The physiological response depends on the specific agent involved but often includes central nervous system depression or stimulation, respiratory compromise, cardiovascular instability, and metabolic disturbances.

For example, opioid overdoses typically present with respiratory depression, pinpoint pupils, and decreased consciousness. Conversely, stimulant overdoses may lead to agitation, hypertension, tachycardia, and hyperthermia. Alcohol overdose primarily causes central nervous system depression, resulting in impaired motor coordination, respiratory depression, and potentially coma.

Management begins with a rapid assessment of airway, breathing, and circulation (ABCs), followed by stabilization of vital functions. Administering activated charcoal can limit absorption if the patient presents within an hour of ingestion. Specific antidotes, such as naloxone for opioids or flumazenil for benzodiazepines, may be employed where applicable. Supportive care is crucial and may include intravenous fluids, oxygen supplementation, or mechanical ventilation.

Monitoring for complications such as aspiration pneumonia or rhabdomyolysis is essential. Nurses must also engage in patient education post-recovery to address underlying issues contributing to substance misuse and to prevent recurrence. Understanding these principles is vital for nurses preparing for the CCRN exam to ensure comprehensive care delivery in overdose scenarios.

1.5.17   Toxin/drug Exposure (including Allergies):

Toxin and drug exposure in critical care refers to the adverse effects on the body due to the introduction of harmful substances, which can include medications, chemicals, or environmental toxins. In critical care settings, it is imperative for nurses to recognize and manage these exposures promptly to prevent further complications.

Toxins can enter the body through various routes, such as inhalation, ingestion, dermal contact, or injection. Once inside the body, they may cause systemic toxicity, affecting multiple organ systems. For instance, acetaminophen overdose can lead to hepatotoxicity, whereas carbon monoxide poisoning affects oxygen delivery by binding to hemoglobin.

Drug exposure involves unintended or excessive intake of pharmaceutical agents, leading to toxicity. This can occur due to medication errors, polypharmacy, or patient non-compliance. Symptoms vary depending on the drug class but often include altered mental status, cardiovascular instability, or respiratory depression.

Allergies are hypersensitive immune responses to specific antigens found in drugs or environmental substances. They can range from mild reactions, such as rashes, to severe anaphylaxis, characterized by airway obstruction and circulatory collapse. Quick identification and intervention with antihistamines or epinephrine are crucial in managing allergic reactions.

In critical care, nurses must be adept at assessing clinical signs of toxin/drug exposure and allergies, utilizing diagnostic tools such as laboratory tests and imaging studies. They should also be proficient in initiating appropriate treatment protocols, including decontamination, administration of antidotes, and supportive care measures to stabilize patients effectively.

2   Ethical Practice in Professional Caring:

PROFESSIONAL CARING & ETHICAL PRACTICE:

Professional Caring & Ethical Practice in critical care nursing encompasses the integration of compassionate patient care with ethical principles to ensure high-quality and morally sound healthcare delivery. It involves a commitment to understanding and respecting the unique needs, values, and preferences of each patient while adhering to ethical standards and guidelines.

At its core, professional caring requires nurses to demonstrate empathy, compassion, and respect for patients and their families. It involves active listening, effective communication, and providing emotional support, all of which are essential in building trust and rapport. Ethical practice demands adherence to principles such as autonomy, beneficence, non-maleficence, and justice. Nurses must advocate for patients' rights, ensuring informed consent and confidentiality while balancing risks and benefits in care decisions.

Critical care nurses must navigate complex ethical dilemmas often encountered in high-stakes environments. This includes end-of-life decisions, resource allocation, and managing conflicts between patient wishes and medical recommendations. Nurses are expected to collaborate with interdisciplinary teams to address these challenges while maintaining professional integrity.

Continuous professional development is vital for staying informed about evolving ethical standards and best practices. Engaging in reflective practice allows nurses to critically evaluate their actions and learn from experiences to enhance future care delivery.

Ultimately, Professional Caring & Ethical Practice ensures that critical care nurses provide holistic, patient-centered care that upholds the dignity and rights of individuals while fostering a therapeutic environment conducive to healing and recovery.

2.1 Advocacy/Moral Agency:

Advocacy in critical care nursing involves the active support and representation of patients' interests, ensuring that their needs and preferences are respected and prioritized. It requires nurses to act as intermediaries between patients, families, and other healthcare professionals, ensuring that patients' voices are heard and their rights are upheld. This role is crucial in critical care settings, where patients often cannot advocate for themselves due to their medical conditions.

Moral agency refers to the capacity of nurses to make ethical decisions and take actions that align with professional values and standards. It involves recognizing moral dilemmas, evaluating options based on ethical principles, and making choices that reflect integrity, compassion, and respect for human dignity. In critical care environments, moral agency is essential, as nurses frequently encounter complex situations that demand ethical judgment.

Together, advocacy and moral agency empower nurses to uphold the highest standards of ethical practice. They require a deep understanding of ethical principles such as autonomy, beneficence, non-maleficence, and justice. Critical care nurses must navigate these principles while considering the unique circumstances of each patient.

By fostering advocacy and moral agency, nurses contribute to a culture of ethical practice within healthcare settings. They ensure that patient care is guided by empathy and respect while promoting a collaborative approach to decision-making. This commitment not only enhances patient outcomes but also strengthens the trust and communication between healthcare providers, patients, and their families.

2.2 Caring Practices:

Caring practices in critical care nursing are actions and behaviors that demonstrate compassion, empathy, and a commitment to patient-centered care. These practices are essential in creating a therapeutic environment that promotes healing and well-being for critically ill patients. Caring practices involve recognizing the unique needs and preferences of each patient and their family, ensuring that care is tailored to meet those needs.

Critical care nurses utilize caring practices by actively listening to patients and their families, providing emotional support, and advocating for the patient's best interests. This includes maintaining clear communication, respecting patient autonomy, and involving patients in decision-making processes related to their care. These practices also encompass the provision of comfort measures, such as pain management, maintaining dignity, and addressing psychological and spiritual needs.

Furthermore, caring practices extend to the interdisciplinary team, promoting collaboration and mutual respect among healthcare professionals to ensure comprehensive care delivery. Nurses must be culturally competent, understanding the diverse backgrounds and beliefs that may impact patient care.

Incorporating caring practices into daily routines requires self-awareness and reflection by nurses on their own values and biases. Continuous professional development in emotional intelligence and ethical decision-making enhances a nurse's ability to provide compassionate care.

Ultimately, caring practices are integral to fostering trust, reducing anxiety, and improving patient outcomes in the critical care setting. By prioritizing these practices, nurses can ensure a holistic approach to patient care that respects the dignity and humanity of each individual under their care.

2.3 Response To Diversity:

Response to diversity in the context of critical care nursing refers to the ability of nurses to recognize, respect, and appropriately respond to the varied cultural, ethnic, and individual differences among patients. This concept is crucial for delivering personalized and effective care that meets the unique needs of each patient.

A comprehensive understanding of response to diversity involves acknowledging that patients come from diverse backgrounds with different beliefs, values, and practices that influence their health perceptions and behaviors. Critical care nurses must be adept at identifying these differences and adapting their care plans accordingly. This includes being sensitive to language barriers, religious practices, dietary preferences, and family dynamics that may impact the patient's care experience.

An effective response to diversity requires ongoing education and self-awareness. Nurses should engage in continuous learning about cultural competence and seek to understand their own biases and assumptions. By doing so, they can foster a therapeutic environment that promotes trust and collaboration with patients and their families.

In practice, responding to diversity might involve using interpreter services for non-English-speaking patients, accommodating specific cultural rituals during treatment, or involving family members in decision-making processes according to the patient's cultural norms. Ultimately, a nurse's ability to effectively respond to diversity enhances patient satisfaction, improves health outcomes, and upholds ethical standards by ensuring equitable care for all individuals, regardless of their background.

2.4 Facilitation Of Learning:

Facilitation of learning in the context of critical care nursing involves creating an environment and utilizing strategies that enhance the acquisition and application of knowledge, skills, and attitudes necessary for high-quality patient care. This concept is integral to professional caring and ethical practice, as it empowers both nurses and patients to engage in a continuous learning process.

For nurses, the facilitation of learning means adopting a lifelong learning mindset, where they actively seek out new information, stay updated with the latest evidence-based practices, and reflect on their experiences to improve their clinical skills. It involves participating in formal education programs, attending workshops, engaging in simulation training, and utilizing technology-based resources. Critical care nurses must also cultivate critical thinking and problem-solving skills to adapt to rapidly changing clinical environments.

In patient care, the facilitation of learning requires nurses to assess the educational needs of patients and their families, considering factors such as literacy levels, cultural backgrounds, and emotional states. Nurses must communicate effectively, using clear language and appropriate educational materials to ensure understanding. They should encourage patient participation in care decisions by providing relevant information about their conditions and treatment options.

Overall, the facilitation of learning fosters a culture of safety and excellence in critical care settings. By prioritizing education for both themselves and their patients, nurses enhance their professional development while promoting informed decision-making and improved health outcomes. This dual focus on continuous education underscores the ethical responsibility of nurses to provide competent and compassionate care.

2.5 Collaboration:

Collaboration in the context of critical care nursing is a dynamic, interactive process that involves a partnership between healthcare professionals, patients, and their families to achieve optimal health outcomes. It is a fundamental component of professional caring and ethical practice, emphasizing shared decision-making and mutual respect among team members. Effective collaboration requires open communication, trust, and a commitment to working together toward common goals.

In critical care settings, collaboration is vital due to the complexity of patient needs and the multidisciplinary nature of care. Nurses must work closely with physicians, respiratory therapists, pharmacists, dietitians, social workers, and other specialists to develop comprehensive care plans. This teamwork ensures that all aspects of a patient's health are addressed, from medical management to emotional support.

Successful collaboration involves active listening, recognizing each team member's expertise, and valuing diverse perspectives. It also requires nurses to advocate for their patients by clearly articulating their needs and preferences during care discussions. By doing so, nurses help ensure that patient-centered care remains at the forefront of decision-making processes.

Barriers to effective collaboration can include hierarchical structures, communication breakdowns, and differing priorities among team members. Overcoming these challenges involves fostering an environment of mutual respect and continuous learning. Regular interdisciplinary meetings and debriefings can enhance understanding and cooperation among team members.

Ultimately, collaboration in critical care nursing leads to improved patient outcomes, increased job satisfaction among healthcare providers, and a more cohesive healthcare delivery system. Through collaborative efforts, nurses can ensure that ethical principles guide patient care while addressing the complex needs of critically ill individuals.

2.6 Systems Thinking:

Systems Thinking is a holistic approach to analysis that focuses on how a system's constituent parts interrelate and how systems function over time within the context of larger systems. In the realm of critical care nursing, Systems Thinking is pivotal, as it enables nurses to understand complex healthcare environments, identify patterns, and anticipate potential outcomes. It involves recognizing the interdependencies within healthcare systems, including patients, healthcare providers, processes, and technologies.

For critical care nurses, Systems Thinking requires a shift from linear thinking to seeing the bigger picture. It emphasizes understanding how changes in one part of the system can impact other parts. For instance, a change in medication protocol not only affects patient outcomes but also influences workflow, resource allocation, and communication among healthcare teams.

In practice, Systems Thinking encourages critical care nurses to consider multiple perspectives and engage in reflective practice. By doing so, they can identify the root causes of problems rather than just addressing symptoms. This approach supports more effective decision-making and problem-solving.

Moreover, Systems Thinking fosters collaboration among interdisciplinary teams by promoting a shared understanding of goals and challenges. It aids in designing interventions that are sustainable and adaptable to changing circumstances. Ultimately, embracing Systems Thinking enhances patient safety and quality of care by ensuring that all elements of the healthcare system are aligned toward optimal patient outcomes.

For CCRN exam preparation, understanding Systems Thinking is essential, as it underpins many aspects of professional caring and ethical practice in critical care settings.

2.7 Clinical Inquiry:

Clinical inquiry is a critical component of professional caring and ethical practice in the field of critical care nursing. It refers to the ongoing process by which nurses question and evaluate their clinical practices, incorporating evidence-based knowledge to improve patient outcomes. Clinical inquiry involves a systematic approach to questioning current practices, identifying gaps in knowledge, and seeking out the best available evidence to inform clinical decisions.

This process begins with the identification of a clinical issue or question that arises during patient care. Nurses then engage in a thorough review of existing literature, research findings, and clinical guidelines relevant to the issue at hand. The goal is to gather comprehensive data that can shed light on the problem and suggest potential solutions or improvements.

Once evidence is gathered, critical care nurses analyze and synthesize the information, considering its applicability to their specific patient population and clinical setting. This step is crucial, as it ensures that any changes in practice are grounded in reliable evidence and tailored to meet the needs of patients.

Clinical inquiry also involves collaboration with other healthcare professionals to discuss findings and implement evidence-based interventions. This collaborative approach fosters a culture of continuous learning and improvement within the healthcare team.

Ultimately, clinical inquiry empowers nurses to deliver high-quality, patient-centered care by integrating scientific evidence with clinical expertise. It enhances decision-making processes, promotes accountability, and upholds ethical standards in nursing practice. By engaging in clinical inquiry, nurses contribute to the advancement of healthcare quality and safety.

CCRN Practice Questions [SET 1]

Question 1: In the management of Heparin-Induced Thrombocytopenia (HIT), which anticoagulant is preferred due to its ability to inhibit thrombin generation without cross-reacting with heparin-platelet factor 4 complexes?
A) Warfarin
B) Fondaparinux
C) Argatroban
D) Enoxaparin

Question 2: In the context of acute genitourinary trauma, which of the following management strategies is most appropriate for a hemodynamically unstable patient with suspected renal laceration?
A) Immediate surgical exploration
B) Observation and supportive care
C) Angiographic embolization
D) Bed rest and fluid resuscitation

Question 3: Emily, a 52-year-old patient with a history of breast cancer, presents to the emergency department with confusion, nausea, and muscle weakness. Her laboratory results show elevated calcium levels. As a critical care nurse, what is the most likely oncologic complication Emily is experiencing?
A) Syndrome of Inappropriate Antidiuretic Hormone Secretion (SIADH)
B) Hypercalcemia of Malignancy
C) Tumor Lysis Syndrome
D) Febrile Neutropenia

Question 4: In the context of pelvic fractures, which of the following interventions is most critical to address first in a hemodynamically unstable patient?
A) Administering intravenous fluids
B) Applying a pelvic binder
C) Performing external fixation
D) Initiating blood transfusion

Question 5: In the management of chronic osteomyelitis, which of the following is the most effective long-term treatment strategy to eradicate infection and prevent recurrence?
A) Prolonged oral antibiotic therapy
B) Surgical debridement with adjunctive antibiotic therapy
C) Hyperbaric oxygen therapy alone
D) Use of bone cement impregnated with antibiotics

Question 6: In the context of adrenal insufficiency, which laboratory finding is most indicative of primary adrenal insufficiency (Addison's disease)?
A) Low serum sodium and high serum potassium
B) High serum sodium and low serum potassium
C) Low serum calcium and high serum phosphate
D) High serum calcium and low serum phosphate

Question 7: In critically ill patients, which micronutrient deficiency is most commonly associated with impaired wound healing and increased risk of infections due to its role in immune function and collagen synthesis?
A) Vitamin C
B) Zinc
C) Vitamin D
D) Magnesium

Question 8: In the context of ischemic (embolic) stroke, which of the following factors is most directly associated with the formation of emboli that can lead to a stroke?
A) Atrial fibrillation
B) Hypertension
C) Hyperlipidemia
D) Diabetes mellitus

Question 9: In the context of Diabetes Insipidus (DI), which laboratory finding is most indicative of central DI rather than nephrogenic DI?
A) Low serum sodium levels
B) High urine osmolality after desmopressin administration
C) Low plasma vasopressin levels
D) High serum potassium levels

Question 10: John, a 55-year-old male with a history of cirrhosis, presents to the emergency department with hematemesis and signs of hypovolemic shock. Which initial management step is most critical in stabilizing John's condition related to esophageal varices?
A) Administering intravenous vasopressin
B) Performing an urgent endoscopy
C) Initiating intravenous octreotide
D) Transfusing packed red blood cells

Question 11: In the context of bacterial infections affecting the central nervous system, which of the following bacteria is most commonly associated with meningitis in adults?
A) Streptococcus pneumoniae
B) Neisseria meningitidis
C) Haemophilus influenzae
D) Listeria monocytogenes

Question 12: Which of the following interventions is most effective in reducing the risk of suicide in patients with suicidal ideation and/or behaviors within a clinical setting?
A) Implementing a no-suicide contract with the patient
B) Conducting regular cognitive-behavioral therapy sessions
C) Increasing medication dosage for anxiety management
D) Establishing a strong therapeutic alliance with the patient

Question 13: In the context of managing a tension pneumothorax in a critical care setting, which immediate intervention is most appropriate to stabilize the patient?
A) Administering high-flow oxygen via non-rebreather mask
B) Performing needle decompression in the second intercostal space, midclavicular line
C) Initiating chest tube insertion in the fifth intercostal space, midaxillary line
D) Providing positive pressure ventilation with a bag-valve mask

Question 14: In the context of malnutrition and malabsorption, which of the following conditions is most commonly associated with steatorrhea due to pancreatic insufficiency?
A) Celiac Disease
B) Crohn's Disease
C) Chronic Pancreatitis
D) Lactose Intolerance

Question 15: Which of the following interventions is most effective in preventing aspiration pneumonia in a critically ill patient receiving enteral nutrition?
A) Elevating the head of the bed to 30-45 degrees
B) Administering antiemetics prophylactically
C) Using a post-pyloric feeding tube
D) Performing regular oral hygiene

Question 16: In the context of dysrhythmias, which of the following is the most accurate indicator for initiating synchronized cardioversion in a hemodynamically unstable patient?
A) Atrial Fibrillation with Rapid Ventricular Response
B) Ventricular Tachycardia without a pulse
C) Supraventricular Tachycardia with hypotension
D) Sinus Bradycardia with syncope

Question 17: A 45-year-old patient named Lisa presents to the emergency department with palpitations, weight loss despite increased appetite, and heat intolerance. Her laboratory results reveal elevated free T4 and suppressed TSH levels. As a critical care nurse, which immediate intervention is most appropriate to address Lisa's symptoms of hyperthyroidism?
A) Administer propranolol to manage tachycardia
B) Start methimazole to reduce thyroid hormone synthesis
C) Initiate iodine therapy to inhibit thyroid hormone release
D) Prepare for radioactive iodine therapy for definitive treatment

Question 18: A 45-year-old patient named Sarah is admitted to the ICU with severe fatigue, recurrent infections, and a recent history of chemotherapy for breast cancer. Her lab results show significant leukopenia. As her critical care nurse, which of the following interventions is most crucial to prioritize in managing Sarah's condition?
A) Administering broad-spectrum antibiotics prophylactically
B) Implementing strict neutropenic precautions
C) Initiating granulocyte colony-stimulating factor (G-CSF) therapy
D) Providing nutritional support with high-protein diet

Question 19: Which of the following interventions is most effective in improving medication adherence among patients with chronic musculoskeletal pain, according to contemporary research?
A) Providing detailed written instructions about the medication regimen.
B) Implementing a digital reminder system with personalized messages.
C) Conducting monthly in-person counseling sessions with healthcare providers.
D) Offering financial incentives for medication adherence.

Question 20: A 45-year-old patient named John is admitted to the ICU following a severe motor vehicle accident. He has multiple lacerations and a significant open wound on his left thigh. The wound is heavily contaminated with debris and there are signs of necrotic tissue. As the critical care nurse, what is the most appropriate initial step in managing John's wound to prevent infection and promote healing?
A) Apply topical antibiotics immediately.
B) Perform surgical debridement of necrotic tissue.
C) Initiate systemic antibiotic therapy.
D) Cover the wound with a sterile dressing.

Question 21: In the context of mesenteric ischemia, which clinical finding is most indicative of acute mesenteric ischemia in a critically ill patient?
A) Abdominal pain out of proportion to physical findings
B) Hematochezia
C) Hypoactive bowel sounds
D) Elevated serum lactate levels

Question 22: John, a 65-year-old male, presents to the emergency department after a motor vehicle accident. He exhibits signs of respiratory distress, hypotension, and decreased breath sounds on the left side. A chest X-ray confirms the presence of a hemothorax. What is the most immediate intervention to stabilize John's condition?
A) Administer high-flow oxygen and monitor vital signs
B) Perform needle decompression on the affected side
C) Initiate large-bore chest tube insertion
D) Start intravenous fluid resuscitation

Question 23: In the context of a prolonged QT interval, which electrolyte imbalance is most commonly associated with this cardiac conduction abnormality?
A) Hyperkalemia
B) Hypocalcemia
C) Hypermagnesemia
D) Hypomagnesemia

Question 24: A 45-year-old patient named John presents to the emergency department with sudden onset of dyspnea and unilateral chest pain. A chest X-ray confirms a pneumothorax. As a critical care nurse, what is the most appropriate initial management step for John?
A) Administer high-flow oxygen therapy.
B) Perform needle decompression immediately.
C) Prepare for chest tube insertion.
D) Place the patient in a semi-Fowler's position.

Question 25: A 3-month-old infant named Emily presents with jaundice, pale stools, and hepatomegaly. After a series of diagnostic tests, she is diagnosed with biliary atresia. As her critical care nurse, you are tasked with monitoring her for potential complications. Which of the following is the most immediate complication that Emily is at risk for if her condition is not promptly treated?
A) Portal hypertension
B) Cirrhosis
C) Hepatic encephalopathy
D) Ascites

Question 26: John, a 65-year-old patient with Parkinson's disease, frequently misses his medication doses, leading to exacerbated symptoms. As his critical care nurse, you need to assess the underlying cause of his non-adherence. Which of the following is the most likely reason for John's medication non-adherence?
A) Cognitive decline related to Parkinson's disease
B) Financial constraints preventing access to medication
C) Lack of understanding about the importance of medication adherence
D) Side effects causing discomfort and reluctance to take medication

Question 27: In the management of Hyperosmolar Hyperglycemic State (HHS), which of the following interventions is most critical in the initial phase of treatment?
A) Administering intravenous insulin to reduce blood glucose levels rapidly
B) Initiating aggressive fluid resuscitation with isotonic saline
C) Correcting electrolyte imbalances, particularly potassium
D) Monitoring and maintaining airway patency

Question 28: In the context of cardiac tamponade, which of the following hemodynamic changes is most indicative of this condition?
A) Decreased central venous pressure (CVP)
B) Increased stroke volume index (SVI)
C) Pulsus paradoxus greater than 10 mmHg
D) Elevated left ventricular end-diastolic pressure (LVEDP)

Question 29: Emily, a 58-year-old patient, has been admitted to the ICU following a severe gastrointestinal bleed and received multiple blood transfusions. Within six hours of transfusion, she developed acute respiratory distress with hypoxemia. As a critical care nurse, which clinical intervention is most appropriate for managing suspected Transfusion-related Acute Lung Injury (TRALI) in this scenario?
A) Administer diuretics to reduce pulmonary edema
B) Initiate mechanical ventilation with high PEEP
C) Provide supportive care with oxygen therapy
D) Administer corticosteroids to reduce inflammation

Question 30: Which of the following clinical signs is most indicative of IV infiltration in a patient receiving intravenous therapy?
A) Erythema and warmth at the site
B) Coolness and pallor at the site
C) Rapid infusion rate with no resistance
D) Localized throbbing pain

Question 31: A 58-year-old male patient, Mr. Thompson, is admitted to the ICU with severe liver cirrhosis. He presents with prolonged bleeding after a minor cut, petechiae, and a recent history of gastrointestinal bleeding. Laboratory tests reveal prolonged prothrombin time (PT) and activated partial thromboplastin time (aPTT), along with thrombocytopenia. Based on this scenario, what is the most likely underlying coagulopathy contributing to his symptoms?
A) Vitamin K deficiency
B) Disseminated Intravascular Coagulation (DIC)
C) Liver failure-induced coagulopathy
D) Hemophilia A

Question 32: In the context of compartment syndrome, which clinical finding is most indicative of the need for immediate surgical intervention?
A) Persistent pain unrelieved by analgesics and elevation
B) Swelling and bruising in the affected limb
C) Decreased sensation in the toes or fingers
D) Weak distal pulses in the affected extremity

Question 33: A 45-year-old patient named John is admitted to the ICU with severe muscle pain, weakness, and dark urine following a marathon. Blood tests reveal elevated creatine kinase levels. As a critical care nurse, which immediate intervention is most crucial to prevent acute kidney injury in this case of rhabdomyolysis?
A) Administering intravenous fluids
B) Initiating hemodialysis
C) Administering diuretics
D) Providing bicarbonate therapy

Question 34: Sarah, a 68-year-old patient with a recent hip fracture, has been immobile for several weeks. During her rehabilitation, she reports experiencing sudden shortness of breath and chest pain. As her critical care nurse, which immediate complication should you suspect given her immobility?
A) Deep vein thrombosis (DVT)
B) Pulmonary embolism (PE)
C) Atelectasis
D) Pneumonia

Question 35: A 68-year-old patient named Mr. Thompson, who has a history of diabetes mellitus, presents with a non-healing ulcer on his left foot. The wound is surrounded by erythema and is exuding purulent discharge. As a critical care nurse, which intervention should be prioritized to prevent further infectious complications?
A) Administer broad-spectrum antibiotics immediately.
B) Perform wound debridement to remove necrotic tissue.
C) Apply a moisture-retentive dressing to promote healing.
D) Initiate glycemic control measures to stabilize blood sugar levels.

Question 36: Sarah, a 32-year-old patient with a history of myasthenia gravis, presents to the emergency department with acute respiratory distress. As her critical care nurse, what is the most appropriate immediate intervention to manage her condition?
A) Administer intravenous corticosteroids
B) Initiate non-invasive ventilation
C) Prepare for plasmapheresis
D) Administer pyridostigmine

Question 37: A 45-year-old patient named John presents with persistent pain and swelling in his right leg following a recent fracture. After a series of diagnostic tests, he is suspected to have osteomyelitis. As the critical care nurse, which of the following interventions is most appropriate to initiate first in managing John's condition?
A) Administer intravenous antibiotics immediately.
B) Schedule surgical debridement to remove necrotic tissue.
C) Initiate hyperbaric oxygen therapy for enhanced healing.
D) Conduct a bone biopsy to confirm the diagnosis.

Question 38: John, a 58-year-old male, has undergone a craniotomy for the removal of a meningioma. Postoperatively, he exhibits signs of increased intracranial pressure (ICP). As his critical care nurse, which of the following interventions is most appropriate to manage his ICP?
A) Elevate the head of the bed to 30 degrees.
B) Administer hypertonic saline.
C) Encourage coughing exercises.
D) Provide continuous sedation.

Question 39: In the management of Guillain-Barré Syndrome (GBS), which of the following treatments is considered most effective in the acute phase to reduce disease severity and improve outcomes?
A) Intravenous Immunoglobulin (IVIG)
B) Corticosteroids
C) Plasma Exchange (Plasmapheresis)
D) Antiviral Medications

Question 40: A 75-year-old patient named Mr. Johnson is admitted to the ICU following hip surgery. On the second post-operative day, he becomes confused, agitated, and disoriented. The nurse suspects delirium. Which of the following interventions is most appropriate to address his condition?
A) Administer a low-dose antipsychotic medication.
B) Reorient the patient frequently and ensure a calm environment.
C) Increase opioid analgesics to manage pain effectively.
D) Restrict fluids to prevent potential fluid overload.

Question 41: In the management of empyema, which intervention is most critical for ensuring successful treatment and preventing recurrence?
A) Broad-spectrum antibiotics alone
B) Thoracentesis with pleural fluid analysis
C) Video-assisted thoracoscopic surgery (VATS) for drainage
D) High-dose corticosteroids

Question 42: In the context of Heparin-Induced Thrombocytopenia (HIT), which laboratory test is most commonly used to confirm the diagnosis after a clinical suspicion has been raised?
A) Prothrombin Time (PT)
B) Activated Partial Thromboplastin Time (aPTT)
C) Serotonin Release Assay (SRA)
D) D-dimer test

Question 43: In patients with COPD, which of the following interventions is most effective in reducing mortality and improving quality of life?
A) Long-term oxygen therapy for patients with resting hypoxemia
B) Routine use of inhaled corticosteroids in all COPD patients

C) Continuous positive airway pressure (CPAP) therapy for stable COPD
D) Use of oral antibiotics during acute exacerbations

Question 44: Sarah, a 45-year-old woman with a history of myasthenia gravis, presents to the emergency department with severe muscle weakness and difficulty breathing. Her medication regimen includes pyridostigmine. After further assessment, which intervention is most appropriate to address her current symptoms?
A) Increase the dose of pyridostigmine.
B) Administer intravenous immunoglobulin (IVIG).
C) Start high-dose corticosteroids immediately.
D) Initiate plasmapheresis.

Question 45: John, a 35-year-old male, arrives at the emergency department after a high-speed motor vehicle accident. He presents with abdominal pain, hypotension, and tachycardia. A focused assessment with sonography for trauma (FAST) reveals free fluid in the abdomen. What is the most appropriate immediate intervention for John's condition?
A) Initiate aggressive fluid resuscitation
B) Perform an urgent exploratory laparotomy
C) Administer broad-spectrum antibiotics
D) Order a CT scan of the abdomen

Question 46: In the context of pleural space abnormalities, which of the following is most indicative of a tension pneumothorax in a critically ill patient?
A) Tracheal deviation towards the affected side
B) Hypotension and distended neck veins
C) Dullness to percussion on the affected side
D) Decreased breath sounds bilaterally

Question 47: Sarah, a 45-year-old patient with a history of hypokalemia, presents to the emergency department with palpitations and dizziness. Her ECG reveals a prolonged QT interval. Which of the following medications is most appropriate to avoid in her treatment plan due to its potential to further prolong the QT interval?
A) Metoprolol
B) Amiodarone
C) Lisinopril
D) Furosemide

Question 48: In the management of a patient presenting with an ST-Elevation Myocardial Infarction (STEMI), which of the following is the most critical first-line treatment to reduce mortality?
A) Beta-blockers
B) Angiotensin-converting enzyme (ACE) inhibitors
C) Percutaneous coronary intervention (PCI)
D) Thrombolytic therapy

Question 49: Sarah, a 58-year-old patient with stage 3 chronic kidney disease (CKD), presents with fatigue, decreased appetite, and swelling in her lower extremities. Her lab results show elevated serum creatinine and blood urea nitrogen (BUN) levels. Considering her condition, which of the following interventions is most appropriate to manage her symptoms and slow the progression of CKD?
A) Increase dietary protein intake
B) Initiate angiotensin-converting enzyme (ACE) inhibitor therapy
C) Restrict fluid intake to prevent edema
D) Prescribe erythropoietin-stimulating agents for anemia

Question 50: John, a 58-year-old male with a history of chronic kidney disease, presents to the emergency department with muscle weakness, lethargy, and cardiac arrhythmias. His laboratory tests reveal a serum potassium level of 7.2 mEq/L. Which of the following interventions should be prioritized to address his life-threatening electrolyte imbalance?
A) Administer intravenous calcium gluconate
B) Initiate sodium polystyrene sulfonate (Kayexalate) therapy
C) Start a continuous insulin and glucose infusion
D) Perform urgent hemodialysis

Question 51: John, a 45-year-old male, was brought to the emergency department after a motorcycle accident. He briefly lost consciousness at the scene but regained it shortly after. A CT scan reveals a biconvex, hyperdense lesion. Based on this information, what is the most likely diagnosis?
A) Epidural hematoma
B) Subdural hematoma
C) Concussion
D) Diffuse axonal injury

Question 52: In the management of Syndrome of Inappropriate Antidiuretic Hormone Secretion (SIADH), which of the following interventions is most critical in preventing severe complications?
A) Administering isotonic saline to correct hyponatremia.
B) Initiating fluid restriction to manage water retention.
C) Providing oral salt tablets to increase serum sodium levels.
D) Using loop diuretics to promote water excretion.

Question 53: A 65-year-old patient named Mr. Johnson is admitted to the ICU with a diagnosis of delirium. His medical history includes hypertension and type 2 diabetes. The nurse observes that Mr. Johnson is experiencing fluctuating levels of consciousness and disorganized thinking. Which intervention should be prioritized to manage his delirium effectively?
A) Administer haloperidol as prescribed.
B) Ensure adequate hydration and nutrition.
C) Implement early mobilization strategies.
D) Provide a quiet and well-lit environment.

Question 54: In the context of clinical judgment for a patient presenting with acute coronary syndrome (ACS), which of the following interventions should be prioritized to reduce myocardial oxygen demand?
A) Administering aspirin
B) Providing supplemental oxygen
C) Initiating nitroglycerin therapy
D) Positioning the patient in a semi-Fowler's position

Question 55: John, a 45-year-old patient, was admitted to the ICU following a severe traumatic brain injury. After 48 hours of observation, the medical team suspects brain death. Which of the following assessments is crucial in confirming brain death in John?
A) Absence of brainstem reflexes
B) Presence of decerebrate posturing
C) Positive Babinski sign
D) Spontaneous respiratory effort

Question 56: In the context of hypertrophic cardiomyopathy (HCM), which of the following echocardiographic findings is most indicative of a poor prognosis?
A) Asymmetric septal hypertrophy
B) Left ventricular outflow tract obstruction
C) Apical hypertrophy
D) Mitral valve systolic anterior motion

Question 57: A 45-year-old patient named John presents

to the emergency department with severe pain in his left leg, swelling, and a rapidly spreading area of erythema. His medical history reveals poorly controlled diabetes mellitus. Laboratory results show elevated white blood cell count and C-reactive protein levels. Considering the clinical presentation and history, what is the most appropriate initial step in managing John's suspected necrotizing fasciitis?
A) Start broad-spectrum antibiotics immediately.
B) Perform urgent surgical debridement.
C) Initiate hyperbaric oxygen therapy.
D) Administer intravenous fluids aggressively.

Question 58: A 68-year-old patient named Mr. Thompson, who is recovering from a stroke, presents with severe agitation in the ICU. His medical history includes hypertension and diabetes. The healthcare team needs to manage his agitation effectively. Which of the following interventions is most appropriate to address Mr. Thompson's agitation while considering his neurological status?
A) Administering lorazepam intravenously
B) Initiating a haloperidol infusion
C) Providing a calm and quiet environment
D) Using physical restraints

Question 59: A 56-year-old patient named Mr. Johnson is admitted to the ICU with acute respiratory failure. He has a history of myasthenia gravis and is currently experiencing worsening muscle weakness. Which of the following interventions is most appropriate to improve his respiratory function?
A) Administer intravenous immunoglobulin (IVIG)
B) Initiate plasmapheresis
C) Increase pyridostigmine dosage
D) Provide non-invasive ventilation

Question 60: A 55-year-old patient named John, who has been receiving heparin therapy for deep vein thrombosis, presents with a sudden drop in platelet count. As the critical care nurse, you suspect heparin-induced thrombocytopenia (HIT). Which of the following actions is most appropriate to take next?
A) Continue heparin and monitor platelet count closely.
B) Discontinue heparin and switch to warfarin immediately.
C) Discontinue heparin and initiate a direct thrombin inhibitor.
D) Continue heparin and start aspirin therapy.

Question 61: In the management of acute gastrointestinal hemorrhage, which of the following interventions is most critical in stabilizing a hemodynamically unstable patient?
A) Initiating proton pump inhibitor (PPI) therapy
B) Performing an urgent endoscopy
C) Administering intravenous crystalloids
D) Transfusing packed red blood cells

Question 62: During a post-operative assessment of Mr. Johnson, who recently underwent a craniotomy for tumor resection, you observe that he exhibits right-sided weakness and slurred speech. Which of the following immediate interventions is most appropriate to address these symptoms?
A) Administer intravenous mannitol to reduce intracranial pressure.
B) Perform a neurological assessment and notify the neurosurgeon immediately.
C) Elevate the head of the bed to 30 degrees to promote venous drainage.
D) Initiate seizure precautions and administer prophylactic anticonvulsants.

Question 63: In the context of myocardial conduction system abnormalities, which of the following conditions is most likely to result in a complete heart block due to disruption at the level of the atrioventricular (AV) node?
A) First-degree AV block
B) Mobitz Type I (Wenckebach)
C) Mobitz Type II
D) Left bundle branch block

Question 64: A 45-year-old patient named John is admitted to the ICU following a severe car accident. Despite being physically stable, John exhibits signs of intense anxiety, including restlessness and hypervigilance. As a critical care nurse, which intervention is most appropriate to address John's anxiety while considering his musculoskeletal and neurological condition?
A) Administering a low-dose benzodiazepine as prescribed.
B) Encouraging deep breathing exercises and guided imagery.
C) Providing continuous reassurance about his physical stability.
D) Limiting environmental stimuli to reduce sensory overload.

Question 65: A 65-year-old patient named Mr. Johnson, with a history of diabetes and chronic kidney disease, is admitted to the ICU with signs of sepsis. Blood cultures reveal the presence of a multidrug-resistant organism. As part of the critical care team, what is the most important initial step in managing Mr. Johnson's infection?
A) Start broad-spectrum antibiotics immediately
B) Initiate renal replacement therapy
C) Implement strict infection control measures
D) Adjust diabetes management protocol

Question 66: In the context of transfusion reactions, which of the following is most indicative of an acute hemolytic transfusion reaction (AHTR) in a patient receiving a blood transfusion?
A) Fever and chills within 24 hours post-transfusion
B) Hypotension and dark urine immediately after starting the transfusion
C) Urticaria and pruritus during the transfusion
D) Shortness of breath and wheezing several hours after transfusion

Question 67: A 45-year-old patient named John is admitted to the ICU with severe agitation and confusion. His history reveals chronic alcohol use disorder, and he has not consumed alcohol for the past 48 hours. Which of the following interventions is most appropriate to address his current condition?
A) Administer lorazepam intravenously
B) Initiate haloperidol treatment
C) Provide thiamine supplementation
D) Start intravenous fluids

Question 68: A 45-year-old male patient, Mr. Johnson, presents with polyuria and polydipsia. His urine output is significantly high, and laboratory tests reveal a low urine osmolality. The endocrinologist suspects Diabetes Insipidus (DI). Which of the following findings would most likely confirm a diagnosis of Central Diabetes Insipidus in Mr. Johnson?
A) Increased urine osmolality after water deprivation test
B) Decreased serum sodium levels
C) Increased urine osmolality after desmopressin administration
D) Decreased plasma vasopressin levels

Question 69: In the management of status asthmaticus,

which of the following interventions is most critical to initiate immediately upon diagnosis to prevent respiratory failure?
A) Administration of intravenous corticosteroids
B) Continuous nebulization of short-acting beta-agonists
C) Initiation of non-invasive positive pressure ventilation
D) Administration of intravenous magnesium sulfate

Question 70: John, a 58-year-old male, underwent a Whipple procedure (pancreaticoduodenectomy) for pancreatic cancer. Post-operatively, he is experiencing malabsorption and significant weight loss. As his critical care nurse, what is the most appropriate intervention to address his nutritional needs?
A) Initiate total parenteral nutrition (TPN) immediately.
B) Start a high-fat diet to increase calorie intake.
C) Administer pancreatic enzyme replacement therapy with meals.
D) Increase oral intake of simple carbohydrates.

Question 71: In the management of a patient with a hemorrhagic stroke, which of the following interventions is most critical to prevent further neurological damage?
A) Administration of intravenous thrombolytics
B) Tight blood pressure control with antihypertensives
C) Immediate anticoagulation therapy
D) Surgical evacuation of hematoma

Question 72: In the context of acute genitourinary trauma, which of the following is the most critical initial step in managing a patient with suspected renal injury?
A) Administering intravenous fluids to maintain blood pressure
B) Performing an immediate CT scan with contrast
C) Inserting a Foley catheter for urinary output monitoring
D) Conducting a focused assessment with sonography for trauma (FAST)

Question 73: A 55-year-old patient named Mr. Thompson presents to the ICU with signs of increased intracranial pressure (ICP) following a traumatic brain injury. As the critical care nurse, you need to prioritize interventions to manage his condition. Which of the following interventions is most appropriate for reducing ICP in this scenario?
A) Administering hypertonic saline
B) Elevating the head of the bed to 30 degrees
C) Initiating deep sedation
D) Performing therapeutic hypothermia

Question 74: A 45-year-old patient named Lisa has been diagnosed with Immune Thrombocytopenic Purpura (ITP). She presents with petechiae and a platelet count of 20,000/µL. After initial treatment with corticosteroids, her platelet count remains low. The healthcare team is considering second-line treatment options. Which of the following is the most appropriate next step in managing Lisa's condition?
A) Intravenous immunoglobulin (IVIG)
B) Splenectomy
C) Rituximab
D) Thrombopoietin receptor agonists

Question 75: In the context of recognizing signs of elder abuse in a critical care setting, which of the following indicators is most likely to suggest psychological abuse rather than physical or neglectful abuse?
A) Unexplained bruises on the arms and legs
B) Sudden withdrawal from social interactions and activities
C) Poor hygiene and malnutrition
D) Repeated falls without medical explanation

Question 76: In the management of urosepsis, which of the following interventions is most critical to initiate promptly to reduce mortality in critically ill patients?
A) Initiation of broad-spectrum antibiotics
B) Administration of intravenous fluids
C) Monitoring of urine output
D) Blood glucose control

Question 77: In patients with cellulitis, which of the following clinical signs is most indicative of a severe infection requiring immediate medical intervention?
A) Localized erythema and warmth
B) Presence of purulent discharge
C) Rapid progression of erythema with systemic symptoms
D) Mild edema and tenderness

Question 78: In the context of immune deficiencies, which of the following conditions is most commonly associated with a defect in the NADPH oxidase enzyme, leading to impaired reactive oxygen species production by phagocytes?
A) Severe Combined Immunodeficiency (SCID)
B) Chronic Granulomatous Disease (CGD)
C) Common Variable Immunodeficiency (CVID)
D) Hyper-IgM Syndrome

Question 79: Mr. Johnson, a 78-year-old patient with severe aortic stenosis, is undergoing Transcatheter Aortic Valve Replacement (TAVR). Post-procedure, he develops hypotension and bradycardia. As a critical care nurse, what is the most appropriate initial intervention to manage this complication?
A) Administer intravenous atropine.
B) Increase intravenous fluid administration.
C) Initiate transcutaneous pacing.
D) Start norepinephrine infusion.

Question 80: John, a 65-year-old male with a history of hypertension, presents to the emergency department with palpitations and dizziness. An ECG reveals a prolonged PR interval, indicating first-degree atrioventricular (AV) block. Which of the following is the most appropriate initial management for John's condition?
A) Immediate administration of atropine
B) Observation and monitoring
C) Initiation of pacemaker therapy
D) Administration of beta-blockers

Question 81: In the context of postoperative care for patients undergoing a Whipple procedure (pancreaticoduodenectomy), which of the following complications is most critical to monitor for during the initial 48 hours post-surgery?
A) Anastomotic leak
B) Delayed gastric emptying
C) Pancreatic fistula
D) Bile duct obstruction

Question 82: In the management of Abdominal Compartment Syndrome (ACS), which of the following interventions is considered the most definitive treatment to relieve intra-abdominal hypertension and prevent organ dysfunction?
A) Administration of diuretics to reduce fluid overload
B) Surgical decompression through laparotomy
C) Optimization of fluid resuscitation and vasopressors
D) Use of neuromuscular blockers to reduce abdominal wall tension

Question 83: In the context of critical care management for patients with musculoskeletal injuries, which of the following interventions is most effective in preventing deep vein thrombosis (DVT) in immobilized patients?

A) Early ambulation and physical therapy
B) Administration of low molecular weight heparin (LMWH)
C) Use of intermittent pneumatic compression devices
D) Elevation of the affected limb above heart level

Question 84: Which of the following clinical signs is most indicative of increased intracranial pressure due to a space-occupying lesion in the brain?
A) Bradycardia
B) Hypertension
C) Papilledema
D) Tachypnea

Question 85: In the context of drug-induced hepatic failure, which of the following drugs is most commonly associated with acute liver failure due to overdose?
A) Ibuprofen
B) Acetaminophen
C) Aspirin
D) Metformin

Question 86: In patients with cirrhosis, which of the following laboratory findings is most indicative of hepatic encephalopathy?
A) Elevated serum bilirubin levels
B) Increased serum ammonia levels
C) Decreased albumin levels
D) Elevated alkaline phosphatase levels

Question 87: In the context of managing acute peripheral vascular insufficiency, which of the following is the most critical consideration for a nurse when monitoring a patient post-endarterectomy?
A) Monitoring for signs of bleeding and hematoma formation at the surgical site
B) Assessing neurological status to detect potential stroke symptoms
C) Ensuring adequate hydration to prevent thrombosis
D) Evaluating blood pressure to maintain cerebral perfusion

Question 88: In managing chronic obstructive pulmonary disease (COPD) exacerbations, which of the following interventions is most effective in reducing mortality according to contemporary research?
A) Long-term oxygen therapy
B) Inhaled corticosteroids
C) Pulmonary rehabilitation
D) Non-invasive ventilation

Question 89: Which of the following interventions is most effective in reducing the incidence of delirium in critically ill patients?
A) Administering low-dose antipsychotics prophylactically
B) Ensuring adequate hydration and nutrition
C) Implementing early mobilization and physical therapy
D) Providing continuous sedation to promote rest

Question 90: John, a 68-year-old male with a history of hypertension and diabetes, presents with acute kidney injury (AKI) after starting a new antihypertensive medication. His lab results show elevated creatinine levels and hyperkalemia. Which of the following medications is most likely responsible for his renal condition?
A) Lisinopril
B) Amlodipine
C) Hydrochlorothiazide
D) Metoprolol

Question 91: A 55-year-old patient named Mr. Johnson is admitted to the ICU with a suspected acute gastrointestinal hemorrhage. He presents with hypotension, tachycardia, and melena. As the critical care nurse, you are preparing to manage his condition. Which initial intervention is most crucial in stabilizing Mr. Johnson's hemodynamic status?
A) Administer intravenous proton pump inhibitors (PPIs).
B) Begin rapid infusion of isotonic crystalloid fluids.
C) Initiate vasopressor therapy.
D) Start blood transfusion immediately.

Question 92: In the context of functional issues in critical care, which intervention is most effective in preventing muscle atrophy in a patient with prolonged immobility?
A) Passive range of motion exercises
B) Administration of muscle relaxants
C) Application of heat therapy
D) High-protein nutritional support

Question 93: In the context of thoracic trauma, which of the following clinical findings is most indicative of a tension pneumothorax?
A) Diminished breath sounds on the affected side
B) Tracheal deviation away from the affected side
C) Hyperresonance on percussion over the affected area
D) Jugular venous distension

Question 94: John, a 55-year-old male with a history of liver cirrhosis, presents to the ICU with signs of bleeding and bruising. Laboratory tests reveal prolonged prothrombin time (PT), partial thromboplastin time (PTT), and decreased fibrinogen levels. What is the most likely underlying cause of John's coagulopathy?
A) Vitamin K deficiency
B) Disseminated Intravascular Coagulation (DIC)
C) Liver failure
D) Hemophilia A

Question 95: A critical care nurse is assessing a patient with a severe burn injury. Which of the following integumentary assessments indicates the need for immediate intervention?
A) Decreased capillary refill in the affected area
B) Presence of eschar on the burn site
C) Increased blister formation on the burn site
D) Pale, cool skin distal to the burn injury

Question 96: In the context of gastrointestinal surgeries, which surgical procedure is most commonly performed to manage refractory gastroesophageal reflux disease (GERD) when medical therapy fails?
A) Roux-en-Y Gastric Bypass
B) Nissen Fundoplication
C) Partial Gastrectomy
D) Heller Myotomy

Question 97: In the context of gastrointestinal resections, which of the following is the most critical factor in determining the success of an ileal resection?
A) Length of ileum remaining post-resection
B) Presence of ileocecal valve
C) Patient's nutritional status pre-surgery
D) Extent of bowel adaptation post-surgery

Question 98: In the context of pericardial effusion, which of the following clinical signs is most indicative of cardiac tamponade, requiring immediate intervention?
A) Elevated jugular venous pressure
B) Pulsus paradoxus
C) Distant heart sounds
D) Hypotension

Question 99: Which of the following neurotransmitter systems is primarily implicated in the pathophysiology of PTSD, particularly in relation to hyperarousal

symptoms?
A) Dopaminergic system
B) Serotonergic system
C) Noradrenergic system
D) GABAergic system

Question 100: Which of the following interventions is most effective in preventing pressure injuries in critically ill patients with limited mobility?
A) Regularly turning the patient every two hours
B) Utilizing a high-density foam mattress
C) Implementing a moisture-wicking barrier cream
D) Ensuring adequate protein intake

Question 101: In the context of Biliary Atresia, which of the following interventions is most critical for improving long-term outcomes in infants diagnosed with this condition?
A) Immediate initiation of corticosteroid therapy
B) Early surgical intervention via the Kasai procedure
C) Administration of ursodeoxycholic acid
D) Nutritional support with medium-chain triglycerides

Question 102: In critically ill patients, which of the following is the most accurate explanation for the mechanism leading to stress-induced hyperglycemia?
A) Increased insulin secretion due to pancreatic beta-cell hyperactivity
B) Enhanced gluconeogenesis due to elevated cortisol levels
C) Decreased glucagon secretion resulting from alpha-cell suppression
D) Increased peripheral glucose uptake due to elevated insulin sensitivity

Question 103: In the context of Transient Ischemic Attack (TIA), which of the following is the most critical initial step in clinical management to prevent subsequent stroke?
A) Immediate administration of intravenous thrombolytics
B) Initiation of dual antiplatelet therapy
C) Comprehensive risk factor assessment and management
D) Urgent carotid endarterectomy

Question 104: In the context of musculoskeletal injuries, which neurotransmitter is primarily involved in the modulation of pain signals in the central nervous system?
A) Dopamine
B) Serotonin
C) Norepinephrine
D) Substance P

Question 105: In the context of restrictive cardiomyopathy, which of the following echocardiographic findings is most indicative of this condition?
A) Left ventricular hypertrophy with preserved ejection fraction
B) Biatrial enlargement with normal ventricular wall thickness
C) Dilated ventricles with reduced ejection fraction
D) Asymmetric septal hypertrophy

Question 106: A 55-year-old male patient named John is admitted to the ICU with confusion, polyuria, and polydipsia. His blood tests reveal a serum sodium level of 150 mmol/L, serum osmolality of 310 mOsm/kg, and urine osmolality of 100 mOsm/kg. Which condition is most likely causing John's symptoms?
A) Syndrome of Inappropriate Antidiuretic Hormone Secretion (SIADH)
B) Diabetes Insipidus
C) Hyperaldosteronism
D) Addison's Disease

Question 107: In the management of a tension pneumothorax, what is the most immediate intervention that should be performed to stabilize the patient?
A) Administer high-flow oxygen therapy
B) Perform needle decompression in the second intercostal space, midclavicular line
C) Insert a chest tube in the fifth intercostal space, anterior axillary line
D) Initiate mechanical ventilation with positive end-expiratory pressure (PEEP)

Question 108: In the context of neurosurgery, which of the following is the most critical factor in determining the need for surgical intervention in a patient with a subdural hematoma?
A) The size of the hematoma
B) The patient's neurological status
C) The patient's age
D) The presence of midline shift

Question 109: Emily, a 67-year-old patient, is admitted to the ICU with an acute ischemic stroke. Her CT scan shows no hemorrhage. The team considers thrombolytic therapy. What is the most critical factor in determining her eligibility for this treatment?
A) Blood pressure levels
B) Time since symptom onset
C) Blood glucose levels
D) Previous stroke history

Question 110: In the management of status epilepticus, which of the following medications is considered the first-line treatment for rapid seizure control in a critical care setting?
A) Phenytoin
B) Lorazepam
C) Valproic Acid
D) Levetiracetam

Question 111: Mrs. Thompson, a 78-year-old patient with a history of dementia, is admitted to the critical care unit following a fall at home. She is confused and agitated, frequently attempting to remove her IV lines. Which of the following interventions is most appropriate to address Mrs. Thompson's current condition?
A) Apply physical restraints to prevent her from removing IV lines.
B) Administer a low-dose antipsychotic medication to reduce agitation.
C) Provide a calm and familiar environment with continuous orientation cues.
D) Increase sedation to ensure she remains calm and does not harm herself.

Question 112: In the context of managing acute respiratory distress syndrome (ARDS) in critically ill patients, which of the following strategies is most effective in improving oxygenation while minimizing ventilator-induced lung injury?
A) High tidal volume ventilation
B) Low tidal volume ventilation
C) Permissive hypercapnia
D) High-frequency oscillatory ventilation

Question 113: Emily, a 56-year-old patient with a history of hypertension and diabetes, presents to the ICU with acute kidney injury (AKI). Her lab results show hyperkalemia and metabolic acidosis. As her critical care nurse, which intervention is most appropriate to rapidly manage her hyperkalemia?
A) Administer calcium gluconate intravenously
B) Administer sodium bicarbonate intravenously

C) Initiate continuous renal replacement therapy (CRRT)
D) Administer insulin and glucose intravenously

Question 114: In the context of critical care, which approach is most effective in managing anxiety in patients with neurological disorders according to contemporary research?
A) Cognitive Behavioral Therapy (CBT)
B) Pharmacological intervention using benzodiazepines
C) Mindfulness-Based Stress Reduction (MBSR)
D) Progressive Muscle Relaxation (PMR)

Question 115: In the context of thoracic surgery, which of the following interventions is most critical in preventing postoperative pulmonary complications in patients undergoing lobectomy?
A) Early ambulation
B) Prophylactic antibiotic administration
C) Fluid restriction
D) Incentive spirometry

Question 116: A 45-year-old patient named John presents to the emergency department with severe pain in his right lower leg following a recent tibial fracture. The pain is disproportionate to the injury and worsens with passive stretching of the toes. Upon examination, the leg appears swollen and tight. What is the most appropriate initial intervention to prevent complications associated with compartment syndrome?
A) Administer intravenous analgesics for pain relief
B) Elevate the limb above heart level
C) Apply ice packs to reduce swelling
D) Prepare for fasciotomy

Question 117: In the management of Hyperosmolar Hyperglycemic State (HHS), which of the following interventions is most critical to initiate first in a hemodynamically stable patient?
A) Administering insulin to reduce blood glucose levels
B) Initiating intravenous fluid replacement with isotonic saline
C) Correcting electrolyte imbalances, particularly potassium
D) Monitoring and adjusting for potential cerebral edema

Question 118: Emily, a 55-year-old female with a history of type 2 diabetes mellitus, presents to the ICU with altered mental status and severe dehydration. Her lab results reveal a blood glucose level of 900 mg/dL, serum osmolality of 320 mOsm/kg, and no significant ketonemia. Based on these findings, what is the most likely diagnosis?
A) Diabetic ketoacidosis (DKA)
B) Hyperosmolar hyperglycemic state (HHS)
C) Lactic acidosis
D) Hypoglycemic encephalopathy

Question 119: John, a 68-year-old male with a history of atrial fibrillation, presents to the emergency department with sudden onset of severe abdominal pain, out of proportion to physical findings. He also reports nausea and vomiting. Given his medical history and symptoms, what is the most likely initial diagnostic test to confirm mesenteric ischemia?
A) Abdominal X-ray
B) CT Angiography
C) MRI Abdomen
D) Ultrasound of the Abdomen

Question 120: In the context of acute kidney injury (AKI), which of the following is the most accurate indicator of renal function recovery?
A) Serum creatinine levels
B) Blood urea nitrogen (BUN) levels
C) Urine output
D) Glomerular filtration rate (GFR)

Question 121: In the management of acute pulmonary edema, which pharmacological intervention is most effective in rapidly reducing preload and improving symptoms?
A) Intravenous Furosemide
B) Sublingual Nitroglycerin
C) Intravenous Morphine
D) Intravenous Dobutamine

Question 122: In the context of neurologic infectious diseases, which of the following is the most indicative clinical feature for differentiating bacterial meningitis from viral meningitis in adult patients?
A) Elevated protein levels in cerebrospinal fluid (CSF)
B) Presence of neutrophils in CSF analysis
C) Low glucose concentration in CSF
D) High opening pressure during lumbar puncture

Question 123: In the context of bacterial infections affecting the central nervous system, which organism is most commonly associated with causing bacterial meningitis in adults?
A) Streptococcus pneumoniae
B) Neisseria meningitidis
C) Haemophilus influenzae
D) Listeria monocytogenes

Question 124: In the context of intraventricular hemorrhage (IVH) management, which of the following interventions is most critical in preventing secondary brain injury in critically ill patients?
A) Maintaining normothermia
B) Administering prophylactic anticonvulsants
C) Ensuring adequate cerebral perfusion pressure
D) Implementing early surgical evacuation

Question 125: In the management of Non-ST Elevation Myocardial Infarction (NSTEMI), which of the following medications is most critical for reducing mortality in high-risk patients with ongoing ischemia?
A) Nitroglycerin
B) Aspirin
C) Clopidogrel
D) Beta-blockers

ANSWER WITH DETAILED EXPLANATION SET [1]

Question 1: Correct Answer: C) Argatroban
Rationale: Argatroban is a direct thrombin inhibitor that does not cross-react with heparin-PF4 complexes, making it the preferred choice in HIT management. Warfarin (A) is contraindicated initially due to risk of venous limb gangrene. Fondaparinux (B), though not a heparin derivative, has limited data supporting its use in HIT. Enoxaparin (D), a low molecular weight heparin, can exacerbate HIT. The key difference lies in argatroban's mechanism, directly inhibiting thrombin, reducing further thrombotic events in HIT patients without exacerbating the condition.

Question 2: Correct Answer: A) Immediate surgical exploration
Rationale: Immediate surgical exploration is necessary for hemodynamically unstable patients with suspected renal laceration due to acute genitourinary trauma. This approach addresses potential life-threatening hemorrhage. Option B, observation, is suitable for stable patients. Option C, angiographic embolization, is effective for controlling bleeding in stable cases but not initial treatment for instability. Option D, bed rest and fluid resuscitation, supports stabilization but does not address active bleeding requiring surgical intervention. The correct choice prioritizes rapid intervention to prevent further deterioration.

Question 3: Correct Answer: B) Hypercalcemia of Malignancy
Rationale: Hypercalcemia of Malignancy is common in cancer patients and can cause confusion, nausea, and muscle weakness due to elevated calcium levels. Option A (SIADH) involves hyponatremia rather than hypercalcemia. Option C (Tumor Lysis Syndrome) presents with electrolyte imbalances like hyperkalemia and hyperuricemia, not hypercalcemia. Option D (Febrile Neutropenia) involves infection risk due to low neutrophil count, unrelated to calcium levels. Therefore, Emily's symptoms and lab results align most closely with Hypercalcemia of Malignancy.

Question 4: Correct Answer: B) Applying a pelvic binder
Rationale: Applying a pelvic binder is crucial in hemodynamically unstable patients with pelvic fractures as it reduces pelvic volume and controls hemorrhage. While intravenous fluids (A) and blood transfusions (D) are essential for managing shock, they do not directly address bleeding source control. External fixation (C) is more definitive but not immediately feasible in an unstable setting. The priority is to stabilize the pelvis quickly to prevent further hemorrhage, making option B the most immediate and effective intervention.

Question 5: Correct Answer: B) Surgical debridement with adjunctive antibiotic therapy
Rationale: Surgical debridement with adjunctive antibiotic therapy is the most effective long-term treatment for chronic osteomyelitis. Debridement removes necrotic tissue, reducing bacterial load, while antibiotics target residual infection. Option A (prolonged oral antibiotics) may not penetrate well into bone tissue. Option C (hyperbaric oxygen therapy alone) lacks evidence as a standalone treatment. Option D (antibiotic-impregnated bone cement) is useful but typically an adjunct to surgery and antibiotics, not a primary treatment. Thus, option B combines essential surgical and pharmacological approaches for optimal outcomes.

Question 6: Correct Answer: A) Low serum sodium and high serum potassium
Rationale: Primary adrenal insufficiency, or Addison's disease, is characterized by low aldosterone production, leading to hyponatremia (low sodium) and hyperkalemia (high potassium). Option A correctly identifies these electrolyte imbalances. Option B suggests the opposite electrolyte pattern, which is not typical in Addison's disease. Options C and D involve calcium and phosphate imbalances, which are not primary indicators of adrenal insufficiency. The correct understanding of aldosterone's role in sodium retention and potassium excretion makes option A the valid choice.

Question 7: Correct Answer: B) Zinc
Rationale: Zinc is crucial for immune function and collagen synthesis, making it essential for wound healing. Its deficiency is linked to delayed healing and increased infection risk. While Vitamin C (Option A) also supports collagen synthesis, it primarily acts as an antioxidant. Vitamin D (Option C) modulates immune response but does not directly influence wound healing. Magnesium (Option D) is vital for numerous biochemical reactions but not specifically for collagen synthesis or immune enhancement. Thus, zinc's direct involvement in these processes makes it the correct choice.

Question 8: Correct Answer: A) Atrial fibrillation
Rationale: Atrial fibrillation is most directly associated with embolic stroke due to irregular heart rhythms causing blood clots in the atria, which can dislodge and travel to the brain. Hypertension (B), while a risk factor for stroke, primarily contributes to hemorrhagic strokes or atherosclerosis. Hyperlipidemia (C) increases risk by promoting atherosclerosis but is less directly linked to embolic events. Diabetes mellitus (D) contributes to vascular damage over time but does not directly cause emboli formation like atrial fibrillation does. Understanding these distinctions is crucial for effective clinical judgment in stroke prevention.

Question 9: Correct Answer: B) High urine osmolality after desmopressin administration
Rationale: Central DI is characterized by a deficiency in vasopressin production, leading to dilute urine. Desmopressin, a vasopressin analog, increases urine osmolality in central DI but not in nephrogenic DI, where the kidneys don't respond to vasopressin. Option A is incorrect because low serum sodium suggests hyponatremia, not typical in DI. Option C is incorrect as low plasma vasopressin can indicate both central and nephrogenic DI. Option D is unrelated to DI diagnosis. Thus, option B effectively differentiates central from nephrogenic DI.

Question 10: Correct Answer: C) Initiating intravenous octreotide
Rationale: Initiating intravenous octreotide is crucial as it reduces portal hypertension by decreasing splanchnic blood flow, thus controlling variceal bleeding. While vasopressin (A) also reduces portal pressure, it has more systemic side effects. Urgent endoscopy (B) is essential but follows stabilization. Transfusing packed red blood cells (D) addresses blood loss but doesn't control bleeding source. Octreotide's targeted action makes it the optimal first step in this scenario.

Question 11: Correct Answer: A) Streptococcus pneumoniae

Rationale: Streptococcus pneumoniae is the leading cause of bacterial meningitis in adults, due to its prevalence and virulence factors. Neisseria meningitidis is also a common cause but more prevalent in younger populations or during outbreaks. Haemophilus influenzae has become less common due to vaccination. Listeria monocytogenes affects primarily immunocompromised individuals and the elderly. The differentiation lies in understanding epidemiology and age-related susceptibility, making Streptococcus pneumoniae the correct choice for adult meningitis.

Question 12: Correct Answer: D) Establishing a strong therapeutic alliance with the patient
Rationale: Establishing a strong therapeutic alliance is crucial as it builds trust, encourages open communication, and increases patient engagement, which are key factors in suicide prevention. While cognitive-behavioral therapy (Option B) is effective, its success heavily relies on the therapeutic relationship. A no-suicide contract (Option A) lacks empirical support for effectiveness. Increasing medication dosage (Option C) may help manage symptoms but does not directly address the underlying issues or enhance therapeutic engagement as effectively as Option D.

Question 13: Correct Answer: B) Performing needle decompression in the second intercostal space, midclavicular line
Rationale: Needle decompression is the immediate intervention for tension pneumothorax to rapidly relieve pressure. Option A provides oxygen but doesn't address pressure. Option C is definitive but not immediate. Option D may worsen tension pneumothorax by increasing intrathoracic pressure. Thus, Option B is correct as it directly alleviates life-threatening pressure quickly, aligning with emergency protocols.

Question 14: Correct Answer: C) Chronic Pancreatitis
Rationale: Chronic pancreatitis leads to pancreatic insufficiency, causing inadequate production of digestive enzymes, particularly lipase, resulting in steatorrhea. Celiac disease and Crohn's disease can cause malabsorption but are not directly linked to enzyme deficiencies from the pancreas. Lactose intolerance involves carbohydrate malabsorption due to lactase deficiency, not fat malabsorption. Thus, while all options involve gastrointestinal issues, only chronic pancreatitis directly causes steatorrhea through pancreatic enzyme deficiency.

Question 15: Correct Answer: C) Using a post-pyloric feeding tube
Rationale: Using a post-pyloric feeding tube is most effective as it bypasses the stomach, reducing the risk of aspiration. While elevating the head of the bed (Option A) reduces reflux risk, it's less effective than direct bypass. Antiemetics (Option B) address nausea but not anatomical aspiration risks. Oral hygiene (Option D) minimizes bacterial load but doesn't prevent aspiration mechanically. Post-pyloric feeding directly addresses gastric content management, significantly lowering aspiration pneumonia risk compared to other measures.

Question 16: Correct Answer: C) Supraventricular Tachycardia with hypotension
Rationale: Synchronized cardioversion is indicated for hemodynamically unstable tachyarrhythmias. Option C, Supraventricular Tachycardia with hypotension, directly aligns with this indication as the instability (hypotension) necessitates immediate intervention. Option A may also require cardioversion but primarily if rate control fails. Option B requires defibrillation, not synchronized cardioversion, due to pulselessness. Option D involves bradyarrhythmia management, not requiring cardioversion. Thus, understanding specific arrhythmias and their clinical presentations is crucial for selecting appropriate interventions.

Question 17: Correct Answer: A) Administer propranolol to manage tachycardia
Rationale: Propranolol is the immediate intervention of choice as it quickly alleviates cardiovascular symptoms like tachycardia by blocking beta-adrenergic receptors. Methimazole (Option B) is used long-term to decrease hormone synthesis but does not provide rapid relief. Iodine therapy (Option C) can inhibit hormone release but requires time. Radioactive iodine (Option D) is definitive but inappropriate for acute symptom management. The key distinction lies in the need for rapid symptom control versus long-term treatment strategies.

Question 18: Correct Answer: C) Initiating granulocyte colony-stimulating factor (G-CSF) therapy
Rationale: Initiating G-CSF therapy is crucial as it stimulates the bone marrow to produce more white blood cells, directly addressing leukopenia. Option A, while important in preventing infections, does not address the root cause of leukopenia. Option B involves preventive measures but does not actively increase white blood cell counts. Option D supports overall health but does not specifically target white blood cell production. Thus, G-CSF therapy is prioritized for its direct impact on increasing neutrophil counts and reducing infection risk in leukopenic patients like Sarah.

Question 19: Correct Answer: B) Implementing a digital reminder system with personalized messages.
Rationale: Digital reminder systems with personalized messages are shown to significantly improve adherence by integrating into daily routines and providing tailored support. While detailed instructions (Option A) and counseling (Option C) are beneficial, they lack ongoing engagement. Financial incentives (Option D) may offer short-term compliance but do not foster intrinsic motivation. Contemporary research supports digital interventions as they combine accessibility and personalization, effectively addressing barriers to adherence in chronic conditions like musculoskeletal pain.

Question 20: Correct Answer: B) Perform surgical debridement of necrotic tissue.
Rationale: Surgical debridement is crucial to remove necrotic tissue and contaminants, reducing infection risk and promoting healing. Topical antibiotics (Option A) are less effective without debridement. Systemic antibiotics (Option C) may be necessary but do not address necrosis directly. A sterile dressing (Option D) protects the wound but doesn't treat underlying issues. Debridement directly addresses the primary concern of necrotic tissue presence, crucial for effective management in trauma cases like John's.

Question 21: Correct Answer: A) Abdominal pain out of proportion to physical findings
Rationale: Acute mesenteric ischemia is characterized by severe abdominal pain that is disproportionate to the physical examination findings, making it a key diagnostic indicator. While hematochezia (Option B) can occur, it typically presents later. Hypoactive bowel sounds (Option C) are non-specific and common in various conditions. Elevated serum lactate levels (Option D) indicate tissue hypoperfusion but are not exclusive to mesenteric ischemia. Therefore, the distinctive feature of disproportionate pain helps differentiate acute mesenteric ischemia from other gastrointestinal issues.

Question 22: Correct Answer: C) Initiate large-bore chest

tube insertion
Rationale: The immediate intervention for a hemothorax is large-bore chest tube insertion to evacuate blood from the pleural space, restoring lung expansion and improving ventilation. While high-flow oxygen (A) supports breathing, it doesn't address the underlying issue. Needle decompression (B) is used for tension pneumothorax, not hemothorax. Intravenous fluids (D) are important for hemodynamic stability but do not directly resolve the pleural blood accumulation. Chest tube insertion directly targets and resolves the cause of respiratory distress in hemothorax cases.

Question 23: Correct Answer: B) Hypocalcemia
Rationale: Hypocalcemia is most commonly associated with a prolonged QT interval due to its effect on phase 2 of the cardiac action potential, prolonging repolarization. While hypomagnesemia can also cause QT prolongation, it is less common than hypocalcemia. Hyperkalemia typically leads to peaked T waves and shortened QT intervals, while hypermagnesemia is rare and usually does not affect the QT interval significantly. Understanding these differences helps in identifying the correct electrolyte disturbance linked to QT prolongation in clinical practice.

Question 24: Correct Answer: B) Perform needle decompression immediately.
Rationale: Needle decompression is the immediate intervention for tension pneumothorax to relieve pressure and restore hemodynamic stability. Option A, high-flow oxygen, helps reabsorb air but does not address acute tension. Option C, chest tube insertion, follows decompression. Option D, semi-Fowler's position, aids breathing but doesn't relieve pressure. Therefore, B is correct as it directly addresses life-threatening tension pneumothorax by rapidly decompressing pleural space pressure.

Question 25: Correct Answer: A) Portal hypertension
Rationale: Portal hypertension is the most immediate complication in untreated biliary atresia due to bile duct obstruction leading to increased pressure in the portal vein. While cirrhosis (Option B) and hepatic encephalopathy (Option C) are long-term complications resulting from chronic liver damage, they occur after persistent portal hypertension and liver failure. Ascites (Option D), an accumulation of fluid in the peritoneal cavity, can result from portal hypertension but is not as immediate as the pressure increase itself. Understanding these progression stages helps prioritize clinical interventions effectively.

Question 26: Correct Answer: A) Cognitive decline related to Parkinson's disease
Rationale: Cognitive decline is a common issue in Parkinson's patients, affecting memory and executive function, leading to non-adherence. While financial constraints (B), lack of understanding (C), and side effects (D) can contribute, they are less directly linked to Parkinson's cognitive symptoms. Option B might be relevant if financial issues were reported; C would be plausible if education was lacking; D could apply if side effects were prominent. However, cognitive decline is most directly associated with missed doses in this context due to its impact on memory and planning.

Question 27: Correct Answer: B) Initiating aggressive fluid resuscitation with isotonic saline
Rationale: The primary concern in HHS is severe dehydration due to osmotic diuresis. Initial treatment focuses on aggressive fluid resuscitation with isotonic saline to restore intravascular volume, improve renal perfusion, and dilute hyperglycemia. While insulin administration (A) is essential for glucose control, it follows fluid replacement. Correcting electrolytes (C) is crucial but secondary to fluids. Airway monitoring (D) is important but not specific to HHS management. Fluid resuscitation directly addresses the critical pathophysiology of HHS, making it the priority intervention.

Question 28: Correct Answer: C) Pulsus paradoxus greater than 10 mmHg
Rationale: Pulsus paradoxus, a drop in blood pressure during inspiration by more than 10 mmHg, is a hallmark sign of cardiac tamponade due to impaired ventricular filling. While elevated LVEDP and CVP can occur, they are not as specific as pulsus paradoxus. An increased SVI is incorrect because cardiac output typically decreases in tamponade. Thus, pulsus paradoxus is the most distinctive indicator among these options for cardiac tamponade, highlighting its diagnostic importance over other hemodynamic changes.

Question 29: Correct Answer: C) Provide supportive care with oxygen therapy
Rationale: In TRALI, supportive care with oxygen therapy is crucial as it addresses hypoxemia without exacerbating fluid balance issues. Diuretics (Option A) are ineffective as TRALI is not due to fluid overload. High PEEP (Option B) may worsen lung injury by increasing alveolar pressure. Corticosteroids (Option D) lack evidence in improving outcomes in TRALI cases. Therefore, providing oxygen therapy ensures adequate oxygenation while monitoring and managing respiratory distress effectively, aligning with contemporary research and clinical guidelines.

Question 30: Correct Answer: B) Coolness and pallor at the site
Rationale: Coolness and pallor at the site are classic signs of IV infiltration, indicating fluid leakage into surrounding tissue. Erythema and warmth (Option A) suggest phlebitis or infection. Rapid infusion with no resistance (Option C) may not indicate infiltration but rather normal function. Localized throbbing pain (Option D) can occur in both infiltration and other complications, but without coolness, it is less specific. Understanding these distinctions is crucial for accurate diagnosis and intervention in clinical practice.

Question 31: Correct Answer: C) Liver failure-induced coagulopathy
Rationale: Liver failure-induced coagulopathy is characterized by impaired synthesis of clotting factors due to liver dysfunction, leading to prolonged PT and aPTT, thrombocytopenia, and bleeding tendencies. Vitamin K deficiency also causes prolonged PT but is less likely given the liver cirrhosis context. DIC involves systemic activation of coagulation pathways leading to consumption of platelets and clotting factors but typically shows more acute onset and organ dysfunction. Hemophilia A primarily affects factor VIII and presents differently, often without liver involvement. Thus, Mr. Thompson's symptoms align best with liver failure-induced coagulopathy.

Question 32: Correct Answer: A) Persistent pain unrelieved by analgesics and elevation
Rationale: Persistent pain unrelieved by analgesics and elevation is a hallmark sign of compartment syndrome, indicating increased intracompartmental pressure requiring fasciotomy. While swelling (B), decreased sensation (C), and weak pulses (D) are associated with compartment syndrome, they are less definitive for urgent intervention. Swelling and bruising can occur without severe complications; decreased sensation may develop

over time; weak pulses suggest arterial compromise but are not as immediate an indicator as unrelenting pain. The key difference lies in the critical nature of persistent pain as a direct signal for surgical decompression.

Question 33: Correct Answer: A) Administering intravenous fluids
Rationale: Administering intravenous fluids is crucial in rhabdomyolysis to prevent acute kidney injury by diluting myoglobin and maintaining renal perfusion. Hemodialysis (B) is reserved for severe cases with established renal failure. Diuretics (C) are not first-line as they may exacerbate dehydration. Bicarbonate therapy (D) can be used to alkalinize urine but is secondary to fluid resuscitation. The primary goal is hydration to support kidney function and flush out myoglobin, making option A the most immediate and effective intervention.

Question 34: Correct Answer: B) Pulmonary embolism (PE)
Rationale: Pulmonary embolism (PE) is a common and severe complication of prolonged immobility, where a blood clot travels to the lungs, causing acute respiratory symptoms like shortness of breath and chest pain. While deep vein thrombosis (DVT) is related to immobility, it typically presents with leg pain or swelling rather than respiratory symptoms. Atelectasis involves collapsed lung tissue but does not usually cause sudden chest pain. Pneumonia can cause similar symptoms but develops over time with fever and productive cough. Thus, PE is the most likely immediate complication in this scenario.

Question 35: Correct Answer: B) Perform wound debridement to remove necrotic tissue.
Rationale: Debridement is crucial for removing necrotic tissue, which can harbor bacteria and impede healing. While antibiotics (A) are important, they are not effective without addressing the source of infection. Moisture-retentive dressings (C) can trap bacteria if used prematurely. Glycemic control (D) supports overall health but does not directly address the infected wound. Debridement directly reduces bacterial load and promotes healing, making it the priority intervention in this scenario.

Question 36: Correct Answer: B) Initiate non-invasive ventilation
Rationale: In cases of acute respiratory distress in myasthenia gravis, non-invasive ventilation is crucial to support breathing and prevent respiratory failure. While corticosteroids (A) and pyridostigmine (D) are treatments for myasthenia gravis, they do not provide immediate respiratory support. Plasmapheresis (C) is effective for severe exacerbations but is not an immediate intervention. Non-invasive ventilation directly addresses the respiratory compromise, offering immediate relief and stabilization, making it the most appropriate choice in this scenario.

Question 37: Correct Answer: A) Administer intravenous antibiotics immediately.
Rationale: Administering intravenous antibiotics immediately is crucial as it addresses the infection promptly, reducing complications. Surgical debridement (B) is important but typically follows antibiotic therapy. Hyperbaric oxygen therapy (C) can aid healing but isn't a primary intervention. Conducting a bone biopsy (D) is essential for confirmation but may delay urgent treatment. Thus, initiating antibiotic therapy first is vital for effective management, aligning with current guidelines and research on osteomyelitis treatment protocols.

Question 38: Correct Answer: A) Elevate the head of the bed to 30 degrees.
Rationale: Elevating the head of the bed to 30 degrees is a primary intervention to reduce ICP by promoting venous drainage. Hypertonic saline (B) can also reduce ICP but is typically used when initial measures are insufficient. Encouraging coughing (C) increases ICP and should be avoided. Continuous sedation (D) may assist in reducing metabolic demand but does not directly address ICP management as effectively as positioning. The correct choice reflects immediate and non-invasive management aligned with established guidelines for managing increased ICP post-neurosurgery.

Question 39: Correct Answer: A) Intravenous Immunoglobulin (IVIG)
Rationale: Intravenous Immunoglobulin (IVIG) is a first-line treatment for Guillain-Barré Syndrome, particularly effective in the acute phase to reduce disease severity. It works by modulating immune response. Plasma Exchange (Option C) is also effective but less convenient than IVIG. Corticosteroids (Option B) have not shown consistent benefit in GBS treatment. Antiviral Medications (Option D) are not relevant as GBS is not caused by viral infections. The choice of IVIG over plasma exchange often depends on availability and patient-specific factors, but both are considered primary therapies.

Question 40: Correct Answer: B) Reorient the patient frequently and ensure a calm environment.
Rationale: Frequent reorientation and maintaining a calm environment are critical in managing delirium, as they help reduce confusion without pharmacological intervention. Option A, while sometimes used, should be reserved for severe agitation due to potential side effects. Option C could exacerbate delirium by increasing sedation and confusion. Option D is not directly related to delirium management and could worsen dehydration-related confusion. Thus, non-pharmacological strategies like reorientation are preferred first-line interventions according to contemporary guidelines on delirium management in postoperative patients.

Question 41: Correct Answer: C) Video-assisted thoracoscopic surgery (VATS) for drainage
Rationale: Video-assisted thoracoscopic surgery (VATS) is crucial as it allows effective drainage of pus and debridement of the pleural space, reducing the risk of recurrence. While broad-spectrum antibiotics (Option A) are essential for infection control, they do not address the physical removal of infected material. Thoracentesis (Option B) is diagnostic and may provide temporary relief but often insufficient for complete resolution. High-dose corticosteroids (Option D) are not standard in empyema management and can suppress immune function, potentially worsening infection. Therefore, VATS offers a comprehensive solution by directly addressing the source of infection.

Question 42: Correct Answer: C) Serotonin Release Assay (SRA)
Rationale: The Serotonin Release Assay (SRA) is considered the gold standard for confirming HIT due to its high specificity and sensitivity. While aPTT (Option B) is used to monitor heparin therapy, it does not confirm HIT. Prothrombin Time (Option A) and D-dimer test (Option D) are unrelated to HIT diagnosis. The SRA detects platelet activation in the presence of heparin, distinguishing it from other coagulopathies. This makes Option C the most accurate choice for confirming HIT, whereas other tests may only provide indirect or unrelated information.

Question 43: Correct Answer: A) Long-term oxygen therapy for patients with resting hypoxemia
Rationale: Long-term oxygen therapy significantly reduces mortality in COPD patients with severe resting hypoxemia by improving oxygenation and reducing

pulmonary hypertension. While inhaled corticosteroids (Option B) can help manage symptoms, they do not reduce mortality. CPAP (Option C) is primarily used for sleep apnea, not stable COPD. Oral antibiotics (Option D) are beneficial during exacerbations but do not impact long-term survival. Thus, Option A is the most effective intervention for reducing mortality in this context, supported by substantial clinical evidence.

Question 44: Correct Answer: D) Initiate plasmapheresis.
Rationale: Plasmapheresis is often used in acute exacerbations of myasthenia gravis to rapidly remove circulating antibodies. While increasing pyridostigmine may seem logical, it doesn't address antibody-mediated symptoms quickly. IVIG and corticosteroids are valid treatments but act slower than plasmapheresis. Plasmapheresis provides immediate relief by reducing antibody levels, making it the best choice for severe symptoms like respiratory distress. The key difference is the rapid onset of action needed in acute scenarios, which makes plasmapheresis more effective than other options in this context.

Question 45: Correct Answer: B) Perform an urgent exploratory laparotomy
Rationale: An urgent exploratory laparotomy is necessary due to the presence of free fluid indicating potential internal bleeding and hemodynamic instability. While fluid resuscitation (Option A) is essential, it does not address the source of bleeding. Broad-spectrum antibiotics (Option C) are important but not immediate priorities in this context. A CT scan (Option D) may delay crucial surgical intervention. The correct choice is based on prioritizing surgical management to control hemorrhage, aligning with contemporary trauma protocols.

Question 46: Correct Answer: B) Hypotension and distended neck veins
Rationale: Tension pneumothorax is characterized by hypotension and distended neck veins due to increased intrathoracic pressure compromising venous return. Option A is incorrect as tracheal deviation occurs away from the affected side. Option C, dullness to percussion, typically suggests pleural effusion rather than pneumothorax. Option D, decreased breath sounds bilaterally, could indicate other conditions like ARDS or bilateral effusions but not specifically tension pneumothorax. Correct identification relies on understanding pathophysiological changes unique to tension pneumothorax.

Question 47: Correct Answer: B) Amiodarone
Rationale: Amiodarone is known to prolong the QT interval, making it unsuitable for Sarah, who already has a prolonged QT interval. Metoprolol (A) and Lisinopril (C) do not typically affect the QT interval significantly. Furosemide (D), while it can exacerbate hypokalemia, does not directly prolong the QT interval like Amiodarone. The choice of Amiodarone as an incorrect treatment highlights the importance of avoiding medications that can worsen cardiac conduction abnormalities in patients with existing prolonged QT intervals.

Question 48: Correct Answer: C) Percutaneous coronary intervention (PCI)
Rationale: PCI is the preferred method for reperfusion in STEMI due to its ability to quickly restore blood flow, reducing myocardial damage and mortality. While thrombolytic therapy (D) is used when PCI is unavailable, it has higher bleeding risks and less efficacy. Beta-blockers (A) and ACE inhibitors (B) are important for long-term management but do not directly address acute coronary artery occlusion. PCI's effectiveness in rapidly revascularizing blocked arteries makes it the optimal choice in contemporary STEMI management, aligning with current guidelines and research.

Question 49: Correct Answer: B) Initiate angiotensin-converting enzyme (ACE) inhibitor therapy
Rationale: Initiating ACE inhibitor therapy is crucial as it reduces proteinuria and slows CKD progression by lowering intraglomerular pressure. Option A is incorrect because high protein intake can worsen kidney function in CKD patients. Option C may help with edema but does not address CKD progression. Option D treats anemia but does not impact CKD progression directly. Thus, ACE inhibitors are the best choice for managing symptoms and slowing disease progression in Sarah's case.

Question 50: Correct Answer: A) Administer intravenous calcium gluconate
Rationale: Administering intravenous calcium gluconate is prioritized as it stabilizes cardiac membranes, reducing the risk of arrhythmias associated with hyperkalemia. While insulin and glucose infusion (Option C) can help shift potassium intracellularly, it is not immediate in preventing arrhythmias. Sodium polystyrene sulfonate (Option B) acts slowly and is not suitable for acute management. Hemodialysis (Option D) effectively removes potassium but requires more time to arrange and initiate. Therefore, Option A is the most immediate intervention to protect cardiac function in severe hyperkalemia.

Question 51: Correct Answer: A) Epidural hematoma
Rationale: An epidural hematoma is characterized by a biconvex, hyperdense lesion on CT and often follows a brief loss of consciousness with a lucid interval. In contrast, a subdural hematoma appears as a crescent-shaped lesion and may not present with such clear intervals of consciousness. A concussion involves transient neurological dysfunction without specific imaging findings. Diffuse axonal injury typically results in widespread brain damage with immediate unconsciousness. Thus, John's presentation aligns most closely with an epidural hematoma due to the characteristic CT findings and clinical history.

Question 52: Correct Answer: B) Initiating fluid restriction to manage water retention.
Rationale: Fluid restriction is crucial in SIADH management as it directly addresses the underlying issue of excessive water retention, thereby preventing dilutional hyponatremia. Option A, administering isotonic saline, can worsen hyponatremia by adding more fluid. Option C, oral salt tablets, may help but are secondary to fluid restriction. Option D, loop diuretics, can be used adjunctively but are not as effective as fluid restriction in controlling water balance. Therefore, B is the most critical intervention based on contemporary management guidelines.

Question 53: Correct Answer: D) Provide a quiet and well-lit environment.
Rationale: Delirium management prioritizes environmental modifications, such as providing a quiet, well-lit space, to reduce sensory overload and confusion. While haloperidol (A) can be used for severe agitation, it is not the first-line intervention. Ensuring hydration and nutrition (B) supports overall health but doesn't directly address delirium symptoms. Early mobilization (C) aids recovery but may not immediately impact delirium severity. Therefore, option D is most effective in stabilizing Mr. Johnson's condition by minimizing disorientation through environmental control.

Question 54: Correct Answer: C) Initiating nitroglycerin therapy

Rationale: Initiating nitroglycerin therapy is prioritized as it directly reduces myocardial oxygen demand by dilating coronary arteries, improving blood flow, and decreasing preload. While administering aspirin (A) is crucial for its antiplatelet effect, it does not immediately reduce oxygen demand. Supplemental oxygen (B) increases oxygen availability but doesn't decrease demand. Semi-Fowler's position (D) aids in respiratory effort but has minimal impact on reducing myocardial workload compared to nitroglycerin. Thus, nitroglycerin is the most effective initial intervention for this purpose.

Question 55: Correct Answer: A) Absence of brainstem reflexes
Rationale: The absence of brainstem reflexes is critical for diagnosing brain death, as it indicates no neurological function. Option B (decerebrate posturing) and C (Babinski sign) suggest some level of neurological activity, inconsistent with brain death. Option D (spontaneous respiratory effort) indicates brainstem activity, ruling out brain death. Thus, only option A aligns with contemporary research and recognized theories on determining brain death by confirming complete loss of neurological function.

Question 56: Correct Answer: B) Left ventricular outflow tract obstruction
Rationale: Left ventricular outflow tract obstruction (LVOTO) in hypertrophic cardiomyopathy is associated with a worse prognosis due to increased risk of heart failure and sudden cardiac death. While asymmetric septal hypertrophy (A) and mitral valve systolic anterior motion (D) are common in HCM, they are not as strongly linked to poor outcomes as LVOTO. Apical hypertrophy (C), though a variant of HCM, generally has a better prognosis compared to LVOTO. The presence of LVOTO requires careful management to prevent complications, making it the most critical finding among the options.

Question 57: Correct Answer: B) Perform urgent surgical debridement.
Rationale: The correct answer is B) Perform urgent surgical debridement. Necrotizing fasciitis requires prompt surgical intervention to remove necrotic tissue and control infection spread. While starting broad-spectrum antibiotics (Option A) is crucial, it cannot replace the necessity of immediate surgical debridement. Hyperbaric oxygen therapy (Option C) may be supportive but is not an initial step. Administering intravenous fluids (Option D) addresses shock but does not directly manage the infection's source. Surgical debridement is vital for survival and preventing further tissue damage, making it the priority in this scenario.

Question 58: Correct Answer: C) Providing a calm and quiet environment
Rationale: Managing agitation in neurologically compromised patients like Mr. Thompson involves non-pharmacological interventions as the first line, such as creating a calm and quiet environment. This approach minimizes sensory overload and promotes recovery without the risks associated with medications or restraints. Lorazepam (Option A) can exacerbate confusion in stroke patients; haloperidol (Option B) may have adverse neurological effects; physical restraints (Option D) can increase agitation and pose ethical concerns. Thus, Option C aligns with contemporary research emphasizing environmental modifications in managing agitation effectively.

Question 59: Correct Answer: B) Initiate plasmapheresis
Rationale: Plasmapheresis is effective in rapidly improving symptoms of myasthenia gravis by removing circulating antibodies, making it ideal for acute exacerbations like Mr. Johnson's. IVIG (Option A) also helps but acts slower than plasmapheresis. Increasing pyridostigmine (Option C), a cholinesterase inhibitor, may not be sufficient during severe exacerbations and could worsen symptoms due to cholinergic crisis. Non-invasive ventilation (Option D) supports breathing but doesn't address the underlying antibody-mediated process. Therefore, initiating plasmapheresis offers immediate symptom relief by directly targeting the pathophysiology of the disorder.

Question 60: Correct Answer: C) Discontinue heparin and initiate a direct thrombin inhibitor.
Rationale: In suspected HIT, it is crucial to discontinue all forms of heparin immediately due to the risk of thrombotic complications. Direct thrombin inhibitors, such as argatroban or bivalirudin, are recommended as they do not cross-react with HIT antibodies. Option A is incorrect as continuing heparin increases risk. Option B is incorrect because warfarin should not be started until platelet count recovers due to initial procoagulant effects. Option D is incorrect as aspirin does not address the underlying cause of HIT-related thrombosis.

Question 61: Correct Answer: C) Administering intravenous crystalloids
Rationale: Administering intravenous crystalloids is crucial for stabilizing a hemodynamically unstable patient by restoring intravascular volume and maintaining perfusion. While PPIs (Option A) are important for reducing gastric acid secretion, they do not immediately stabilize hemodynamics. Urgent endoscopy (Option B) helps identify and treat bleeding sources but is secondary to initial stabilization. Transfusing packed red blood cells (Option D) is essential for significant anemia or ongoing bleeding but follows initial fluid resuscitation with crystalloids to quickly restore circulatory volume.

Question 62: Correct Answer: B) Perform a neurological assessment and notify the neurosurgeon immediately.
Rationale: The immediate priority is to perform a detailed neurological assessment and notify the neurosurgeon, as these symptoms may indicate complications such as hemorrhage or edema requiring urgent intervention. Option A, administering mannitol, addresses intracranial pressure but without further assessment could be inappropriate. Option C is supportive but does not directly address acute changes in neurological status. Option D focuses on seizure prevention, which is not indicated by the current symptoms. Correctly identifying and communicating changes are crucial in post-craniotomy care.

Question 63: Correct Answer: C) Mobitz Type II
Rationale: Mobitz Type II is associated with a higher risk of progression to complete heart block due to its location distal to the AV node. Unlike Mobitz Type I, which typically involves the AV node and is less likely to progress, Mobitz Type II affects the His-Purkinje system. First-degree AV block involves only prolonged conduction time without dropped beats, and left bundle branch block affects ventricular conduction rather than causing complete heart block. Thus, understanding the anatomical site of conduction disturbances aids in predicting progression risks.

Question 64: Correct Answer: A) Administering a low-dose benzodiazepine as prescribed.
Rationale: Administering a low-dose benzodiazepine is effective for acute anxiety management in critical care, especially when other interventions may not suffice due to the patient's condition. Option B, while beneficial for anxiety, may not be feasible if John's neurological status limits his ability to participate actively. Option C provides

emotional support but may not adequately address physiological symptoms of anxiety. Option D helps in reducing stressors but does not directly alleviate severe anxiety symptoms. Benzodiazepines act quickly on the central nervous system, providing necessary relief in acute settings.

Question 65: Correct Answer: A) Start broad-spectrum antibiotics immediately
Rationale: The immediate initiation of broad-spectrum antibiotics (Option A) is crucial in managing sepsis, especially with multidrug-resistant organisms, to prevent further deterioration. While infection control measures (Option C) are important for preventing spread, they do not address the acute treatment need. Renal replacement therapy (Option B) might be necessary later but is not an initial step for sepsis management. Adjusting diabetes management (Option D) is essential for overall care but not the priority in acute sepsis intervention. Thus, starting antibiotics promptly addresses the critical need to control infection and improve outcomes.

Question 66: Correct Answer: B) Hypotension and dark urine immediately after starting the transfusion
Rationale: Option B is correct as acute hemolytic transfusion reactions (AHTR) are characterized by symptoms like hypotension and hemoglobinuria (dark urine), occurring soon after transfusion begins. Option A describes febrile non-hemolytic reactions, which are less severe. Option C indicates allergic reactions, while option D suggests possible TRALI or TACO. The immediate timing and specific symptoms in option B align with AHTR, highlighting the importance of recognizing early signs to prevent severe complications.

Question 67: Correct Answer: A) Administer lorazepam intravenously
Rationale: John's symptoms suggest alcohol withdrawal syndrome, where benzodiazepines like lorazepam are the first-line treatment to manage agitation and prevent seizures. Option B (haloperidol) can worsen withdrawal symptoms. Option C (thiamine) prevents Wernicke's encephalopathy but does not address acute agitation. Option D (intravenous fluids) supports hydration but does not treat withdrawal symptoms. Benzodiazepines are crucial in stabilizing the patient during withdrawal, highlighting their importance over other supportive measures in this scenario.

Question 68: Correct Answer: C) Increased urine osmolality after desmopressin administration
Rationale: Central Diabetes Insipidus is characterized by a deficiency in vasopressin (ADH) production. Desmopressin, an ADH analog, increases urine osmolality by reducing diuresis, confirming the diagnosis. Option A is incorrect as increased urine osmolality post-water deprivation suggests intact ADH function. Option B is misleading; DI typically presents with hypernatremia due to water loss. Option D, while indicative of DI, does not differentiate between central and nephrogenic types without further testing. Thus, option C specifically confirms Central DI by showing responsiveness to desmopressin.

Question 69: Correct Answer: B) Continuous nebulization of short-acting beta-agonists
Rationale: Continuous nebulization of short-acting beta-agonists is crucial as it rapidly alleviates bronchospasm, a primary concern in status asthmaticus. While intravenous corticosteroids (Option A) are essential for reducing inflammation, they act more slowly. Non-invasive positive pressure ventilation (Option C) is supportive but not first-line. Intravenous magnesium sulfate (Option D) is beneficial for severe exacerbations but secondary to beta-agonists. The immediate bronchodilation provided by beta-agonists directly addresses airway constriction, making Option B the most critical initial intervention to prevent respiratory failure.

Question 70: Correct Answer: C) Administer pancreatic enzyme replacement therapy with meals.
Rationale: Administering pancreatic enzyme replacement therapy is crucial post-Whipple due to reduced pancreatic function, aiding in nutrient absorption. Option A, TPN, is invasive and not first-line unless oral intake fails. Option B, a high-fat diet, may worsen malabsorption without enzymes. Option D, increasing simple carbohydrates, doesn't address fat malabsorption and can lead to hyperglycemia. Enzyme therapy directly targets the malabsorption issue by compensating for decreased endogenous enzyme production, making it the most effective initial intervention.

Question 71: Correct Answer: B) Tight blood pressure control with antihypertensives
Rationale: Tight blood pressure control is crucial in hemorrhagic stroke to prevent rebleeding and reduce intracranial pressure. Option A (thrombolytics) is contraindicated as it can worsen bleeding. Option C (anticoagulation) increases bleeding risk, and D (surgical evacuation) is considered based on hematoma size and location but isn't the first step. Controlling hypertension effectively reduces morbidity, aligning with contemporary guidelines and research emphasizing its importance in acute management to stabilize the patient and prevent further damage.

Question 72: Correct Answer: A) Administering intravenous fluids to maintain blood pressure
Rationale: Administering IV fluids is crucial to stabilize hemodynamics in acute renal trauma. While a CT scan (B) provides diagnostic clarity, it's secondary to stabilizing the patient. A Foley catheter (C) helps monitor output but doesn't address immediate stabilization needs. FAST (D) is useful for detecting free fluid but not specific for renal injuries. Prioritizing fluid resuscitation aligns with contemporary trauma protocols emphasizing hemodynamic stability as a primary intervention.

Question 73: Correct Answer: B) Elevating the head of the bed to 30 degrees
Rationale: Elevating the head of the bed to 30 degrees is an effective and immediate intervention to reduce ICP by promoting venous drainage from the brain. While hypertonic saline (Option A) can also reduce ICP, it requires careful monitoring and is not as immediate. Deep sedation (Option C) can help decrease metabolic demand but may not directly reduce ICP. Therapeutic hypothermia (Option D) is more applicable for post-cardiac arrest care rather than acute ICP management. Therefore, Option B is most appropriate given its immediacy and effectiveness in this context.

Question 74: Correct Answer: D) Thrombopoietin receptor agonists
Rationale: Thrombopoietin receptor agonists are recommended as a second-line treatment for ITP when patients do not respond adequately to corticosteroids. They help increase platelet production by stimulating the bone marrow. While IVIG (Option A) can be used for rapid platelet increase, it is not ideal for long-term management. Splenectomy (Option B) is effective but considered when medical treatments fail or are contraindicated. Rituximab (Option C) is another option but typically used if thrombopoietin receptor agonists are ineffective or unsuitable, making Option D the best choice given Lisa's scenario.

Question 75: Correct Answer: B) Sudden withdrawal

from social interactions and activities
Rationale: Sudden withdrawal from social interactions is a key indicator of psychological abuse, reflecting emotional distress. Option A suggests physical abuse due to visible injuries. Option C indicates neglect, as it involves failure to meet basic needs. Option D might imply either physical abuse or neglect but lacks specificity for psychological abuse. Psychological abuse often manifests as behavioral changes, making B the most relevant choice. Understanding these distinctions is crucial for clinical judgment in identifying and addressing different types of elder abuse effectively.

Question 76: Correct Answer: A) Initiation of broad-spectrum antibiotics
Rationale: Initiating broad-spectrum antibiotics promptly is crucial in reducing mortality in urosepsis, as it targets the underlying infection swiftly. While intravenous fluids (Option B) are vital for hemodynamic support, they do not address the infection directly. Monitoring urine output (Option C) is essential for assessing renal function but does not treat the infection. Blood glucose control (Option D) is important in managing sepsis-related metabolic disturbances but is not as immediate a priority as antibiotic therapy. Timely antibiotic administration is supported by contemporary research and recognized clinical guidelines.

Question 77: Correct Answer: C) Rapid progression of erythema with systemic symptoms
Rationale: Rapid progression of erythema with systemic symptoms such as fever or chills indicates a severe cellulitis infection that may lead to complications like sepsis, necessitating urgent care. Option A, localized erythema and warmth, is typical but not necessarily severe. Option B, purulent discharge, suggests possible abscess formation but isn't an immediate systemic threat. Option D, mild edema and tenderness, are common in cellulitis but not alarming for severity. The critical difference is the rapid spread and systemic involvement in option C, which requires prompt intervention.

Question 78: Correct Answer: B) Chronic Granulomatous Disease (CGD)
Rationale: Chronic Granulomatous Disease (CGD) is characterized by a defect in the NADPH oxidase enzyme, which impairs phagocytes' ability to produce reactive oxygen species necessary for killing certain pathogens. This distinguishes it from SCID, which involves defects in T and B cell development, CVID, which features hypogammaglobulinemia due to B cell dysfunction, and Hyper-IgM Syndrome, where there is a class-switching defect in immunoglobulin production. The key difference lies in the specific enzymatic deficiency affecting phagocyte function in CGD.

Question 79: Correct Answer: A) Administer intravenous atropine.
Rationale: Atropine is the first-line treatment for bradycardia, particularly if it's causing hypotension post-TAVR. It acts by increasing heart rate and improving cardiac output. While increasing fluids (Option B) might help hypotension, it won't address bradycardia directly. Transcutaneous pacing (Option C) is more invasive and typically considered if atropine fails. Norepinephrine (Option D) is used for persistent hypotension but isn't first-line for bradycardia-induced hypotension. Thus, atropine directly targets the root cause, making it the most appropriate initial intervention in this scenario.

Question 80: Correct Answer: B) Observation and monitoring
Rationale: First-degree AV block is typically benign and asymptomatic, often requiring only observation unless symptomatic or progressing. Option A (atropine) is used for symptomatic bradycardia. Option C (pacemaker therapy) is reserved for higher-degree blocks or symptomatic patients. Option D (beta-blockers) can worsen conduction delay, making it inappropriate in this context. Monitoring ensures no progression to more severe blocks while avoiding unnecessary interventions.

Question 81: Correct Answer: A) Anastomotic leak
Rationale: An anastomotic leak is a critical complication following a Whipple procedure, especially in the first 48 hours post-surgery. It can lead to severe infection and sepsis, requiring immediate intervention. While pancreatic fistulas and delayed gastric emptying are significant complications, they typically manifest later in the postoperative period. Bile duct obstruction is less common immediately after surgery. Therefore, close monitoring for signs of anastomotic leakage, such as changes in vital signs or abdominal pain, is essential to ensure prompt treatment and improve patient outcomes.

Question 82: Correct Answer: B) Surgical decompression through laparotomy
Rationale: Surgical decompression through laparotomy is the most definitive treatment for ACS as it directly relieves intra-abdominal pressure, preventing organ dysfunction. While diuretics (A) and fluid optimization (C) may help manage symptoms, they do not address the primary cause of pressure. Neuromuscular blockers (D) might reduce tension temporarily but do not resolve underlying compartment syndrome. Thus, surgical intervention remains the gold standard in severe cases where immediate pressure relief is crucial.

Question 83: Correct Answer: B) Administration of low molecular weight heparin (LMWH)
Rationale: Administration of LMWH is widely recognized as a primary intervention for DVT prevention in immobilized patients due to its anticoagulant properties. While early ambulation (A) and pneumatic devices (C) are beneficial, they are adjuncts rather than primary interventions. Elevation (D) helps with edema but not specifically DVT. LMWH is supported by contemporary research as the most effective standalone measure, aligning with evidence-based practices in critical care settings.

Question 84: Correct Answer: C) Papilledema
Rationale: Papilledema, the swelling of the optic disc, is a classic sign of increased intracranial pressure often associated with space-occupying lesions. Unlike bradycardia (A) and hypertension (B), which can be secondary responses, papilledema directly indicates elevated intracranial pressure. Tachypnea (D) might occur in response to other systemic issues but is not specific to intracranial pressure changes. Papilledema's direct link to pressure changes makes it a more reliable indicator compared to other options.

Question 85: Correct Answer: B) Acetaminophen
Rationale: Acetaminophen is the most common cause of drug-induced acute liver failure, particularly in overdose situations. It is metabolized in the liver, and excessive doses lead to the accumulation of a toxic metabolite causing hepatocellular damage. Ibuprofen (A) and aspirin (C), though they can cause liver issues, are more often associated with gastrointestinal or renal complications. Metformin (D) primarily affects lactic acid levels rather than directly causing hepatic failure. The critical distinction lies in acetaminophen's unique metabolic pathway leading to hepatotoxicity when overdosed, unlike the other options.

Question 86: Correct Answer: B) Increased serum ammonia levels

Rationale: Increased serum ammonia levels are most indicative of hepatic encephalopathy in cirrhosis. Ammonia, a byproduct of protein metabolism, accumulates due to impaired liver function and contributes to neurological symptoms. While elevated bilirubin and decreased albumin indicate liver dysfunction, they are not specific for encephalopathy. Elevated alkaline phosphatase suggests biliary obstruction or bone disease rather than encephalopathy. Thus, increased ammonia is the key marker distinguishing hepatic encephalopathy from other complications of cirrhosis.

Question 87: Correct Answer: B) Assessing neurological status to detect potential stroke symptoms
Rationale: Post-endarterectomy, assessing neurological status is crucial due to the risk of stroke from emboli or hypoperfusion. While monitoring for bleeding (A) and maintaining blood pressure (D) are important, they are secondary to detecting early signs of neurological compromise. Ensuring hydration (C) is less directly related to immediate postoperative complications compared to neurological assessment. Detecting changes in neurological status allows timely intervention, reducing morbidity associated with cerebrovascular events.

Question 88: Correct Answer: D) Non-invasive ventilation
Rationale: Non-invasive ventilation (NIV) is the most effective intervention for reducing mortality during COPD exacerbations. It improves gas exchange and reduces the need for intubation. Long-term oxygen therapy (A) is beneficial in chronic management but not specifically during exacerbations. Inhaled corticosteroids (B) help reduce inflammation but don't significantly impact acute mortality rates. Pulmonary rehabilitation (C) improves quality of life and exercise capacity over time but is not an immediate intervention for acute exacerbations. Therefore, NIV stands out as the critical intervention during acute episodes.

Question 89: Correct Answer: C) Implementing early mobilization and physical therapy
Rationale: Early mobilization and physical therapy are proven to reduce the incidence of delirium by enhancing cognitive function and reducing hospital stay. While adequate hydration and nutrition (Option B) are important, they are less directly linked to delirium prevention. Prophylactic antipsychotics (Option A) can have adverse effects without clear evidence of benefit. Continuous sedation (Option D) increases delirium risk by impairing cognitive function. Thus, Option C is most aligned with contemporary research on delirium prevention strategies.

Question 90: Correct Answer: A) Lisinopril
Rationale: Lisinopril, an ACE inhibitor, can cause AKI by reducing glomerular filtration pressure through vasodilation of the efferent arterioles, particularly in patients with compromised renal perfusion. Amlodipine (a calcium channel blocker), Hydrochlorothiazide (a thiazide diuretic), and Metoprolol (a beta-blocker) are less likely to cause AKI in this context. Amlodipine primarily affects vascular smooth muscle without significant renal impact. Hydrochlorothiazide may alter electrolytes but typically doesn't induce AKI. Metoprolol affects cardiac output without directly impacting renal function like ACE inhibitors do.

Question 91: Correct Answer: B) Begin rapid infusion of isotonic crystalloid fluids.
Rationale: The immediate priority in managing acute GI hemorrhage is to stabilize the patient's hemodynamic status, typically achieved by administering isotonic crystalloid fluids to address hypovolemia and maintain perfusion. While PPIs (A) help reduce gastric acid secretion, they do not stabilize hemodynamics. Vasopressors (C) are used if fluid resuscitation fails to restore blood pressure. Blood transfusions (D) are crucial but follow initial fluid resuscitation to correct volume deficit. Thus, option B is vital for immediate stabilization before further interventions.

Question 92: Correct Answer: A) Passive range of motion exercises
Rationale: Passive range of motion exercises are crucial in preventing muscle atrophy as they help maintain joint flexibility and stimulate circulation without requiring active patient participation. Muscle relaxants (B) may reduce spasticity but do not prevent atrophy. Heat therapy (C) can alleviate discomfort but does not directly address muscle preservation. High-protein nutritional support (D) aids in muscle repair but cannot prevent atrophy alone. Thus, option A is the most comprehensive approach to maintaining musculoskeletal function during immobility.

Question 93: Correct Answer: B) Tracheal deviation away from the affected side
Rationale: Tracheal deviation away from the affected side is a hallmark sign of tension pneumothorax, caused by increased intrathoracic pressure. This pressure shift pushes the trachea toward the unaffected side. While diminished breath sounds (A), hyperresonance (C), and jugular venous distension (D) can be present in tension pneumothorax, they are not as definitive as tracheal deviation. Diminished breath sounds and hyperresonance may occur in other conditions like simple pneumothorax, and jugular venous distension can be seen in cardiac tamponade, making option B the most specific indicator.

Question 94: Correct Answer: C) Liver failure
Rationale: The liver synthesizes most clotting factors; thus, liver failure often results in coagulopathy due to reduced production of these factors, explaining John's prolonged PT and PTT. While Vitamin K deficiency can also prolong PT, it typically does not affect fibrinogen levels. DIC involves consumption of clotting factors and platelets but is less common in isolated liver disease without sepsis or trauma. Hemophilia A is characterized by a deficiency in factor VIII, leading to bleeding but not typically associated with liver function impairment.

Question 95: Correct Answer: D) Pale, cool skin distal to the burn injury
Rationale: Pale, cool skin distal to the burn injury suggests compromised circulation and potential compartment syndrome, requiring urgent intervention. Option A, decreased capillary refill, can be concerning but isn't as immediately critical as compromised distal circulation. Option B, presence of eschar, is expected in burns and not an immediate concern unless it leads to constriction. Option C, increased blister formation, indicates ongoing damage but does not imply immediate vascular compromise like option D. Immediate action is necessary to prevent further complications such as tissue necrosis.

Question 96: Correct Answer: B) Nissen Fundoplication
Rationale: Nissen Fundoplication is the preferred surgical procedure for treating refractory GERD, as it involves wrapping the gastric fundus around the lower esophagus to strengthen the sphincter. While Roux-en-Y Gastric Bypass (A) can also reduce GERD symptoms, it is primarily a weight-loss surgery. Partial Gastrectomy (C) and Heller Myotomy (D) address other conditions like peptic ulcers and achalasia, respectively. The key difference lies in Nissen Fundoplication's specific design to prevent acid reflux, distinguishing it from these other

procedures.
Question 97: Correct Answer: B) Presence of ileocecal valve
Rationale: The presence of the ileocecal valve is crucial in determining the success of an ileal resection as it regulates the flow between the small and large intestines, aiding nutrient absorption and preventing bacterial overgrowth. While the length of remaining ileum (A) and extent of bowel adaptation (D) are important, they are secondary to maintaining this anatomical structure. Nutritional status (C) influences recovery but does not directly impact surgical success. Thus, preserving the ileocecal valve is prioritized for optimal postoperative outcomes.

Question 98: Correct Answer: B) Pulsus paradoxus
Rationale: Pulsus paradoxus is a key indicator of cardiac tamponade, a life-threatening complication of pericardial effusion. It involves an exaggerated decrease in systolic blood pressure during inspiration. While elevated jugular venous pressure (A), distant heart sounds (C), and hypotension (D) are associated with cardiac tamponade, they are less specific than pulsus paradoxus. Jugular venous pressure and distant heart sounds can occur in other conditions, while hypotension is a late sign. Therefore, pulsus paradoxus is the most immediate and specific sign necessitating urgent intervention.

Question 99: Correct Answer: C) Noradrenergic system
Rationale: The noradrenergic system is primarily implicated in PTSD, especially concerning hyperarousal symptoms. This is due to its role in stress response and arousal regulation, often leading to heightened vigilance and anxiety. While the serotonergic system (Option B) influences mood and anxiety, it is not as directly linked to hyperarousal as the noradrenergic system. The dopaminergic system (Option A) relates more to reward and motivation processes, whereas the GABAergic system (Option D) is associated with inhibitory control but not specifically with PTSD's hyperarousal symptoms.

Question 100: Correct Answer: A) Regularly turning the patient every two hours
Rationale: Regularly turning the patient every two hours is crucial for preventing pressure injuries by redistributing pressure and enhancing circulation. While high-density foam mattresses (Option B) and moisture-wicking creams (Option C) support pressure injury prevention, they are supplementary. Adequate protein intake (Option D) aids in healing but doesn't directly prevent pressure injuries. Therefore, frequent repositioning remains the primary and most effective intervention.

Question 101: Correct Answer: B) Early surgical intervention via the Kasai procedure
Rationale: The Kasai procedure, performed early, is crucial for improving bile flow and delaying liver transplantation in Biliary Atresia. While corticosteroids (A) and ursodeoxycholic acid (C) may support treatment, they do not address the underlying obstruction. Nutritional support (D) is essential but secondary to restoring bile flow. Early surgery optimizes liver function and growth, distinguishing it from other supportive therapies.

Question 102: Correct Answer: B) Enhanced gluconeogenesis due to elevated cortisol levels
Rationale: Stress-induced hyperglycemia in critically ill patients is primarily driven by enhanced gluconeogenesis, a process intensified by elevated cortisol levels. Cortisol, a stress hormone, promotes glucose production in the liver, contributing significantly to hyperglycemia. Option A is incorrect as stress typically decreases insulin secretion. Option C is misleading because stress increases glucagon secretion. Option D is incorrect since stress reduces insulin sensitivity, not increasing peripheral glucose uptake. Understanding these mechanisms helps in managing hyperglycemia effectively in critical care settings.

Question 103: Correct Answer: C) Comprehensive risk factor assessment and management
Rationale: The most critical initial step in managing TIA is comprehensive risk factor assessment and management. This approach identifies modifiable risks, such as hypertension, diabetes, and lifestyle factors, crucial for preventing subsequent strokes. While options A and B involve treatments that might be considered, they are not immediate priorities for TIA. Option D is a surgical intervention reserved for specific cases with significant carotid stenosis. Therefore, identifying and managing risk factors is pivotal in reducing long-term stroke risk.

Question 104: Correct Answer: D) Substance P
Rationale: Substance P is a key neurotransmitter involved in transmitting pain signals to the central nervous system. It plays a crucial role in pain perception and inflammation. While dopamine (A), serotonin (B), and norepinephrine (C) are neurotransmitters that can influence mood and pain indirectly, they are not primarily responsible for direct pain signal modulation like Substance P. Dopamine is more related to reward pathways, serotonin to mood regulation, and norepinephrine to arousal and alertness. Thus, understanding these distinctions is critical for effective clinical judgment in managing musculoskeletal pain.

Question 105: Correct Answer: B) Biatrial enlargement with normal ventricular wall thickness
Rationale: Restrictive cardiomyopathy is characterized by impaired diastolic filling and reduced ventricular compliance, often leading to biatrial enlargement due to increased atrial pressure. Option A describes hypertrophic cardiomyopathy, while C suggests dilated cardiomyopathy, both unrelated to restrictive pathology. Option D indicates hypertrophic obstructive cardiomyopathy. The correct answer, B, aligns with restrictive physiology where ventricles are stiff but not thickened, causing atrial dilation due to pressure overload. This differentiation is crucial for accurate diagnosis and management in clinical practice.

Question 106: Correct Answer: B) Diabetes Insipidus
Rationale: Diabetes Insipidus (DI) is characterized by hypernatremia, high serum osmolality, and low urine osmolality due to insufficient ADH or renal insensitivity to ADH. SIADH would show hyponatremia and concentrated urine. Hyperaldosteronism typically presents with hypokalemia and hypertension rather than these symptoms. Addison's Disease would present with hyponatremia, hyperkalemia, and hypotension. The key indicators for DI in this scenario are the combination of high serum sodium and low urine osmolality, confirming the diagnosis over other conditions.

Question 107: Correct Answer: B) Perform needle decompression in the second intercostal space, midclavicular line
Rationale: Needle decompression is the immediate intervention for tension pneumothorax to rapidly relieve pressure. Administering oxygen (Option A) supports breathing but doesn't relieve pressure. Chest tube insertion (Option C) follows decompression for definitive treatment but isn't immediate. Mechanical ventilation with PEEP (Option D) could worsen tension by increasing intrathoracic pressure. Thus, Option B is critical to prevent cardiovascular collapse by quickly decompressing trapped air.

Question 108: Correct Answer: B) The patient's

neurological status
Rationale: The patient's neurological status is paramount in deciding surgical intervention for a subdural hematoma. While size (A) and midline shift (D) are important, they are evaluated alongside clinical symptoms. A patient with significant neurological deterioration may require urgent surgery regardless of hematoma size. Age (C) affects prognosis but not immediate surgical decisions. Thus, neurological status provides a direct assessment of brain function and potential for recovery, making it the most critical factor.

Question 109: Correct Answer: B) Time since symptom onset
Rationale: The eligibility for thrombolytic therapy primarily hinges on the time elapsed since stroke symptoms began, ideally within 4.5 hours. Although blood pressure and glucose levels are crucial for management, they are not primary exclusion criteria. Previous stroke history influences risk assessment but does not directly determine immediate eligibility like time does. Understanding this time window is essential, as it directly impacts treatment efficacy and patient outcomes, aligning with current guidelines and research in acute stroke management.

Question 110: Correct Answer: B) Lorazepam
Rationale: Lorazepam is the first-line treatment for status epilepticus due to its rapid onset and efficacy in terminating seizures. It acts quickly compared to Phenytoin, which is used for long-term control and not rapid intervention. Valproic Acid is effective but not preferred for immediate seizure cessation. Levetiracetam is used for maintenance therapy, not acute management. The preference for Lorazepam stems from its benzodiazepine class, providing fast action essential in critical care scenarios, unlike the slower-acting alternatives listed.

Question 111: Correct Answer: C) Provide a calm and familiar environment with continuous orientation cues.
Rationale: Providing a calm and familiar environment with continuous orientation cues is the most appropriate intervention for Mrs. Thompson's agitation due to dementia. This approach addresses confusion by reducing anxiety through environmental familiarity, which aligns with dementia care principles focusing on non-pharmacological strategies. Option A (physical restraints) can increase agitation and risk of injury. Option B (antipsychotics) may have adverse effects in elderly patients with dementia. Option D (increased sedation) could exacerbate confusion and reduce cognitive function, contrary to maintaining alertness and orientation in dementia care.

Question 112: Correct Answer: B) Low tidal volume ventilation
Rationale: Low tidal volume ventilation is the most effective strategy for improving oxygenation and minimizing ventilator-induced lung injury in ARDS patients. It reduces alveolar overdistension and barotrauma. While permissive hypercapnia (C) can be used adjunctively to allow low tidal volumes, it does not directly improve oxygenation. High-frequency oscillatory ventilation (D) may improve oxygenation but lacks consistent evidence of reduced mortality. High tidal volume ventilation (A) is contraindicated as it increases the risk of lung injury. Thus, low tidal volume ventilation remains the preferred approach based on current evidence and guidelines.

Question 113: Correct Answer: D) Administer insulin and glucose intravenously
Rationale: Administering insulin and glucose is effective for rapidly driving potassium back into cells, temporarily reducing serum potassium levels. Calcium gluconate stabilizes cardiac membranes but doesn't lower potassium. Sodium bicarbonate can shift potassium intracellularly but is less rapid. CRRT is useful for long-term management but not immediate correction. Insulin/glucose offers the quickest reduction in serum potassium, crucial in acute settings like Emily's severe hyperkalemia and metabolic acidosis.

Question 114: Correct Answer: C) Mindfulness-Based Stress Reduction (MBSR)
Rationale: Mindfulness-Based Stress Reduction (MBSR) is recognized for its effectiveness in reducing anxiety by promoting awareness and acceptance, particularly beneficial for patients with neurological disorders. While CBT (Option A) is a well-established method for anxiety management, it may not be as immediately effective in acute settings. Benzodiazepines (Option B), though effective short-term, can lead to dependency and adverse effects. Progressive Muscle Relaxation (Option D) aids in physical tension reduction but lacks the comprehensive benefits of mindfulness practices. MBSR uniquely combines mental and physical relaxation, making it superior in this context.

Question 115: Correct Answer: D) Incentive spirometry
Rationale: Incentive spirometry is crucial for preventing atelectasis and enhancing lung expansion post-lobectomy. While early ambulation (Option A) aids in general recovery, it does not directly target pulmonary function. Prophylactic antibiotics (Option B) prevent infections but do not address pulmonary complications. Fluid restriction (Option C) manages fluid balance but is less effective in promoting lung expansion compared to incentive spirometry. Thus, incentive spirometry remains the most direct intervention for maintaining optimal respiratory function post-surgery.

Question 116: Correct Answer: D) Prepare for fasciotomy
Rationale: Fasciotomy is the definitive treatment for compartment syndrome, aimed at relieving pressure and preventing irreversible muscle and nerve damage. While administering analgesics (Option A) addresses pain, it does not address underlying pressure. Elevating the limb (Option B) can worsen perfusion by reducing arterial flow, contrary to treatment goals. Ice application (Option C) might temporarily reduce swelling but doesn't alleviate pressure within the compartment. Thus, preparing for fasciotomy (Option D) is essential as it directly resolves the compartmental pressure issue.

Question 117: Correct Answer: B) Initiating intravenous fluid replacement with isotonic saline
Rationale: Initiating intravenous fluid replacement with isotonic saline is critical in HHS management to address severe dehydration and restore intravascular volume. While insulin administration (Option A) is essential, it follows rehydration. Correcting electrolytes (Option C) and monitoring for cerebral edema (Option D) are also crucial but secondary to fluid resuscitation. The primary focus on fluids helps stabilize hemodynamics and improve renal perfusion, which are foundational before other interventions can be effectively implemented.

Question 118: Correct Answer: B) Hyperosmolar hyperglycemic state (HHS)
Rationale: The presentation of extreme hyperglycemia, high serum osmolality, and absence of significant ketonemia suggests HHS. Unlike DKA, HHS is characterized by minimal ketone production due to some residual insulin activity. Lactic acidosis typically presents with elevated lactate levels and metabolic acidosis, which

are not indicated here. Hypoglycemic encephalopathy involves low blood glucose levels, contrary to Emily's elevated glucose. The key distinction is the lack of ketosis in HHS compared to DKA, making B the correct choice.

Question 119: Correct Answer: B) CT Angiography
Rationale: CT Angiography is the preferred initial diagnostic test for mesenteric ischemia due to its rapidity and accuracy in visualizing blood flow in mesenteric vessels. An abdominal X-ray (Option A) might show non-specific signs like bowel distension but lacks specificity. MRI (Option C) provides detailed images but is not typically used acutely due to time constraints. Ultrasound (Option D) can assess blood flow but is less effective for diagnosing mesenteric ischemia compared to CT Angiography. Thus, CT Angiography is optimal for quick and precise diagnosis in acute settings.

Question 120: Correct Answer: D) Glomerular filtration rate (GFR)
Rationale: GFR is the most accurate indicator of renal function recovery as it directly measures kidney filtration capacity. While serum creatinine (A) and BUN (B) are commonly used, they are influenced by factors like muscle mass and hydration status. Urine output (C), though useful for assessing acute changes, does not reflect true renal function recovery. GFR provides a comprehensive assessment by evaluating how well kidneys filter blood, making it superior in determining long-term recovery compared to the other options.

Question 121: Correct Answer: B) Sublingual Nitroglycerin
Rationale: Sublingual Nitroglycerin is most effective for rapid preload reduction in acute pulmonary edema by causing venodilation, which decreases cardiac filling pressures. Although intravenous furosemide (Option A) is used to reduce fluid overload, it acts slower than nitroglycerin. Intravenous morphine (Option C) can reduce anxiety and preload but is less effective than nitroglycerin. Dobutamine (Option D) increases cardiac output but doesn't primarily target preload reduction. Thus, nitroglycerin's rapid action on venous capacitance makes it the preferred initial choice in acute settings.

Question 122: Correct Answer: C) Low glucose concentration in CSF
Rationale: Low glucose concentration in CSF is a hallmark of bacterial meningitis due to bacterial consumption and impaired transport. While elevated protein levels (A), presence of neutrophils (B), and high opening pressure (D) are also associated with bacterial meningitis, they can be seen in viral infections too. Neutrophilic predominance may occur early in viral infections, and elevated protein can be nonspecific. However, significant hypoglycorrhachia is more distinctively linked to bacterial etiology, making it a key differentiator between bacterial and viral meningitis in adults.

Question 123: Correct Answer: A) Streptococcus pneumoniae
Rationale: Streptococcus pneumoniae is the most common cause of bacterial meningitis in adults, primarily due to its prevalence and virulence. Neisseria meningitidis is also a significant cause but is more common in adolescents and young adults. Haemophilus influenzae has decreased in incidence due to vaccination. Listeria monocytogenes typically affects immunocompromised individuals and the elderly. Understanding these distinctions helps clinicians prioritize diagnostic and therapeutic approaches based on patient demographics and clinical presentation.

Question 124: Correct Answer: C) Ensuring adequate cerebral perfusion pressure
Rationale: Ensuring adequate cerebral perfusion pressure (CPP) is crucial to prevent secondary brain injury by maintaining sufficient blood flow and oxygen delivery to the brain. While maintaining normothermia (A) is important, it does not directly address CPP. Prophylactic anticonvulsants (B) may prevent seizures but do not influence CPP. Early surgical evacuation (D) can be necessary but is contingent on specific clinical indications and does not universally apply like maintaining CPP. Thus, option C is the most comprehensive intervention for preventing further neurological damage in IVH patients.

Question 125: Correct Answer: B) Aspirin
Rationale: Aspirin is crucial in reducing mortality for NSTEMI patients due to its antiplatelet effects, which prevent further thrombus formation. Nitroglycerin (Option A) alleviates chest pain but does not impact mortality. Clopidogrel (Option C) is beneficial but used adjunctively with aspirin. Beta-blockers (Option D) are important for heart rate control and reducing myocardial oxygen demand but are not as directly linked to mortality reduction as aspirin. Thus, aspirin's role in inhibiting platelet aggregation makes it the most critical medication for reducing mortality in this context.

CCRN Exam Practice Questions [SET 2]

Question 1: A 45-year-old patient named Sarah is admitted to the critical care unit following a hip fracture surgery. Over the past week, Sarah has exhibited signs of persistent sadness, loss of interest in activities she once enjoyed, and difficulty concentrating. As her care nurse, which intervention is most appropriate to address Sarah's depressive symptoms while considering her current physical recovery?
A) Encourage Sarah to participate in physical therapy sessions.
B) Refer Sarah to a psychiatrist for medication evaluation.
C) Arrange for daily visits from a hospital chaplain.
D) Facilitate group therapy sessions with other orthopedic patients.

Question 2: John, a 65-year-old male with a history of smoking and occupational exposure to dust, presents with progressive dyspnea and a dry cough. High-resolution CT reveals bilateral reticular opacities predominantly in the lower lobes. Which of the following interventions is most likely to slow the progression of his pulmonary fibrosis?
A) Long-term oxygen therapy
B) Corticosteroid therapy
C) Nintedanib treatment
D) Pulmonary rehabilitation

Question 3: In the management of Type 2 Diabetes Mellitus, which pharmacological agent primarily enhances insulin sensitivity in peripheral tissues?
A) Metformin
B) Sulfonylureas
C) DPP-4 inhibitors
D) Insulin

Question 4: A 58-year-old patient named Mr. Thompson is recovering from a Whipple procedure (pancreaticoduodenectomy) due to pancreatic cancer. On the third postoperative day, he develops tachycardia, hypotension, and abdominal pain. As his critical care nurse, what is the most likely complication you should suspect?
A) Pancreatic fistula
B) Delayed gastric emptying
C) Hemorrhage
D) Anastomotic leak

Question 5: John, a 55-year-old male with a history of Type 2 Diabetes Mellitus, presents to the emergency department with confusion and lethargy. His blood glucose level is measured at 650 mg/dL. Considering his condition, which of the following initial treatments is most appropriate?
A) Administer intravenous insulin
B) Administer oral hypoglycemic agents
C) Provide oral glucose
D) Initiate fluid resuscitation with isotonic saline

Question 6: A 45-year-old patient named John presents to the emergency department with a mid-shaft femur fracture following a motor vehicle accident. The attending nurse must prioritize interventions. Which of the following actions should be the nurse's first priority in managing John's condition?
A) Administer intravenous fluids to prevent hypovolemic shock.
B) Apply a traction splint to stabilize the fracture.
C) Monitor vital signs for any signs of neurovascular compromise.
D) Provide pain relief through prescribed analgesics.

Question 7: Which of the following is the most definitive method to diagnose portal hypertension in a patient with suspected hepatic failure?
A) Measurement of hepatic venous pressure gradient (HVPG)
B) Doppler ultrasound of the portal vein
C) Serum-ascites albumin gradient (SAAG)
D) Liver biopsy

Question 8: A 68-year-old patient named Mr. Thompson is admitted to the ICU with a diagnosis of septic shock. On the second day, he exhibits fluctuating levels of consciousness and disorganized thinking. As a critical care nurse, what is the most appropriate intervention to manage his delirium?
A) Administer low-dose haloperidol
B) Implement early mobilization strategies
C) Increase sedation to promote rest
D) Provide continuous reorientation

Question 9: In the context of aortic aneurysms, which of the following diagnostic tests is most sensitive for detecting an asymptomatic abdominal aortic aneurysm in a high-risk patient?
A) Abdominal ultrasound
B) Computed tomography (CT) scan
C) Magnetic resonance imaging (MRI)
D) Chest X-ray

Question 10: Emily, a 68-year-old patient with a history of hypertension and type 2 diabetes, is admitted to the ICU following hip surgery. She becomes disoriented and agitated on the second postoperative day. Which intervention is most effective in managing her delirium?
A) Administering low-dose haloperidol
B) Increasing environmental stimuli
C) Encouraging family visitation
D) Providing frequent reorientation

Question 11: In the context of critical care, which of the following hormones is primarily responsible for regulating serum calcium levels through its actions on bone, kidney, and intestine?
A) Calcitonin
B) Parathyroid hormone (PTH)
C) Vitamin D
D) Thyroid-stimulating hormone (TSH)

Question 12: A 65-year-old male patient named Mr. Johnson presents to the emergency department with severe muscle weakness, confusion, and an irregular heartbeat. His laboratory results reveal a serum potassium level of 2.3 mEq/L. Which immediate intervention should the critical care nurse prioritize to address this life-threatening electrolyte imbalance?
A) Administer oral potassium supplements.
B) Initiate a potassium-sparing diuretic.
C) Administer intravenous potassium chloride.
D) Provide dietary potassium-rich foods.

Question 13: Mrs. Thompson, a 78-year-old patient with a history of osteoporosis and recent hip replacement surgery, is being assessed for fall risk in the critical care unit. Which intervention should be prioritized to minimize her risk of falling while maintaining her mobility?
A) Encourage independent walking with a cane.
B) Implement scheduled toileting rounds every two hours.
C) Use bed alarms to alert staff when she attempts to get up.
D) Provide physical therapy sessions focused on balance exercises.

Question 14: In the management of a patient with Acute Coronary Syndrome (ACS), which biomarker is most specific for myocardial injury and should be prioritized in diagnostic evaluation?
A) Creatine Kinase-MB (CK-MB)
B) Myoglobin
C) Troponin I
D) Lactate Dehydrogenase (LDH)

Question 15: A 55-year-old male patient, Mr. Johnson, with a history of type 2 diabetes, is admitted to the ICU with confusion and diaphoresis. His blood glucose level is recorded at 45 mg/dL. After administering IV dextrose, what is the next most appropriate step in managing his acute hypoglycemia?
A) Administer glucagon injection.
B) Reassess blood glucose in 15 minutes.
C) Start continuous IV insulin infusion.
D) Provide a high-protein snack.

Question 16: Which of the following brain tumor types is most commonly associated with the production of hormones, leading to endocrine disturbances in patients?
A) Meningioma
B) Glioblastoma
C) Pituitary adenoma
D) Medulloblastoma

Question 17: Sarah, a 45-year-old patient, is recovering from abdominal surgery and presents with a surgical wound that shows signs of delayed healing. Her medical history includes diabetes mellitus and peripheral vascular disease. As her critical care nurse, what is the most appropriate intervention to promote wound healing in this scenario?
A) Apply negative pressure wound therapy
B) Increase caloric intake with high-protein supplements
C) Administer prophylactic antibiotics
D) Implement strict blood glucose control

Question 18: In the context of wound management in critical care, which of the following factors is most likely to impair wound healing in a patient with diabetes mellitus?
A) Increased collagen synthesis
B) Enhanced angiogenesis
C) Impaired leukocyte function
D) Reduced glucose levels

Question 19: A 55-year-old patient named Mr. Thompson is admitted to the ICU with severe hyperglycemia. His blood glucose level is 650 mg/dL, and he presents with polyuria, polydipsia, and altered mental status. As a critical care nurse, you need to prioritize interventions. Which of the following is the most appropriate initial intervention?
A) Administer intravenous insulin infusion.
B) Initiate oral hypoglycemic agents.
C) Start an intravenous fluid bolus with normal saline.
D) Begin potassium replacement therapy.

Question 20: A 68-year-old patient named Mr. Thompson is admitted to the ICU with severe dehydration, altered mental status, and a blood glucose level of 980 mg/dL. His laboratory results show no significant ketonemia. As the critical care nurse, which initial intervention is most appropriate to address Mr. Thompson's condition of Hyperosmolar Hyperglycemic State (HHS)?
A) Administer regular insulin intravenously to rapidly decrease blood glucose levels.
B) Initiate aggressive fluid resuscitation with isotonic saline to correct dehydration.
C) Start potassium replacement therapy to prevent hypokalemia.
D) Begin bicarbonate infusion to correct potential metabolic acidosis.

Question 21: Emily, a 68-year-old female patient with a history of osteoarthritis, is admitted to the critical care unit following a hip replacement surgery. During her recovery, she experiences significant difficulty in ambulating and performing daily activities. As her nurse, what is the most appropriate initial intervention to address Emily's functional mobility issues?
A) Encourage independent ambulation without assistive devices.
B) Implement a physical therapy regimen focusing on passive range of motion exercises.
C) Provide a walker and educate Emily on its use for ambulation support.
D) Administer analgesics before any physical activity to manage pain.

Question 22: In managing a patient with Type 1 Diabetes Mellitus in a critical care setting, which of the following interventions is most critical to prevent diabetic ketoacidosis (DKA)?
A) Administering regular insulin subcutaneously every 4 hours
B) Monitoring blood glucose levels every 2 hours
C) Administering intravenous insulin infusion
D) Providing a high-carbohydrate diet

Question 23: A 45-year-old patient named John presents to the emergency department with acute liver failure symptoms, including jaundice, coagulopathy, and hepatic encephalopathy. His medical history reveals recent use of over-the-counter medications for a cold. In managing fulminant hepatitis, which immediate intervention is most critical to improve John's prognosis?
A) Initiate high-dose corticosteroid therapy
B) Administer intravenous N-acetylcysteine
C) Start broad-spectrum antibiotics
D) Perform an urgent liver biopsy

Question 24: John, a 45-year-old male, presents to the emergency department after a motor vehicle accident with severe left-sided chest pain and difficulty breathing. A chest X-ray confirms a fractured rib on the left side. As a critical care nurse, what is the most appropriate initial intervention to manage John's respiratory status?
A) Administer high-flow oxygen therapy.
B) Initiate non-invasive positive pressure ventilation (NIPPV).
C) Encourage deep breathing exercises and use of an incentive spirometer.
D) Position the patient in a semi-Fowler's position.

Question 25: In the context of neurosurgery, which of the following is the primary purpose of performing burr holes in a patient with a suspected subdural hematoma?
A) To relieve intracranial pressure by draining cerebrospinal

fluid.
B) To provide access for insertion of a ventricular catheter.
C) To evacuate accumulated blood and relieve pressure on the brain.
D) To facilitate biopsy of brain tissue for diagnostic purposes.

Question 26: John, a 68-year-old male with a long history of smoking, presents with worsening shortness of breath and a chronic cough. On examination, you note decreased breath sounds and hyper-resonance on percussion. A chest X-ray reveals flattened diaphragms and increased anterior-posterior diameter. Which intervention is most appropriate to improve his respiratory function?
A) Prescribe inhaled corticosteroids
B) Initiate supplemental oxygen therapy
C) Recommend pulmonary rehabilitation
D) Start long-acting beta-agonists

Question 27: In the context of critical care, which of the following interventions is most effective in managing delirium in a patient with mixed musculoskeletal and neurological issues?
A) Continuous sedation with benzodiazepines
B) Early mobilization and physical therapy
C) Use of antipsychotic medications
D) Implementation of a sleep hygiene protocol

Question 28: Which of the following clinical findings is most indicative of acute mesenteric ischemia in a critical care setting?
A) Sudden onset of severe abdominal pain with minimal physical examination findings
B) Gradual onset of abdominal pain with localized tenderness
C) Abdominal distension with rebound tenderness
D) Presence of bloody diarrhea with fever

Question 29: In patients with Chronic Kidney Disease (CKD), which of the following laboratory findings is most indicative of a progression to end-stage renal disease (ESRD)?
A) Elevated serum creatinine levels
B) Increased blood urea nitrogen (BUN)
C) Decreased glomerular filtration rate (GFR)
D) Hyperkalemia

Question 30: A 45-year-old patient named John presents to the emergency department with acute onset of fever, headache, neck stiffness, and photophobia. He has a history of recent travel to an area with known viral outbreaks. As a critical care nurse, you are tasked with identifying the most likely viral cause of his symptoms. Which viral infection should be suspected given the neurological presentation?
A) Herpes Simplex Virus (HSV) Encephalitis
B) West Nile Virus Meningitis
C) Cytomegalovirus (CMV) Encephalitis
D) Epstein-Barr Virus (EBV) Encephalitis

Question 31: John, a 35-year-old male with a history of depression, presents to the emergency department expressing feelings of hopelessness and stating he has been considering suicide. As his critical care nurse, which initial intervention is most appropriate to ensure John's safety and address his suicidal ideation?
A) Conduct a thorough psychiatric assessment to evaluate John's mental status.
B) Immediately initiate one-on-one observation to prevent self-harm.
C) Administer prescribed antidepressant medication to stabilize mood.
D) Refer John to outpatient psychiatric services for follow-up care.

Question 32: In the management of acute pancreatitis, which of the following is considered the most reliable indicator for assessing the severity of the condition within the first 48 hours?
A) Serum amylase levels
B) Serum lipase levels
C) Ranson's criteria
D) C-reactive protein (CRP) levels

Question 33: In the context of acute abdominal trauma, which of the following diagnostic methods is considered most reliable for identifying free intraperitoneal fluid in a hemodynamically unstable patient?
A) Focused Assessment with Sonography for Trauma (FAST)
B) Diagnostic Peritoneal Lavage (DPL)
C) Computed Tomography (CT) Scan
D) Magnetic Resonance Imaging (MRI)

Question 34: In the context of managing delirium in critically ill patients, which of the following interventions is most strongly supported by contemporary research for reducing the incidence and severity of delirium?
A) Routine use of antipsychotic medications
B) Implementation of early mobility programs
C) Administration of benzodiazepines as needed
D) Regular use of sedative-hypnotics for sleep

Question 35: A 55-year-old patient named Mr. Johnson with a history of Type 2 Diabetes Mellitus is admitted to the ICU with severe hyperglycemia and dehydration. The physician orders an insulin infusion to manage his condition. After initiating treatment, which of the following laboratory values should be closely monitored to prevent a common complication associated with insulin therapy in this scenario?
A) Serum potassium levels
B) Serum sodium levels
C) Blood urea nitrogen (BUN)
D) Serum calcium levels

Question 36: In the context of acute respiratory infections, which of the following interventions is most critical in managing a patient with severe hypoxemia and respiratory distress?
A) Initiating high-flow nasal cannula oxygen therapy
B) Administering broad-spectrum antibiotics immediately
C) Performing endotracheal intubation and mechanical ventilation
D) Providing nebulized bronchodilator therapy

Question 37: John, a 35-year-old male, presents to the emergency department with severe pain in his right lower leg following a motorcycle accident. The leg is swollen, and he reports tingling sensations. Upon examination, the leg is tense and shiny. Which of the following interventions should be prioritized to prevent complications associated with compartment syndrome?
A) Elevate the affected limb above heart level.
B) Apply ice packs to reduce swelling.
C) Administer analgesics for pain relief.
D) Prepare for an emergent fasciotomy.

Question 38: In the context of rhabdomyolysis, which electrolyte imbalance is most commonly associated with this condition and can lead to serious complications if not addressed promptly?
A) Hypokalemia
B) Hyperkalemia
C) Hyponatremia
D) Hypercalcemia

Question 39: A 68-year-old patient named John is admitted to the ICU following a fall that resulted in a femoral neck fracture. He has a history of osteoporosis and is scheduled for surgical repair. Post-operatively, he is at risk for complications related to immobility. Which of the following interventions is most critical to prevent deep vein thrombosis (DVT) in this patient?
A) Administering low-dose aspirin daily
B) Encouraging early ambulation as tolerated
C) Applying ice packs to the surgical site
D) Providing passive range-of-motion exercises

Question 40: In the management of a patient with a flail chest resulting from thoracic trauma, which of the following interventions is most critical to ensure adequate ventilation and oxygenation?
A) Administering high-flow oxygen via non-rebreather mask
B) Initiating positive pressure ventilation with PEEP
C) Performing needle decompression
D) Providing aggressive fluid resuscitation

Question 41: Emily, a 45-year-old patient with diabetes, presents with a non-healing ulcer on her lower extremity. The wound is erythematous, warm to touch, and has purulent drainage. Considering the risk of infection in diabetic patients, which of the following is the most appropriate initial intervention to manage this infectious wound?
A) Initiate broad-spectrum antibiotics immediately
B) Obtain a wound culture before starting antibiotics
C) Debride the wound to remove necrotic tissue
D) Apply topical antiseptic ointment

Question 42: In the context of thrombocytopenia, which of the following mechanisms is primarily responsible for the destruction of platelets in Immune Thrombocytopenic Purpura (ITP)?
A) Increased platelet production by megakaryocytes
B) Platelet destruction mediated by autoantibodies
C) Sequestration of platelets in the spleen
D) Platelet consumption due to widespread clotting

Question 43: A 32-year-old patient named Emily presents to the emergency department with severe shortness of breath, wheezing, and a history of asthma. Despite using her rescue inhaler, her symptoms have not improved. As a critical care nurse, you need to decide on the next immediate intervention. What is the most appropriate action?
A) Administer intravenous corticosteroids
B) Provide supplemental oxygen via nasal cannula
C) Initiate continuous nebulized albuterol treatment
D) Perform endotracheal intubation

Question 44: A 45-year-old patient named John presents to the emergency department with complaints of severe headaches, nausea, and difficulty walking. Upon examination, he shows signs of increased intracranial pressure. An MRI reveals obstructive hydrocephalus. As the critical care nurse, what is the most appropriate initial intervention to manage John's condition?
A) Administer intravenous mannitol to reduce intracranial pressure.
B) Perform a lumbar puncture to relieve cerebrospinal fluid pressure.
C) Prepare for surgical placement of a ventriculoperitoneal shunt.
D) Position the patient in Trendelenburg to improve cerebral perfusion.

Question 45: Emily, a 45-year-old female patient, presents with fatigue, pallor, and shortness of breath. Her laboratory results show microcytic hypochromic anemia. As her nurse, you suspect iron deficiency anemia. Which of the following findings would most strongly support this diagnosis?
A) Elevated ferritin levels
B) Low serum iron levels
C) High total iron binding capacity (TIBC)
D) Increased mean corpuscular volume (MCV)

Question 46: A 65-year-old patient named Mr. Johnson is admitted to the ICU with a sudden severe headache, vomiting, and decreased consciousness. A CT scan confirms a subarachnoid hemorrhage. Which immediate intervention is most critical to prevent rebleeding in this scenario?
A) Administering intravenous mannitol
B) Initiating nimodipine therapy
C) Maintaining systolic blood pressure below 140 mmHg
D) Starting anticoagulation therapy

Question 47: A 58-year-old patient named John presents to the emergency department with chest pain, diaphoresis, and shortness of breath. His ECG shows ST-segment elevation in leads II, III, and aVF. As a critical care nurse, what is the most appropriate initial clinical judgment to make for John's management?
A) Administer aspirin and initiate oxygen therapy
B) Prepare for immediate percutaneous coronary intervention (PCI)
C) Administer nitroglycerin and morphine for pain relief
D) Initiate a beta-blocker infusion immediately

Question 48: A 55-year-old male patient named John is admitted to the ICU with severe sepsis. His laboratory results reveal a platelet count of 45,000/μL and elevated D-dimer levels. He is also experiencing petechiae and ecchymosis. Based on these findings, what is the most likely hematological condition John is experiencing?
A) Thrombotic Thrombocytopenic Purpura (TTP)
B) Disseminated Intravascular Coagulation (DIC)
C) Immune Thrombocytopenic Purpura (ITP)
D) Heparin-Induced Thrombocytopenia (HIT)

Question 49: In the context of neurosurgery, what is the primary purpose of performing burr holes in a patient with a suspected subdural hematoma?
A) To relieve intracranial pressure by draining cerebrospinal fluid
B) To provide access for inserting an intracranial pressure monitor
C) To evacuate accumulated blood and alleviate pressure on the brain
D) To facilitate the insertion of a ventriculoperitoneal shunt

Question 50: Emily, a 65-year-old woman with osteoporosis, presents to the emergency department with severe hip pain after a fall. X-rays confirm an intertrochanteric fracture of the femur. Considering her age and bone condition, which initial management approach is most appropriate for Emily?
A) Non-weight bearing with physical therapy
B) Open reduction and internal fixation (ORIF)
C) Hip arthroplasty
D) Traction followed by delayed surgical intervention

Question 51: In the context of managing withdrawal symptoms in patients with substance use disorders, which of the following medications is primarily used to mitigate severe alcohol withdrawal symptoms and prevent progression to delirium tremens?
A) Lorazepam
B) Haloperidol
C) Clonidine

D) Disulfiram

Question 52: Mr. Thompson, a 68-year-old patient with severe aortic stenosis, is scheduled for valve replacement surgery. Post-operatively, the critical care nurse observes signs of decreased cardiac output. Which of the following is the most appropriate initial intervention to address this issue?
A) Administer intravenous fluids to increase preload.
B) Initiate dobutamine infusion to enhance myocardial contractility.
C) Increase oxygen delivery via high-flow nasal cannula.
D) Adjust ventilator settings to improve respiratory function.

Question 53: Mrs. Thompson, a 78-year-old patient with a history of dementia, is admitted to the ICU after a fall. She exhibits confusion, agitation, and difficulty recognizing family members. As her critical care nurse, what is the most appropriate initial step to manage her symptoms?
A) Administer a low-dose antipsychotic medication.
B) Reorient her to time and place using visual aids.
C) Apply physical restraints to prevent further injury.
D) Conduct a thorough assessment for potential delirium triggers.

Question 54: A patient with suspected autoimmune hemolytic anemia (AIHA) presents with fatigue, pallor, and jaundice. Which laboratory test is most definitive in confirming the diagnosis of AIHA?
A) Peripheral blood smear
B) Direct Coombs test
C) Serum haptoglobin level
D) Reticulocyte count

Question 55: A 68-year-old patient named Mr. Thompson is admitted to the ICU with a diagnosis of hyperactive delirium following hip surgery. As a critical care nurse, you are tasked with managing his symptoms. Which of the following interventions is most appropriate to address Mr. Thompson's hyperactive delirium?
A) Administering lorazepam to reduce agitation.
B) Increasing sensory stimulation to reorient the patient.
C) Providing a calm and quiet environment.
D) Encouraging frequent family visits to reassure the patient.

Question 56: In managing a patient with hypertensive crisis, which of the following medications is most appropriate for rapid blood pressure reduction in a critical care setting?
A) Labetalol
B) Nifedipine
C) Hydralazine
D) Nitroprusside

Question 57: Which of the following is a primary mechanism implicated in the pathophysiology of Transfusion-related Acute Lung Injury (TRALI)?
A) Activation of recipient neutrophils by donor antibodies
B) Direct hemolysis of red blood cells in the pulmonary circulation
C) Increased capillary permeability due to donor leukocytes
D) Immune complex deposition in pulmonary vasculature

Question 58: Sarah, a 55-year-old patient with advanced breast cancer, presents to the emergency department with confusion, nausea, and polyuria. Her laboratory results reveal hypercalcemia. Which of the following is the most appropriate initial management step for her oncologic complication?
A) Administer bisphosphonates
B) Initiate intravenous hydration with normal saline
C) Start calcitonin therapy

D) Begin dialysis

Question 59: Which of the following is the most likely mechanism by which intra-abdominal adhesions lead to bowel obstruction in post-surgical patients?
A) Adhesions cause chronic inflammation leading to fibrosis and narrowing of the bowel lumen.
B) Adhesions create a physical barrier that restricts normal peristalsis, leading to obstruction.
C) Adhesions result in ischemia of the bowel wall, causing necrosis and subsequent obstruction.
D) Adhesions form bands that kink or twist the bowel, obstructing passage of intestinal contents.

Question 60: A 65-year-old patient named Mr. Johnson presents with sudden onset of dyspnea and unilateral chest pain. Upon examination, decreased breath sounds and hyperresonance on percussion are noted on the right side. A chest X-ray reveals a significant shift of the mediastinum to the left. What is the most likely diagnosis?
A) Pleural effusion
B) Tension pneumothorax
C) Simple pneumothorax
D) Atelectasis

Question 61: Mr. Thompson, a 65-year-old male with a history of hypertension and diabetes, presents with acute kidney injury (AKI) following a recent infection. His laboratory results reveal elevated serum creatinine and blood urea nitrogen (BUN). Considering the potential causes of AKI, which of the following is most likely responsible for his condition?
A) Prerenal azotemia due to hypovolemia
B) Intrinsic renal damage due to nephrotoxic drugs
C) Postrenal obstruction from prostatic hypertrophy
D) Glomerulonephritis secondary to infection

Question 62: In managing agitation in critically ill patients, which of the following strategies is most supported by contemporary research for minimizing adverse outcomes?
A) Use of physical restraints to prevent self-harm
B) Administration of high-dose benzodiazepines for sedation
C) Implementation of a multimodal approach including non-pharmacological interventions
D) Sole reliance on continuous infusion of propofol

Question 63: In patients with cirrhosis, which of the following laboratory findings is most indicative of hepatic encephalopathy?
A) Elevated serum bilirubin
B) Decreased albumin levels
C) Increased ammonia levels
D) Prolonged prothrombin time

Question 64: John, a 68-year-old male with a history of hypertension and smoking, presents to the emergency department with sudden onset of severe back pain and hypotension. A CT scan reveals an abdominal aortic aneurysm measuring 6.5 cm. What is the most appropriate immediate management for John?
A) Initiate beta-blocker therapy to control heart rate
B) Schedule elective surgical repair within a month
C) Immediate endovascular aneurysm repair (EVAR)
D) Start intravenous antihypertensives to manage blood pressure

Question 65: John, a 45-year-old male with a history of autoimmune hemolytic anemia, presents to the emergency department with fatigue, jaundice, and dark urine. Lab tests reveal elevated bilirubin and reticulocyte count. Which of the following interventions is most

appropriate to address his acute hemolytic crisis?
A) Initiate high-dose corticosteroids
B) Administer intravenous immunoglobulin (IVIG)
C) Perform plasmapheresis
D) Transfuse packed red blood cells

Question 66: In the management of a patient with a hemorrhagic stroke, which of the following interventions is most critical to prevent further neurological deterioration?
A) Administering intravenous thrombolytics
B) Maintaining systolic blood pressure below 160 mmHg
C) Initiating anticoagulation therapy
D) Providing hypertonic saline to manage cerebral edema

Question 67: John, a 65-year-old male with a history of chronic obstructive pulmonary disease (COPD), presents with fever, pleuritic chest pain, and productive cough. A chest X-ray reveals a pleural effusion. Which of the following is the most appropriate initial step in managing suspected empyema in this patient?
A) Start broad-spectrum antibiotics immediately
B) Perform a diagnostic thoracentesis
C) Schedule a CT scan of the chest
D) Initiate oxygen therapy

Question 68: Sarah, a 55-year-old patient, has undergone a Whipple procedure (pancreaticoduodenectomy) for pancreatic cancer. During her postoperative care in the critical care unit, she exhibits signs of malabsorption and significant weight loss. Which of the following interventions is most appropriate to address these issues?
A) Initiate total parenteral nutrition (TPN)
B) Start enzyme replacement therapy
C) Increase dietary fiber intake
D) Administer proton pump inhibitors

Question 69: A 68-year-old patient named Mr. Thompson presents to the emergency department with sudden onset of right-sided weakness and difficulty speaking. A CT scan confirms an ischemic embolic stroke. As a critical care nurse, which of the following interventions is most crucial to initiate within the first three hours of symptom onset?
A) Administer aspirin immediately.
B) Initiate intravenous thrombolytic therapy.
C) Start anticoagulation with heparin.
D) Provide oxygen supplementation.

Question 70: A 45-year-old patient named John presents to the emergency department with palpitations and dizziness. His ECG reveals a short PR interval and a delta wave. John is diagnosed with Wolff-Parkinson-White syndrome. What is the most appropriate initial treatment for John if he becomes hemodynamically unstable?
A) Intravenous Amiodarone
B) Synchronized Cardioversion
C) Intravenous Adenosine
D) Oral Beta-blockers

Question 71: Sarah, a 45-year-old patient, is admitted to the ICU following a traumatic brain injury. She exhibits symptoms of anxiety and emotional lability. The critical care nurse needs to address her psychosocial needs as part of the care plan. Which intervention is most appropriate to manage Sarah's anxiety and emotional lability?
A) Administering a low-dose benzodiazepine as prescribed.
B) Encouraging Sarah to participate in guided imagery sessions.
C) Providing Sarah with a structured daily routine.
D) Engaging Sarah in cognitive-behavioral therapy (CBT) sessions.

Question 72: In the context of IV infiltration, which clinical sign is most indicative of severe tissue damage requiring immediate intervention?
A) Coolness and pallor at the site
B) Swelling with taut, stretched skin
C) Pain and numbness in the affected limb
D) Redness and warmth around the insertion area

Question 73: Sarah, a 45-year-old patient, presents with polyuria and polydipsia. Her urine output is excessively high, and she is unable to concentrate her urine despite adequate hydration. Lab results show low urine osmolality and normal serum glucose levels. Based on this scenario, which of the following treatments is most appropriate for Sarah's condition?
A) Intravenous fluids
B) Desmopressin
C) Thiazide diuretics
D) Insulin therapy

Question 74: John, a 65-year-old male with a history of hypertension and hyperlipidemia, presents to the emergency department with sudden onset of right-sided weakness and slurred speech lasting for 20 minutes. His symptoms resolved by the time he arrived at the hospital. As a critical care nurse, which immediate intervention is most crucial to prevent a subsequent stroke?
A) Administer aspirin immediately.
B) Schedule an MRI to assess for brain lesions.
C) Initiate intravenous thrombolytic therapy.
D) Perform carotid ultrasound to evaluate stenosis.

Question 75: Which clinical finding is most indicative of hemodynamic compromise in a patient with pericardial effusion?
A) Distant heart sounds
B) Pulsus paradoxus
C) Jugular venous distension
D) Hypotension

Question 76: In the context of acute ischemic stroke management, which of the following statements about the administration of tissue plasminogen activator (tPA) is most accurate?
A) tPA should be administered within 6 hours of symptom onset for maximum effectiveness.
B) The risk of hemorrhagic transformation increases significantly if tPA is administered beyond 4.5 hours.
C) tPA is contraindicated in patients with a history of transient ischemic attacks (TIAs).
D) The use of tPA is recommended only if the patient's blood pressure is below 185/110 mmHg.

Question 77: In the context of critical care, which psychosocial intervention is most effective in reducing anxiety in patients experiencing prolonged mechanical ventilation?
A) Cognitive-behavioral therapy (CBT)
B) Music therapy
C) Mindfulness-based stress reduction (MBSR)
D) Guided imagery

Question 78: In the context of hydrocephalus, which of the following is the most effective initial intervention to manage increased intracranial pressure in a critical care setting?
A) Administering mannitol to decrease cerebral edema
B) Performing a lumbar puncture to relieve pressure
C) Elevating the head of the bed to 30 degrees

D) Initiating hyperventilation to lower carbon dioxide levels

Question 79: Emily, a 55-year-old patient with known cirrhosis, presents to the emergency department with hematemesis and signs of hemodynamic instability. Upon examination, she is diagnosed with portal hypertension. Which of the following interventions should be prioritized to stabilize Emily's condition?
A) Administer intravenous beta-blockers to reduce portal pressure.
B) Initiate a transjugular intrahepatic portosystemic shunt (TIPS) procedure immediately.
C) Start intravenous octreotide to control variceal bleeding.
D) Perform an urgent endoscopic band ligation.

Question 80: In the context of preventing falls in a critical care setting, which of the following interventions is most effective according to recent evidence-based practices?
A) Implementing hourly rounding to assess patient needs
B) Using bed alarms to alert staff of patient movement
C) Providing non-slip socks to all patients
D) Conducting a fall risk assessment upon admission only

Question 81: In the context of valve replacement surgery, which of the following is the most critical factor in deciding between a mechanical valve and a bioprosthetic valve?
A) Patient's age and life expectancy
B) Risk of thromboembolism
C) Anticoagulation therapy compliance
D) Valve durability and longevity

Question 82: A 65-year-old patient named Mr. Johnson, with a history of hypertension and atrial fibrillation, presents to the ICU with sudden onset of severe headache, nausea, and altered consciousness. A CT scan reveals an intraventricular hemorrhage (IVH). Which initial management strategy is most appropriate to prevent further neurological deterioration in this patient?
A) Administering intravenous mannitol to reduce intracranial pressure
B) Initiating antihypertensive therapy to maintain systolic blood pressure below 140 mmHg
C) Performing an external ventricular drain (EVD) placement to relieve hydrocephalus
D) Starting anticoagulation therapy to manage atrial fibrillation

Question 83: In the context of chronic alcohol dependence, which neurotransmitter system is primarily affected, leading to altered mood and behavior?
A) Dopaminergic system
B) Serotonergic system
C) GABAergic system
D) Glutamatergic system

Question 84: In the context of Guillain-Barré Syndrome (GBS), which of the following is the most accurate initial diagnostic test to confirm the diagnosis?
A) Nerve conduction studies
B) Cerebrospinal fluid analysis
C) Magnetic Resonance Imaging (MRI)
D) Electromyography (EMG)

Question 85: John, a 45-year-old male, is admitted to the ICU following a motorcycle accident. A CT scan reveals a biconvex hematoma. He is experiencing severe headache and rapidly declining consciousness. Based on this presentation, which type of traumatic brain injury is most likely?
A) Epidural hematoma
B) Subdural hematoma
C) Concussion
D) Diffuse axonal injury

Question 86: Emily, a 45-year-old patient, was admitted to the ICU following a motor vehicle accident. She sustained a pelvic fracture and is experiencing hemodynamic instability. As her critical care nurse, which intervention should be prioritized to stabilize her condition?
A) Administer intravenous fluids aggressively to maintain blood pressure.
B) Apply a pelvic binder to reduce bleeding and stabilize the fracture.
C) Prepare for immediate surgical intervention to repair the fracture.
D) Initiate vasopressor therapy to support blood pressure.

Question 87: John, a 65-year-old male with a history of type 2 diabetes, presents to the emergency department with redness, warmth, and swelling in his left lower leg. The area is tender to touch and he has a fever of 101°F. Considering his condition and medical history, what is the most appropriate initial treatment for John's cellulitis?
A) Oral amoxicillin
B) Intravenous vancomycin
C) Oral cephalexin
D) Topical mupirocin

Question 88: In the context of neurological hemorrhage, which of the following is the most critical initial intervention to minimize secondary brain injury?
A) Administering mannitol to reduce intracranial pressure
B) Initiating therapeutic hypothermia
C) Ensuring adequate cerebral perfusion pressure
D) Providing supplemental oxygen to maintain normoxia

Question 89: In the context of preventing falls in critically ill patients, which of the following interventions is most supported by contemporary research for reducing fall risk in the intensive care unit (ICU)?
A) Continuous video monitoring of patients
B) Hourly rounding by nursing staff
C) Use of bed alarms for all patients
D) Implementation of individualized patient education programs

Question 90: In the management of acute gastrointestinal (GI) hemorrhage, which of the following interventions is considered most critical in stabilizing a hemodynamically unstable patient before definitive treatment?
A) Administration of proton pump inhibitors (PPIs)
B) Immediate endoscopic intervention
C) Rapid intravenous fluid resuscitation
D) Blood transfusion to maintain hemoglobin above 10 g/dL

Question 91: In the management of a patient with severe trauma and extensive soft tissue injury, which of the following interventions is most critical to prevent wound infection and promote healing?
A) Early administration of broad-spectrum antibiotics
B) Adequate debridement of necrotic tissue
C) Application of negative pressure wound therapy
D) Frequent dressing changes with antiseptic solutions

Question 92: A 68-year-old patient named Mr. Johnson is admitted to the ICU with severe dehydration, confusion, and a blood glucose level of 950 mg/dL. His serum osmolality is significantly elevated, and there is no significant ketoacidosis. As the critical care nurse, what is the primary intervention you should prioritize for

managing Mr. Johnson's condition?
A) Administering intravenous insulin immediately.
B) Initiating aggressive fluid replacement with isotonic saline.
C) Providing bicarbonate therapy to correct acidosis.
D) Starting potassium replacement therapy.

Question 93: In the management of acute esophageal variceal bleeding, which of the following interventions is considered the most effective initial treatment to control bleeding and stabilize the patient?
A) Endoscopic variceal ligation
B) Intravenous octreotide infusion
C) Transjugular intrahepatic portosystemic shunt (TIPS)
D) Balloon tamponade

Question 94: In critically ill patients, prolonged immobility can lead to which of the following musculoskeletal complications that significantly impacts functional recovery?
A) Osteoporosis
B) Muscle atrophy
C) Joint contractures
D) Pressure ulcers

Question 95: Sarah, a 58-year-old patient with a history of diabetes mellitus, presents with fever, flank pain, and dysuria. Her urinalysis shows significant pyuria and bacteriuria. Considering her symptoms and lab findings, which of the following is the most appropriate initial management to prevent potential complications related to her condition?
A) Initiate broad-spectrum intravenous antibiotics
B) Start oral antibiotics targeting gram-negative bacteria
C) Increase fluid intake and monitor closely
D) Prescribe analgesics for pain management

Question 96: In the management of chronic wounds, which factor is most critical in promoting optimal wound healing in patients with diabetes?
A) Maintaining strict glycemic control
B) Regular debridement of necrotic tissue
C) Application of advanced wound dressings
D) Use of systemic antibiotics

Question 97: In the context of hypoactive delirium, which clinical intervention is most effective in improving patient outcomes by addressing underlying causes?
A) Administering antipsychotic medication
B) Implementing a structured reorientation program
C) Increasing sedative medication
D) Initiating physical restraints

Question 98: Sarah, a 45-year-old patient, presents with symptoms of headaches, nausea, and gait disturbances. An MRI confirms the diagnosis of non-communicating hydrocephalus due to an obstructive lesion in the third ventricle. Which of the following is the most appropriate initial intervention to relieve her symptoms?
A) Lumbar puncture
B) Endoscopic third ventriculostomy
C) Ventriculoperitoneal shunt placement
D) Administration of acetazolamide

Question 99: In the management of Intraventricular Hemorrhage (IVH) in critically ill patients, which of the following interventions is most crucial for preventing secondary brain injury?
A) Maintaining cerebral perfusion pressure (CPP) above 70 mmHg
B) Administering prophylactic anticonvulsants
C) Ensuring normothermia and avoiding hyperthermia
D) Utilizing corticosteroids to reduce cerebral edema

Question 100: John, a 62-year-old patient with stage 4 chronic kidney disease (CKD), presents with severe fatigue and pallor. His laboratory results show a hemoglobin level of 8 g/dL. Which of the following interventions is most appropriate to address his anemia in the context of CKD?
A) Start oral iron supplements
B) Administer erythropoiesis-stimulating agents (ESAs)
C) Begin vitamin B12 injections
D) Prescribe folic acid supplements

Question 101: A 45-year-old patient named John presents with fever, headache, neck stiffness, and photophobia. He has a history of sinusitis. The attending nurse suspects bacterial meningitis. Which of the following is the most likely causative organism in this scenario?
A) Streptococcus pneumoniae
B) Neisseria meningitidis
C) Haemophilus influenzae
D) Listeria monocytogenes

Question 102: John, a 65-year-old male with a history of atrial fibrillation, presents to the emergency department with severe abdominal pain out of proportion to physical examination findings. He also reports nausea and vomiting. Laboratory results show elevated lactate levels. Considering the clinical presentation and risk factors, what is the most likely initial diagnostic test to confirm mesenteric ischemia?
A) Abdominal X-ray
B) CT Angiography
C) MRI of the abdomen
D) Ultrasound of the abdomen

Question 103: In the management of heart failure with reduced ejection fraction (HFrEF), which medication class is primarily used to reduce mortality by antagonizing the effects of aldosterone?
A) Angiotensin-converting enzyme inhibitors (ACE inhibitors)
B) Beta-blockers
C) Mineralocorticoid receptor antagonists (MRAs)
D) Loop diuretics

Question 104: In the context of anemia management in critical care, which of the following laboratory findings is most indicative of hemolytic anemia?
A) Decreased serum haptoglobin
B) Elevated mean corpuscular volume (MCV)
C) Increased reticulocyte count
D) Low serum ferritin

Question 105: In the context of lung contusion management, which intervention is most critical to prevent complications in a patient with severe thoracic trauma?
A) Administering high-flow oxygen therapy
B) Implementing aggressive fluid resuscitation
C) Initiating mechanical ventilation with low tidal volumes
D) Providing continuous positive airway pressure (CPAP)

Question 106: John, a 68-year-old male with a history of smoking and occupational exposure to asbestos, presents with progressive dyspnea and a dry cough. A high-resolution CT scan reveals reticular opacities predominantly in the lower lobes. Which of the following interventions is most likely to improve his long-term prognosis?
A) High-dose corticosteroids
B) Lung transplantation
C) Long-term oxygen therapy
D) Pulmonary rehabilitation

Question 107: Mr. Thompson, a 65-year-old male with a history of congestive heart failure, presents with dyspnea and pleuritic chest pain. A chest X-ray reveals a moderate pleural effusion. Based on contemporary management strategies, which initial intervention is most appropriate for managing his pleural effusion?
A) Thoracentesis to remove the fluid
B) Diuretics to manage fluid overload
C) Pleurodesis to prevent recurrence
D) Chest tube insertion for continuous drainage

Question 108: A 45-year-old patient named John presents to the emergency department with fever, headache, neck stiffness, and photophobia. Given his symptoms and recent travel history to an area with a high incidence of viral infections, which viral pathogen is most likely responsible for his condition?
A) Herpes Simplex Virus
B) West Nile Virus
C) Enterovirus
D) Epstein-Barr Virus

Question 109: In the management of biliary atresia, which of the following interventions is considered the most definitive treatment to improve long-term survival and liver function in affected infants?
A) Kasai portoenterostomy
B) Liver transplantation
C) Ursodeoxycholic acid administration
D) Percutaneous transhepatic cholangiography

Question 110: Mr. Thompson, a 68-year-old patient, is recovering from a Coronary Artery Bypass Grafting (CABG) surgery. On the second postoperative day, he develops atrial fibrillation with a rapid ventricular response. As the critical care nurse, what is the most appropriate initial intervention to manage his condition?
A) Administer intravenous amiodarone
B) Initiate synchronized cardioversion
C) Administer intravenous diltiazem
D) Increase beta-blocker dosage

Question 111: Emily, a 68-year-old woman with a history of Parkinson's disease, presents with a shuffling gait and frequent freezing episodes when attempting to walk through doorways. What is the most appropriate initial intervention to help improve her gait and reduce freezing episodes?
A) Increase her levodopa dosage
B) Introduce visual cueing techniques
C) Initiate physical therapy focused on strength training
D) Recommend a walker for stability

Question 112: A 65-year-old patient named Mr. Thompson is admitted to the ICU with multiple fractures and bruises. His medical history reveals frequent visits to different hospitals over the past year for similar injuries. During your assessment, Mr. Thompson appears withdrawn and anxious when questioned about his injuries. What should be your primary consideration as a critical care nurse in this scenario?
A) Focus on managing Mr. Thompson's pain effectively.
B) Prioritize assessing Mr. Thompson's risk for abuse or neglect.
C) Ensure that Mr. Thompson receives adequate nutrition and hydration.
D) Coordinate with physical therapy for rehabilitation planning.

Question 113: In the context of critical care, which hormone is primarily responsible for the regulation of serum calcium levels through its effects on bone resorption and renal tubular reabsorption?
A) Calcitonin
B) Parathyroid hormone (PTH)
C) Vitamin D
D) Aldosterone

Question 114: Emily, a 58-year-old female with a history of hypertension, presents to the emergency department with severe headache, visual disturbances, and confusion. Her blood pressure is recorded at 220/130 mmHg. Which of the following is the most appropriate initial management step for Emily's hypertensive crisis?
A) Administer oral antihypertensive medication
B) Start intravenous labetalol infusion
C) Initiate continuous nitroglycerin infusion
D) Provide oxygen therapy

Question 115: Sarah, a 45-year-old patient with a history of rheumatoid arthritis, presents with acute right knee pain and swelling. She reports difficulty in weight-bearing and has a fever of 38.5°C. As a critical care nurse, what is the most appropriate initial action to take in this scenario?
A) Administer non-steroidal anti-inflammatory drugs (NSAIDs) for pain relief.
B) Perform an arthrocentesis to obtain synovial fluid for analysis.
C) Apply ice packs to reduce swelling and manage symptoms.
D) Initiate broad-spectrum antibiotics immediately.

Question 116: Which of the following interventions is most effective in managing acute anxiety in a critically ill patient, according to contemporary research and recognized theories?
A) Deep breathing exercises
B) Administration of benzodiazepines
C) Cognitive Behavioral Therapy (CBT)
D) Progressive muscle relaxation

Question 117: A 55-year-old male patient named John presents to the emergency department with severe ascites, jaundice, and confusion. His medical history reveals chronic alcohol use and liver cirrhosis. Considering his symptoms and condition, what is the most appropriate initial management step to address his portal hypertension?
A) Initiate intravenous albumin infusion
B) Administer lactulose to reduce ammonia levels
C) Perform a large-volume paracentesis
D) Start propranolol to decrease portal pressure

Question 118: In the management of acute coronary syndrome (ACS), which biomarker is considered most specific for diagnosing myocardial infarction?
A) Myoglobin
B) Creatine kinase-MB (CK-MB)
C) Troponin I
D) Lactate dehydrogenase (LDH)

Question 119: John, a 58-year-old male with a history of hypertension, presents to the emergency department with sudden onset severe chest pain radiating to his back. His blood pressure is markedly different between his arms. What is the most appropriate initial imaging study to confirm a diagnosis of aortic dissection?
A) Chest X-ray
B) CT angiography
C) Transthoracic echocardiography
D) Magnetic resonance imaging (MRI)

Question 120: A 65-year-old patient named Mr. Thompson is admitted to the ICU with a diagnosis of sepsis. He becomes increasingly agitated and attempts

to remove his IV lines. Considering his condition and potential causes of agitation, what is the most appropriate initial intervention?
A) Administer a sedative to calm the patient.
B) Assess for hypoxia and provide supplemental oxygen if needed.
C) Restrain the patient to prevent self-harm.
D) Increase environmental stimulation to distract the patient.

Question 121: Emily, a 68-year-old patient with type 2 diabetes, presents to the emergency department with confusion and diaphoresis. Her blood glucose level is measured at 45 mg/dL. After initial treatment with intravenous dextrose, what is the next most appropriate step in managing her acute hypoglycemia?
A) Administer glucagon intramuscularly
B) Initiate a continuous glucose infusion
C) Provide a complex carbohydrate snack once she is alert
D) Reassess blood glucose every 30 minutes

Question 122: A 55-year-old patient named John presents to the emergency department with severe pain and an inability to bear weight on his right leg after a fall. An X-ray reveals a displaced femoral neck fracture. Considering the patient's age and fracture type, which management strategy is most appropriate to ensure optimal recovery?
A) Closed reduction and casting
B) Open reduction and internal fixation (ORIF)
C) Total hip arthroplasty
D) Conservative management with bed rest

Question 123: In a patient suspected of adrenal insufficiency, which laboratory finding is most indicative of primary adrenal insufficiency (Addison's disease)?
A) Low serum sodium and high serum potassium
B) High serum sodium and low serum potassium
C) Low serum cortisol and high ACTH levels
D) High serum cortisol and low ACTH levels

Question 124: In the context of leukopenia, which of the following conditions is most likely to cause a decrease in neutrophil count, thereby increasing the risk of infection in critical care patients?
A) Aplastic anemia
B) Iron deficiency anemia
C) Vitamin B12 deficiency
D) Hemolytic anemia

Question 125: Emily, a 45-year-old female patient with a history of chronic kidney disease, presents with fatigue and pallor. Her laboratory results show hemoglobin of 9 g/dL and low serum ferritin levels. Considering her condition and lab results, which is the most appropriate initial treatment for her anemia?
A) Oral iron supplementation
B) Intravenous iron therapy
C) Erythropoiesis-stimulating agents (ESAs)
D) Blood transfusion

ANSWER WITH DETAILED EXPLANATION SET [2]

Question 1: Correct Answer: B) Refer Sarah to a psychiatrist for medication evaluation.
Rationale: The correct answer is B because referral to a psychiatrist can provide an expert evaluation and potentially initiate pharmacotherapy, which is crucial for managing depression effectively. Option A may aid physical recovery but does not directly address depression. Option C might offer emotional support but lacks specificity in treating depression. Option D could provide social interaction but doesn't target individual depressive symptoms. Medication evaluation is essential for comprehensive care, aligning with contemporary research emphasizing pharmacological intervention in depression management.

Question 2: Correct Answer: C) Nintedanib treatment
Rationale: Nintedanib is an antifibrotic agent shown to slow disease progression in idiopathic pulmonary fibrosis by inhibiting pathways involved in fibrogenesis. Long-term oxygen therapy (A) aids symptom management but doesn't alter disease progression. Corticosteroids (B) are less effective for idiopathic pulmonary fibrosis and may cause adverse effects. Pulmonary rehabilitation (D) improves quality of life but does not directly impact disease progression. Thus, while all options contribute to managing pulmonary fibrosis, Nintedanib specifically targets and slows its advancement.

Question 3: Correct Answer: A) Metformin
Rationale: Metformin is the first-line treatment for Type 2 Diabetes Mellitus, enhancing insulin sensitivity in peripheral tissues, particularly muscle and liver. It decreases hepatic glucose production and improves glucose uptake. Sulfonylureas (B) increase insulin secretion but do not directly affect insulin sensitivity. DPP-4 inhibitors (C) enhance incretin activity, indirectly affecting insulin secretion. Insulin (D), while essential for managing hyperglycemia, does not primarily enhance peripheral insulin sensitivity. Understanding these mechanisms is crucial for effective diabetes management and illustrates why Metformin is the preferred choice.

Question 4: Correct Answer: D) Anastomotic leak
Rationale: Anastomotic leak is a serious complication post-Whipple procedure, presenting with signs of sepsis like tachycardia, hypotension, and abdominal pain. While pancreatic fistula (A) can occur, it typically presents with fluid drainage issues rather than acute systemic symptoms. Delayed gastric emptying (B) usually manifests as nausea or vomiting without systemic instability. Hemorrhage (C) could cause hypotension but is less likely to present with abdominal pain in this context. Thus, anastomotic leak (D) aligns most closely with Mr. Thompson's clinical presentation due to its acute and severe nature.

Question 5: Correct Answer: D) Initiate fluid resuscitation with isotonic saline
Rationale: In cases of hyperglycemic hyperosmolar state (HHS), as seen in John's scenario, the priority is fluid resuscitation to address dehydration, which is critical before insulin administration. Option A (intravenous insulin) is necessary but secondary to fluids. Option B (oral hypoglycemics) is ineffective due to his acute condition. Option C (oral glucose) would exacerbate hyperglycemia. Fluid resuscitation stabilizes hemodynamics and improves renal perfusion, crucial for subsequent insulin therapy.

Question 6: Correct Answer: A) Administer intravenous fluids to prevent hypovolemic shock.
Rationale: Administering intravenous fluids is crucial as femur fractures can lead to significant blood loss, risking hypovolemic shock. While applying a traction splint (B) and monitoring for neurovascular compromise (C) are important, they follow stabilization of circulation. Pain relief (D) is essential but not the immediate priority over preventing shock. Prioritizing fluid administration aligns with the ABCs (Airway, Breathing, Circulation), ensuring John's hemodynamic stability before addressing other concerns like pain or fracture stabilization.

Question 7: Correct Answer: A) Measurement of hepatic venous pressure gradient (HVPG)
Rationale: Measurement of HVPG is the gold standard for diagnosing portal hypertension, as it directly assesses the pressure difference between the portal vein and hepatic veins. Doppler ultrasound, while non-invasive, estimates blood flow but not pressure. SAAG helps differentiate types of ascites but doesn't measure portal pressure. Liver biopsy provides information on liver pathology but not specific hemodynamic data. HVPG's direct measurement makes it superior in confirming portal hypertension compared to other methods that provide indirect or ancillary information.

Question 8: Correct Answer: B) Implement early mobilization strategies
Rationale: Early mobilization is crucial in managing delirium as it helps reduce its duration and severity by promoting normal sleep-wake cycles and enhancing cognitive function. While low-dose haloperidol (Option A) can be used, it's typically reserved for severe agitation due to potential side effects. Increasing sedation (Option C) can worsen delirium by disrupting sleep-wake cycles. Continuous reorientation (Option D) is supportive but less effective alone compared to physical activity in preventing or managing delirium. Therefore, mobilization is prioritized based on current research and guidelines.

Question 9: Correct Answer: A) Abdominal ultrasound
Rationale: Abdominal ultrasound is the most sensitive and cost-effective method for detecting asymptomatic abdominal aortic aneurysms, especially in high-risk patients. It provides accurate measurements of the aneurysm's size and can be easily repeated for monitoring. CT scans, while precise, involve radiation and are typically reserved for pre-surgical evaluation. MRI offers detailed imaging but is less accessible and more expensive. Chest X-rays are not used for abdominal assessment and lack sensitivity for detecting aneurysms. Thus, ultrasound remains the first-line choice due to its non-invasive nature and reliability.

Question 10: Correct Answer: D) Providing frequent reorientation
Rationale: Frequent reorientation is crucial in managing delirium, as it helps patients regain their sense of time and place. While low-dose haloperidol (Option A) can be used, it is generally reserved for severe agitation due to potential side effects. Increasing environmental stimuli (Option B) may worsen confusion. Encouraging family visitation (Option C) can be beneficial but is not as directly impactful as consistent reorientation. Therefore, Option D effectively addresses the underlying disorientation typical in delirium cases by reinforcing reality orientation through repeated cues and reminders.

Question 11: Correct Answer: B) Parathyroid hormone (PTH)
Rationale: Parathyroid hormone (PTH) is crucial for maintaining serum calcium levels by increasing bone resorption, enhancing renal calcium reabsorption, and promoting intestinal absorption of calcium via activation of vitamin D. Calcitonin also affects bone metabolism but primarily decreases serum calcium. Vitamin D aids in calcium absorption but does not directly regulate it. Thyroid-stimulating hormone (TSH) influences thyroid function, not calcium homeostasis. The nuanced roles of these hormones make understanding their specific functions essential in critical care settings, particularly in managing electrolyte imbalances.

Question 12: Correct Answer: C) Administer intravenous potassium chloride.
Rationale: Administering intravenous potassium chloride is crucial for rapidly correcting severe hypokalemia (serum potassium <3.0 mEq/L), especially when life-threatening symptoms like cardiac arrhythmias are present. Oral supplements (Option A) are too slow for acute correction. Potassium-sparing diuretics (Option B) are not effective in immediate correction and may not address acute deficits. Dietary changes (Option D) are inadequate in emergencies due to delayed absorption. Prompt IV administration ensures rapid restoration of normal cardiac and muscular function, preventing further complications.

Question 13: Correct Answer: D) Provide physical therapy sessions focused on balance exercises.
Rationale: Prioritizing physical therapy sessions focused on balance exercises addresses both fall prevention and mobility enhancement. While scheduled toileting (B) and bed alarms (C) are useful, they do not actively improve balance or strength. Encouraging independent walking with a cane (A) may increase fall risk if balance is not first addressed. Balance exercises have been shown to significantly reduce fall risks in elderly patients by improving proprioception and muscle strength, which are crucial for safe mobility post-surgery.

Question 14: Correct Answer: C) Troponin I
Rationale: Troponin I is the most specific biomarker for myocardial injury, as it is highly sensitive and specific to cardiac muscle damage. Unlike CK-MB, which can also be elevated in skeletal muscle injury, Troponin I remains elevated longer, providing a more reliable indication of myocardial infarction. Myoglobin rises quickly but lacks specificity, while LDH is less specific and slower to rise. Therefore, Troponin I's specificity and sensitivity make it the preferred choice for diagnosing ACS.

Question 15: Correct Answer: B) Reassess blood glucose in 15 minutes.
Rationale: After initial treatment with IV dextrose, reassessing blood glucose in 15 minutes ensures effective resolution of hypoglycemia and guides further management. Option A (glucagon) is used when IV access isn't available; here, it is unnecessary. Option C (IV insulin infusion) could worsen hypoglycemia. Option D (high-protein snack) helps prevent future episodes but isn't immediate post-IV dextrose care. The emphasis on timely reassessment aligns with guidelines for acute hypoglycemia management in critical care settings.

Question 16: Correct Answer: C) Pituitary adenoma
Rationale: Pituitary adenomas are known for their ability to secrete hormones, causing endocrine disturbances such as Cushing's disease or acromegaly. Meningiomas (A) and glioblastomas (B) are typically non-hormone-secreting tumors, although they can cause neurological symptoms due to mass effect. Medulloblastomas (D), primarily seen in children, originate in the cerebellum and are not associated with hormone production. The key difference is the pituitary adenoma's location and function, directly affecting hormone levels, unlike the other options which do not primarily involve endocrine disruption.

Question 17: Correct Answer: D) Implement strict blood glucose control
Rationale: Strict blood glucose control is crucial for promoting wound healing in patients with diabetes, as hyperglycemia impairs leukocyte function and collagen synthesis. Although negative pressure wound therapy (A) aids in healing, it may not address underlying glycemic issues. Increasing caloric intake (B) helps but does not directly target hyperglycemia. Prophylactic antibiotics (C) prevent infection but do not enhance healing directly related to glycemic control. Thus, controlling blood glucose addresses the root cause of impaired healing in diabetic patients like Sarah.

Question 18: Correct Answer: C) Impaired leukocyte function
Rationale: Impaired leukocyte function in diabetic patients hinders effective wound healing due to reduced phagocytic activity and delayed inflammatory response. While increased collagen synthesis (Option A) and enhanced angiogenesis (Option B) are beneficial for healing, they are often compromised in diabetes. Reduced glucose levels (Option D) can actually improve healing by reducing hyperglycemia-related damage. Thus, impaired leukocyte function is the primary factor that negatively impacts wound healing in diabetic patients, making it the correct answer.

Question 19: Correct Answer: C) Start an intravenous fluid bolus with normal saline.
Rationale: The initial treatment for severe hyperglycemia involves starting an intravenous fluid bolus with normal saline to address dehydration and improve circulation. While insulin administration (Option A) is crucial, it follows fluid resuscitation. Oral hypoglycemics (Option B) are inappropriate in acute settings due to delayed onset and potential ineffectiveness in severe cases. Potassium replacement (Option D) is necessary but should be considered after initiating fluids and insulin due to the risk of hypokalemia during treatment.

Question 20: Correct Answer: B) Initiate aggressive fluid resuscitation with isotonic saline to correct dehydration.
Rationale: The primary concern in HHS is severe dehydration due to osmotic diuresis, making fluid resuscitation with isotonic saline the initial priority (Option B). While insulin administration (Option A) is necessary, it follows fluid replacement to prevent circulatory collapse. Potassium replacement (Option C) is essential but secondary, as initial potassium levels are often normal or elevated. Bicarbonate infusion (Option D) is not indicated due to the absence of significant acidosis in HHS. Prioritizing fluid resuscitation addresses the critical volume deficit and stabilizes hemodynamics before other interventions.

Question 21: Correct Answer: C) Provide a walker and educate Emily on its use for ambulation support.
Rationale: Providing a walker addresses Emily's immediate need for mobility support post-surgery, promoting safety and independence. Option A is incorrect as independent ambulation without support can risk falls. Option B focuses on passive exercises, which do not immediately aid functional mobility. Option D addresses pain but does not directly improve mobility or safety. The correct option ensures balance between safety and functional improvement by offering practical support

aligned with contemporary rehabilitation strategies.

Question 22: Correct Answer: C) Administering intravenous insulin infusion
Rationale: Intravenous insulin infusion is crucial in preventing DKA by providing rapid and precise control of blood glucose levels. While monitoring blood glucose (Option B) is important, it doesn't directly prevent DKA without appropriate insulin administration. Subcutaneous insulin (Option A) acts slower than intravenous, delaying necessary intervention. A high-carbohydrate diet (Option D) can exacerbate hyperglycemia, increasing the risk of DKA. Therefore, Option C is the most effective intervention in this context.

Question 23: Correct Answer: B) Administer intravenous N-acetylcysteine
Rationale: The administration of intravenous N-acetylcysteine is crucial in cases of acetaminophen-induced fulminant hepatitis, as it acts as a glutathione precursor, aiding in detoxifying the liver. Option A is incorrect because corticosteroids are not effective in acetaminophen toxicity. Option C is inappropriate without evidence of infection. Option D poses unnecessary risk and does not address the immediate need for detoxification. Therefore, option B directly targets the underlying cause and enhances liver recovery prospects effectively.

Question 24: Correct Answer: C) Encourage deep breathing exercises and use of an incentive spirometer.
Rationale: Encouraging deep breathing exercises and using an incentive spirometer is crucial for preventing atelectasis and promoting lung expansion, especially with rib fractures that can lead to shallow breathing due to pain. While high-flow oxygen (A) might improve oxygenation temporarily, it does not address underlying ventilation issues. NIPPV (B) may be excessive initially unless respiratory failure is evident. Positioning in semi-Fowler's (D) aids comfort but doesn't directly enhance lung expansion like incentive spirometry does. Thus, option C addresses both prevention and management of potential respiratory complications effectively.

Question 25: Correct Answer: C) To evacuate accumulated blood and relieve pressure on the brain.
Rationale: Burr holes are primarily used to evacuate blood from a subdural hematoma, alleviating pressure on the brain. Option A is incorrect as burr holes are not typically used for cerebrospinal fluid drainage; this is more commonly achieved via lumbar puncture or shunt placement. Option B involves ventricular catheters, which require different surgical access. Option D pertains to biopsies, which may use burr holes but are not their primary purpose in subdural hematomas. The focus is on decompression, aligning with contemporary neurosurgical practices.

Question 26: Correct Answer: C) Recommend pulmonary rehabilitation
Rationale: Pulmonary rehabilitation is crucial in managing emphysema as it improves exercise tolerance and quality of life by enhancing respiratory muscle function. While inhaled corticosteroids (A) and long-acting beta-agonists (D) are part of the pharmacological management, they do not directly enhance physical conditioning. Supplemental oxygen therapy (B) is vital for hypoxemia but does not improve overall respiratory function like rehabilitation does. Pulmonary rehabilitation focuses on exercise training, education, and behavioral changes that help patients manage their symptoms more effectively than medication alone.

Question 27: Correct Answer: B) Early mobilization and physical therapy
Rationale: Early mobilization and physical therapy are crucial in managing delirium, as they help maintain cognitive function and reduce the duration of delirium. While continuous sedation (A) can exacerbate delirium, antipsychotic medications (C) are not always effective and may have side effects. Sleep hygiene (D) is beneficial but not as impactful as early mobilization. Mobilization addresses both musculoskeletal and neurological components by enhancing circulation, reducing muscle atrophy, and stimulating cognitive engagement, making it the most comprehensive intervention for this mixed condition.

Question 28: Correct Answer: A) Sudden onset of severe abdominal pain with minimal physical examination findings
Rationale: Acute mesenteric ischemia typically presents as sudden, severe abdominal pain that is disproportionate to physical examination findings due to bowel necrosis. Option B suggests gradual pain, which is less characteristic. Option C indicates peritoneal signs, which usually occur later. Option D suggests colitis or infection rather than ischemia. The key difference lies in the acute nature and severity of pain in option A, emphasizing the urgency and often subtle initial physical signs associated with mesenteric ischemia.

Question 29: Correct Answer: C) Decreased glomerular filtration rate (GFR)
Rationale: A decreased GFR is the most definitive indicator of CKD progression to ESRD, as it directly reflects kidney function. While elevated creatinine and increased BUN are common in CKD, they are less specific for staging. Hyperkalemia indicates electrolyte imbalance but not necessarily ESRD progression. GFR decline provides a direct measure of kidney filtering capacity, making it the most reliable marker for advancing CKD stages compared to other lab values that may fluctuate due to various factors.

Question 30: Correct Answer: B) West Nile Virus Meningitis
Rationale: The clinical presentation of fever, headache, neck stiffness, and photophobia in a patient with recent travel history is highly indicative of viral meningitis. West Nile Virus is known for causing meningitis and encephalitis, especially in areas with outbreaks. HSV typically causes encephalitis rather than meningitis. CMV encephalitis is more common in immunocompromised patients. EBV rarely causes neurological symptoms like meningitis or encephalitis. Thus, given the travel history and symptomatology, West Nile Virus Meningitis is the most plausible diagnosis.

Question 31: Correct Answer: B) Immediately initiate one-on-one observation to prevent self-harm.
Rationale: The immediate priority in managing a patient with suicidal ideation is ensuring their safety, making one-on-one observation crucial. While conducting a psychiatric assessment (A) and administering medication (C) are important, they are secondary in an acute crisis. Referring John to outpatient services (D) is inappropriate without stabilizing the current risk. The correct option ensures immediate safety, aligning with contemporary guidelines on managing acute suicidal ideation.

Question 32: Correct Answer: C) Ranson's criteria
Rationale: Ranson's criteria are a set of clinical and laboratory parameters used to assess the severity and predict the prognosis of acute pancreatitis within the first 48 hours. Unlike serum amylase and lipase levels (Options A and B), which indicate pancreatic injury but not severity, and CRP levels (Option D), which rise later in response to inflammation, Ranson's criteria provide a

comprehensive assessment by considering multiple factors such as age, white blood cell count, blood glucose, and liver function tests. This makes Ranson's criteria more reliable for early severity assessment.

Question 33: Correct Answer: A) Focused Assessment with Sonography for Trauma (FAST)
Rationale: FAST is the preferred method for detecting free intraperitoneal fluid in hemodynamically unstable patients due to its rapidity and non-invasiveness. DPL, while sensitive, is more invasive and less commonly used. CT scans provide detailed images but are not ideal in unstable patients due to time and radiation exposure. MRI is rarely used in acute settings due to time constraints and availability. Therefore, FAST remains the most efficient and effective initial assessment tool in these critical situations.

Question 34: Correct Answer: B) Implementation of early mobility programs
Rationale: Early mobility programs are supported by research as an effective strategy to reduce delirium in critical care settings. Unlike antipsychotics (A), which lack consistent evidence for delirium prevention, or benzodiazepines (C), which can worsen delirium, early mobilization promotes physical activity and cognitive engagement. Sedative-hypnotics (D) may also exacerbate delirium risk. Early mobility improves outcomes by maintaining muscle strength and promoting neurological function, thus effectively reducing both incidence and severity compared to pharmacological interventions.

Question 35: Correct Answer: A) Serum potassium levels
Rationale: Insulin therapy can cause hypokalemia by driving potassium into cells, thus serum potassium levels must be closely monitored. While serum sodium and BUN may be affected by dehydration, they are not directly altered by insulin infusion. Serum calcium is less likely to fluctuate acutely due to insulin administration. Monitoring potassium is crucial because hypokalemia can lead to life-threatening cardiac arrhythmias, making it a priority in managing patients with severe hyperglycemia receiving insulin therapy.

Question 36: Correct Answer: C) Performing endotracheal intubation and mechanical ventilation
Rationale: Endotracheal intubation and mechanical ventilation are crucial for patients with severe hypoxemia and respiratory distress when non-invasive methods fail. While high-flow nasal cannula (Option A) can improve oxygenation, it may not suffice in severe cases. Broad-spectrum antibiotics (Option B) address infection but do not directly manage acute hypoxemia. Nebulized bronchodilators (Option D) are beneficial for bronchospasm but inadequate alone for severe hypoxemia. Intubation ensures airway protection and adequate ventilation, crucial in critical care settings.

Question 37: Correct Answer: D) Prepare for an emergent fasciotomy.
Rationale: Emergent fasciotomy is crucial in preventing irreversible damage from compartment syndrome by relieving pressure. While elevation (A) might reduce swelling, it can decrease perfusion in compartment syndrome. Ice packs (B) can cause vasoconstriction, worsening ischemia. Analgesics (C) address symptoms but not the underlying pressure issue. Thus, D is correct as it directly addresses the cause of compartment syndrome by releasing pressure and restoring blood flow, which is supported by contemporary research emphasizing timely surgical intervention as critical in such cases.

Question 38: Correct Answer: B) Hyperkalemia
Rationale: Rhabdomyolysis often results in hyperkalemia due to the release of intracellular potassium from damaged muscle cells into the bloodstream. This can cause cardiac arrhythmias, making it a critical concern. Hypokalemia (A) is incorrect as it involves low potassium levels. Hyponatremia (C) and hypercalcemia (D) are less directly linked to rhabdomyolysis. Hyponatremia involves low sodium levels, while hypercalcemia involves high calcium levels, neither of which are primary concerns in rhabdomyolysis compared to hyperkalemia's cardiac implications.

Question 39: Correct Answer: B) Encouraging early ambulation as tolerated
Rationale: Early ambulation is crucial in preventing DVT by promoting venous return and reducing stasis. While low-dose aspirin (A) can reduce clotting risk, it is less effective than mechanical movement. Ice packs (C) are used for swelling, not DVT prevention. Passive range-of-motion exercises (D) help maintain joint function but do not actively prevent DVT like ambulation does. Therefore, encouraging early ambulation directly addresses the primary risk factor of immobility associated with post-operative care in musculoskeletal injuries.

Question 40: Correct Answer: B) Initiating positive pressure ventilation with PEEP
Rationale: Positive pressure ventilation with PEEP is crucial in managing flail chest as it stabilizes the chest wall and improves oxygenation. While administering high-flow oxygen (Option A) can help, it does not address paradoxical breathing. Needle decompression (Option C) is relevant for tension pneumothorax, not flail chest. Aggressive fluid resuscitation (Option D) may worsen pulmonary edema without directly improving ventilation. Thus, Option B effectively addresses the pathophysiology of flail chest by maintaining alveolar stability and enhancing gas exchange.

Question 41: Correct Answer: B) Obtain a wound culture before starting antibiotics
Rationale: Obtaining a wound culture before starting antibiotics ensures targeted therapy, crucial for effective treatment and antibiotic stewardship. While initiating broad-spectrum antibiotics (Option A) can be necessary in severe cases, it risks resistance without culture guidance. Debridement (Option C) is important but secondary to identifying pathogens. Topical antiseptics (Option D) may help but do not address systemic infection risks. Thus, Option B is prioritized for accurate diagnosis and management based on contemporary guidelines for diabetic wound infections.

Question 42: Correct Answer: B) Platelet destruction mediated by autoantibodies
Rationale: In ITP, autoantibodies target platelets, leading to their destruction, primarily in the spleen. Option A is incorrect as increased production does not cause thrombocytopenia. Option C, sequestration, contributes but isn't primary. Option D describes disseminated intravascular coagulation (DIC), not ITP. The key distinction lies in autoantibody involvement specific to ITP, differentiating it from other thrombocytopenic mechanisms.

Question 43: Correct Answer: C) Initiate continuous nebulized albuterol treatment
Rationale: Continuous nebulized albuterol is crucial for acute asthma exacerbations when initial inhaler use fails. It rapidly relieves bronchospasm. Option A (intravenous corticosteroids) helps reduce inflammation but acts slower than albuterol. Option B (supplemental oxygen) addresses hypoxia but doesn't relieve bronchospasm.

Option D (endotracheal intubation) is reserved for severe cases with respiratory failure and not an immediate step in this scenario. Thus, continuous nebulized albuterol directly addresses Emily's acute bronchospasm effectively and promptly.

Question 44: Correct Answer: A) Administer intravenous mannitol to reduce intracranial pressure.
Rationale: Administering intravenous mannitol is the correct initial intervention as it acts as an osmotic diuretic, reducing cerebral edema and intracranial pressure rapidly. Option B is incorrect because a lumbar puncture can worsen symptoms in obstructive hydrocephalus by causing brain herniation. Option C, while necessary eventually, is not an immediate intervention. Option D is incorrect as Trendelenburg positioning can increase intracranial pressure rather than decrease it. Understanding these interventions requires knowledge of pathophysiology and appropriate acute management strategies in hydrocephalus.

Question 45: Correct Answer: C) High total iron binding capacity (TIBC)
Rationale: High TIBC is indicative of iron deficiency anemia because the body increases transferrin production to capture more iron due to low stores. While low serum iron (Option B) is also seen in this condition, it is not as specific without considering TIBC. Elevated ferritin (Option A) usually suggests adequate or excessive iron stores, which contradicts iron deficiency. Increased MCV (Option D) typically indicates macrocytic anemias such as B12 or folate deficiency, not microcytic anemias like iron deficiency.

Question 46: Correct Answer: C) Maintaining systolic blood pressure below 140 mmHg
Rationale: In subarachnoid hemorrhage, controlling systolic blood pressure below 140 mmHg is crucial to prevent rebleeding. Option A (mannitol) addresses intracranial pressure but not rebleeding. Option B (nimodipine) prevents vasospasm, not rebleeding. Option D (anticoagulation) increases bleeding risk and is contraindicated. Managing blood pressure directly reduces the risk of recurrent hemorrhage, aligning with contemporary guidelines and research.

Question 47: Correct Answer: B) Prepare for immediate percutaneous coronary intervention (PCI)
Rationale: The presence of ST-segment elevation in leads II, III, and aVF indicates an inferior STEMI, requiring urgent reperfusion therapy. Option B is correct as PCI is the preferred treatment to restore coronary blood flow. Option A is supportive but not definitive. Option C addresses symptoms but not the underlying cause. Option D can be harmful if contraindicated by conditions such as hypotension or bradycardia. Therefore, prioritizing PCI aligns with contemporary guidelines for managing acute coronary syndrome effectively.

Question 48: Correct Answer: B) Disseminated Intravascular Coagulation (DIC)
Rationale: John's symptoms and lab findings suggest DIC, characterized by low platelets, elevated D-dimer, and bleeding signs. TTP also presents with thrombocytopenia but typically includes neurological symptoms and normal D-dimer levels. ITP involves isolated thrombocytopenia without elevated D-dimer or systemic signs of sepsis. HIT would be considered if he had recent heparin exposure, characterized by thrombocytopenia and possible thrombotic events rather than bleeding. Therefore, the combination of sepsis, low platelets, elevated D-dimer, and bleeding points to DIC as the correct diagnosis.

Question 49: Correct Answer: C) To evacuate accumulated blood and alleviate pressure on the brain
Rationale: Burr holes are primarily used to evacuate blood from a subdural hematoma, relieving pressure on the brain. Option A is incorrect as it refers to cerebrospinal fluid drainage, not blood. Option B involves monitoring, not evacuation. Option D pertains to hydrocephalus treatment, unrelated to hematomas. The correct choice, C, aligns with contemporary neurosurgical practices where burr holes enable direct access to remove clotted blood and reduce intracranial pressure effectively.

Question 50: Correct Answer: B) Open reduction and internal fixation (ORIF)
Rationale: ORIF is preferred for intertrochanteric fractures in osteoporotic patients due to its ability to stabilize the fracture and allow early mobilization, reducing complications. Option A is less effective as non-weight bearing can lead to prolonged immobility. Option C, hip arthroplasty, is more common for displaced femoral neck fractures rather than intertrochanteric ones. Option D delays definitive treatment, increasing risk of complications like deep vein thrombosis or pneumonia. Thus, ORIF offers the best balance between stabilization and recovery in this scenario.

Question 51: Correct Answer: A) Lorazepam
Rationale: Lorazepam, a benzodiazepine, is the first-line treatment for severe alcohol withdrawal due to its efficacy in reducing symptoms and preventing delirium tremens. Haloperidol (B) may be used for agitation but does not address withdrawal symptoms. Clonidine (C) can manage autonomic symptoms but is not primary for alcohol withdrawal. Disulfiram (D) is used for alcohol aversion therapy, not acute withdrawal management. The key difference lies in lorazepam's ability to modulate GABA receptors effectively, thus stabilizing neuronal activity during withdrawal.

Question 52: Correct Answer: A) Administer intravenous fluids to increase preload.
Rationale: Administering intravenous fluids is crucial for increasing preload and enhancing cardiac output in post-operative valve replacement patients. This intervention directly addresses hypovolemia often seen post-surgery. Option B (dobutamine infusion) may be considered if fluid resuscitation is inadequate but isn't the first-line intervention. Option C (oxygen delivery) and D (ventilator adjustments) are supportive measures but do not directly address decreased cardiac output due to low preload. Thus, A is prioritized based on physiological principles of hemodynamic management in post-surgical care.

Question 53: Correct Answer: D) Conduct a thorough assessment for potential delirium triggers.
Rationale: The initial step in managing Mrs. Thompson's symptoms should be conducting a thorough assessment for potential delirium triggers (Option D). Delirium can exacerbate dementia symptoms and may be caused by factors such as infections, medications, or metabolic imbalances. Identifying these triggers allows for targeted interventions. Option A (antipsychotics) is not first-line due to potential side effects; Option B (reorientation) is supportive but not primary; Option C (restraints) can increase agitation and should be avoided unless absolutely necessary. Understanding and addressing underlying causes is crucial in dementia care.

Question 54: Correct Answer: B) Direct Coombs test
Rationale: The Direct Coombs test is crucial for diagnosing AIHA as it detects antibodies bound to red blood cells, confirming immune-mediated hemolysis. While a peripheral blood smear (A) shows spherocytes,

it's not definitive. Serum haptoglobin (C) decreases in hemolysis but isn't specific to AIHA. Reticulocyte count (D) indicates increased erythropoiesis but doesn't confirm AIHA's immune basis. The Direct Coombs test directly identifies the presence of autoantibodies on RBCs, making it the most specific diagnostic tool for AIHA among the options provided.

Question 55: Correct Answer: C) Providing a calm and quiet environment.
Rationale: The correct answer is C) Providing a calm and quiet environment, as it helps reduce external stimuli that may exacerbate hyperactive delirium. Option A, lorazepam, can worsen delirium in elderly patients due to its sedative effects. Option B, increasing sensory stimulation, may further disorient the patient. Option D, while supportive, might increase stimulation and confusion if not managed carefully. Creating a low-stimulus environment aligns with contemporary research on managing delirium by minimizing stressors and promoting recovery through environmental control.

Question 56: Correct Answer: D) Nitroprusside
Rationale: Nitroprusside is the most appropriate medication for rapid blood pressure reduction in hypertensive crisis due to its immediate onset and ability to be titrated easily. Labetalol, while effective, has a slower onset compared to nitroprusside. Nifedipine is not recommended due to unpredictable effects and potential harm. Hydralazine can cause reflex tachycardia and is less predictable in effect. Therefore, nitroprusside's rapid action and controllability make it the preferred choice in acute settings where swift management is crucial.

Question 57: Correct Answer: A) Activation of recipient neutrophils by donor antibodies
Rationale: TRALI is primarily caused by the activation of recipient neutrophils by donor antibodies, leading to acute lung injury. Option B is incorrect as hemolysis is not a mechanism in TRALI. Option C, while related to immune response, does not accurately describe TRALI's pathophysiology. Option D involves immune complexes, which are not central to TRALI's development. The key difference lies in the specific immune activation by donor antibodies, which distinguishes TRALI from other transfusion reactions.

Question 58: Correct Answer: B) Initiate intravenous hydration with normal saline
Rationale: The initial management of hypercalcemia in cancer patients like Sarah involves aggressive intravenous hydration with normal saline to dilute serum calcium and promote renal excretion. While bisphosphonates (Option A) and calcitonin (Option C) are important for longer-term management, they are not immediate interventions. Dialysis (Option D) is reserved for severe cases unresponsive to other treatments. Hydration addresses both the confusion and polyuria by correcting dehydration and facilitating calcium excretion, which is crucial in acute settings.

Question 59: Correct Answer: D) Adhesions form bands that kink or twist the bowel, obstructing passage of intestinal contents.
Rationale: Option D is correct as adhesions often form fibrous bands that can kink or twist the bowel, physically blocking passage and leading to obstruction. Option A is incorrect; while inflammation can occur, it does not primarily cause lumen narrowing. Option B suggests restriction of peristalsis but does not account for mechanical obstruction as effectively as option D. Option C involves ischemia but fails to directly address adhesion-induced twisting or kinking as a primary mechanism for obstruction.

Question 60: Correct Answer: B) Tension pneumothorax
Rationale: The clinical presentation of dyspnea, unilateral chest pain, decreased breath sounds, hyperresonance, and mediastinal shift to the opposite side strongly suggests a tension pneumothorax. This condition occurs when air becomes trapped in the pleural space, causing increased pressure that shifts mediastinal structures. Option A (Pleural effusion) would typically present with dullness on percussion and no mediastinal shift unless massive. Option C (Simple pneumothorax) lacks significant mediastinal shift due to less pressure build-up. Option D (Atelectasis) usually results in mediastinal shift towards the affected side, not away from it.

Question 61: Correct Answer: A) Prerenal azotemia due to hypovolemia
Rationale: Prerenal azotemia is often caused by decreased renal perfusion, commonly from hypovolemia, especially in the context of infection. Mr. Thompson's recent infection could have led to fluid losses and decreased kidney perfusion. Option B is incorrect as there's no mention of nephrotoxic drug use. Option C is unlikely without urinary symptoms or evidence of obstruction. Option D is possible but less common compared to prerenal causes in this scenario. Understanding these distinctions helps identify prerenal azotemia as the most plausible cause in Mr. Thompson's case.

Question 62: Correct Answer: C) Implementation of a multimodal approach including non-pharmacological interventions
Rationale: Contemporary research supports a multimodal approach, including non-pharmacological interventions, as it effectively reduces agitation without the adverse effects associated with pharmacological methods. Option A, using physical restraints, can increase agitation and risk for injury. Option B, high-dose benzodiazepines, may lead to delirium and prolonged sedation. Option D, continuous propofol infusion alone, lacks comprehensive management and can cause hypotension. Thus, integrating environmental modifications and therapeutic communication alongside medication is most beneficial.

Question 63: Correct Answer: C) Increased ammonia levels
Rationale: Increased ammonia levels are most indicative of hepatic encephalopathy in cirrhosis. Ammonia accumulates due to impaired liver function, leading to neurotoxicity. While elevated bilirubin (Option A), decreased albumin (Option B), and prolonged prothrombin time (Option D) also reflect liver dysfunction, they are not specific markers for hepatic encephalopathy. Bilirubin indicates jaundice; low albumin suggests poor protein synthesis; and prolonged prothrombin time indicates coagulation issues. Therefore, increased ammonia levels directly correlate with neurological symptoms, making it the most relevant indicator of hepatic encephalopathy in cirrhotic patients.

Question 64: Correct Answer: C) Immediate endovascular aneurysm repair (EVAR)
Rationale: The correct answer is C) Immediate endovascular aneurysm repair (EVAR). Given John's symptomatic presentation and the size of the aneurysm, immediate intervention is necessary to prevent rupture. Option A, initiating beta-blocker therapy, does not address the acute risk of rupture. Option B, scheduling elective repair, is inappropriate due to the emergent nature of his condition. Option D, managing blood pressure alone, fails to resolve the life-threatening aneurysm itself. EVAR is preferred for its minimally invasive approach in emergencies like John's.

Question 65: Correct Answer: A) Initiate high-dose corticosteroids
Rationale: High-dose corticosteroids are the first-line treatment for autoimmune hemolytic anemia to suppress the immune response causing red blood cell destruction. While IVIG (B) can be used, it is typically reserved for refractory cases. Plasmapheresis (C) is less effective in this context as it removes antibodies from circulation temporarily. Transfusing packed red blood cells (D) can manage severe anemia but does not address the underlying immune-mediated hemolysis. Therefore, corticosteroids are preferred for their efficacy in reducing antibody production and hemolysis in acute crises.

Question 66: Correct Answer: B) Maintaining systolic blood pressure below 160 mmHg
Rationale: Maintaining systolic blood pressure below 160 mmHg is crucial in hemorrhagic stroke to prevent rebleeding and reduce intracranial pressure. Option A is incorrect as thrombolytics are contraindicated in hemorrhagic stroke. Option C is inappropriate due to the risk of exacerbating bleeding. Option D, while relevant for managing cerebral edema, does not address the primary concern of preventing further hemorrhage. Thus, controlling blood pressure is paramount, aligning with contemporary research and guidelines on managing hemorrhagic strokes effectively.

Question 67: Correct Answer: B) Perform a diagnostic thoracentesis
Rationale: The correct answer is B) Perform a diagnostic thoracentesis because it confirms empyema by analyzing pleural fluid. A) Starting antibiotics is crucial but should follow fluid analysis to target pathogens effectively. C) A CT scan helps assess the extent but isn't the initial step. D) Oxygen therapy addresses respiratory distress but doesn't diagnose empyema. Thus, thoracentesis is critical for accurate diagnosis and guides subsequent treatment decisions, making it the most appropriate initial step in managing suspected empyema.

Question 68: Correct Answer: B) Start enzyme replacement therapy
Rationale: The Whipple procedure often leads to exocrine pancreatic insufficiency, causing malabsorption. Enzyme replacement therapy compensates for reduced pancreatic enzyme production, aiding digestion and nutrient absorption. While TPN (Option A) provides nutrients intravenously, it doesn't address the underlying enzyme deficiency. Increasing dietary fiber (Option C) might worsen malabsorption symptoms by further hindering digestion. Proton pump inhibitors (Option D) reduce stomach acid but don't improve enzyme function. Therefore, enzyme replacement is the most direct and effective intervention for Sarah's malabsorption post-Whipple procedure.

Question 69: Correct Answer: B) Initiate intravenous thrombolytic therapy.
Rationale: Intravenous thrombolytic therapy, such as tissue plasminogen activator (tPA), is crucial within the first three hours to dissolve the clot and restore cerebral blood flow in ischemic embolic strokes. Option A (aspirin) is not effective for acute clot dissolution. Option C (heparin) is used for prevention rather than acute treatment. Option D (oxygen supplementation) addresses hypoxia but does not resolve the embolism. The timely administration of tPA significantly improves neurological outcomes by directly targeting the cause of ischemic embolism, distinguishing it from other supportive measures.

Question 70: Correct Answer: B) Synchronized Cardioversion
Rationale: In cases of hemodynamic instability in Wolff-Parkinson-White syndrome, synchronized cardioversion is the preferred treatment due to its rapid action in restoring normal rhythm. Amiodarone (A) and Adenosine (C) may exacerbate accessory pathway conduction, worsening tachyarrhythmias. Oral Beta-blockers (D) are inappropriate for acute management due to delayed onset and potential risk of worsening symptoms. Synchronized cardioversion effectively addresses the immediate threat posed by unstable arrhythmias, aligning with contemporary clinical guidelines for acute intervention in WPW syndrome.

Question 71: Correct Answer: B) Encouraging Sarah to participate in guided imagery sessions.
Rationale: Guided imagery helps reduce anxiety by promoting relaxation through mental visualization, making it effective for managing emotional lability post-injury. While benzodiazepines (Option A) can alleviate anxiety, they may worsen cognitive function in brain injuries. A structured routine (Option C) aids stability but doesn't specifically target anxiety. CBT (Option D), though effective for long-term management, requires cognitive engagement that may be challenging immediately post-injury. Thus, guided imagery is optimal for immediate psychosocial support without adverse effects on cognition.

Question 72: Correct Answer: B) Swelling with taut, stretched skin
Rationale: Swelling with taut, stretched skin is a critical sign of significant infiltration that may lead to compartment syndrome, necessitating urgent intervention. While coolness and pallor (A) indicate reduced circulation, pain and numbness (C) suggest nerve involvement, and redness and warmth (D) can indicate phlebitis or infection, none are as directly linked to severe tissue damage as option B. The distinction lies in the potential for increased pressure compromising circulation, making B the most urgent indicator.

Question 73: Correct Answer: B) Desmopressin
Rationale: Desmopressin is the treatment of choice for central Diabetes Insipidus (DI), as it replaces the deficient antidiuretic hormone (ADH). Option A (Intravenous fluids) may manage dehydration but does not address the underlying ADH deficiency. Option C (Thiazide diuretics) can paradoxically reduce urine output in nephrogenic DI but not in central DI. Option D (Insulin therapy) is irrelevant here as Sarah's serum glucose levels are normal, indicating that her polyuria is not due to diabetes mellitus. Desmopressin directly targets the cause of Sarah's symptoms, making it the correct choice.

Question 74: Correct Answer: A) Administer aspirin immediately.
Rationale: Administering aspirin immediately is crucial as it reduces the risk of subsequent strokes by inhibiting platelet aggregation. Option B, scheduling an MRI, while useful for diagnosis, does not provide immediate prevention. Option C, thrombolytic therapy, is inappropriate for TIA as it carries unnecessary risks. Option D, carotid ultrasound, helps in assessing stenosis but does not offer immediate prevention. The key difference lies in the immediacy and preventive nature of aspirin compared to diagnostic or treatment planning approaches in other options.

Question 75: Correct Answer: B) Pulsus paradoxus
Rationale: Pulsus paradoxus, an exaggerated decrease in systolic blood pressure during inspiration, is a key indicator of cardiac tamponade, suggesting hemodynamic compromise due to pericardial effusion. While distant heart sounds (Option A) and jugular venous distension

(Option C) are associated signs, they are not as specific for hemodynamic instability. Hypotension (Option D) can occur but is a later sign. The presence of pulsus paradoxus directly reflects impaired ventricular filling, making it the most critical sign among the options provided.

Question 76: Correct Answer: B) The risk of hemorrhagic transformation increases significantly if tPA is administered beyond 4.5 hours.
Rationale: Option B is correct because administering tPA beyond 4.5 hours significantly raises the risk of hemorrhagic transformation, as established in clinical guidelines and research studies. Option A is incorrect since the window for effective tPA administration is typically within 4.5 hours, not 6. Option C is misleading; a history of TIAs does not contraindicate tPA use, though other factors might. Option D highlights an important consideration regarding blood pressure control but doesn't directly address timing and risks associated with tPA administration, making it less accurate than option B.

Question 77: Correct Answer: B) Music therapy
Rationale: Music therapy has been shown to effectively reduce anxiety in patients undergoing prolonged mechanical ventilation by promoting relaxation and providing a distraction from stressors. While CBT is effective for long-term anxiety management, it requires active participation and time, making it less suitable for immediate relief in critical care settings. MBSR also requires practice and commitment. Guided imagery can be helpful but is less effective than music therapy in this specific context due to its reliance on patient visualization skills. Therefore, music therapy stands out as the optimal choice for immediate anxiety reduction.

Question 78: Correct Answer: C) Elevating the head of the bed to 30 degrees
Rationale: Elevating the head of the bed to 30 degrees is crucial as it enhances venous drainage and reduces intracranial pressure. Mannitol (Option A) is effective but not an immediate intervention; it acts over time by reducing cerebral edema. Lumbar puncture (Option B) is contraindicated in acute settings due to risk of brain herniation. Hyperventilation (Option D) temporarily decreases intracranial pressure by reducing CO2 levels, but it can lead to cerebral vasoconstriction and ischemia if prolonged. Thus, Option C is preferred for immediate management.

Question 79: Correct Answer: C) Start intravenous octreotide to control variceal bleeding.
Rationale: In cases of acute variceal bleeding due to portal hypertension, intravenous octreotide is prioritized as it effectively reduces splanchnic blood flow and portal pressure, thereby controlling bleeding. Option A is incorrect as beta-blockers are not used in acute settings. Option B, TIPS, is considered after stabilization if bleeding persists. Option D, endoscopic band ligation, is effective but typically follows pharmacological stabilization. Octreotide acts quickly in acute scenarios, making it the most appropriate initial intervention compared to the other options.

Question 80: Correct Answer: A) Implementing hourly rounding to assess patient needs
Rationale: Hourly rounding is the most effective intervention as it proactively addresses patient needs, reducing fall risks by ensuring timely assistance. While bed alarms (B) alert staff, they react rather than prevent. Non-slip socks (C) offer some protection but do not address underlying risks. Conducting a fall risk assessment upon admission only (D) fails to account for changes in patient condition. Thus, regular assessments and proactive engagement through hourly rounding provide comprehensive fall prevention strategies, aligning with contemporary research emphasizing continuous monitoring and intervention.

Question 81: Correct Answer: A) Patient's age and life expectancy
Rationale: The choice between a mechanical and bioprosthetic valve primarily hinges on the patient's age and life expectancy. Younger patients often receive mechanical valves due to their durability, despite requiring lifelong anticoagulation. Conversely, older patients may benefit from bioprosthetic valves, which have a lower risk of thromboembolism and don't require long-term anticoagulation. Although options B), C), and D) are important considerations, they are secondary to age and life expectancy when determining the appropriate type of valve replacement.

Question 82: Correct Answer: C) Performing an external ventricular drain (EVD) placement to relieve hydrocephalus
Rationale: EVD placement is crucial for managing acute hydrocephalus caused by IVH, preventing further neurological decline. Option A, mannitol, reduces ICP but doesn't address CSF drainage directly. Option B, controlling BP, is vital but not immediate for hydrocephalus relief. Option D is contraindicated due to bleeding risk. Thus, EVD directly addresses CSF buildup caused by IVH, making it the immediate priority compared to other options focused on secondary aspects or contraindicated interventions.

Question 83: Correct Answer: C) GABAergic system
Rationale: Chronic alcohol dependence primarily affects the GABAergic system, enhancing its inhibitory effects and contributing to mood alterations and behavioral changes. While the dopaminergic system (Option A) is involved in reward pathways, it is not primarily affected by alcohol. The serotonergic system (Option B) influences mood but is less directly impacted by alcohol compared to GABA. The glutamatergic system (Option D) is involved in excitatory signaling and becomes more active during withdrawal, but it is not the primary target during chronic use. Understanding these distinctions helps in managing substance use disorders effectively.

Question 84: Correct Answer: B) Cerebrospinal fluid analysis
Rationale: Cerebrospinal fluid analysis is crucial in diagnosing Guillain-Barré Syndrome, typically revealing elevated protein levels with normal white cell count. Nerve conduction studies (A) and electromyography (D) can show demyelination but are not as immediate or definitive as CSF analysis. MRI (C) is not typically used for GBS diagnosis but can rule out other conditions. The CSF finding of albuminocytologic dissociation is a hallmark in GBS, distinguishing it from other neuromuscular disorders, making option B the most accurate choice.

Question 85: Correct Answer: A) Epidural hematoma
Rationale: An epidural hematoma typically presents with a biconvex shape on CT and is associated with rapid neurological deterioration due to arterial bleeding. Subdural hematomas (Option B) are crescent-shaped and progress more slowly as they involve venous bleeding. Concussions (Option C) do not show structural lesions on imaging like hematomas do. Diffuse axonal injury (Option D) involves widespread brain damage rather than localized bleeding. The key difference lies in the CT appearance and the speed of symptom progression, which aligns with an epidural hematoma in this scenario.

Question 86: Correct Answer: B) Apply a pelvic binder to reduce bleeding and stabilize the fracture.
Rationale: Applying a pelvic binder is crucial in managing hemodynamic instability from a pelvic fracture as it helps control bleeding by stabilizing the fractured pelvis. Option A (aggressive fluid administration) may worsen bleeding without stabilization. Option C (immediate surgery) is not prioritized before initial stabilization. Option D (vasopressors) may be necessary but only after mechanical stabilization. The binder effectively reduces pelvic volume, thus controlling hemorrhage, making it the priority intervention in this scenario.

Question 87: Correct Answer: B) Intravenous vancomycin
Rationale: In patients with cellulitis who have risk factors such as diabetes, intravenous vancomycin is preferred due to its efficacy against MRSA and severe infections. While oral cephalexin (Option C) could be used for mild cases without complicating factors, John's diabetes and systemic symptoms necessitate more aggressive treatment. Oral amoxicillin (Option A) lacks sufficient coverage for MRSA. Topical mupirocin (Option D) is inappropriate for systemic infections like cellulitis. Vancomycin provides broad-spectrum coverage necessary in this scenario, especially given John's compromised immune status due to diabetes.

Question 88: Correct Answer: C) Ensuring adequate cerebral perfusion pressure
Rationale: Ensuring adequate cerebral perfusion pressure (CPP) is crucial as it maintains blood flow to the brain, preventing ischemia and further neurological damage. While mannitol (Option A) reduces intracranial pressure, it does not directly address CPP. Therapeutic hypothermia (Option B) can be beneficial post-cardiac arrest but is not primary for hemorrhage management. Supplemental oxygen (Option D) helps maintain normoxia but does not specifically target CPP. Thus, maintaining CPP directly prevents secondary injury, making it the most critical intervention in this context.

Question 89: Correct Answer: B) Hourly rounding by nursing staff
Rationale: Hourly rounding by nursing staff is supported by research as an effective intervention to reduce fall risk in ICUs. It proactively addresses patient needs, such as toileting and repositioning, reducing the likelihood of falls. Continuous video monitoring (A) is more passive and doesn't directly prevent falls. Bed alarms (C), while useful, can lead to alarm fatigue and may not prevent falls proactively. Individualized education (D) is important but less immediate in impact compared to the direct oversight provided by hourly rounding.

Question 90: Correct Answer: C) Rapid intravenous fluid resuscitation
Rationale: Rapid intravenous fluid resuscitation is crucial for stabilizing hemodynamically unstable patients with acute GI hemorrhage, as it restores intravascular volume and maintains perfusion. While PPIs (A) and endoscopy (B) are important, they do not address immediate hemodynamic instability. Blood transfusions (D) are essential but should aim to maintain hemoglobin at safe levels rather than an arbitrary high threshold. The key difference is that fluid resuscitation directly impacts circulation and organ perfusion, which is critical in acute settings.

Question 91: Correct Answer: B) Adequate debridement of necrotic tissue
Rationale: Adequate debridement of necrotic tissue is crucial as it removes dead tissue that can harbor bacteria, thereby reducing infection risk and promoting healing. While early antibiotic use (Option A) is important, it does not address existing necrotic tissue. Negative pressure therapy (Option C) aids in wound healing but is less effective if necrotic tissue remains. Frequent dressing changes (Option D) help maintain cleanliness but are secondary to removing necrotic matter. Debridement directly addresses the root cause, making it the most critical initial intervention.

Question 92: Correct Answer: B) Initiating aggressive fluid replacement with isotonic saline.
Rationale: The primary intervention for Hyperosmolar Hyperglycemic State (HHS) is aggressive fluid replacement with isotonic saline to address severe dehydration and restore circulatory volume. Option A, administering insulin, is important but secondary after initial fluid resuscitation. Option C, bicarbonate therapy, is not indicated as there is no significant acidosis in HHS. Option D, potassium replacement, may be necessary later but only after ensuring adequate renal function and initial fluid resuscitation. Therefore, option B directly addresses the immediate need for rehydration in HHS.

Question 93: Correct Answer: B) Intravenous octreotide infusion
Rationale: Intravenous octreotide infusion is considered the most effective initial treatment for acute esophageal variceal bleeding due to its ability to reduce portal venous pressure by inhibiting splanchnic blood flow. While endoscopic variceal ligation (A) is a definitive treatment, it is not typically the first step. TIPS (C) is more invasive and used when other treatments fail. Balloon tamponade (D) is a temporary measure with significant risks. Octreotide's rapid action in reducing portal pressure makes it the preferred initial choice in stabilizing patients with active bleeding.

Question 94: Correct Answer: C) Joint contractures
Rationale: Joint contractures are a significant musculoskeletal complication of prolonged immobility, leading to reduced range of motion and functional impairment. Unlike osteoporosis (A), which affects bone density over time, joint contractures develop from muscle shortening and joint stiffness due to immobility. Muscle atrophy (B) involves muscle wasting but does not directly cause joint immobility. Pressure ulcers (D), while a concern in immobile patients, affect the skin rather than musculoskeletal function. Understanding these distinctions is crucial for managing and preventing complications associated with immobility in critical care settings.

Question 95: Correct Answer: A) Initiate broad-spectrum intravenous antibiotics
Rationale: Initiating broad-spectrum intravenous antibiotics is crucial in managing severe urinary tract infections (UTIs), especially in diabetic patients like Sarah who are at higher risk for complications such as pyelonephritis or sepsis. Option B may be less effective initially due to potential severity and resistance issues. Option C alone is inadequate for addressing infection. Option D addresses symptom relief but not the underlying infection. Prompt IV antibiotic therapy reduces complication risks by rapidly addressing systemic infection signs in high-risk patients like Sarah.

Question 96: Correct Answer: A) Maintaining strict glycemic control
Rationale: Strict glycemic control is paramount in diabetic patients as hyperglycemia impairs leukocyte function, collagen synthesis, and angiogenesis, all crucial for wound healing. Although regular debridement (B) and advanced dressings (C) are important, they do not address the systemic issue of high blood sugar. Systemic

antibiotics (D) are only necessary if infection is present. Therefore, while all options contribute to wound management, maintaining glycemic control directly influences the physiological processes essential for effective healing.

Question 97: Correct Answer: B) Implementing a structured reorientation program
Rationale: Implementing a structured reorientation program effectively addresses hypoactive delirium by promoting cognitive engagement and orientation, targeting the root cause rather than symptoms. Option A, administering antipsychotics, may not address underlying causes and can have adverse effects. Option C, increasing sedatives, exacerbates hypoactivity. Option D, physical restraints, can worsen delirium and lead to complications. Reorientation programs align with contemporary research emphasizing non-pharmacological interventions for delirium management, making it the most effective choice.

Question 98: Correct Answer: B) Endoscopic third ventriculostomy
Rationale: Endoscopic third ventriculostomy (ETV) is the preferred initial intervention for non-communicating hydrocephalus caused by obstruction in the ventricular system, particularly in the third ventricle. It creates a bypass for cerebrospinal fluid flow, alleviating pressure without external hardware. Option A (Lumbar puncture) is contraindicated due to risk of herniation. Option C (Ventriculoperitoneal shunt) is more invasive and typically considered if ETV fails. Option D (Acetazolamide) can reduce CSF production but is not definitive for obstructive hydrocephalus.

Question 99: Correct Answer: C) Ensuring normothermia and avoiding hyperthermia
Rationale: Ensuring normothermia is crucial as hyperthermia can exacerbate neuronal injury and increase metabolic demand, worsening outcomes in IVH. Option A is important but CPP targets vary; B lacks evidence for routine use in IVH; D has limited efficacy in this context. Normothermia directly mitigates secondary brain injury by stabilizing physiological processes, making it a critical intervention.

Question 100: Correct Answer: B) Administer erythropoiesis-stimulating agents (ESAs)
Rationale: In CKD, anemia is often due to decreased erythropoietin production by the kidneys. Administering ESAs directly addresses this deficiency, making it the most appropriate intervention. Oral iron supplements (A) are beneficial if iron deficiency is present but do not stimulate erythropoiesis. Vitamin B12 injections (C) and folic acid supplements (D) are useful for specific deficiencies but do not target the primary cause of anemia in CKD. ESAs effectively increase hemoglobin levels, improving symptoms like fatigue and pallor in CKD patients.

Question 101: Correct Answer: A) Streptococcus pneumoniae
Rationale: Streptococcus pneumoniae is the most common cause of bacterial meningitis in adults with predisposing conditions such as sinusitis. Neisseria meningitidis typically affects younger populations or those in close quarters. Haemophilus influenzae is less common due to vaccination, and Listeria monocytogenes is more prevalent in immunocompromised individuals or the elderly. The patient's age and history of sinusitis strongly suggest S. pneumoniae as the causative agent, making option A the correct choice based on contemporary understanding and clinical guidelines.

Question 102: Correct Answer: B) CT Angiography
Rationale: CT Angiography is the preferred initial diagnostic test for mesenteric ischemia due to its high sensitivity and specificity in detecting vascular occlusions. While an abdominal X-ray (Option A) can identify bowel obstruction or perforation, it is not specific for mesenteric ischemia. MRI (Option C) provides detailed images but is less practical in acute settings. Ultrasound (Option D) is useful for evaluating blood flow but may miss early ischemic changes. Therefore, CT Angiography is favored for rapid and accurate diagnosis in suspected cases of mesenteric ischemia.

Question 103: Correct Answer: C) Mineralocorticoid receptor antagonists (MRAs)
Rationale: MRAs, such as spironolactone and eplerenone, specifically target aldosterone receptors, reducing mortality in HFrEF by mitigating cardiac remodeling and fibrosis. While ACE inhibitors (Option A) and beta-blockers (Option B) also reduce mortality, they do so through different mechanisms, primarily affecting the renin-angiotensin system and sympathetic nervous system, respectively. Loop diuretics (Option D), while crucial for symptom management via fluid removal, do not directly impact mortality. Thus, MRAs are distinct in their specific action against aldosterone's detrimental effects in heart failure.

Question 104: Correct Answer: A) Decreased serum haptoglobin
Rationale: Decreased serum haptoglobin is a key indicator of hemolytic anemia because haptoglobin binds free hemoglobin released from lysed red blood cells. In hemolysis, haptoglobin levels drop as it gets depleted. Elevated MCV (Option B) suggests macrocytic anemia, not specifically hemolytic. Increased reticulocyte count (Option C) occurs in various anemias and indicates bone marrow response but is not specific to hemolysis. Low serum ferritin (Option D) typically points to iron deficiency anemia, unrelated to hemolytic processes. Thus, Option A is most indicative of hemolytic anemia in critical care settings.

Question 105: Correct Answer: C) Initiating mechanical ventilation with low tidal volumes
Rationale: Initiating mechanical ventilation with low tidal volumes is crucial to prevent further lung injury in patients with lung contusion. High tidal volumes can exacerbate alveolar damage. While high-flow oxygen (A) supports oxygenation, it does not address ventilator-induced injury. Aggressive fluid resuscitation (B) may worsen pulmonary edema. CPAP (D) can improve oxygenation but may not be sufficient alone for severe cases. Understanding these nuances is essential for managing lung contusions effectively and preventing complications like acute respiratory distress syndrome (ARDS).

Question 106: Correct Answer: B) Lung transplantation
Rationale: Lung transplantation is the only intervention that can significantly improve long-term survival in patients with advanced pulmonary fibrosis. High-dose corticosteroids (Option A) may reduce inflammation but do not alter disease progression. Long-term oxygen therapy (Option C) alleviates hypoxemia but does not improve prognosis. Pulmonary rehabilitation (Option D) enhances quality of life and exercise capacity but does not impact survival. The correct answer, lung transplantation, directly addresses end-stage lung disease by replacing damaged lungs, thus offering a potential for extended survival compared to other options.

Question 107: Correct Answer: B) Diuretics to manage fluid overload
Rationale: In patients with pleural effusions secondary to congestive heart failure, diuretics are the initial treatment

of choice as they address the underlying cause by reducing fluid overload. Thoracentesis (Option A) is typically reserved for diagnostic purposes or if diuretic therapy fails. Pleurodesis (Option C) is not indicated unless recurrent effusions are present and refractory to medical management. Chest tube insertion (Option D) is more invasive and generally unnecessary unless there is significant respiratory compromise or an empyema. Thus, diuretics offer the most effective initial intervention in this scenario.

Question 108: Correct Answer: B) West Nile Virus
Rationale: The symptoms presented by John—fever, headache, neck stiffness, and photophobia—are indicative of viral meningitis or encephalitis. Considering his travel history to an area with high viral infection rates, West Nile Virus is a probable cause due to its prevalence in certain geographic regions and its ability to cause neurological symptoms. Herpes Simplex Virus typically causes encephalitis but is less geographically influenced. Enterovirus can cause similar symptoms but is more common in children. Epstein-Barr Virus primarily causes infectious mononucleosis rather than acute neurological symptoms.

Question 109: Correct Answer: B) Liver transplantation
Rationale: Liver transplantation is the most definitive treatment for biliary atresia, offering improved long-term survival and liver function. While Kasai portoenterostomy (Option A) is a crucial initial surgical intervention that can delay disease progression, it often does not prevent eventual liver failure. Ursodeoxycholic acid (Option C) may aid bile flow but does not address the underlying obstruction. Percutaneous transhepatic cholangiography (Option D) is diagnostic, not therapeutic. Thus, transplantation remains the ultimate solution when other treatments fail to restore adequate liver function.

Question 110: Correct Answer: C) Administer intravenous diltiazem
Rationale: Intravenous diltiazem is often used as an initial intervention to control heart rate in postoperative atrial fibrillation due to its efficacy and rapid onset. While amiodarone (Option A) is effective for rhythm control, it is typically not the first-line treatment for rate control. Synchronized cardioversion (Option B) may be considered if pharmacological interventions fail or if the patient is hemodynamically unstable. Increasing beta-blocker dosage (Option D) might be beneficial but lacks the immediate effect needed in acute settings. Diltiazem's ability to quickly manage rate makes it the preferred initial choice.

Question 111: Correct Answer: B) Introduce visual cueing techniques
Rationale: Visual cueing techniques are effective in reducing freezing episodes in Parkinson's patients by providing external stimuli that help initiate movement. Option A, increasing levodopa, may not specifically target freezing episodes. Option C, while beneficial for overall mobility, does not directly address freezing. Option D provides stability but does not address the specific issue of freezing. Visual cues like floor markings or laser lines can help overcome motor blocks associated with freezing, making it the most targeted intervention for Emily's symptoms.

Question 112: Correct Answer: B) Prioritize assessing Mr. Thompson's risk for abuse or neglect.
Rationale: The correct answer is B because recognizing patterns of injury and behavioral cues are crucial in identifying potential abuse or neglect, especially given the repeated injuries and anxiety observed in Mr. Thompson. Option A, while important, doesn't address the underlying issue of potential abuse. Option C focuses on general care needs but misses the critical aspect of assessing safety and well-being related to abuse. Option D is relevant for recovery but does not address immediate concerns about potential harm or neglect that could be life-threatening if unaddressed.

Question 113: Correct Answer: B) Parathyroid hormone (PTH)
Rationale: Parathyroid hormone (PTH) is crucial in regulating serum calcium levels by increasing bone resorption and enhancing renal tubular reabsorption of calcium. While calcitonin (Option A) also affects calcium levels, it lowers them by inhibiting bone resorption. Vitamin D (Option C) aids in intestinal absorption of calcium but does not directly influence renal reabsorption or bone resorption like PTH. Aldosterone (Option D), involved in sodium and potassium balance, does not regulate calcium. Understanding these hormonal functions is vital for managing electrolyte imbalances in critical care settings.

Question 114: Correct Answer: B) Start intravenous labetalol infusion
Rationale: In hypertensive crises with end-organ damage symptoms like those Emily presents, immediate reduction of blood pressure is crucial. Intravenous labetalol is effective due to its rapid onset and controllable effects. Option A (oral medication) is inappropriate as it acts too slowly in emergencies. Option C (nitroglycerin) primarily targets coronary vasodilation and isn't first-line for acute BP control. Option D (oxygen therapy) doesn't address the underlying hypertensive crisis. Thus, option B is correct as it aligns with current best practices for managing hypertensive emergencies effectively.

Question 115: Correct Answer: B) Perform an arthrocentesis to obtain synovial fluid for analysis.
Rationale: Arthrocentesis is crucial for diagnosing septic arthritis, indicated by acute joint pain, swelling, and fever. NSAIDs (Option A) may relieve symptoms but don't address potential infection. Ice packs (Option C) are supportive but not diagnostic. Broad-spectrum antibiotics (Option D) should be delayed until after synovial fluid analysis confirms infection, preventing inappropriate treatment. The procedure allows for accurate diagnosis and tailored therapy, aligning with contemporary practices in musculoskeletal/neurological care.

Question 116: Correct Answer: B) Administration of benzodiazepines
Rationale: Benzodiazepines are the most effective for immediate relief of acute anxiety due to their rapid onset, which is crucial in critical care settings. Deep breathing (A) and progressive muscle relaxation (D), though beneficial, take longer to impact anxiety levels. Cognitive Behavioral Therapy (C), while effective long-term, is not suitable for immediate anxiety relief. Contemporary research supports benzodiazepines as first-line treatment for acute episodes, given their efficacy and quick action compared to other interventions that require more time and patient participation.

Question 117: Correct Answer: C) Perform a large-volume paracentesis
Rationale: Large-volume paracentesis is the correct initial management for severe ascites due to portal hypertension, providing rapid symptomatic relief. Option A (albumin infusion) supports circulatory function post-paracentesis but isn't the initial step. Option B (lactulose) targets hepatic encephalopathy, not directly addressing ascites. Option D (propranolol) reduces portal pressure long-term but doesn't provide immediate relief from ascites.

Question 118: Correct Answer: C) Troponin I
Rationale: Troponin I is the most specific biomarker for myocardial infarction due to its high specificity and sensitivity. It remains elevated longer than CK-MB, making it more reliable for late diagnosis. Myoglobin (Option A) rises quickly but lacks specificity. CK-MB (Option B) is less specific than troponins and returns to normal sooner. LDH (Option D) is a non-specific enzyme that peaks later, making it less useful for early diagnosis compared to troponins. The specificity of Troponin I in detecting cardiac injury makes it the superior choice in ACS management.

Question 119: Correct Answer: B) CT angiography
Rationale: CT angiography is the preferred initial imaging modality for suspected aortic dissection due to its rapid availability, high sensitivity, and specificity. While a chest X-ray (Option A) might show mediastinal widening, it lacks specificity. Transthoracic echocardiography (Option C) can be useful but may not visualize the entire aorta. MRI (Option D), though detailed, is less practical in emergencies due to time constraints and availability. Thus, CT angiography provides the most accurate and immediate assessment for confirming an aortic dissection in acute settings.

Question 120: Correct Answer: B) Assess for hypoxia and provide supplemental oxygen if needed.
Rationale: Agitation in critically ill patients like Mr. Thompson can often be due to hypoxia, which should be assessed and corrected first. Administering a sedative (Option A) may mask symptoms without addressing the underlying cause. Restraints (Option C) are a last resort due to potential harm and ethical concerns. Increasing environmental stimulation (Option D) could exacerbate agitation in this context. Therefore, addressing potential hypoxia directly targets a common reversible cause of agitation in ICU settings, aligning with best practices in critical care management.

Question 121: Correct Answer: C) Provide a complex carbohydrate snack once she is alert
Rationale: Once Emily is alert after receiving IV dextrose, providing a complex carbohydrate snack helps sustain normal blood glucose levels and prevent recurrent hypoglycemia. Option A (glucagon) is used when IV access isn't available. Option B (continuous glucose infusion) isn't standard for routine post-treatment care. Option D (reassessing every 30 minutes) is essential but not the immediate next step. Providing a snack stabilizes glucose levels more effectively than relying solely on monitoring or additional interventions without addressing dietary needs.

Question 122: Correct Answer: C) Total hip arthroplasty
Rationale: Total hip arthroplasty is preferred for displaced femoral neck fractures in older adults due to better functional outcomes and reduced risk of complications compared to ORIF. Closed reduction and casting are unsuitable for this fracture type, while conservative management increases morbidity in elderly patients. ORIF is often used in younger patients where bone healing potential is higher. The choice of total hip arthroplasty considers John's age and fracture displacement, aligning with contemporary research emphasizing improved mobility and quality of life post-surgery.

Question 123: Correct Answer: C) Low serum cortisol and high ACTH levels
Rationale: Primary adrenal insufficiency (Addison's disease) is characterized by low serum cortisol due to adrenal gland failure, leading to compensatory high ACTH levels. Option A is incorrect because while electrolyte imbalances like low sodium and high potassium can occur, they are not definitive without cortisol/ACTH evaluation. Option B is misleading as it suggests opposite electrolyte changes. Option D suggests secondary or tertiary adrenal insufficiency with intact adrenal response but impaired pituitary or hypothalamic function, making C the accurate indicator of primary adrenal insufficiency.

Question 124: Correct Answer: A) Aplastic anemia
Rationale: Aplastic anemia leads to pancytopenia, including neutropenia, significantly increasing infection risk. Iron deficiency anemia primarily affects red blood cells, not white cells. Vitamin B12 deficiency may cause leukopenia but is more associated with macrocytic anemia. Hemolytic anemia involves red cell destruction without directly affecting white cell production. Therefore, aplastic anemia is the most relevant condition causing leukopenia due to bone marrow failure, leading to decreased production of all blood cells, including neutrophils, unlike the other options.

Question 125: Correct Answer: B) Intravenous iron therapy
Rationale: Intravenous iron therapy is the most appropriate initial treatment for Emily's anemia due to chronic kidney disease and low ferritin, indicating iron deficiency. Oral iron (A) may be less effective due to poor absorption in CKD. ESAs (C) require adequate iron stores to be effective, making IV iron a priority. Blood transfusion (D) is reserved for severe anemia or acute situations. The choice of IV iron addresses the root cause efficiently, optimizing hemoglobin synthesis and improving symptoms more rapidly than oral supplementation or ESAs alone.

CCRN Exam Practice Questions [SET 3]

Question 1: Sarah, a 35-year-old patient, has been admitted to the ICU following a traumatic brain injury. She exhibits signs of agitation and confusion, frequently attempting to remove her IV lines and get out of bed. As a critical care nurse, what is the most appropriate initial intervention to address Sarah's behavioral symptoms while considering her safety and psychosocial needs?
A) Administer a low-dose sedative to manage agitation.
B) Apply physical restraints to prevent self-harm.
C) Implement environmental modifications and provide frequent orientation.
D) Increase family visitation to provide reassurance.

Question 2: A 56-year-old male named John is admitted to the ICU with confusion, asterixis, and altered mental status. His medical history reveals chronic liver disease. As the critical care nurse, you suspect hepatic encephalopathy. Which of the following initial management strategies is most appropriate for John?
A) Administering intravenous thiamine
B) Initiating lactulose therapy
C) Starting high-protein diet
D) Prescribing antiepileptic medication

Question 3: Sarah, a 32-year-old nurse, has been experiencing flashbacks, hypervigilance, and emotional numbness since witnessing a traumatic event at her workplace. She is seeking therapy and considering pharmacological options to manage her PTSD symptoms. Which of the following medications is most appropriate as a first-line treatment for Sarah's PTSD?
A) Benzodiazepines
B) Selective Serotonin Reuptake Inhibitors (SSRIs)
C) Antipsychotics
D) Beta-blockers

Question 4: A 56-year-old male patient named John is admitted to the ICU with severe abdominal pain, vomiting, and signs of shock. His history includes chronic alcohol use. Imaging reveals acute pancreatitis. As a critical care nurse, which of the following interventions is most crucial in managing John's condition during the initial phase?
A) Initiate enteral nutrition immediately.
B) Administer intravenous fluids aggressively.
C) Provide opioid analgesics for pain management.
D) Start prophylactic antibiotics to prevent infection.

Question 5: Which of the following is a primary mechanism believed to contribute to the pathophysiology of Transfusion-related Acute Lung Injury (TRALI)?
A) Antibody-mediated activation of neutrophils in the pulmonary vasculature
B) Direct hemolysis of red blood cells in the bloodstream
C) Activation of the coagulation cascade leading to disseminated intravascular coagulation (DIC)
D) Increased capillary permeability due to cytokine release from donor leukocytes

Question 6: John, a 58-year-old male with a history of myocardial infarction, presents with sudden onset of dyspnea and hypotension. On examination, he has a new systolic murmur at the apex. Echocardiography reveals severe mitral regurgitation. What is the most likely underlying cause of his condition?
A) Left ventricular free wall rupture
B) Papillary muscle rupture
C) Ventricular septal defect
D) Acute pericarditis

Question 7: In the context of encephalopathy, which of the following conditions is most likely to lead to hepatic encephalopathy due to its impact on liver function?
A) Chronic kidney disease
B) Cirrhosis
C) Type 2 diabetes mellitus
D) Hypertension

Question 8: A 45-year-old male patient named John is admitted to the ICU following a motor vehicle accident. He presents with signs of increased intra-abdominal pressure, oliguria, and difficulty breathing. The medical team suspects abdominal compartment syndrome (ACS). Which of the following interventions is most appropriate to manage John's condition?
A) Administering diuretics to reduce fluid overload
B) Increasing intravenous fluid administration to maintain blood pressure
C) Performing a decompressive laparotomy
D) Elevating the head of the bed to improve respiratory function

Question 9: Which of the following is the most appropriate initial antibiotic treatment for a patient with uncomplicated cellulitis and no known drug allergies, according to current clinical guidelines?
A) Clindamycin
B) Vancomycin
C) Cephalexin
D) Doxycycline

Question 10: John, a 68-year-old patient with chronic obstructive pulmonary disease (COPD), has been on mechanical ventilation for two weeks following an acute exacerbation. Despite multiple weaning attempts, he remains ventilator-dependent. Which of the following factors is most likely contributing to John's failure to wean from mechanical ventilation?
A) Inadequate nutritional support
B) Unresolved pulmonary infection
C) Poor pain management
D) Fluid overload

Question 11: In the management of acute hypoglycemia in a critically ill patient, which of the following interventions is most appropriate for rapidly restoring blood glucose levels?
A) Administering 10% dextrose intravenously
B) Administering 50% dextrose intravenously
C) Providing oral glucose tablets
D) Initiating a continuous insulin infusion

Question 12: Emily, a 68-year-old patient with a history of COPD, is admitted to the ICU with acute respiratory distress. Her arterial blood gas (ABG) results show pH 7.30, PaCO2 55 mmHg, and HCO3- 26 mEq/L. Based on these findings, what is the most likely primary acid-base disorder she is experiencing?
A) Metabolic acidosis
B) Respiratory acidosis
C) Metabolic alkalosis
D) Respiratory alkalosis

Question 13: In the management of hyperthyroidism, which medication is primarily used to inhibit thyroid

hormone synthesis by blocking the iodination of tyrosine residues in thyroglobulin?
A) Methimazole
B) Propranolol
C) Radioactive iodine
D) Levothyroxine

Question 14: Mr. Thompson, a 67-year-old male with a history of congestive heart failure, presents with dyspnea and chest discomfort. A chest X-ray reveals a pleural effusion. Which of the following is the most appropriate initial step in managing his pleural effusion?
A) Perform a diagnostic thoracentesis
B) Start diuretics to reduce fluid overload
C) Administer antibiotics empirically
D) Schedule an immediate pleurodesis

Question 15: John, a 65-year-old male with a history of Crohn's disease, undergoes an ileocecal resection. Post-operatively, he develops symptoms of vitamin B12 deficiency. Which of the following is the most likely cause for this deficiency following his surgery?
A) Loss of gastric intrinsic factor production
B) Resection of the terminal ileum
C) Impaired pancreatic enzyme secretion
D) Reduced dietary intake

Question 16: A 55-year-old male named John is admitted to the ICU with acute liver failure. His medical history reveals chronic use of acetaminophen for osteoarthritis pain. Despite adhering to recommended dosages, he developed symptoms of hepatic failure. What is the most likely mechanism by which acetaminophen induced John's liver failure?
A) Inhibition of hepatic glucuronidation
B) Depletion of glutathione leading to toxic metabolite accumulation
C) Increased hepatic blood flow causing hepatocyte damage
D) Enhanced renal excretion reducing hepatic clearance

Question 17: A 45-year-old patient named John is admitted to the ICU with a history of cerebral palsy (CP) and presents with acute respiratory distress. As a critical care nurse, what is the most appropriate initial intervention to manage his respiratory status, considering his neuromuscular disorder?
A) Administer supplemental oxygen via nasal cannula
B) Perform chest physiotherapy to clear secretions
C) Initiate non-invasive positive pressure ventilation (NIPPV)
D) Intubate and initiate mechanical ventilation

Question 18: A 55-year-old female patient named Mary presents to the emergency department with fatigue, weight gain, and cold intolerance. Her lab results reveal elevated TSH and low free T4 levels. As the critical care nurse, you suspect hypothyroidism. Which of the following initial management strategies is most appropriate for Mary?
A) Administer intravenous levothyroxine immediately.
B) Initiate oral levothyroxine therapy.
C) Start a high-dose corticosteroid regimen.
D) Provide symptomatic treatment with warm blankets and fluids.

Question 19: A 45-year-old patient named John is admitted to the ICU with severe blunt abdominal trauma following a motor vehicle accident. He presents with hypotension, tachycardia, and abdominal distension. A CT scan reveals a large retroperitoneal hematoma. What is the most appropriate initial management step for John in this scenario?
A) Immediate surgical exploration
B) Aggressive fluid resuscitation

C) Administration of vasopressors
D) Monitoring and observation

Question 20: Mrs. Thompson, a 65-year-old patient with a history of hypertension and diabetes, presents to the ICU with oliguria and elevated serum creatinine levels. Her recent medication history includes NSAIDs for arthritis. Which of the following interventions is most appropriate to address her Acute Kidney Injury (AKI)?
A) Initiate aggressive intravenous hydration
B) Administer loop diuretics
C) Discontinue NSAIDs and monitor renal function
D) Start renal replacement therapy immediately

Question 21: In the context of pleural space abnormalities, which of the following is the most definitive diagnostic procedure for identifying the presence of a pleural effusion?
A) Chest X-ray
B) Thoracentesis
C) Ultrasound
D) CT Scan

Question 22: Emily, a 45-year-old patient with a history of rheumatic fever, presents with exertional dyspnea and fatigue. An echocardiogram reveals thickening and calcification of the mitral valve leaflets with restricted movement. Which valvular condition is most likely responsible for her symptoms?
A) Mitral Valve Prolapse
B) Mitral Stenosis
C) Aortic Stenosis
D) Tricuspid Regurgitation

Question 23: In the context of a traumatic brain injury, which of the following types of hemorrhage is most likely to lead to rapid neurological deterioration due to arterial bleeding?
A) Subdural Hematoma
B) Epidural Hematoma
C) Intracerebral Hemorrhage
D) Subarachnoid Hemorrhage

Question 24: In the management of hydrocephalus, which of the following interventions is primarily aimed at reducing increased intracranial pressure?
A) Administration of osmotic diuretics
B) Use of anticonvulsants
C) Implementation of fluid restriction
D) Surgical placement of a ventriculoperitoneal shunt

Question 25: In the context of thrombocytopenia, which of the following laboratory findings is most indicative of Immune Thrombocytopenic Purpura (ITP)?
A) Increased mean platelet volume (MPV)
B) Decreased platelet-associated IgG
C) Elevated platelet count with normal bleeding time
D) Presence of schistocytes on peripheral blood smear

Question 26: In the context of a Whipple procedure, which of the following complications is most commonly associated with delayed gastric emptying?
A) Pancreatic fistula
B) Bile leak
C) Gastrojejunostomy dysfunction
D) Duodenal stump leakage

Question 27: A 68-year-old patient named Mr. Thompson presents with a chronic venous ulcer on his lower leg that has been resistant to healing despite standard wound care interventions. As a critical care nurse, which of the following advanced interventions is most appropriate to promote wound healing in this scenario?

A) Application of negative pressure wound therapy (NPWT)
B) Use of hydrocolloid dressings
C) Implementation of hyperbaric oxygen therapy
D) Administration of systemic antibiotics

Question 28: A 65-year-old patient named Mr. Johnson with a history of COPD is admitted to the ICU with acute respiratory failure. He is on mechanical ventilation. The arterial blood gas (ABG) analysis shows pH 7.30, PaCO2 60 mmHg, and PaO2 55 mmHg. Which of the following interventions is most appropriate to improve his condition?
A) Increase the FiO2
B) Decrease the tidal volume
C) Increase the respiratory rate
D) Initiate prone positioning

Question 29: In the management of increased intracranial pressure (ICP), which of the following interventions is most effective in reducing ICP by decreasing cerebral blood volume?
A) Hyperventilation
B) Administration of mannitol
C) Elevation of the head of the bed to 30 degrees
D) Use of sedatives to reduce metabolic demand

Question 30: In the management of myasthenia gravis, which of the following treatments is primarily used to provide rapid improvement in muscle strength during a myasthenic crisis?
A) Pyridostigmine
B) Plasmapheresis
C) Azathioprine
D) Thymectomy

Question 31: John, a 45-year-old male with a history of chronic alcohol dependence, is admitted to the ICU with acute pancreatitis. During his stay, he experiences tremors, agitation, and confusion. As a critical care nurse, which intervention is most appropriate to manage John's symptoms and prevent further complications?
A) Administering intravenous thiamine
B) Initiating a high-calorie diet
C) Providing intravenous glucose
D) Administering antipsychotic medication

Question 32: A 55-year-old patient named John is admitted to the ICU following a sudden, severe headache and loss of consciousness. A CT scan confirms a subarachnoid hemorrhage. As part of the management plan, which of the following interventions is most critical in preventing secondary complications associated with aneurysmal subarachnoid hemorrhage?
A) Administering nimodipine to prevent vasospasm
B) Initiating anticoagulation therapy to prevent clot formation
C) Performing therapeutic hypothermia to reduce metabolic demand
D) Administering mannitol to decrease intracranial pressure

Question 33: A 3-month-old infant named Emma presents with jaundice, pale stools, and hepatomegaly. Laboratory tests reveal elevated conjugated bilirubin levels. As the critical care nurse evaluating Emma, which of the following interventions is most crucial to initiate promptly for suspected biliary atresia?
A) Initiate phototherapy to manage jaundice.
B) Schedule an immediate Kasai procedure consultation.
C) Begin oral ursodeoxycholic acid therapy.
D) Administer intravenous vitamin K to prevent bleeding.

Question 34: In the management of status asthmaticus, which of the following interventions is most critical for preventing respiratory failure in a patient unresponsive to initial bronchodilator therapy?
A) Administering intravenous corticosteroids
B) Initiating high-flow oxygen therapy
C) Implementing non-invasive ventilation
D) Providing continuous nebulized albuterol

Question 35: In the management of a traumatic hemothorax, which intervention is most critical to prevent complications and ensure effective treatment?
A) Immediate administration of intravenous fluids
B) Needle decompression of the pleural space
C) Insertion of a chest tube for drainage
D) Application of positive end-expiratory pressure (PEEP)

Question 36: Sarah, a 35-year-old patient with cerebral palsy (CP), presents to the emergency department with complaints of muscle weakness and difficulty swallowing. As her care nurse, you need to determine the most appropriate immediate intervention. Which of the following should be prioritized in managing her condition?
A) Administering oral muscle relaxants
B) Initiating a swallow assessment
C) Providing respiratory support
D) Starting physical therapy exercises

Question 37: A 45-year-old male named John is admitted to the ICU with progressive muscle weakness and difficulty breathing. His medical history reveals recent gastrointestinal infection. After conducting a nerve conduction study, the neurologist suspects a neuromuscular disorder. Which of the following is the most likely diagnosis?
A) Myasthenia Gravis
B) Guillain-Barré Syndrome
C) Amyotrophic Lateral Sclerosis (ALS)
D) Lambert-Eaton Myasthenic Syndrome

Question 38: A 55-year-old patient named Mr. Johnson, recently diagnosed with acute lymphoblastic leukemia, is undergoing chemotherapy. He presents with muscle cramps, fatigue, and dark urine. Laboratory tests reveal hyperkalemia, hyperuricemia, and elevated lactate dehydrogenase levels. What is the most appropriate initial management step for Mr. Johnson's suspected tumor lysis syndrome?
A) Administer allopurinol
B) Initiate aggressive IV hydration
C) Start rasburicase therapy
D) Provide calcium gluconate

Question 39: Mr. Thompson, a 68-year-old patient with diabetes, is admitted to the ICU with renal failure. During your assessment, you notice a stage 2 pressure injury on his sacrum. Which intervention is most appropriate to promote healing and prevent further deterioration of the pressure injury?
A) Apply a hydrocolloid dressing and reposition every 4 hours.
B) Use a foam dressing and reposition every 2 hours.
C) Implement a low-air-loss mattress and reposition every 6 hours.
D) Cleanse the wound with saline and apply an antibiotic ointment.

Question 40: A 45-year-old patient named John is admitted to the ICU with recurrent bacterial infections, poor wound healing, and chronic diarrhea. His laboratory tests reveal low immunoglobulin levels and a reduced number of B cells. Based on these findings, which of the following is the most likely diagnosis?
A) Severe Combined Immunodeficiency (SCID)
B) Common Variable Immunodeficiency (CVID)

C) X-linked Agammaglobulinemia (XLA)
D) Hyper-IgM Syndrome

Question 41: Nurse Emma is caring for a patient, Mr. Johnson, who has suffered a severe traumatic brain injury. The healthcare team is considering the diagnosis of brain death. Which of the following clinical assessments is essential to confirm brain death in Mr. Johnson?
A) Presence of deep tendon reflexes
B) Absence of pupillary light reflex
C) Presence of spontaneous breathing
D) Absence of corneal reflex

Question 42: In the management of carotid artery stenosis, which of the following is considered the most effective intervention for symptomatic patients with severe stenosis to prevent stroke?
A) Antiplatelet therapy
B) Carotid endarterectomy
C) Carotid artery stenting
D) Statin therapy

Question 43: A 65-year-old male patient named Mr. Johnson presents to the emergency department with severe abdominal pain, distension, and vomiting. His medical history includes atrial fibrillation and recent abdominal surgery. On examination, he is hypotensive and tachycardic. A CT scan reveals bowel wall thickening and pneumatosis intestinalis. Based on this clinical presentation, what is the most likely diagnosis?
A) Bowel Obstruction
B) Bowel Perforation
C) Mesenteric Ischemia
D) Acute Pancreatitis

Question 44: Which of the following hemodynamic changes is most characteristic of pulmonary hypertension in a critical care setting?
A) Increased pulmonary artery wedge pressure
B) Decreased mean pulmonary artery pressure
C) Increased right ventricular afterload
D) Decreased systemic vascular resistance

Question 45: In the context of medical non-adherence, which of the following factors is most strongly associated with unintentional non-adherence in patients with chronic musculoskeletal conditions?
A) Complexity of medication regimen
B) Patient's belief in the necessity of medication
C) Side effects experienced by the patient
D) Poor patient-provider communication

Question 46: In the context of managing infectious wounds, which of the following interventions is most critical in preventing the spread of infection in a healthcare setting?
A) Regularly changing wound dressings using sterile technique
B) Administering prophylactic antibiotics to all patients with wounds
C) Isolating patients with infectious wounds in a separate ward
D) Implementing strict hand hygiene protocols for healthcare workers

Question 47: In the context of papillary muscle rupture following a myocardial infarction, which clinical finding is most indicative of this complication?
A) New-onset systolic murmur at the apex
B) Jugular venous distention
C) Widened pulse pressure
D) Decreased breath sounds at lung bases

Question 48: John, a 65-year-old patient with a history of metastatic lung cancer, presents with shortness of breath and hypotension. An echocardiogram reveals a significant pericardial effusion. As the critical care nurse, what is the most appropriate initial intervention to stabilize John's hemodynamics?
A) Administer intravenous diuretics to reduce fluid overload
B) Prepare for an emergency pericardiocentesis
C) Initiate high-flow oxygen therapy
D) Start vasopressor support to maintain blood pressure

Question 49: A 75-year-old patient named Mr. Johnson is admitted to the ICU with a hip fracture. During your assessment, you notice multiple bruises in various stages of healing on his arms and back. Mr. Johnson seems hesitant to answer questions about his home environment. As a critical care nurse, what is the most appropriate initial action to take regarding suspected elder abuse or neglect?
A) Document your findings and report them to the attending physician immediately.
B) Ask Mr. Johnson directly if he feels safe at home.
C) Contact social services to investigate the situation further.
D) Discuss your concerns with Mr. Johnson's family members.

Question 50: In the context of acute hypoglycemia management in critical care, which of the following interventions is most appropriate for a patient who is unconscious with a blood glucose level of 40 mg/dL?
A) Administer 50% dextrose intravenously
B) Provide oral glucose gel
C) Initiate a glucagon injection intramuscularly
D) Start an intravenous insulin infusion

Question 51: In the postoperative care of a patient who has undergone an esophagectomy, which of the following is the most critical intervention to prevent respiratory complications?
A) Early ambulation
B) Incentive spirometry
C) Nasogastric tube management
D) Fluid restriction

Question 52: In the context of critical care nursing, which neurotransmitter imbalance is most commonly associated with the pathophysiology of depression, affecting mood regulation and requiring careful clinical judgment in patient management?
A) Dopamine
B) Serotonin
C) GABA
D) Acetylcholine

Question 53: A 45-year-old patient named John has been admitted to the ICU following a generalized tonic-clonic seizure. As a critical care nurse, you are assessing his postictal state. Which of the following is the most appropriate initial intervention to ensure John's safety and recovery?
A) Administering intravenous lorazepam
B) Positioning John on his side
C) Monitoring vital signs every hour
D) Starting continuous EEG monitoring

Question 54: Which of the following clinical signs is most indicative of systemic involvement in a patient with severe burns covering more than 30% of total body surface area?
A) Localized erythema
B) Hypovolemic shock
C) Hyperkalemia

D) Increased risk of infection

Question 55: Sarah, a 34-year-old patient, is admitted to the ICU following a severe panic attack. She reports feeling overwhelmed by her inability to control her emotions and fears another attack. As a critical care nurse, what is the most appropriate initial intervention to manage Sarah's anxiety?
A) Administer a low-dose benzodiazepine as prescribed.
B) Encourage deep breathing exercises and relaxation techniques.
C) Provide reassurance and maintain a calm environment.
D) Refer Sarah for cognitive-behavioral therapy.

Question 56: John, a 45-year-old male, presents to the emergency department with symptoms of fatigue, shortness of breath, and palpitations. After a series of diagnostic tests, he is diagnosed with idiopathic dilated cardiomyopathy. Which of the following is the most appropriate initial management strategy for John?
A) Start beta-blockers immediately
B) Initiate ACE inhibitors
C) Prescribe diuretics for symptom relief
D) Recommend lifestyle modifications only

Question 57: Emily, a 32-year-old female patient with a recent diagnosis of Immune Thrombocytopenic Purpura (ITP), presents with petechiae and mild gingival bleeding. Her platelet count is 28,000/µL. Considering her condition, which of the following treatment options is most appropriate to initiate at this stage?
A) Intravenous Immunoglobulin (IVIG)
B) Splenectomy
C) Platelet transfusion
D) Corticosteroids

Question 58: John, a 45-year-old male, presents to the emergency department after a motor vehicle accident with suspected rib fractures. He is experiencing severe pain on inspiration and has shallow breathing. Which of the following interventions is most appropriate to address John's respiratory status?
A) Administer high-flow oxygen therapy.
B) Encourage deep breathing exercises and use of incentive spirometry.
C) Provide intravenous morphine for pain management.
D) Position the patient in a semi-Fowler's position.

Question 59: A 45-year-old patient named John presents to the emergency department with fatigue, recurrent infections, and a recent history of chemotherapy for lymphoma. His complete blood count reveals significant leukopenia. As a critical care nurse, what is the most appropriate initial action to address John's leukopenia?
A) Administer broad-spectrum antibiotics immediately.
B) Initiate granulocyte colony-stimulating factor (G-CSF) therapy.
C) Isolate the patient to prevent infection.
D) Transfuse white blood cells.

Question 60: In the context of compartment syndrome, which of the following clinical findings is most indicative of this condition in its early stages?
A) Loss of pulse in the affected limb
B) Severe pain disproportionate to the injury
C) Numbness and tingling in the affected area
D) Swelling and tightness over the compartment

Question 61: In the management of myasthenia gravis, which of the following medications is primarily used to improve neuromuscular transmission by inhibiting the breakdown of acetylcholine?
A) Prednisone
B) Azathioprine
C) Pyridostigmine
D) Methotrexate

Question 62: Emily, a 45-year-old female, presents to the emergency department with severe fatigue, hypotension, and hyperpigmentation of her skin. Her laboratory results reveal hyponatremia and hyperkalemia. Considering these findings, which initial treatment should be prioritized for Emily's suspected adrenal insufficiency?
A) Administer IV hydrocortisone
B) Start oral fludrocortisone
C) Initiate IV saline infusion
D) Provide oral glucose

Question 63: In the context of trauma management, which of the following interventions is most critical in the initial assessment and stabilization of a patient with a suspected tension pneumothorax?
A) Administering high-flow oxygen therapy
B) Initiating needle decompression
C) Performing an immediate chest X-ray
D) Starting intravenous fluid resuscitation

Question 64: Emily, a 45-year-old patient with newly diagnosed hyperthyroidism, presents with palpitations, weight loss, and increased sweating. Her laboratory results show elevated free T4 and suppressed TSH levels. As her critical care nurse, which immediate intervention is most appropriate to address her symptoms?
A) Administer propranolol to control palpitations and anxiety.
B) Initiate methimazole therapy to reduce thyroid hormone synthesis.
C) Provide a high-calorie diet to counteract weight loss.
D) Start levothyroxine to stabilize thyroid hormone levels.

Question 65: In the context of managing infections in critically ill patients with renal complications, which of the following statements regarding the use of antibiotics is most accurate?
A) Antibiotic dosing should be reduced in all renal failure patients to prevent toxicity.
B) Renal replacement therapy has no impact on antibiotic clearance.
C) Loading doses of antibiotics are often required despite renal impairment.
D) All antibiotics are equally affected by renal dysfunction.

Question 66: Sarah, a 45-year-old female, presents to the emergency department with severe abdominal pain, nausea, and vomiting. She has a history of alcohol abuse and is diagnosed with acute pancreatitis. Which laboratory finding is most indicative of this condition?
A) Elevated serum amylase
B) Elevated serum lipase
C) Elevated serum bilirubin
D) Elevated alkaline phosphatase

Question 67: In the management of central Diabetes Insipidus (DI), which of the following is the most appropriate first-line treatment to reduce polyuria and polydipsia?
A) Thiazide diuretics
B) Desmopressin acetate
C) Indomethacin
D) Amiloride

Question 68: A 68-year-old patient named Mr. Johnson is scheduled for a carotid endarterectomy due to significant carotid artery stenosis. During preoperative assessment, which clinical finding would most likely

indicate the need for urgent surgical intervention?
A) Transient ischemic attacks (TIAs) in the past month
B) Mild dizziness with no neurological deficits
C) Asymptomatic carotid bruit
D) Controlled hypertension with no other symptoms

Question 69: A 65-year-old patient named Mr. Thompson, who has a history of hypertension and diabetes, presents to the emergency department with severe flank pain, hematuria, and oliguria. Laboratory tests reveal elevated creatinine levels and hyperkalemia. Considering these symptoms and laboratory findings, what is the most likely cause of his acute kidney injury?
A) Acute tubular necrosis
B) Prerenal azotemia
C) Postrenal obstruction
D) Glomerulonephritis

Question 70: In the context of idiopathic cardiomyopathies, which of the following is most characteristic of idiopathic dilated cardiomyopathy (IDC)?
A) Thickened ventricular walls with decreased chamber size
B) Dilated ventricles with systolic dysfunction
C) Restrictive filling pattern with preserved ejection fraction
D) Hypertrophied septum causing outflow obstruction

Question 71: In the management of septic shock, which intervention is primarily aimed at reversing the underlying pathophysiological process?
A) Administration of broad-spectrum antibiotics
B) Initiation of mechanical ventilation
C) Use of vasopressors to maintain blood pressure
D) Fluid resuscitation with crystalloids

Question 72: John, a 58-year-old male with a history of chronic alcoholism, is admitted to the ICU with hepatic encephalopathy. His ammonia levels are elevated, and he exhibits confusion and lethargy. Which of the following interventions is most critical in managing his condition?
A) Administering lactulose to reduce ammonia levels
B) Providing high-protein diet to support liver regeneration
C) Administering diuretics to manage ascites
D) Initiating broad-spectrum antibiotics to prevent infection

Question 73: A 45-year-old patient named John presents to the emergency department with fever, headache, neck stiffness, and photophobia. After a lumbar puncture, cerebrospinal fluid (CSF) analysis reveals elevated protein levels and decreased glucose concentration. Which of the following is the most likely diagnosis?
A) Viral meningitis
B) Bacterial meningitis
C) Fungal meningitis
D) Tuberculous meningitis

Question 74: In the management of open fractures, which of the following interventions is most critical in reducing the risk of infection and promoting optimal healing?
A) Immediate immobilization of the fracture site
B) Administration of prophylactic antibiotics within 3 hours
C) Application of sterile dressing to the wound
D) Surgical debridement within 24 hours

Question 75: A 45-year-old male patient named John is admitted to the ICU with a history of chronic alcohol use. He is now experiencing symptoms of alcohol withdrawal, including tremors, anxiety, and hypertension. As the critical care nurse, you need to prioritize his care. Which of the following interventions should be your primary focus to manage John's withdrawal symptoms effectively?
A) Administering intravenous fluids to prevent dehydration
B) Providing thiamine supplementation to prevent Wernicke's encephalopathy
C) Initiating benzodiazepine therapy to manage withdrawal symptoms
D) Monitoring vital signs closely for any changes

Question 76: A 45-year-old patient named John is admitted to the ICU with acute liver failure suspected to be fulminant hepatitis. He presents with jaundice, coagulopathy, and encephalopathy. Which of the following interventions is most critical in managing John's condition to prevent further complications?
A) Administering broad-spectrum antibiotics
B) Initiating lactulose therapy
C) Starting intravenous N-acetylcysteine
D) Performing plasmapheresis

Question 77: In the management of Disseminated Intravascular Coagulation (DIC), which of the following interventions is most critical to address the underlying cause of coagulopathy?
A) Administering fresh frozen plasma
B) Initiating anticoagulation therapy with heparin
C) Treating the underlying infection or condition
D) Providing platelet transfusions

Question 78: A 45-year-old patient named John is admitted to the ICU with rapidly progressing muscle weakness and areflexia. He has a recent history of an upper respiratory infection. As a critical care nurse, you need to prioritize interventions. Which of the following should be your primary focus in managing John's condition?
A) Initiating corticosteroid therapy
B) Monitoring respiratory function closely
C) Starting plasmapheresis immediately
D) Administering intravenous immunoglobulin (IVIG)

Question 79: A 45-year-old patient named John presents to the emergency department with signs of bleeding, including petechiae and oozing from venipuncture sites. His laboratory tests reveal thrombocytopenia, prolonged prothrombin time (PT), and elevated D-dimer levels. As a critical care nurse, what is the most appropriate initial management step for John, considering he is suspected to have disseminated intravascular coagulation (DIC)?
A) Administer fresh frozen plasma
B) Initiate intravenous heparin therapy
C) Provide platelet transfusion
D) Correct underlying cause of DIC

Question 80: A 65-year-old male patient named Mr. Johnson with a history of chronic obstructive pulmonary disease (COPD) presents to the emergency department with increased shortness of breath, wheezing, and productive cough. His arterial blood gas analysis shows pH 7.32, PaCO2 55 mmHg, and PaO2 60 mmHg. What is the most appropriate initial intervention to address his current condition?
A) Administer high-flow oxygen therapy.
B) Initiate non-invasive positive pressure ventilation (NIPPV).
C) Start intravenous corticosteroids.
D) Increase bronchodilator dosage.

Question 81: A 45-year-old male patient named John presents to the emergency department with severe shortness of breath, wheezing, and chest tightness. Despite receiving high-dose bronchodilators and corticosteroids, his symptoms persist. Which of the following interventions is most appropriate to consider next in managing John's status asthmaticus?

A) Administer intravenous magnesium sulfate
B) Increase the dose of inhaled corticosteroids
C) Initiate non-invasive positive pressure ventilation (NIPPV)
D) Provide continuous nebulization of beta-agonists

Question 82: A 55-year-old patient named Mr. Thompson is admitted to the ICU with severe hyperglycemia and a history of type 2 diabetes. His blood glucose level is 450 mg/dL, and he exhibits signs of dehydration and confusion. As the critical care nurse, what is the most appropriate initial intervention to address his condition?
A) Administer intravenous insulin immediately.
B) Start an intravenous infusion of normal saline.
C) Provide oral hypoglycemic agents.
D) Begin continuous glucose monitoring.

Question 83: A 68-year-old patient named Mr. Thompson, who recently suffered a stroke, is being evaluated for his ability to perform activities of daily living (ADLs) independently. During the assessment, it is noted that he has difficulty with fine motor skills and coordination, affecting his ability to dress himself. Which intervention should the nurse prioritize to enhance Mr. Thompson's functional independence?
A) Encourage the use of adaptive clothing with Velcro fasteners.
B) Recommend daily physical therapy focused on strength training.
C) Suggest cognitive-behavioral therapy to improve motivation.
D) Advise the use of assistive devices for ambulation.

Question 84: In managing a patient with acute pancreatitis, which of the following interventions is most critical in the initial phase to prevent complications?
A) Administering antibiotics prophylactically
B) Initiating early enteral nutrition
C) Providing aggressive intravenous fluid resuscitation
D) Monitoring serum calcium levels closely

Question 85: A patient with a suspected subarachnoid hemorrhage presents with a sudden, severe headache described as "the worst headache of their life." Which diagnostic test is considered the gold standard for confirming this condition?
A) Magnetic Resonance Imaging (MRI)
B) Computed Tomography (CT) Scan without contrast
C) Lumbar Puncture
D) Cerebral Angiography

Question 86: In the management of acute peripheral vascular insufficiency, which of the following clinical interventions is most critical in preventing tissue necrosis?
A) Administering anticoagulants to prevent thrombosis
B) Elevating the affected limb to reduce edema
C) Initiating thrombolytic therapy to dissolve clots
D) Applying warm compresses to improve circulation

Question 87: In patients with Chronic Kidney Disease (CKD), which of the following laboratory findings is most indicative of a progression towards end-stage renal disease (ESRD)?
A) Elevated serum creatinine levels
B) Reduced glomerular filtration rate (GFR)
C) Increased serum potassium levels
D) Elevated blood urea nitrogen (BUN)

Question 88: John, a 67-year-old male with a history of hypertension and recent chest trauma, is admitted to the ICU with signs of hypotension, jugular venous distention, and muffled heart sounds. An echocardiogram confirms cardiac tamponade. Which immediate intervention is most appropriate to stabilize John's condition?
A) Administer IV fluids rapidly
B) Perform pericardiocentesis
C) Start vasopressor therapy
D) Administer diuretics

Question 89: In the context of surgical wound management, which of the following is considered the most effective method for promoting healing in a chronic wound with necrotic tissue?
A) Autolytic debridement
B) Mechanical debridement
C) Enzymatic debridement
D) Sharp surgical debridement

Question 90: In the context of dementia care, which of the following interventions is most effective in managing agitation in patients with Alzheimer's disease according to contemporary research?
A) Pharmacological treatment with antipsychotics
B) Implementation of personalized music therapy
C) Regular physical exercise programs
D) Cognitive-behavioral therapy sessions

Question 91: In assessing a critically ill patient with suspected musculoskeletal functional issues, which of the following assessments is most indicative of early functional impairment in the context of neurological and musculoskeletal integration?
A) Decreased deep tendon reflexes
B) Reduced grip strength
C) Limited range of motion in joints
D) Altered gait pattern

Question 92: Emily, a 45-year-old patient, is admitted to the ICU following a severe trauma and requires multiple blood transfusions. Within six hours of receiving the transfusion, she develops acute respiratory distress with hypoxemia and bilateral pulmonary infiltrates on chest X-ray. Which of the following is the most likely diagnosis for Emily's condition?
A) Transfusion-associated circulatory overload (TACO)
B) Transfusion-related acute lung injury (TRALI)
C) Acute respiratory distress syndrome (ARDS) unrelated to transfusion
D) Anaphylactic transfusion reaction

Question 93: Emily, a 68-year-old patient with a history of recurrent urinary tract infections, presents to the emergency department with fever, confusion, and hypotension. Her lab results show leukocytosis and elevated lactate levels. What is the most immediate intervention to improve her condition based on the current guidelines for managing urosepsis?
A) Administer broad-spectrum antibiotics
B) Initiate aggressive fluid resuscitation
C) Perform blood cultures before antibiotics
D) Start vasopressor therapy immediately

Question 94: During a cardiac catheterization procedure, Mr. Thompson, a 65-year-old male with a history of hypertension and hyperlipidemia, suddenly develops hypotension and bradycardia. As the critical care nurse, what is the most appropriate initial action to take?
A) Administer intravenous atropine.
B) Initiate fluid resuscitation with normal saline.
C) Prepare for transcutaneous pacing.
D) Administer intravenous epinephrine.

Question 95: Emily, a 45-year-old patient, presents with fever, headache, neck stiffness, and photophobia. A lumbar puncture reveals elevated white blood cell count

and protein levels in the cerebrospinal fluid (CSF), along with decreased glucose levels. Based on these findings, what is the most likely causative organism for her condition?
A) Streptococcus pneumoniae
B) Neisseria meningitidis
C) Listeria monocytogenes
D) Haemophilus influenzae

Question 96: John, a 58-year-old male, presents with progressive headaches, nausea, and blurred vision. An MRI reveals a large mass in the frontal lobe. As his critical care nurse, you must consider potential complications related to brain tumors. Which of the following complications should be prioritized due to its immediate threat to life?
A) Seizures
B) Hydrocephalus
C) Hemorrhagic stroke
D) Increased intracranial pressure (ICP)

Question 97: In the postoperative management of a patient who has undergone a craniotomy, which of the following interventions is most critical to monitor for signs of increased intracranial pressure (ICP)?
A) Elevate the head of the bed to 30 degrees
B) Administer sedatives as prescribed
C) Maintain normothermia
D) Monitor electrolyte levels

Question 98: In the context of a fractured rib, which of the following interventions is most critical to prevent complications such as atelectasis and pneumonia?
A) Administering high-flow oxygen therapy
B) Encouraging incentive spirometry use
C) Applying a rib belt for support
D) Initiating early ambulation

Question 99: Sarah, a 45-year-old patient with a history of systemic sclerosis, presents with exertional dyspnea and fatigue. Right heart catheterization confirms pulmonary arterial hypertension (PAH). Which of the following therapeutic approaches is most appropriate to initiate in managing her condition based on contemporary guidelines?
A) Oral endothelin receptor antagonists
B) High-dose calcium channel blockers
C) Long-term oxygen therapy
D) Intravenous prostacyclin analogs

Question 100: In patients with portal hypertension, which of the following is the most likely initial physiological change leading to the development of esophageal varices?
A) Increased hepatic arterial pressure
B) Collateral circulation formation
C) Splanchnic vasodilation
D) Decreased portal venous inflow

Question 101: In the context of lung contusion management, which of the following interventions is most crucial to prevent further respiratory compromise in a patient with significant thoracic trauma?
A) Administering high-flow oxygen therapy
B) Initiating mechanical ventilation with low tidal volumes
C) Performing aggressive fluid resuscitation
D) Providing continuous positive airway pressure (CPAP)

Question 102: Emily, a 68-year-old woman with a history of hypertension and diabetes, presents to the emergency department with sudden onset of unilateral weakness and slurred speech. Her symptoms resolve within an hour. As a critical care nurse, what is the most appropriate immediate action to take in managing Emily's condition?
A) Administer aspirin immediately.
B) Schedule an MRI to assess for ischemic changes.
C) Initiate thrombolytic therapy.
D) Monitor vital signs and neurological status closely.

Question 103: In the management of aortic stenosis, which intervention is most appropriate for symptomatic patients with a high surgical risk who are not candidates for traditional open-heart surgery?
A) Transcatheter Aortic Valve Replacement (TAVR)
B) Balloon Aortic Valvuloplasty
C) Medical Management with Beta-blockers
D) Surgical Aortic Valve Replacement

Question 104: Sarah, a 35-year-old patient with a history of depression, is admitted to the critical care unit following an overdose. During your assessment, she expresses feelings of hopelessness and mentions that she has been "thinking about ending it all." Based on contemporary research and recognized theories, which of the following interventions should be prioritized to ensure Sarah's safety?
A) Initiate a no-suicide contract with Sarah.
B) Conduct a comprehensive suicide risk assessment.
C) Increase the frequency of monitoring to every 15 minutes.
D) Administer antidepressant medication immediately.

Question 105: John, a 65-year-old male with a history of smoking and hypertension, presents with sudden onset of severe pain in his left leg, accompanied by pallor and pulselessness. As a critical care nurse, what is the most appropriate initial intervention to address acute arterial occlusion in this patient?
A) Administer intravenous heparin
B) Perform an urgent embolectomy
C) Apply warm compresses to the affected limb
D) Elevate the affected limb

Question 106: In the context of Acute Kidney Injury (AKI), which of the following laboratory findings is most indicative of a prerenal cause?
A) Elevated serum creatinine with a low fractional excretion of sodium (FeNa < 1%)
B) High urine osmolality with elevated urinary sodium concentration
C) Low urine osmolality with high fractional excretion of sodium (FeNa > 2%)
D) Normal serum creatinine with high urinary protein levels

Question 107: Mr. Thompson, a 62-year-old male with a history of hypertension and hyperlipidemia, presents to the emergency department with chest pain radiating to his left arm. An ECG confirms ST-segment elevation myocardial infarction (STEMI). Which of the following is the most critical initial treatment to improve Mr. Thompson's survival?
A) Administering aspirin
B) Administering nitroglycerin
C) Initiating thrombolytic therapy
D) Providing supplemental oxygen

Question 108: In the context of acute pulmonary embolism (PE), which clinical finding is most indicative of a massive PE requiring immediate intervention?
A) Sudden onset dyspnea with pleuritic chest pain
B) Hypotension with elevated central venous pressure
C) Tachycardia with low-grade fever
D) Hemoptysis with mild hypoxemia

Question 109: Sarah, a 45-year-old patient with a history of deep vein thrombosis, presents to the emergency

department with sudden onset of dyspnea, chest pain, and hemoptysis. Her vital signs reveal tachycardia and hypotension. Which diagnostic test is most appropriate to confirm the suspicion of an acute pulmonary embolism in Sarah?
A) Chest X-ray
B) D-dimer test
C) CT Pulmonary Angiography
D) Ventilation-Perfusion (V/Q) scan

Question 110: Which electrolyte imbalance is most commonly associated with the initial presentation of Tumor Lysis Syndrome (TLS) in critically ill patients?
A) Hypercalcemia
B) Hypocalcemia
C) Hyperkalemia
D) Hypokalemia

Question 111: In the context of hepatic encephalopathy, which of the following neurotransmitter alterations is most commonly implicated in its pathophysiology?
A) Increased dopamine levels
B) Elevated serotonin levels
C) Increased gamma-aminobutyric acid (GABA) activity
D) Elevated acetylcholine levels

Question 112: A 35-year-old male named John is admitted to the emergency department following a motor vehicle accident. He presents with hematuria, flank pain, and hypotension. As a critical care nurse, which of the following is the most appropriate initial diagnostic test to assess for acute genitourinary trauma in this patient?
A) Ultrasound of the abdomen
B) CT scan of the abdomen and pelvis with contrast
C) Intravenous pyelogram (IVP)
D) Abdominal X-ray

Question 113: In the context of acute kidney injury (AKI) management, which of the following interventions is most effective in preventing contrast-induced nephropathy in high-risk patients?
A) Administration of N-acetylcysteine before and after contrast exposure
B) Intravenous hydration with isotonic saline before and after contrast exposure
C) Use of low-osmolar or iso-osmolar contrast media
D) Administration of sodium bicarbonate infusion during contrast exposure

Question 114: John, a 55-year-old patient with a history of chronic kidney disease, is undergoing a blood transfusion. Shortly after the transfusion begins, he experiences chills, fever, and back pain. As his nurse, what is the most appropriate immediate action to take?
A) Administer antipyretics to manage the fever.
B) Slow down the transfusion rate and monitor vital signs closely.
C) Stop the transfusion immediately and notify the physician.
D) Continue the transfusion while preparing for potential allergic reaction treatment.

Question 115: Sarah, a 45-year-old patient, is receiving intravenous fluids for dehydration. During your shift, you notice her IV site is swollen, cool to the touch, and the patient reports discomfort. Which of the following actions should be prioritized to manage this situation effectively?
A) Apply a warm compress to the affected area.
B) Elevate the affected limb above heart level.
C) Discontinue the IV infusion immediately.
D) Notify the physician before taking any action.

Question 116: In the context of traumatic brain injuries, which of the following is a characteristic feature distinguishing an epidural hematoma from a subdural hematoma?
A) An epidural hematoma often results from venous bleeding.
B) An epidural hematoma typically presents with a lucid interval.
C) A subdural hematoma is usually associated with arterial bleeding.
D) A subdural hematoma commonly causes immediate loss of consciousness.

Question 117: Sarah, a 58-year-old patient with diabetes, presents with a non-healing ulcer on her left foot. Despite standard wound care, the ulcer has not improved over the past four weeks. Which of the following is the most appropriate next step in managing Sarah's wound to promote healing?
A) Increase frequency of dressing changes
B) Initiate negative pressure wound therapy (NPWT)
C) Begin systemic antibiotic therapy
D) Refer for hyperbaric oxygen therapy

Question 118: In the context of aortic dissection, which clinical feature is most indicative of an acute type A aortic dissection?
A) Sudden onset of tearing chest pain radiating to the back
B) Gradual onset of dull chest pain with dyspnea
C) Intermittent chest pain with palpitations
D) Sharp chest pain relieved by sitting forward

Question 119: A 45-year-old patient named John presents to the emergency department after a high-speed motor vehicle accident. He is experiencing severe respiratory distress, decreased breath sounds on the right side, and hypotension. A chest X-ray reveals a large pleural effusion on the right. What is the most appropriate initial intervention for John?
A) Administer high-flow oxygen and observe
B) Insert a chest tube to drain the pleural effusion
C) Perform an emergency thoracotomy
D) Initiate mechanical ventilation immediately

Question 120: In the context of necrotizing fasciitis, which of the following is the most critical initial step in management to improve patient outcomes?
A) Initiation of broad-spectrum antibiotics
B) Immediate surgical debridement
C) Hyperbaric oxygen therapy
D) Fluid resuscitation

Question 121: In the management of Acute Respiratory Distress Syndrome (ARDS), which of the following strategies is most effective in improving oxygenation while minimizing ventilator-induced lung injury?
A) High tidal volume ventilation
B) Low tidal volume ventilation
C) High positive end-expiratory pressure (PEEP)
D) Prone positioning

Question 122: John, a 58-year-old male with a history of chronic alcohol abuse, presents to the ICU with confusion, jaundice, and ascites. His laboratory results show elevated liver enzymes, prolonged prothrombin time, and elevated ammonia levels. Which intervention is most crucial in managing John's hepatic encephalopathy?
A) Administering lactulose to reduce ammonia levels
B) Providing high-protein diet to support liver function
C) Administering diuretics to manage ascites
D) Initiating corticosteroid therapy to reduce inflammation

Question 123: In the context of fulminant hepatitis, which of the following laboratory findings is most indicative of severe hepatic encephalopathy?
A) Elevated serum bilirubin levels
B) Increased prothrombin time (PT)
C) Elevated serum ammonia levels
D) Decreased albumin levels

Question 124: Which of the following diagnostic imaging techniques is most sensitive for identifying small space-occupying lesions in the brain?
A) Computed Tomography (CT) Scan
B) Magnetic Resonance Imaging (MRI)
C) Positron Emission Tomography (PET) Scan
D) Ultrasound

Question 125: In the context of acute kidney injury (AKI), which of the following laboratory findings is most indicative of prerenal azotemia?
A) Elevated blood urea nitrogen (BUN) to creatinine ratio greater than 20:1
B) Urine sodium concentration greater than 40 mEq/L
C) Fractional excretion of sodium (FENa) greater than 2%
D) Presence of muddy brown casts in urine sediment

ANSWER WITH DETAILED EXPLANATION SET [3]

Question 1: Correct Answer: C) Implement environmental modifications and provide frequent orientation.
Rationale: The correct answer is C. Environmental modifications and frequent orientation are crucial for managing agitation in patients with brain injuries, promoting safety without restraint use. Option A (sedatives) may be necessary but should not be the initial intervention due to potential side effects. Option B (restraints) can increase agitation and are used only as a last resort. Option D (family visitation) helps but isn't sufficient alone for immediate safety concerns. This approach aligns with contemporary research emphasizing non-pharmacological interventions in managing behavioral symptoms post-injury.

Question 2: Correct Answer: B) Initiating lactulose therapy
Rationale: Lactulose is used to treat hepatic encephalopathy by reducing ammonia levels in the blood. Option A (thiamine) is more relevant for Wernicke's encephalopathy. Option C (high-protein diet) can worsen ammonia levels in liver disease. Option D (antiepileptics) is not first-line treatment for hepatic encephalopathy. Lactulose effectively decreases ammonia absorption in the gut, addressing the root cause of John's symptoms related to his liver condition.

Question 3: Correct Answer: B) Selective Serotonin Reuptake Inhibitors (SSRIs)
Rationale: SSRIs are the first-line pharmacological treatment for PTSD due to their efficacy in reducing core symptoms such as re-experiencing and avoidance. Benzodiazepines (Option A) may offer short-term relief but can worsen symptoms long-term and lead to dependency. Antipsychotics (Option C) are reserved for severe cases with psychotic features. Beta-blockers (Option D) may help with peripheral symptoms like anxiety but do not address core PTSD symptoms effectively. Thus, SSRIs are preferred due to their proven benefit in managing PTSD's primary symptoms.

Question 4: Correct Answer: B) Administer intravenous fluids aggressively.
Rationale: The primary concern in acute pancreatitis is maintaining hemodynamic stability due to potential fluid shifts and hypovolemia. Aggressive IV fluid resuscitation is crucial to prevent shock and organ failure. Option A is incorrect as early enteral nutrition may exacerbate pancreatic stimulation. Option C, while important for comfort, does not address the underlying hemodynamic instability. Option D is not routinely recommended as prophylactic antibiotics have not shown benefit in preventing infections in acute pancreatitis without evidence of infection.

Question 5: Correct Answer: A) Antibody-mediated activation of neutrophils in the pulmonary vasculature
Rationale: TRALI is primarily caused by antibody-mediated activation of neutrophils, leading to lung injury. Option A is correct because antibodies in transfused blood can react with recipient leukocytes, activating neutrophils and causing damage. Option B is incorrect as it describes hemolytic reactions, not TRALI. Option C is related to coagulation disorders, not directly linked to TRALI's mechanism. Option D mentions cytokines, which play a role but are not the primary cause; it's the antibody-neutrophil interaction that initiates TRALI.

Question 6: Correct Answer: B) Papillary muscle rupture
Rationale: Papillary muscle rupture is a complication of myocardial infarction leading to acute mitral regurgitation, characterized by sudden dyspnea and hypotension. The new systolic murmur at the apex is indicative of this condition. Option A (left ventricular free wall rupture) would cause cardiac tamponade rather than a murmur. Option C (ventricular septal defect) would present with a different murmur pattern. Option D (acute pericarditis) typically presents with chest pain and friction rub, not acute mitral regurgitation. Thus, papillary muscle rupture is the most plausible explanation given John's symptoms and echocardiographic findings.

Question 7: Correct Answer: B) Cirrhosis
Rationale: Cirrhosis is a chronic liver disease characterized by scarring and impaired liver function, leading to hepatic encephalopathy due to the accumulation of toxins like ammonia in the bloodstream. Chronic kidney disease (A), while affecting toxin clearance, primarily impacts renal rather than hepatic systems. Type 2 diabetes mellitus (C) can cause neurological issues but does not directly result in hepatic encephalopathy. Hypertension (D), although it can affect multiple organs, does not specifically impair liver function to cause hepatic encephalopathy as cirrhosis does.

Question 8: Correct Answer: C) Performing a decompressive laparotomy
Rationale: Decompressive laparotomy is the definitive treatment for ACS, as it directly relieves intra-abdominal pressure. Option A is incorrect because diuretics can worsen hypoperfusion in ACS. Option B is misleading; while fluids support blood pressure, they can exacerbate intra-abdominal hypertension. Option D might temporarily aid respiration but doesn't address the underlying issue. Therefore, surgical intervention (Option C) is critical for resolving ACS and preventing organ dysfunction.

Question 9: Correct Answer: C) Cephalexin
Rationale: Cephalexin is the recommended initial antibiotic for uncomplicated cellulitis due to its effectiveness against common causative organisms like Streptococcus and Staphylococcus aureus. Clindamycin (A) and Doxycycline (D) are alternatives, often used in cases of penicillin allergy or suspected MRSA. Vancomycin (B) is reserved for severe cases or confirmed MRSA. The choice of Cephalexin reflects guidelines emphasizing coverage for typical skin flora, balancing efficacy and patient safety.

Question 10: Correct Answer: B) Unresolved pulmonary infection
Rationale: Unresolved pulmonary infection is a critical factor impeding weaning due to its impact on respiratory mechanics and gas exchange. While inadequate nutritional support (A) can affect muscle strength, it is less immediate in this context. Poor pain management (C) might contribute to discomfort but does not directly affect respiratory function significantly. Fluid overload (D) can impair lung function but is typically managed more easily than infections. Therefore, addressing the infection directly impacts respiratory recovery and facilitates successful weaning from mechanical ventilation.

Question 11: Correct Answer: B) Administering 50% dextrose intravenously
Rationale: Administering 50% dextrose intravenously is the most effective intervention for rapidly increasing blood

glucose levels in acute hypoglycemia. This option provides a concentrated source of glucose directly into the bloodstream, ensuring swift correction. Option A, while beneficial, offers a less concentrated solution, making it slower to act. Option C is ineffective in unconscious patients or those unable to swallow. Option D is inappropriate as insulin would further lower glucose levels.

Question 12: Correct Answer: B) Respiratory acidosis
Rationale: The ABG results indicate a low pH (acidemia), elevated PaCO2, and normal HCO3-, suggesting respiratory acidosis due to CO2 retention. In metabolic acidosis (A), HCO3- would be decreased. Metabolic alkalosis (C) would present with elevated pH and HCO3-. Respiratory alkalosis (D) would show low PaCO2 and high pH. The patient's COPD history supports CO2 retention as the cause of respiratory acidosis, differentiating it from other disorders.

Question 13: Correct Answer: A) Methimazole
Rationale: Methimazole is the correct answer as it inhibits thyroid hormone synthesis by blocking the iodination of tyrosine residues in thyroglobulin. Propranolol (B) is a beta-blocker used to manage symptoms but does not inhibit hormone synthesis. Radioactive iodine (C) destroys thyroid tissue, reducing hormone production but not by blocking iodination. Levothyroxine (D) is a synthetic thyroid hormone, not an inhibitor. Methimazole's mechanism directly targets the synthesis process, distinguishing it from options B and C, which manage symptoms or reduce tissue function differently.

Question 14: Correct Answer: A) Perform a diagnostic thoracentesis
Rationale: Diagnostic thoracentesis is crucial to ascertain the nature of the effusion, distinguishing between transudative and exudative causes. While diuretics (Option B) address fluid overload in heart failure, they don't provide diagnostic clarity. Empirical antibiotics (Option C) are premature without infection confirmation. Pleurodesis (Option D) is for recurrent effusions, not initial management. Hence, thoracentesis guides subsequent treatment by analyzing pleural fluid characteristics, ensuring appropriate intervention based on whether the effusion is transudative or exudative.

Question 15: Correct Answer: B) Resection of the terminal ileum
Rationale: The terminal ileum is critical for vitamin B12 absorption due to its role in absorbing the vitamin-intrinsic factor complex. Resection leads to malabsorption and deficiency. Option A is incorrect as intrinsic factor production occurs in the stomach, not affected by ileocecal resection. Option C is unrelated as pancreatic enzymes do not influence B12 absorption directly. Option D is incorrect since dietary intake post-surgery is usually managed to prevent deficiencies. Thus, option B accurately addresses the physiological changes post-resection impacting B12 absorption.

Question 16: Correct Answer: B) Depletion of glutathione leading to toxic metabolite accumulation
Rationale: Acetaminophen overdose leads to liver damage primarily through the depletion of glutathione, resulting in the accumulation of a toxic metabolite, N-acetyl-p-benzoquinone imine (NAPQI). Option A is incorrect as glucuronidation inhibition is not the primary mechanism. Option C is unrelated; increased blood flow does not cause hepatocyte damage in this context. Option D incorrectly suggests renal excretion affects hepatic clearance. Thus, option B correctly identifies the pathophysiological process responsible for John's condition.

Question 17: Correct Answer: C) Initiate non-invasive positive pressure ventilation (NIPPV)
Rationale: NIPPV is preferred for patients with CP experiencing respiratory distress due to weakened respiratory muscles, as it supports breathing without invasive procedures. Option A may not suffice in severe cases. Option B is beneficial but not immediate. Option D is more invasive and reserved for failure of less invasive measures. NIPPV offers a balance of support and patient comfort while minimizing risks associated with intubation, making it the optimal initial intervention in this scenario.

Question 18: Correct Answer: B) Initiate oral levothyroxine therapy.
Rationale: Initiating oral levothyroxine is the standard treatment for hypothyroidism, addressing Mary's low free T4 levels. Option A (IV levothyroxine) is reserved for myxedema coma, a severe form of hypothyroidism. Option C (corticosteroids) is inappropriate without adrenal insufficiency. Option D addresses symptoms but not the underlying thyroid deficiency. The correct choice directly targets the hormonal imbalance, while others either apply to more severe conditions or provide only symptomatic relief.

Question 19: Correct Answer: B) Aggressive fluid resuscitation
Rationale: The primary goal in managing trauma patients with signs of shock and potential hemorrhage is to restore hemodynamic stability through aggressive fluid resuscitation. This approach helps to maintain perfusion to vital organs while further diagnostic evaluations or surgical interventions are considered. Option A, immediate surgical exploration, may be necessary if there is evidence of ongoing bleeding or organ injury but is not the initial step without stabilization. Option C, administration of vasopressors, is inappropriate before adequate volume resuscitation. Option D, monitoring and observation, is insufficient given John's hemodynamic instability.

Question 20: Correct Answer: C) Discontinue NSAIDs and monitor renal function
Rationale: The most appropriate intervention is to discontinue NSAIDs, as they can exacerbate AKI by reducing renal blood flow. Option A may worsen fluid overload if not carefully managed. Option B, while useful in certain contexts, does not address the underlying cause here. Option D is premature without first attempting less invasive measures. Identifying and removing nephrotoxic agents is critical in managing AKI, especially when linked to medication use like NSAIDs in this scenario.

Question 21: Correct Answer: B) Thoracentesis
Rationale: Thoracentesis is the most definitive diagnostic procedure for identifying and analyzing pleural effusions, as it allows direct sampling of pleural fluid. While a chest X-ray (A) can suggest effusion presence, it lacks specificity. Ultrasound (C) aids in detection and guidance but doesn't provide fluid analysis. A CT scan (D) offers detailed imaging but cannot sample fluid directly. Thoracentesis provides both diagnostic and therapeutic benefits by enabling fluid analysis for infection, malignancy, or other causes, making it superior in confirming pleural effusion etiology.

Question 22: Correct Answer: B) Mitral Stenosis
Rationale: Mitral stenosis is characterized by thickening and calcification of the mitral valve leaflets, leading to restricted movement, which aligns with Emily's echocardiogram findings. This condition often results from rheumatic fever, explaining her exertional dyspnea and fatigue. Mitral valve prolapse (A) typically involves

leaflet displacement without calcification. Aortic stenosis (C) affects the aortic valve rather than the mitral valve. Tricuspid regurgitation (D) involves backflow through the tricuspid valve, unrelated to Emily's presentation. Thus, mitral stenosis is the most accurate diagnosis given the clinical scenario.

Question 23: Correct Answer: B) Epidural Hematoma
Rationale: An epidural hematoma involves arterial bleeding, typically from the middle meningeal artery, leading to rapid neurological decline. This makes it distinct from a subdural hematoma (A), which involves venous bleeding and usually progresses more slowly. An intracerebral hemorrhage (C) occurs within brain tissue and varies in progression. A subarachnoid hemorrhage (D) involves bleeding into the space around the brain and may not cause immediate deterioration unless massive. The rapid arterial nature of an epidural hematoma necessitates swift intervention, highlighting its critical impact on patient outcomes.

Question 24: Correct Answer: D) Surgical placement of a ventriculoperitoneal shunt
Rationale: The surgical placement of a ventriculoperitoneal shunt is the primary intervention for reducing increased intracranial pressure in hydrocephalus by diverting excess cerebrospinal fluid. While osmotic diuretics (A) can temporarily reduce pressure by removing fluid, they do not address the underlying cause. Anticonvulsants (B) are used to manage seizures, not directly decrease intracranial pressure. Fluid restriction (C) may help in managing fluid balance but is not sufficient to control intracranial pressure effectively. Thus, option D provides a definitive and long-term solution.

Question 25: Correct Answer: A) Increased mean platelet volume (MPV)
Rationale: Increased mean platelet volume (MPV) is indicative of Immune Thrombocytopenic Purpura (ITP), as it reflects larger, younger platelets due to increased turnover. Option B is incorrect because ITP usually involves increased, not decreased, platelet-associated IgG. Option C is incorrect as ITP typically presents with low platelet count and prolonged bleeding time. Option D suggests microangiopathic processes like thrombotic thrombocytopenic purpura, not ITP. The correct answer highlights the characteristic laboratory finding in ITP, distinguishing it from other thrombocytopenic disorders.

Question 26: Correct Answer: C) Gastrojejunostomy dysfunction
Rationale: Delayed gastric emptying after a Whipple procedure is most commonly due to gastrojejunostomy dysfunction, where the anastomosis between the stomach and jejunum fails to function properly. Pancreatic fistula (A) and bile leak (B) are potential complications but relate more to pancreatic and biliary anastomoses, respectively. Duodenal stump leakage (D) is less common as the duodenum is typically resected. Understanding these distinctions is crucial for managing postoperative care effectively.

Question 27: Correct Answer: A) Application of negative pressure wound therapy (NPWT)
Rationale: Negative pressure wound therapy (NPWT) is effective for chronic venous ulcers by promoting granulation tissue formation and reducing edema. While hydrocolloid dressings (Option B) provide a moist environment, they are less effective for deep or heavily exudative wounds. Hyperbaric oxygen therapy (Option C) can enhance healing in certain cases but is not typically first-line for venous ulcers. Systemic antibiotics (Option D) are indicated if there is an infection, not solely for healing promotion. NPWT's ability to manage exudate and stimulate tissue makes it the most suitable choice here.

Question 28: Correct Answer: C) Increase the respiratory rate
Rationale: Increasing the respiratory rate helps reduce PaCO2 by enhancing alveolar ventilation, which is crucial in this hypercapnic respiratory failure scenario. Option A (Increase the FiO2) primarily addresses hypoxemia but does not correct hypercapnia. Option B (Decrease the tidal volume) could worsen hypercapnia by reducing ventilation. Option D (Initiate prone positioning) is more beneficial for improving oxygenation in ARDS rather than correcting hypercapnia. Therefore, increasing the respiratory rate effectively targets Mr. Johnson's elevated PaCO2 and acidosis while maintaining adequate oxygenation.

Question 29: Correct Answer: A) Hyperventilation
Rationale: Hyperventilation reduces ICP by causing cerebral vasoconstriction, which decreases cerebral blood volume. While mannitol (B) reduces ICP by osmotic diuresis, it does not specifically target cerebral blood volume. Elevating the head (C) aids venous drainage but is less direct in altering blood volume. Sedatives (D) lower metabolic demand but do not primarily affect blood volume. Hyperventilation's direct impact on cerebral vasculature makes it uniquely effective in this context, aligning with contemporary research on ICP management.

Question 30: Correct Answer: B) Plasmapheresis
Rationale: Plasmapheresis is the correct answer as it rapidly removes circulating antibodies responsible for muscle weakness in myasthenia gravis, providing quick symptom relief during a crisis. Pyridostigmine (A), while useful for symptomatic control, does not act as quickly. Azathioprine (C) is an immunosuppressant used for long-term management, not immediate crisis intervention. Thymectomy (D) may offer long-term benefits but is not suitable for acute symptom relief. The key distinction lies in the rapidity and mechanism of action, making plasmapheresis the optimal choice for immediate improvement.

Question 31: Correct Answer: A) Administering intravenous thiamine
Rationale: Administering intravenous thiamine is crucial for patients with chronic alcohol dependence to prevent Wernicke's encephalopathy, characterized by confusion, tremors, and agitation. Thiamine deficiency is common in alcohol-dependent individuals due to poor nutritional intake. Option B (high-calorie diet) addresses nutritional needs but doesn't immediately resolve neurological symptoms. Option C (intravenous glucose) can exacerbate symptoms if given without thiamine due to increased metabolic demands. Option D (antipsychotic medication) may manage agitation but doesn't address the underlying thiamine deficiency crucial for preventing neurological complications.

Question 32: Correct Answer: A) Administering nimodipine to prevent vasospasm
Rationale: Nimodipine is crucial in preventing cerebral vasospasm, a common and severe complication after an aneurysmal subarachnoid hemorrhage. Anticoagulation (B) increases bleeding risk; therapeutic hypothermia (C) lacks efficacy for this condition; mannitol (D) is used for elevated intracranial pressure but doesn't address vasospasm. Thus, administering nimodipine (A) is the most effective intervention for preventing vasospasm-related ischemia, aligning with contemporary research and clinical guidelines for managing aneurysmal

subarachnoid hemorrhage.

Question 33: Correct Answer: B) Schedule an immediate Kasai procedure consultation.
Rationale: The Kasai procedure is critical for biliary atresia as it can restore bile flow if performed early. Phototherapy (A) is ineffective for conjugated hyperbilirubinemia. Ursodeoxycholic acid (C) aids bile flow but doesn't address atresia directly. Vitamin K (D) prevents bleeding but doesn't treat the underlying cause. Prompt surgical intervention through the Kasai procedure is vital to improve prognosis and liver function, distinguishing it as the essential intervention in suspected biliary atresia cases.

Question 34: Correct Answer: D) Providing continuous nebulized albuterol
Rationale: Continuous nebulized albuterol is crucial as it provides sustained bronchodilation, essential for reversing severe airway obstruction in status asthmaticus. While intravenous corticosteroids (A) are important for reducing inflammation, their effects are not immediate. High-flow oxygen therapy (B) improves oxygenation but does not address bronchospasm directly. Non-invasive ventilation (C) can assist with ventilation but may not be suitable if bronchospasm persists. Continuous nebulization ensures persistent delivery of the bronchodilator, directly targeting the cause of respiratory distress, thus preventing progression to respiratory failure.

Question 35: Correct Answer: C) Insertion of a chest tube for drainage
Rationale: Insertion of a chest tube is crucial for draining blood from the pleural space, preventing complications like lung collapse or infection. While intravenous fluids (A) are essential for hemodynamic stability, they don't address the underlying issue. Needle decompression (B) is more appropriate for tension pneumothorax, not hemothorax. PEEP (D) can improve oxygenation but may worsen bleeding if not carefully managed. The primary goal in hemothorax management is to evacuate blood efficiently, making chest tube insertion the most appropriate intervention.

Question 36: Correct Answer: C) Providing respiratory support
Rationale: In patients with CP experiencing muscle weakness and difficulty swallowing, respiratory support is critical due to the risk of aspiration and compromised breathing. While a swallow assessment (Option B) is important, it follows stabilization of breathing. Oral muscle relaxants (Option A) may exacerbate swallowing difficulties, increasing aspiration risk. Physical therapy exercises (Option D) are beneficial long-term but not immediately life-saving. Therefore, ensuring adequate respiratory function takes precedence to prevent further complications and stabilize the patient.

Question 37: Correct Answer: B) Guillain-Barré Syndrome
Rationale: Guillain-Barré Syndrome (GBS) is characterized by acute onset of muscle weakness and often follows an infection, such as a gastrointestinal one. The nerve conduction study in GBS typically shows demyelination patterns. Myasthenia Gravis (A) involves fluctuating muscle weakness without preceding infection. ALS (C) presents with progressive motor neuron degeneration, not an acute presentation post-infection. Lambert-Eaton Myasthenic Syndrome (D) involves proximal muscle weakness and is often associated with malignancies, not infections. Therefore, the acute presentation post-infection points to GBS as the correct diagnosis.

Question 38: Correct Answer: B) Initiate aggressive IV hydration
Rationale: Aggressive IV hydration is crucial to prevent renal failure by enhancing uric acid excretion in tumor lysis syndrome (TLS). While allopurinol (A) prevents new uric acid formation, it doesn't address existing hyperuricemia. Rasburicase (C) reduces uric acid levels but isn't an initial step. Calcium gluconate (D) addresses severe hyperkalemia symptoms but doesn't treat TLS's root cause. Thus, hydration is prioritized to manage electrolyte imbalances and prevent renal complications effectively in TLS scenarios.

Question 39: Correct Answer: B) Use a foam dressing and reposition every 2 hours.
Rationale: Option B is correct because using a foam dressing provides cushioning and moisture balance, while repositioning every 2 hours alleviates pressure, crucial for healing. Option A offers less frequent repositioning, risking further injury. Option C's extended intervals between repositioning are inadequate for effective prevention of pressure injuries. Option D focuses on infection control but lacks the necessary mechanical relief from pressure that foam dressings provide. Hence, B is the most comprehensive approach to managing pressure injuries in this scenario.

Question 40: Correct Answer: B) Common Variable Immunodeficiency (CVID)
Rationale: CVID is characterized by low immunoglobulin levels and reduced B cells, causing recurrent infections and poor wound healing. SCID involves both T and B cell deficiencies, making it less likely given John's specific symptoms. XLA primarily affects males with absent B cells from infancy, not aligning with John's age. Hyper-IgM Syndrome involves normal or elevated IgM levels with other immunoglobulins decreased, which doesn't match John's lab results. CVID's adult onset and symptom profile best fit the scenario described.

Question 41: Correct Answer: B) Absence of pupillary light reflex
Rationale: The absence of the pupillary light reflex is crucial in confirming brain death, as it indicates a lack of brainstem function. While deep tendon reflexes (Option A) may persist due to spinal cord activity, they do not indicate brainstem function. Spontaneous breathing (Option C) would suggest some brainstem activity, ruling out brain death. The absence of the corneal reflex (Option D) is also significant but less definitive than the pupillary response for confirming brainstem inactivity. Therefore, Option B correctly identifies a critical assessment for diagnosing brain death.

Question 42: Correct Answer: B) Carotid endarterectomy
Rationale: Carotid endarterectomy is the most effective intervention for symptomatic patients with severe carotid artery stenosis (70-99%) to prevent stroke, as supported by clinical trials. While antiplatelet therapy (Option A) and statin therapy (Option D) are crucial for managing atherosclerosis, they are less effective in preventing strokes in severe cases compared to surgery. Carotid artery stenting (Option C) is an alternative but generally reserved for patients at high surgical risk. The choice between endarterectomy and stenting depends on individual patient factors, but surgery remains the gold standard for most.

Question 43: Correct Answer: C) Mesenteric Ischemia
Rationale: Mesenteric ischemia is suggested by Mr. Johnson's risk factors (atrial fibrillation), symptoms (abdominal pain, distension), and CT findings (pneumatosis intestinalis). Bowel obstruction (A) typically presents with similar symptoms but lacks ischemic signs

like pneumatosis. Bowel perforation (B) would likely show free air under the diaphragm rather than bowel wall thickening alone. Acute pancreatitis (D) would present with elevated pancreatic enzymes and different imaging findings. The combination of clinical presentation and imaging strongly indicates mesenteric ischemia in this scenario.

Question 44: Correct Answer: C) Increased right ventricular afterload
Rationale: Pulmonary hypertension primarily leads to increased right ventricular afterload due to elevated pressures in the pulmonary circulation, which the right ventricle must overcome. Option A is incorrect as increased pulmonary artery wedge pressure is more indicative of left-sided heart issues. Option B is incorrect because pulmonary hypertension involves increased, not decreased, mean pulmonary artery pressure. Option D is incorrect as systemic vascular resistance typically pertains to systemic circulation, not directly related to pulmonary hypertension. Understanding these distinctions is crucial for managing patients with this condition.

Question 45: Correct Answer: A) Complexity of medication regimen
Rationale: Complexity of medication regimen is a primary factor leading to unintentional non-adherence, as it can overwhelm patients, causing confusion and forgetfulness. While beliefs about medication necessity (B) and side effects (C) relate to intentional non-adherence, they are less impactful for unintentional cases. Poor communication (D) can affect adherence but primarily influences understanding and trust, not directly causing unintentional lapses. Therefore, simplifying regimens can significantly improve adherence in patients with chronic conditions.

Question 46: Correct Answer: D) Implementing strict hand hygiene protocols for healthcare workers
Rationale: Implementing strict hand hygiene protocols is the most effective intervention to prevent the spread of infections in healthcare settings. Hand hygiene reduces transmission of pathogens, as hands are a primary vector. While regularly changing dressings (A) and isolating patients (C) are important, they do not address pathogen spread as directly as hand hygiene. Prophylactic antibiotics (B) can lead to resistance and are not universally recommended. Therefore, hand hygiene remains paramount due to its broad impact on infection control.

Question 47: Correct Answer: A) New-onset systolic murmur at the apex
Rationale: A new-onset systolic murmur at the apex is most indicative of papillary muscle rupture due to acute mitral regurgitation. Jugular venous distention (B) can occur in heart failure but is not specific to papillary muscle rupture. Widened pulse pressure (C) is typically associated with conditions like aortic regurgitation. Decreased breath sounds (D) may suggest pleural effusion or pneumothorax, not directly linked to papillary muscle rupture. The murmur results from turbulent blood flow through an incompetent mitral valve, a direct consequence of papillary muscle dysfunction.

Question 48: Correct Answer: B) Prepare for an emergency pericardiocentesis
Rationale: Pericardiocentesis is crucial in relieving cardiac tamponade caused by pericardial effusion, which is likely given John's symptoms. While diuretics (Option A) might reduce volume overload, they do not address the immediate risk of tamponade. High-flow oxygen (Option C) can help with hypoxia but does not resolve hemodynamic instability. Vasopressors (Option D) may temporarily support blood pressure but do not treat the underlying cause. Therefore, Option B directly addresses the life-threatening condition by removing excess fluid from the pericardium.

Question 49: Correct Answer: A) Document your findings and report them to the attending physician immediately.
Rationale: The correct action is to document findings and report them to the attending physician as it ensures proper protocol for suspected abuse cases, aligning with legal obligations and safeguarding patient welfare. Option B, while important, may not yield truthful responses due to fear or intimidation. Option C should follow initial reporting, ensuring thorough investigation by professionals. Option D could compromise patient safety if family members are involved in the abuse. Reporting first ensures that appropriate steps are taken in a structured manner consistent with healthcare protocols.

Question 50: Correct Answer: A) Administer 50% dextrose intravenously
Rationale: In cases of acute hypoglycemia with unconsciousness, intravenous administration of 50% dextrose is the fastest and most effective method to rapidly increase blood glucose levels. Option B is incorrect as oral glucose is not feasible in unconscious patients. Option C, glucagon injection, can be used if IV access is unavailable but is slower than IV dextrose. Option D, insulin infusion, would exacerbate hypoglycemia and is contraindicated. The correct choice ensures prompt reversal of hypoglycemia and prevents neurological damage.

Question 51: Correct Answer: B) Incentive spirometry
Rationale: Incentive spirometry is crucial for preventing respiratory complications post-esophagectomy by promoting lung expansion and preventing atelectasis. While early ambulation (Option A) aids in overall recovery and circulation, it does not directly target lung function. Nasogastric tube management (Option C) is important for gastrointestinal recovery but does not address respiratory risks. Fluid restriction (Option D) may be necessary for specific cases but does not primarily prevent respiratory issues. Thus, incentive spirometry specifically addresses the risk of pulmonary complications by enhancing lung capacity and function.

Question 52: Correct Answer: B) Serotonin
Rationale: Serotonin is the neurotransmitter most closely linked to depression, playing a crucial role in mood regulation. Its imbalance can lead to depressive symptoms, making it a primary target for antidepressant therapies like SSRIs. Dopamine (A) also influences mood but is more associated with reward pathways. GABA (C) primarily affects anxiety and inhibitory control, while acetylcholine (D) is linked to memory and learning processes. Understanding these differences aids in precise clinical interventions for depression in critical care settings.

Question 53: Correct Answer: B) Positioning John on his side
Rationale: Positioning John on his side is crucial to maintain airway patency and prevent aspiration, common concerns in the postictal state. While administering lorazepam (Option A) is essential during active seizures, it is not the priority postictally. Monitoring vital signs (Option C) is important but not as immediate as airway management. Continuous EEG monitoring (Option D) helps assess seizure activity but is secondary to ensuring immediate safety. The lateral position directly addresses airway protection, differentiating it as the primary intervention compared to other supportive measures.

Question 54: Correct Answer: B) Hypovolemic shock
Rationale: Hypovolemic shock is the most indicative sign of systemic involvement in severe burns due to significant fluid loss. Localized erythema (A) is a local response, while hyperkalemia (C) can occur but is not as immediate. Increased risk of infection (D) is a later complication. Hypovolemic shock requires immediate attention, distinguishing it from the other options which are less acute or secondary concerns, thus making it the most critical systemic indicator among patients with extensive burns.

Question 55: Correct Answer: C) Provide reassurance and maintain a calm environment.
Rationale: Providing reassurance and maintaining a calm environment is crucial in managing acute anxiety, as it helps stabilize the patient's immediate emotional state. Option A, while effective for quick relief, may not address the underlying anxiety triggers initially. Option B is beneficial but secondary to establishing safety and reassurance. Option D is more long-term and not suitable as an immediate intervention. Thus, option C aligns with clinical judgment in acute anxiety scenarios by prioritizing immediate emotional support.

Question 56: Correct Answer: B) Initiate ACE inhibitors
Rationale: Initiating ACE inhibitors is the most appropriate initial management strategy for idiopathic dilated cardiomyopathy as they help reduce afterload and improve cardiac output. While beta-blockers (Option A) are also used in treatment, they are typically introduced after stabilization with ACE inhibitors. Diuretics (Option C) provide symptom relief but do not address underlying pathophysiology. Lifestyle modifications (Option D) are supportive but insufficient alone. The correct choice reflects contemporary guidelines emphasizing ACE inhibitors as first-line therapy due to their beneficial effects on survival and cardiac function in heart failure patients.

Question 57: Correct Answer: D) Corticosteroids
Rationale: Corticosteroids are the first-line treatment for ITP to increase platelet count by dampening the immune response. IVIG (Option A) is used when rapid platelet increase is necessary or in refractory cases. Splenectomy (Option B) is typically considered for chronic ITP unresponsive to medical therapy. Platelet transfusion (Option C) is reserved for severe bleeding due to its transient effect on platelet counts. Hence, corticosteroids are the most appropriate initial treatment in this scenario due to their effectiveness in managing mild bleeding symptoms and increasing platelet levels.

Question 58: Correct Answer: B) Encourage deep breathing exercises and use of incentive spirometry.
Rationale: Encouraging deep breathing exercises and using incentive spirometry helps prevent atelectasis and promotes lung expansion, crucial in managing fractured ribs. While high-flow oxygen (A) addresses hypoxia, it doesn't promote lung expansion. Intravenous morphine (C) alleviates pain but may suppress respiration if not carefully monitored. Semi-Fowler's position (D) aids comfort but doesn't directly enhance lung function. Thus, option B directly targets improving respiratory mechanics compromised by rib fractures, aligning with contemporary practices in thoracic trauma care.

Question 59: Correct Answer: B) Initiate granulocyte colony-stimulating factor (G-CSF) therapy.
Rationale: Initiating G-CSF therapy is crucial as it stimulates bone marrow to produce more white blood cells, addressing leukopenia effectively. Option A is incorrect as antibiotics do not address the underlying cause of leukopenia. Option C is preventive but does not actively treat leukopenia. Option D is rarely performed due to risks and limited efficacy compared to G-CSF. Thus, B is the most appropriate action for promoting white cell production in chemotherapy-induced leukopenia.

Question 60: Correct Answer: B) Severe pain disproportionate to the injury
Rationale: Severe pain disproportionate to the injury is an early hallmark of compartment syndrome due to increased intracompartmental pressure. While loss of pulse (Option A) indicates severe vascular compromise and occurs later, numbness and tingling (Option C) are sensory changes that can develop as pressure increases but are not as early as pain. Swelling and tightness (Option D) can be present but are less specific compared to severe pain. Recognizing early signs like disproportionate pain is crucial for timely intervention, differentiating it from other symptoms that manifest later.

Question 61: Correct Answer: C) Pyridostigmine
Rationale: Pyridostigmine is a cholinesterase inhibitor that prevents the breakdown of acetylcholine, enhancing neuromuscular transmission in myasthenia gravis. Prednisone (A) and azathioprine (B) are immunosuppressants used to reduce autoantibody production but do not directly enhance neuromuscular transmission. Methotrexate (D), also an immunosuppressant, is less commonly used in this context. Pyridostigmine's direct action on neuromuscular junctions makes it distinct from the other options, which target immune modulation rather than neurotransmitter availability.

Question 62: Correct Answer: A) Administer IV hydrocortisone
Rationale: In acute adrenal insufficiency, immediate administration of IV hydrocortisone is crucial to replace deficient cortisol levels and stabilize the patient. Option B (oral fludrocortisone) addresses mineralocorticoid deficiency but is not suitable for acute management. Option C (IV saline infusion) aids in correcting electrolyte imbalances but does not address cortisol deficiency directly. Option D (oral glucose) might help with hypoglycemia but isn't a primary treatment for adrenal crisis. The correct choice ensures rapid response to adrenal crisis symptoms, emphasizing cortisol replacement over other therapies.

Question 63: Correct Answer: B) Initiating needle decompression
Rationale: Needle decompression is crucial for rapidly relieving pressure in a tension pneumothorax, which can be life-threatening due to compromised cardiopulmonary function. While high-flow oxygen (A) supports respiration and fluid resuscitation (D) addresses potential shock, neither directly resolves the underlying issue. An immediate chest X-ray (C) is diagnostic but delays treatment. Needle decompression directly addresses the cause by allowing trapped air to escape, stabilizing the patient more effectively than other interventions in this acute scenario.

Question 64: Correct Answer: A) Administer propranolol to control palpitations and anxiety.
Rationale: Propranolol is used for symptomatic relief in hyperthyroidism by controlling palpitations and anxiety through beta-blockade. Methimazole (Option B) addresses hormone synthesis but isn't immediate for symptom relief. A high-calorie diet (Option C) supports weight management but doesn't address acute symptoms. Levothyroxine (Option D) is inappropriate as it increases thyroid hormone levels, worsening hyperthyroidism. Thus, propranolol is the immediate

choice for symptomatic control in hyperthyroid patients like Emily.

Question 65: Correct Answer: C) Loading doses of antibiotics are often required despite renal impairment.
Rationale: Option C is correct because loading doses ensure therapeutic levels quickly, even in renal impairment. Option A is incorrect as not all antibiotics require dose reduction; some need adjustment based on specific pharmacokinetics. Option B is false since renal replacement therapy can significantly alter drug clearance, necessitating dose adjustments. Option D is misleading as antibiotics vary in how renal dysfunction affects their pharmacokinetics, requiring individualized dosing strategies. Understanding these nuances is crucial for effective infection management in critically ill patients with renal issues.

Question 66: Correct Answer: B) Elevated serum lipase
Rationale: Elevated serum lipase is the most specific marker for acute pancreatitis due to its longer half-life and higher specificity compared to amylase. While elevated serum amylase (Option A) can also indicate pancreatitis, it is less specific and can be elevated in other conditions. Elevated bilirubin (Option C) suggests possible biliary obstruction or liver disease, not directly pancreatitis. Elevated alkaline phosphatase (Option D) indicates biliary obstruction or bone disease. Thus, lipase elevation is the key indicator for diagnosing acute pancreatitis in this scenario.

Question 67: Correct Answer: B) Desmopressin acetate
Rationale: Desmopressin acetate is a synthetic analog of vasopressin and is the first-line treatment for central DI due to its ability to reduce urine output and thirst. Thiazide diuretics (A) are used in nephrogenic DI to decrease polyuria but are not suitable for central DI. Indomethacin (C), a nonsteroidal anti-inflammatory drug, can potentiate antidiuretic effects but is not first-line. Amiloride (D) is used in lithium-induced nephrogenic DI, not central DI. Desmopressin's efficacy in directly addressing vasopressin deficiency makes it superior in this context.

Question 68: Correct Answer: A) Transient ischemic attacks (TIAs) in the past month
Rationale: TIAs in the past month suggest unstable plaque or severe stenosis, indicating an increased risk of stroke, thus necessitating urgent intervention. Option B, mild dizziness, lacks specificity to carotid pathology. Option C, an asymptomatic carotid bruit, may not require immediate surgery without symptoms. Option D, controlled hypertension, does not directly correlate with urgent endarterectomy needs unless accompanied by neurological symptoms. The presence of recent TIAs directly points to increased cerebrovascular risk and justifies prioritizing surgical management over other findings.

Question 69: Correct Answer: C) Postrenal obstruction
Rationale: The combination of severe flank pain, hematuria, and oliguria suggests a postrenal cause such as an obstruction, which is consistent with the diagnosis of postrenal obstruction. Acute tubular necrosis (A) often results from ischemia or toxins but lacks flank pain. Prerenal azotemia (B) is linked to volume depletion or decreased renal perfusion without hematuria. Glomerulonephritis (D) typically involves proteinuria and hypertension rather than acute flank pain. Thus, Mr. Thompson's presentation aligns most closely with postrenal obstruction due to obstructive uropathy leading to acute kidney injury.

Question 70: Correct Answer: B) Dilated ventricles with systolic dysfunction
Rationale: Idiopathic dilated cardiomyopathy (IDC) is characterized by the dilation of ventricles and impaired systolic function, leading to reduced ejection fraction. Option A describes hypertrophic cardiomyopathy, where thickened walls and reduced chamber size are seen. Option C refers to restrictive cardiomyopathy, which maintains ejection fraction but impairs diastolic filling. Option D describes hypertrophic obstructive cardiomyopathy, where septal hypertrophy causes outflow obstruction. Understanding these differences is crucial for diagnosing IDC accurately.

Question 71: Correct Answer: A) Administration of broad-spectrum antibiotics
Rationale: Administration of broad-spectrum antibiotics is crucial in septic shock as it targets the underlying infection causing the systemic inflammatory response. While fluid resuscitation (D) and vasopressors (C) address hemodynamic instability, they do not resolve the infection. Mechanical ventilation (B) supports respiratory function but also does not target the root cause. Antibiotics effectively combat the infectious source, thus addressing the primary pathophysiological process, distinguishing it from supportive measures that manage symptoms rather than causes.

Question 72: Correct Answer: A) Administering lactulose to reduce ammonia levels
Rationale: Lactulose is critical for reducing ammonia levels by trapping ammonia in the gut and promoting its excretion, addressing the root cause of hepatic encephalopathy. Option B is incorrect as a high-protein diet can exacerbate ammonia production. Option C, while helpful for ascites, does not address encephalopathy directly. Option D may be useful if infection is present but does not target ammonia reduction. Therefore, lactulose remains the primary intervention for mitigating symptoms of hepatic encephalopathy in this context.

Question 73: Correct Answer: B) Bacterial meningitis
Rationale: The CSF findings of elevated protein and decreased glucose concentration are indicative of bacterial meningitis. Viral meningitis typically presents with normal glucose levels. Fungal meningitis can show similar CSF characteristics but is less common and usually occurs in immunocompromised individuals. Tuberculous meningitis also shows low glucose but often has a more gradual onset compared to bacterial meningitis. The acute presentation with these specific CSF findings makes bacterial meningitis the most likely diagnosis for John.

Question 74: Correct Answer: B) Administration of prophylactic antibiotics within 3 hours
Rationale: Administering prophylactic antibiotics within 3 hours is crucial in preventing infection in open fractures, as bacteria can quickly colonize exposed tissues. While immediate immobilization (A) and sterile dressing (C) are important for stabilization and protection, they do not directly address bacterial contamination. Surgical debridement (D), though necessary, is often performed later. The timing of antibiotics has a direct impact on reducing infection rates, aligning with contemporary research that emphasizes early antibiotic administration as a key factor in fracture management.

Question 75: Correct Answer: C) Initiating benzodiazepine therapy to manage withdrawal symptoms
Rationale: Benzodiazepines are the first-line treatment for managing alcohol withdrawal symptoms due to their efficacy in reducing excitability and preventing seizures. Option A is important but not the primary intervention for acute withdrawal. Option B addresses a complication of chronic alcoholism but not immediate withdrawal

management. Option D is essential for overall care but does not directly alleviate withdrawal symptoms. Thus, initiating benzodiazepine therapy is prioritized due to its direct impact on symptom management and prevention of severe complications like delirium tremens.

Question 76: Correct Answer: C) Starting intravenous N-acetylcysteine
Rationale: Intravenous N-acetylcysteine is crucial for treating fulminant hepatitis, especially if acetaminophen toxicity is suspected. It acts as an antioxidant, reducing liver damage. Option A (broad-spectrum antibiotics) is used for infection prevention but not directly for liver protection. Option B (lactulose therapy) addresses hepatic encephalopathy but doesn't halt liver damage progression. Option D (plasmapheresis) may help remove toxins but isn't as immediate or effective as N-acetylcysteine in acute settings. Understanding the primary cause and addressing it promptly is vital in fulminant hepatitis management.

Question 77: Correct Answer: C) Treating the underlying infection or condition
Rationale: The primary intervention in managing DIC is addressing the underlying cause, such as infection or trauma, to halt the pathological activation of coagulation. While options A and D (administering fresh frozen plasma and platelet transfusions) provide supportive care by replacing depleted clotting factors and platelets, they do not address the root cause. Option B (anticoagulation therapy with heparin) can be used in chronic DIC but is not universally applicable. Thus, treating the underlying condition is crucial for resolving DIC effectively.

Question 78: Correct Answer: B) Monitoring respiratory function closely
Rationale: Monitoring respiratory function is crucial due to the risk of respiratory failure in Guillain-Barré Syndrome (GBS). While options C and D (plasmapheresis and IVIG) are treatments for GBS, they do not address immediate life-threatening complications like respiratory failure. Option A, corticosteroids, are not typically effective in GBS management. Prioritizing respiratory monitoring ensures timely intervention if ventilation support is needed, highlighting the critical role of clinical judgment in preventing severe complications associated with neuromuscular disorders like GBS.

Question 79: Correct Answer: D) Correct underlying cause of DIC
Rationale: The primary management of DIC involves treating the underlying cause, as this can halt the progression of coagulopathy. Options A and C focus on symptom management but do not address the root cause. Option B, heparin therapy, may be considered in chronic DIC but is not an initial step. Addressing the underlying condition stabilizes coagulation pathways more effectively than supportive treatments alone, which are often adjuncts.

Question 80: Correct Answer: B) Initiate non-invasive positive pressure ventilation (NIPPV).
Rationale: The correct answer is B) Initiate non-invasive positive pressure ventilation (NIPPV). In patients with COPD exacerbation presenting with respiratory acidosis (pH <7.35 and elevated PaCO2), NIPPV can improve gas exchange by reducing CO2 retention and supporting alveolar ventilation. While A) administering high-flow oxygen may worsen hypercapnia due to V/Q mismatch, C) starting corticosteroids is beneficial but not immediately corrective for acidosis, and D) increasing bronchodilators alone may not adequately address acute ventilatory failure. Therefore, NIPPV is the most effective immediate intervention in this scenario.

Question 81: Correct Answer: A) Administer intravenous magnesium sulfate
Rationale: Administering intravenous magnesium sulfate is an evidence-based intervention for patients with refractory status asthmaticus who do not respond to initial treatments. It acts as a bronchodilator by relaxing smooth muscle. While increasing inhaled corticosteroids (B) and continuous nebulization of beta-agonists (D) are part of initial management, they may not be sufficient alone in refractory cases. Non-invasive positive pressure ventilation (C) can assist in respiratory support but does not address bronchospasm directly. Magnesium sulfate's role in acute severe asthma is supported by contemporary research, making it the most appropriate choice here.

Question 82: Correct Answer: B) Start an intravenous infusion of normal saline.
Rationale: The initial treatment for severe hyperglycemia with dehydration is fluid resuscitation using intravenous normal saline to restore intravascular volume and improve perfusion. While insulin administration (Option A) is crucial, it follows fluid replacement to avoid exacerbating hypotension. Oral hypoglycemic agents (Option C) are inappropriate in acute settings due to delayed action and potential ineffectiveness in severe cases. Continuous glucose monitoring (Option D) is supportive but not an immediate corrective measure. Thus, prioritizing fluid resuscitation aligns with clinical guidelines for managing hyperglycemia-induced dehydration.

Question 83: Correct Answer: A) Encourage the use of adaptive clothing with Velcro fasteners.
Rationale: Encouraging the use of adaptive clothing with Velcro fasteners directly addresses Mr. Thompson's specific issue with fine motor skills and coordination, facilitating his independence in dressing. While physical therapy (Option B) can improve overall strength, it may not immediately address fine motor challenges. Cognitive-behavioral therapy (Option C) targets motivation but not physical limitations directly. Assistive devices for ambulation (Option D) are unrelated to dressing tasks. Thus, Option A is most appropriate for improving his functional independence in this context.

Question 84: Correct Answer: C) Providing aggressive intravenous fluid resuscitation
Rationale: Aggressive intravenous fluid resuscitation is crucial in the initial management of acute pancreatitis to prevent hypovolemia and organ failure. While early enteral nutrition (B) supports gut integrity, it is secondary to hemodynamic stabilization. Prophylactic antibiotics (A) are not routinely recommended unless infection is confirmed. Monitoring serum calcium (D) is important but not as immediate as fluid resuscitation. The focus on fluid management aligns with current guidelines emphasizing the prevention of systemic complications through maintaining adequate perfusion and oxygenation.

Question 85: Correct Answer: D) Cerebral Angiography
Rationale: Cerebral angiography is the gold standard for diagnosing subarachnoid hemorrhage as it provides detailed images of blood vessels, identifying any aneurysms or vascular malformations. While a CT scan without contrast (Option B) is often the first step due to its speed and availability, it may miss smaller bleeds. An MRI (Option A) is less sensitive in acute settings, and a lumbar puncture (Option C) can confirm bleeding if CT is inconclusive but does not locate the source. Thus, cerebral angiography remains definitive for diagnosis and treatment planning.

Question 86: Correct Answer: C) Initiating thrombolytic

therapy to dissolve clots
Rationale: Thrombolytic therapy is critical as it directly dissolves clots, restoring blood flow and preventing tissue necrosis, a key goal in acute peripheral vascular insufficiency. Anticoagulants (A) prevent new clot formation but don't dissolve existing ones. Elevating the limb (B) reduces edema but doesn't address occlusion. Warm compresses (D) may improve circulation superficially but are ineffective against deep occlusions. Thrombolytics offer a direct approach to resolving the underlying issue, making option C the most effective intervention in acute scenarios.

Question 87: Correct Answer: B) Reduced glomerular filtration rate (GFR)
Rationale: A reduced GFR is the most definitive indicator of CKD progression towards ESRD, reflecting diminished kidney function. While elevated serum creatinine (A), increased serum potassium (C), and elevated BUN (D) are related to impaired renal function, they can fluctuate due to various factors and do not directly measure the filtration capacity. GFR provides a comprehensive assessment of renal function, making it the preferred marker in evaluating CKD severity and progression. Understanding these differences is crucial for accurate clinical judgment in CKD management.

Question 88: Correct Answer: B) Perform pericardiocentesis
Rationale: Pericardiocentesis is the definitive treatment for cardiac tamponade as it directly relieves pressure on the heart by removing excess fluid from the pericardial space. While administering IV fluids (Option A) can temporarily stabilize hemodynamics by increasing preload, it does not address the root cause. Vasopressor therapy (Option C) may support blood pressure but fails to relieve cardiac compression. Diuretics (Option D) are contraindicated as they reduce preload further, worsening tamponade symptoms. Thus, pericardiocentesis effectively resolves the underlying issue by decompressing the heart.

Question 89: Correct Answer: D) Sharp surgical debridement
Rationale: Sharp surgical debridement is the most effective method for promoting healing in chronic wounds with necrotic tissue as it allows precise removal of devitalized tissue, reducing infection risk and facilitating healing. While autolytic debridement (A) uses the body's enzymes and moisture to rehydrate, soften, and liquefy hard eschar and slough, it is slower. Mechanical debridement (B), involving physical removal, can be painful and less precise. Enzymatic debridement (C) involves topical agents to break down necrotic tissue but is less immediate than sharp surgical methods.

Question 90: Correct Answer: B) Implementation of personalized music therapy
Rationale: Personalized music therapy has been shown to significantly reduce agitation in Alzheimer's patients by engaging their emotional memory and providing comfort. While antipsychotics (Option A) can be used, they carry risks of side effects. Physical exercise (Option C) improves overall health but is less effective for immediate agitation relief. Cognitive-behavioral therapy (Option D), though beneficial for some cognitive symptoms, is less impactful on agitation compared to music therapy. Music therapy's ability to tap into preserved musical memory offers a unique calming effect, distinguishing it from other interventions.

Question 91: Correct Answer: B) Reduced grip strength
Rationale: Reduced grip strength is a sensitive indicator of early functional impairment as it reflects both neuromuscular function and overall muscle health. It can signal issues in neurological pathways affecting muscle control. Decreased deep tendon reflexes (A) may indicate neurological issues but are less specific to functional capacity. Limited range of motion (C) often indicates joint-specific problems, while altered gait (D) may occur later in disease progression. Grip strength is a comprehensive measure encompassing both neurological and musculoskeletal systems, making it the most indicative of early impairment.

Question 92: Correct Answer: B) Transfusion-related acute lung injury (TRALI)
Rationale: TRALI is characterized by acute respiratory distress, hypoxemia, and bilateral pulmonary infiltrates within six hours of transfusion, aligning with Emily's symptoms. TACO (Option A) involves volume overload but typically presents with hypertension and cardiac issues. ARDS (Option C), while similar, lacks the direct temporal link to transfusion. Anaphylactic reactions (Option D) involve rapid onset with additional systemic symptoms like rash or hypotension. The temporal relationship and symptomatology in this scenario specifically point to TRALI as the correct diagnosis.

Question 93: Correct Answer: B) Initiate aggressive fluid resuscitation
Rationale: In cases of urosepsis, immediate fluid resuscitation is crucial to stabilize hemodynamics and improve perfusion. While administering antibiotics (Option A) is essential, fluids must be given first to address hypotension. Blood cultures (Option C) should be done promptly but not delay fluid resuscitation. Vasopressors (Option D) are considered only if hypotension persists after adequate fluid replacement. Therefore, Option B is prioritized as it aligns with sepsis management guidelines emphasizing early hemodynamic support.

Question 94: Correct Answer: A) Administer intravenous atropine.
Rationale: Administering intravenous atropine is the correct initial action as it directly addresses bradycardia by blocking vagal influences on the heart, thus increasing heart rate and stabilizing blood pressure. Option B, initiating fluid resuscitation, may help hypotension but does not directly address bradycardia. Option C, preparing for pacing, is more invasive and typically considered if atropine fails. Option D, administering epinephrine, is generally reserved for severe cases or cardiac arrest scenarios. Atropine effectively targets the root cause in this scenario by counteracting vagal stimulation.

Question 95: Correct Answer: A) Streptococcus pneumoniae
Rationale: Streptococcus pneumoniae is the most common cause of bacterial meningitis in adults, presenting with fever, headache, neck stiffness, and altered CSF profile. Neisseria meningitidis can present similarly but is more common in younger populations or those in close quarters. Listeria monocytogenes is typically seen in immunocompromised patients or those over 50 years old. Haemophilus influenzae was historically common but has decreased due to vaccination. The CSF findings of elevated WBCs and protein with low glucose are classic for bacterial meningitis, supporting Streptococcus pneumoniae as the likely pathogen.

Question 96: Correct Answer: D) Increased intracranial pressure (ICP)
Rationale: Increased intracranial pressure (ICP) is the most immediate life-threatening complication of brain tumors due to potential herniation and compromised

cerebral perfusion. While seizures (A), hydrocephalus (B), and hemorrhagic stroke (C) are significant concerns, they are either secondary effects or less immediately fatal compared to unchecked ICP. Seizures can be managed with medication, hydrocephalus often requires surgical intervention, and hemorrhagic stroke is less common than ICP issues in this context. Recognizing ICP as an urgent priority aligns with contemporary neurological care standards for space-occupying lesions.

Question 97: Correct Answer: A) Elevate the head of the bed to 30 degrees
Rationale: Elevating the head of the bed to 30 degrees is crucial for facilitating venous drainage and reducing ICP. While administering sedatives (B) can prevent agitation that might increase ICP, it does not directly address ICP management. Maintaining normothermia (C) is important but primarily prevents metabolic demands that could indirectly affect ICP. Monitoring electrolyte levels (D) is essential for overall neurological function but doesn't specifically target ICP reduction. Thus, option A directly addresses ICP control through positioning, making it the most critical intervention post-craniotomy.

Question 98: Correct Answer: B) Encouraging incentive spirometry use
Rationale: Encouraging incentive spirometry use is crucial in preventing atelectasis and pneumonia by promoting lung expansion and improving ventilation. While high-flow oxygen therapy (A) supports oxygenation, it doesn't directly address lung expansion. Rib belts (C) can restrict breathing and are not recommended. Early ambulation (D) aids recovery but is less effective than incentive spirometry in specifically preventing pulmonary complications. The correct option targets the direct prevention of respiratory issues through enhanced lung function, aligning with contemporary respiratory care practices.

Question 99: Correct Answer: A) Oral endothelin receptor antagonists
Rationale: Oral endothelin receptor antagonists are recommended as first-line therapy for PAH due to their efficacy in improving exercise capacity and hemodynamics. High-dose calcium channel blockers are only effective if the patient is a vasoreactive responder, which Sarah is not confirmed to be. Long-term oxygen therapy is indicated for hypoxemia rather than PAH specifically. Intravenous prostacyclin analogs are reserved for severe cases or those unresponsive to oral agents. Therefore, option A is most suitable given Sarah's diagnosis and typical treatment protocols.

Question 100: Correct Answer: C) Splanchnic vasodilation
Rationale: Splanchnic vasodilation is the initial physiological change in portal hypertension, leading to increased blood flow and pressure in the portal vein. This triggers collateral circulation formation, contributing to esophageal varices. While collateral circulation (Option B) is a consequence, it is not the initiating event. Increased hepatic arterial pressure (Option A) and decreased portal venous inflow (Option D) are not primary contributors to variceal formation. Understanding these mechanisms highlights splanchnic vasodilation as the critical starting point for subsequent pathophysiological changes.

Question 101: Correct Answer: B) Initiating mechanical ventilation with low tidal volumes
Rationale: Initiating mechanical ventilation with low tidal volumes is crucial in managing lung contusion to minimize barotrauma and volutrauma, preventing further respiratory compromise. High-flow oxygen (A) may not address underlying ventilatory issues. Aggressive fluid resuscitation (C) can exacerbate pulmonary edema in contused lungs. CPAP (D) can improve oxygenation but may not be sufficient for severe cases requiring controlled ventilation. Understanding the pathophysiology of lung contusion and appropriate ventilatory strategies is essential for effective management.

Question 102: Correct Answer: A) Administer aspirin immediately.
Rationale: Administering aspirin is crucial as it reduces the risk of subsequent strokes by preventing platelet aggregation. While scheduling an MRI (Option B) is important for assessment, it is not the immediate priority. Thrombolytic therapy (Option C) is inappropriate for TIA since symptoms have resolved. Monitoring vital signs (Option D) is essential but secondary to initiating antiplatelet therapy. The focus on immediate aspirin administration aligns with current guidelines emphasizing rapid antiplatelet therapy post-TIA to mitigate future risks.

Question 103: Correct Answer: A) Transcatheter Aortic Valve Replacement (TAVR)
Rationale: TAVR is recommended for symptomatic aortic stenosis patients at high surgical risk, offering a less invasive alternative to open-heart surgery. Balloon aortic valvuloplasty provides only temporary relief and is less effective. Medical management with beta-blockers does not address the underlying valve issue. Surgical aortic valve replacement is not suitable due to high surgical risk. TAVR's minimally invasive nature and effectiveness make it the preferred choice in this scenario, aligning with contemporary research and guidelines for managing high-risk patients.

Question 104: Correct Answer: B) Conduct a comprehensive suicide risk assessment.
Rationale: Conducting a comprehensive suicide risk assessment is crucial as it provides detailed insights into Sarah's current mental state and risk factors, allowing for tailored interventions. While a no-suicide contract (A) might seem helpful, its efficacy is debated in contemporary research. Increasing monitoring (C) is supportive but not a primary intervention. Immediate administration of antidepressants (D) lacks immediate effect on acute suicidal ideation. Thus, option B ensures an evidence-based approach to prioritizing Sarah's safety by understanding her specific needs and risks.

Question 105: Correct Answer: A) Administer intravenous heparin
Rationale: The administration of intravenous heparin is crucial as it prevents further clot propagation in acute arterial occlusion. While an urgent embolectomy (Option B) may be necessary, anticoagulation is the immediate priority to stabilize the condition. Applying warm compresses (Option C) can exacerbate ischemia, and elevating the limb (Option D) may worsen perfusion. Heparin's role in preventing additional clotting is fundamental in managing acute arterial occlusion, distinguishing it from other interventions which may not directly address the immediate risk of thrombus extension.

Question 106: Correct Answer: A) Elevated serum creatinine with a low fractional excretion of sodium (FeNa < 1%)
Rationale: Option A is correct as it reflects prerenal AKI, characterized by reduced renal perfusion leading to concentrated urine and low FeNa. Option B suggests intrinsic renal damage, where the kidney cannot concentrate urine effectively. Option C indicates intrinsic or postrenal AKI due to impaired sodium reabsorption. Option D is irrelevant to AKI diagnosis as normal creatinine and proteinuria are not typical indicators.

Understanding these distinctions helps in differentiating prerenal causes from intrinsic or postrenal issues in AKI.

Question 107: Correct Answer: C) Initiating thrombolytic therapy
Rationale: Initiating thrombolytic therapy is crucial in STEMI for reperfusion, reducing mortality by restoring coronary blood flow. While aspirin (A) is essential for antiplatelet action, it does not directly dissolve clots like thrombolytics. Nitroglycerin (B) alleviates symptoms but doesn't address the underlying clot. Supplemental oxygen (D) is beneficial if hypoxemia is present but isn't as pivotal in acute reperfusion. Thrombolytics directly target the occlusion causing STEMI, making them vital for immediate survival improvement, unlike other supportive measures.

Question 108: Correct Answer: B) Hypotension with elevated central venous pressure
Rationale: Hypotension with elevated central venous pressure suggests right ventricular strain or failure due to a massive PE, necessitating urgent treatment. While A) sudden dyspnea and pleuritic chest pain are common in PE, they do not specifically indicate massive PE. C) Tachycardia and low-grade fever can occur in various conditions and are not specific to massive PE. D) Hemoptysis and mild hypoxemia may be present in smaller PEs but do not indicate severity. The correct answer reflects critical hemodynamic compromise associated with massive PE, demanding immediate intervention.

Question 109: Correct Answer: C) CT Pulmonary Angiography
Rationale: CT Pulmonary Angiography is the gold standard for diagnosing acute pulmonary embolism due to its high sensitivity and specificity. While a D-dimer test (Option B) can suggest PE presence, it is not definitive. A chest X-ray (Option A) can rule out other conditions but does not confirm PE. The V/Q scan (Option D) is used when CT is contraindicated but is less definitive than CT Pulmonary Angiography. Therefore, CT Pulmonary Angiography remains the most reliable diagnostic tool in this scenario.

Question 110: Correct Answer: C) Hyperkalemia
Rationale: Tumor Lysis Syndrome (TLS) is characterized by rapid cell lysis leading to the release of intracellular contents, including potassium, resulting in hyperkalemia. This condition can cause severe cardiac complications if not managed promptly. While hypocalcemia (Option B) is also seen in TLS due to phosphate release binding calcium, hyperkalemia is more immediate and common. Hypercalcemia (Option A) and hypokalemia (Option D) are not typically associated with TLS. Understanding these imbalances is crucial for effective clinical management of TLS in critical care settings.

Question 111: Correct Answer: C) Increased gamma-aminobutyric acid (GABA) activity
Rationale: Hepatic encephalopathy is primarily associated with increased GABAergic activity, leading to inhibitory neurotransmission and altered mental status. While dopamine and serotonin alterations can influence neurological conditions, they are not central to hepatic encephalopathy. Acetylcholine is more relevant in other disorders like Alzheimer's disease. The focus on GABA underscores its role in neural inhibition, differentiating it from other neurotransmitters that may contribute to neurological changes but not as directly as GABA in hepatic encephalopathy.

Question 112: Correct Answer: B) CT scan of the abdomen and pelvis with contrast
Rationale: The CT scan of the abdomen and pelvis with contrast is the gold standard for diagnosing acute genitourinary trauma due to its high sensitivity and specificity in detecting renal injuries. Option A, ultrasound, is less detailed for complex injuries. Option C, IVP, is outdated and less informative. Option D, an abdominal X-ray, provides limited information on soft tissue structures. The CT scan offers comprehensive imaging, crucial for identifying both renal parenchymal injuries and associated vascular damage in trauma cases like John's.

Question 113: Correct Answer: B) Intravenous hydration with isotonic saline before and after contrast exposure
Rationale: Intravenous hydration with isotonic saline is the most effective intervention to prevent contrast-induced nephropathy by maintaining renal perfusion and diluting nephrotoxic agents. While N-acetylcysteine (Option A) has been considered, evidence supporting its efficacy is inconsistent. Low-osmolar or iso-osmolar contrast media (Option C) reduces risk but is less effective than hydration. Sodium bicarbonate infusion (Option D) is also used but lacks strong evidence compared to saline. Therefore, saline hydration remains the cornerstone for prevention based on contemporary research and clinical guidelines.

Question 114: Correct Answer: C) Stop the transfusion immediately and notify the physician.
Rationale: The symptoms suggest an acute hemolytic transfusion reaction, requiring immediate cessation of the transfusion to prevent further hemolysis and complications. Option A is incorrect as antipyretics do not address underlying causes. Option B is inappropriate because slowing does not halt immune-mediated damage. Option D risks exacerbating reactions without addressing root cause. Immediate action (Option C) halts antigen-antibody interaction, allowing for evaluation and intervention, aligning with contemporary protocols for managing suspected transfusion reactions.

Question 115: Correct Answer: C) Discontinue the IV infusion immediately.
Rationale: The priority in managing IV infiltration is to discontinue the infusion to prevent further tissue damage. Option C is correct because it stops additional fluid from entering the tissue. While applying a warm compress (Option A) and elevating the limb (Option B) can help reduce swelling and pain, they are secondary measures after discontinuing the infusion. Notifying the physician (Option D) is important but should follow after stopping the infusion to mitigate further harm.

Question 116: Correct Answer: B) An epidural hematoma typically presents with a lucid interval.
Rationale: An epidural hematoma is characterized by a lucid interval, where the patient temporarily regains consciousness before deteriorating, due to arterial bleeding between the dura mater and skull. Option A is incorrect as it describes subdural hematomas, which involve venous bleeding. Option C incorrectly associates subdural hematomas with arterial bleeding; they are typically venous. Option D inaccurately suggests immediate loss of consciousness is common in subdural hematomas; this is more typical of severe brain injuries rather than specific to subdural hematomas.

Question 117: Correct Answer: D) Refer for hyperbaric oxygen therapy
Rationale: Hyperbaric oxygen therapy (HBOT) is effective in promoting healing in chronic, non-healing diabetic ulcers by enhancing oxygen delivery to tissues, which is crucial for wound healing. While increasing dressing changes (A) and NPWT (B) can be beneficial, they may not address underlying ischemia. Systemic antibiotics (C)

are indicated only if infection is present. HBOT specifically targets ischemia and hypoxia in chronic wounds, making it a more suitable choice when standard care fails.

Question 118: Correct Answer: A) Sudden onset of tearing chest pain radiating to the back
Rationale: The sudden onset of tearing chest pain radiating to the back is characteristic of an acute type A aortic dissection, as it reflects the rapid separation of the aortic wall layers. Option B suggests myocardial ischemia or heart failure, while option C indicates arrhythmias. Option D is more typical of pericarditis. The acute nature and specific pain pattern in option A are crucial for distinguishing aortic dissection from other cardiovascular conditions, making it the correct answer.

Question 119: Correct Answer: B) Insert a chest tube to drain the pleural effusion
Rationale: In cases of traumatic hemothorax indicated by decreased breath sounds and hypotension, immediate chest tube insertion is critical to evacuate blood and relieve pressure on the lung, restoring normal respiratory function. Option A is incorrect as observation alone does not address the underlying issue. Option C, thoracotomy, is invasive and reserved for specific indications like massive hemothorax or cardiac tamponade. Option D, mechanical ventilation, may be necessary later but does not directly resolve the pleural effusion causing John's symptoms.

Question 120: Correct Answer: B) Immediate surgical debridement
Rationale: Immediate surgical debridement is crucial for managing necrotizing fasciitis because it removes necrotic tissue, halting the spread of infection. While broad-spectrum antibiotics (Option A) are essential, they cannot penetrate necrotic tissue alone. Hyperbaric oxygen therapy (Option C) may aid healing but isn't a primary intervention. Fluid resuscitation (Option D) supports hemodynamics but doesn't address the source. Surgical intervention directly targets the root cause, distinguishing it from other supportive measures, making it the definitive initial step according to contemporary research and clinical guidelines.

Question 121: Correct Answer: B) Low tidal volume ventilation
Rationale: Low tidal volume ventilation is crucial in ARDS management to minimize ventilator-induced lung injury by reducing barotrauma and volutrauma, thereby improving oxygenation. High tidal volumes (Option A) can exacerbate lung injury. High PEEP (Option C) may improve oxygenation but risks hemodynamic compromise. Prone positioning (Option D) improves oxygenation but does not directly address lung protection as effectively as low tidal volumes. Contemporary research supports low tidal volume as a cornerstone strategy for ARDS, emphasizing its role in reducing mortality and improving patient outcomes.

Question 122: Correct Answer: A) Administering lactulose to reduce ammonia levels
Rationale: Lactulose is essential in treating hepatic encephalopathy as it reduces intestinal ammonia absorption by acidifying the colon. Option B is incorrect as high-protein diets can exacerbate encephalopathy by increasing ammonia production. Option C addresses ascites but not directly encephalopathy. Option D is not typically used for hepatic encephalopathy and doesn't address ammonia levels.

Question 123: Correct Answer: C) Elevated serum ammonia levels
Rationale: Elevated serum ammonia levels are most indicative of severe hepatic encephalopathy in fulminant hepatitis. Ammonia, a byproduct of protein metabolism, accumulates due to impaired liver function and contributes to neurotoxicity. While elevated bilirubin and increased PT indicate liver dysfunction severity, they do not directly correlate with encephalopathy. Decreased albumin reflects chronic liver disease but is less specific for acute encephalopathy. Therefore, serum ammonia is the key marker distinguishing encephalopathy from other hepatic failure complications.

Question 124: Correct Answer: B) Magnetic Resonance Imaging (MRI)
Rationale: MRI is the most sensitive imaging technique for detecting small space-occupying lesions in the brain due to its superior contrast resolution and ability to differentiate between soft tissues. CT scans, while useful for initial assessment, are less effective in identifying small lesions. PET scans are primarily used for metabolic activity analysis rather than structural detail. Ultrasound is not typically used for intracranial evaluations due to poor penetration through bone. Therefore, MRI is preferred for its detailed imaging capabilities, making it the optimal choice in this context.

Question 125: Correct Answer: A) Elevated blood urea nitrogen (BUN) to creatinine ratio greater than 20:1
Rationale: Prerenal azotemia is characterized by an elevated BUN to creatinine ratio (>20:1), reflecting reduced renal perfusion. Option B and C suggest intrinsic renal causes due to higher urine sodium and FENa, indicating impaired tubular function. Option D indicates acute tubular necrosis, not prerenal azotemia. The high BUN/creatinine ratio in prerenal azotemia results from increased urea reabsorption due to low renal perfusion, making option A the most indicative finding.

CCRN Exam Practice Questions [SET 4]

Question 1: John, a 68-year-old male with a history of smoking and diabetes, underwent a femoral-popliteal (fem-pop) bypass surgery to address critical limb ischemia. Post-operatively, he is experiencing significant pain in the affected leg. As his critical care nurse, what is the most appropriate initial action to assess for graft patency?
A) Check the pedal pulse on the affected leg.
B) Measure the ankle-brachial index (ABI).
C) Assess capillary refill time in the toes.
D) Monitor for changes in skin color and temperature.

Question 2: In the context of anemia management in critical care settings, which of the following laboratory findings is most indicative of iron deficiency anemia?
A) Elevated serum ferritin
B) Low serum iron and high total iron-binding capacity (TIBC)
C) High mean corpuscular volume (MCV)
D) Increased reticulocyte count

Question 3: John, a 45-year-old male with a history of alcohol use disorder, presents to the emergency department with severe abdominal pain radiating to his back, nausea, and vomiting. His serum amylase and lipase levels are markedly elevated. As a critical care nurse, what is the most appropriate initial management step for John's acute pancreatitis?
A) Administer intravenous antibiotics
B) Initiate aggressive intravenous fluid resuscitation
C) Start nasogastric suction
D) Provide parenteral nutrition

Question 4: In the management of status epilepticus, which medication is considered the first-line treatment due to its rapid action and effectiveness in terminating seizures?
A) Phenytoin
B) Lorazepam
C) Levetiracetam
D) Valproic Acid

Question 5: Which of the following neurotransmitter systems is primarily implicated in the pathophysiology of PTSD, particularly in relation to hyperarousal symptoms?
A) Dopaminergic system
B) Serotonergic system
C) Noradrenergic system
D) GABAergic system

Question 6: In the context of femur fractures, which of the following statements about the management of an intertrochanteric fracture is most accurate?
A) Closed reduction and casting are typically sufficient for stable intertrochanteric fractures.
B) Open reduction and internal fixation (ORIF) with a dynamic hip screw is commonly used for unstable intertrochanteric fractures.
C) External fixation is the preferred method for all types of intertrochanteric fractures.
D) Total hip arthroplasty is the first-line treatment for young patients with intertrochanteric fractures.

Question 7: In a patient suspected of bowel infarction, which clinical finding is most indicative of transmural necrosis requiring immediate surgical intervention?
A) Severe abdominal pain with rebound tenderness
B) Intermittent abdominal cramping with diarrhea
C) Hyperactive bowel sounds with palpable mass
D) Abdominal distension with absent bowel sounds

Question 8: In the context of hypoactive delirium in critically ill patients, which of the following interventions is most effective in managing this condition according to contemporary research?
A) Administering benzodiazepines to promote sedation
B) Implementing a structured reorientation program
C) Increasing environmental stimuli to engage the patient
D) Using antipsychotic medications as a first-line treatment

Question 9: A 45-year-old patient named John presents to the emergency department with sudden onset dyspnea and pleuritic chest pain. On examination, there is decreased breath sounds and hyperresonance on percussion over the right hemithorax. A chest X-ray reveals a large pneumothorax. Which of the following is the most appropriate initial management step for this condition?
A) Administer supplemental oxygen
B) Perform needle decompression
C) Start high-dose corticosteroids
D) Initiate broad-spectrum antibiotics

Question 10: In the context of increased intracranial pressure (ICP) management, which of the following interventions is most effective in reducing ICP through osmotic diuresis?
A) Administering Mannitol
B) Providing Hypertonic Saline
C) Elevating the head of the bed to 30 degrees
D) Implementing controlled hyperventilation

Question 11: In the context of surgical wound management, which of the following strategies is most effective in preventing surgical site infections (SSIs) in patients with compromised integumentary systems?
A) Administering prophylactic antibiotics within 24 hours post-surgery
B) Maintaining normothermia during the perioperative period
C) Using antiseptic solutions for preoperative skin preparation
D) Applying occlusive dressings immediately after surgery

Question 12: During cardiac catheterization, which of the following hemodynamic changes is most indicative of left ventricular dysfunction?
A) Elevated right atrial pressure
B) Increased pulmonary capillary wedge pressure
C) Decreased cardiac output
D) Elevated systemic vascular resistance

Question 13: In the management of Tumor Lysis Syndrome (TLS), which electrolyte imbalance is most critical to monitor and correct promptly to prevent cardiac complications?
A) Hyperkalemia
B) Hypocalcemia
C) Hyperphosphatemia
D) Hyperuricemia

Question 14: John, a 58-year-old male with a history of hypertension, presents to the emergency department with sudden onset of severe headache, vomiting, and altered consciousness. A CT scan confirms an intracranial hemorrhage. In managing John's condition,

which of the following interventions is most crucial in the acute phase to prevent further neurological deterioration?
A) Administering antihypertensive medication to maintain systolic blood pressure below 160 mmHg
B) Initiating anticoagulation therapy to prevent thromboembolic events
C) Performing immediate surgical evacuation of the hematoma
D) Providing high-dose corticosteroids to reduce cerebral edema

Question 15: John, a 55-year-old male, presents with severe abdominal pain, distension, and decreased urine output. He was recently involved in a motor vehicle accident and underwent extensive abdominal surgery. His intra-abdominal pressure is measured at 22 mmHg. Which of the following interventions should be prioritized to manage his suspected Abdominal Compartment Syndrome?
A) Increase intravenous fluid administration.
B) Administer diuretics to reduce fluid overload.
C) Perform decompressive laparotomy.
D) Elevate the head of the bed to 30 degrees.

Question 16: In the context of pulmonary fibrosis, which of the following pathophysiological processes is primarily responsible for the progressive decline in lung function?
A) Excessive mucus production in the airways
B) Alveolar epithelial cell injury and fibroblast proliferation
C) Bronchial smooth muscle hypertrophy
D) Pulmonary vasoconstriction

Question 17: A 32-year-old patient named Alex has been admitted to the critical care unit following a motorcycle accident. Despite multiple injuries, Alex insists on being discharged early to participate in an extreme sports event. As a critical care nurse, how should you assess Alex's risk-taking behavior in this scenario?
A) Consider Alex's cognitive function and decision-making capacity.
B) Evaluate the potential influence of peer pressure on Alex's decisions.
C) Assess Alex's past medical history for previous risk-taking incidents.
D) Determine if Alex understands the consequences of his actions.

Question 18: Which of the following is the most common complication associated with abdominal adhesions in post-surgical patients?
A) Bowel obstruction
B) Perforation of the bowel
C) Intra-abdominal abscess formation
D) Ischemic bowel disease

Question 19: A 68-year-old patient named Mr. Thompson is admitted to the ICU with sepsis and develops signs of disseminated intravascular coagulation (DIC). As his critical care nurse, you are assessing his lab results. Which of the following laboratory findings is most indicative of DIC?
A) Elevated fibrinogen levels
B) Decreased platelet count
C) Increased hemoglobin levels
D) Normal prothrombin time (PT)

Question 20: A 55-year-old patient named John is scheduled for a craniotomy to remove a brain tumor. During the preoperative assessment, the critical care nurse must evaluate John's neurological status. Which of the following assessments is most crucial in determining potential complications related to increased intracranial pressure post-craniotomy?
A) Monitoring blood pressure for hypertension
B) Assessing pupillary response to light
C) Evaluating respiratory rate and pattern
D) Checking for signs of infection at the surgical site

Question 21: In a critical care setting, which of the following is the most definitive laboratory test for diagnosing hyperthyroidism in a patient with suspected thyroid storm?
A) Elevated Free T4 level
B) Suppressed Thyroid-Stimulating Hormone (TSH) level
C) Increased Total T3 level
D) Elevated Reverse T3 level

Question 22: A 28-year-old patient named Lisa presents to the emergency department with symptoms of nausea, vomiting, abdominal pain, and deep rapid breathing. Her blood glucose level is 450 mg/dL, and arterial blood gas analysis shows a pH of 7.25 with elevated anion gap metabolic acidosis. Based on this scenario, what is the most critical initial treatment step for Lisa's suspected Diabetic Ketoacidosis (DKA)?
A) Administering intravenous insulin
B) Providing oral glucose
C) Initiating intravenous fluid resuscitation
D) Administering sodium bicarbonate

Question 23: In a critically ill patient with acute pancreatitis, which of the following laboratory findings is most indicative of severe disease and a poor prognosis?
A) Elevated amylase levels
B) Decreased serum calcium levels
C) Elevated lipase levels
D) Increased bilirubin levels

Question 24: In the management of hepatic encephalopathy associated with hepatic failure, which of the following interventions primarily targets the reduction of ammonia production in the gastrointestinal tract?
A) Administration of lactulose
B) Restriction of dietary protein
C) Use of neomycin
D) Supplementation with branched-chain amino acids

Question 25: Emily, a 45-year-old patient with a history of Crohn's disease, presents with fatigue, weight loss, and diarrhea. Her lab results show low levels of serum albumin and vitamin B12. As her critical care nurse, which intervention is most appropriate to address her malnutrition and malabsorption issues?
A) Initiate a high-calorie diet with oral B12 supplements.
B) Start total parenteral nutrition (TPN) immediately.
C) Administer intramuscular vitamin B12 injections and a low-residue diet.
D) Recommend an increase in dietary fiber intake.

Question 26: After an esophagectomy, which postoperative complication is most critical to monitor in the immediate recovery period?
A) Anastomotic leak
B) Chylothorax
C) Recurrent laryngeal nerve injury
D) Pulmonary embolism

Question 27: In the context of immune deficiencies, which of the following conditions is characterized by a defect in both humoral and cell-mediated immunity, often due to a genetic mutation affecting T-cell development?

A) Chronic Granulomatous Disease
B) Severe Combined Immunodeficiency (SCID)
C) Common Variable Immunodeficiency (CVID)
D) Selective IgA Deficiency

Question 28: A 68-year-old patient named Mr. Johnson is admitted to the ICU following a high-impact car accident resulting in a closed femur fracture. The orthopedic team plans an intramedullary nailing procedure. As a critical care nurse, what is your primary concern during the preoperative period for Mr. Johnson?
A) Monitoring for signs of fat embolism syndrome
B) Ensuring adequate hydration to prevent renal failure
C) Maintaining immobilization to prevent further injury
D) Assessing for potential compartment syndrome

Question 29: Which of the following medications is most commonly associated with drug-induced hepatic failure leading to coma in patients with pre-existing liver conditions?
A) Acetaminophen
B) Ibuprofen
C) Aspirin
D) Metformin

Question 30: Sarah, a 58-year-old female patient with a history of atrial fibrillation, has been on heparin therapy for the past week. She presents with a sudden drop in platelet count and new thrombotic events. As a critical care nurse, what is the most appropriate immediate intervention to address suspected Heparin-Induced Thrombocytopenia (HIT)?
A) Discontinue heparin and start warfarin immediately.
B) Discontinue heparin and initiate argatroban.
C) Continue heparin and monitor platelet count closely.
D) Switch from heparin to low molecular weight heparin.

Question 31: A 45-year-old patient named John presents to the emergency department with a history of blunt chest trauma from a motor vehicle accident. He exhibits signs of respiratory distress, decreased breath sounds on the left side, and hypotension. A chest X-ray reveals fluid accumulation in the pleural space. Which immediate intervention is most appropriate for managing John's condition?
A) Administer high-flow oxygen therapy.
B) Perform needle decompression on the affected side.
C) Initiate intravenous fluid resuscitation.
D) Insert a chest tube on the affected side.

Question 32: In the management of empyema, which intervention is considered most effective in promoting drainage and resolution of the infection?
A) Intravenous antibiotic therapy
B) Thoracentesis
C) Video-assisted thoracoscopic surgery (VATS)
D) Chest tube placement

Question 33: In the context of ischemic (embolic) stroke management, which of the following interventions is most critical in minimizing long-term neurological damage if administered within the appropriate time window?
A) Administration of intravenous thrombolytics
B) Initiation of aspirin therapy
C) Control of blood pressure
D) Use of anticoagulants

Question 34: A 17-year-old patient named Alex presents to the critical care unit with progressive muscle weakness and difficulty breathing. The healthcare team suspects a neuromuscular disorder and is considering muscular dystrophy as a potential diagnosis. Which of the following diagnostic tests is most definitive in confirming muscular dystrophy?
A) Serum Creatine Kinase (CK) levels
B) Electromyography (EMG)
C) Muscle Biopsy
D) Genetic Testing

Question 35: John, a 68-year-old male with a history of hypertension and smoking, presents to the emergency department with sudden onset of severe chest and back pain. His blood pressure is significantly different between his arms, and he appears pale and diaphoretic. Given the suspicion of an aortic rupture, which diagnostic test should be prioritized to confirm the diagnosis rapidly?
A) Transthoracic echocardiography (TTE)
B) Chest X-ray
C) Computed tomography angiography (CTA)
D) Magnetic resonance imaging (MRI)

Question 36: In the context of neurosurgery, which intervention is most critical in reducing intracranial pressure (ICP) following traumatic brain injury?
A) Hyperventilation to reduce CO2 levels
B) Administration of mannitol
C) Elevation of the head of the bed to 30 degrees
D) Inducing mild hypothermia

Question 37: In the clinical assessment of brain death, which of the following tests is considered definitive for confirming the absence of cerebral blood flow?
A) Electroencephalogram (EEG)
B) Transcranial Doppler ultrasound
C) Apnea test
D) Cerebral angiography

Question 38: In the management of a patient with intracerebral hemorrhage (ICH), which of the following is the most critical initial step to prevent further neurological deterioration?
A) Immediate surgical evacuation of the hematoma
B) Administration of antihypertensive medication to control blood pressure
C) Initiation of anticoagulant therapy
D) Hyperventilation to reduce intracranial pressure

Question 39: A 55-year-old patient named John is admitted to the ICU with severe acute pancreatitis. He presents with hypotension, tachycardia, and abdominal pain. Laboratory tests reveal elevated serum lipase and amylase levels. Which of the following interventions is most critical in managing John's condition at this stage?
A) Administering intravenous fluids to maintain hemodynamic stability
B) Initiating early enteral nutrition to prevent gut atrophy
C) Providing prophylactic antibiotics to prevent infection
D) Starting analgesics for pain management

Question 40: A 55-year-old patient named John presents to the emergency department with dyspnea, fatigue, and peripheral edema. His echocardiogram reveals a dilated left ventricle with reduced ejection fraction. Considering John's symptoms and echocardiographic findings, what is the most likely type of cardiomyopathy he is experiencing?
A) Hypertrophic Cardiomyopathy
B) Dilated Cardiomyopathy
C) Restrictive Cardiomyopathy
D) Arrhythmogenic Right Ventricular Cardiomyopathy

Question 41: John, a 68-year-old male with a history of hypertension, presents to the emergency department

with sudden severe headache, nausea, and confusion. A CT scan confirms a hemorrhagic stroke. Which immediate management step is crucial to prevent further neurological damage?
A) Administer intravenous mannitol
B) Initiate nimodipine therapy
C) Control blood pressure aggressively
D) Start anticoagulation therapy

Question 42: Emily, a 57-year-old patient, presents to the ICU with sudden onset of severe headache, neck stiffness, and photophobia. A CT scan reveals a subarachnoid hemorrhage. Which of the following is the most critical initial management step to prevent further neurological deterioration in Emily?
A) Administer nimodipine
B) Initiate IV mannitol
C) Start anticoagulation therapy
D) Perform immediate lumbar puncture

Question 43: Mr. Thompson, a 68-year-old male with a history of diabetes mellitus, is recovering from abdominal surgery. During a postoperative assessment, the nurse notices that the surgical wound is showing signs of delayed healing. Which of the following interventions is most appropriate to promote wound healing in this patient?
A) Increase dietary protein intake.
B) Apply heat packs to the wound area.
C) Encourage increased oral fluid intake.
D) Initiate prophylactic antibiotic therapy.

Question 44: A 45-year-old male patient named John, undergoing chemotherapy for acute lymphoblastic leukemia, presents with symptoms of fatigue, nausea, and muscle cramps. Laboratory tests reveal hyperkalemia, hyperuricemia, and elevated serum creatinine levels. As his critical care nurse, what is the most appropriate initial management step to prevent further complications of Tumor Lysis Syndrome?
A) Administer intravenous calcium gluconate
B) Initiate aggressive intravenous hydration
C) Provide oral allopurinol
D) Start renal replacement therapy

Question 45: A 35-year-old patient named John has been admitted to the critical care unit following a traumatic brain injury. He exhibits increased aggression and agitation, especially during nursing interventions. As a critical care nurse, what is the most appropriate initial intervention to manage John's aggressive behavior while ensuring his safety and the safety of the staff?
A) Restrain John physically to prevent harm.
B) Administer a prescribed sedative immediately.
C) Use verbal de-escalation techniques and maintain a calm environment.
D) Increase environmental stimuli to distract John.

Question 46: Sarah, a 58-year-old patient with a history of hypertension and diabetes, is admitted to the ICU with acute kidney injury (AKI) following a severe gastrointestinal bleed. Her lab results show elevated blood urea nitrogen (BUN) and creatinine levels. Which intervention is most appropriate to prevent further renal damage in this scenario?
A) Administer diuretics to increase urine output.
B) Initiate continuous renal replacement therapy (CRRT).
C) Optimize fluid resuscitation to maintain hemodynamic stability.
D) Restrict protein intake to reduce nitrogenous waste.

Question 47: A 55-year-old patient named John presents with a sudden onset of severe headache, nausea, and altered mental status. An MRI reveals a large mass in the left temporal lobe causing midline shift. What is the most appropriate initial management step for this space-occupying lesion?
A) Immediate surgical resection
B) Administration of corticosteroids
C) Initiation of chemotherapy
D) Observation and serial imaging

Question 48: In the management of cerebral palsy (CP) with spasticity, which pharmacological agent is most commonly used to reduce muscle tone and improve functional mobility?
A) Baclofen
B) Diazepam
C) Dantrolene
D) Botulinum toxin

Question 49: Mr. Johnson, a 68-year-old male with a history of hypertension and coronary artery disease, presents to the emergency department with acute shortness of breath, orthopnea, and frothy pink sputum. His vital signs reveal tachycardia and hypertension. Which initial intervention is most critical in managing his acute pulmonary edema?
A) Administering intravenous furosemide
B) Providing supplemental oxygen via nasal cannula
C) Initiating non-invasive positive pressure ventilation (NIPPV)
D) Administering sublingual nitroglycerin

Question 50: In the management of fulminant hepatitis, which of the following is the most critical initial intervention to prevent cerebral edema?
A) Administering intravenous glucose to maintain normoglycemia
B) Initiating lactulose therapy to reduce ammonia levels
C) Implementing strict fluid restriction to prevent hyponatremia
D) Monitoring intracranial pressure and initiating mannitol therapy if needed

Question 51: Which of the following pathogens is most commonly associated with community-acquired pneumonia in adults, requiring consideration for empirical antibiotic therapy?
A) Mycoplasma pneumoniae
B) Streptococcus pneumoniae
C) Haemophilus influenzae
D) Legionella pneumophila

Question 52: A 65-year-old patient named Mr. Thompson presents with sudden onset of pain, pallor, and pulselessness in his right lower limb. As a critical care nurse, you suspect acute peripheral vascular insufficiency. Which of the following immediate interventions is most appropriate to prevent further complications?
A) Administer intravenous heparin immediately.
B) Elevate the affected limb above heart level.
C) Apply a warm compress to the affected area.
D) Initiate aggressive fluid resuscitation.

Question 53: In the context of hyperactive delirium management in critically ill patients, which of the following pharmacological interventions is considered most effective for immediate symptom control?
A) Lorazepam
B) Haloperidol
C) Quetiapine
D) Risperidone

Question 54: John, a 45-year-old male, was admitted to

the ICU following a motor vehicle accident. He presents with respiratory distress, hemoptysis, and decreased breath sounds on auscultation. A chest X-ray reveals patchy infiltrates bilaterally. Based on these findings, what is the most appropriate initial management step for his lung contusion?
A) Administer high-flow oxygen therapy
B) Initiate mechanical ventilation with positive end-expiratory pressure (PEEP)
C) Perform immediate bronchoscopy
D) Administer prophylactic antibiotics

Question 55: Emily, a 45-year-old patient with acute respiratory distress syndrome (ARDS), is being managed in the ICU. Her PaO2/FiO2 ratio is currently 150, and she is on mechanical ventilation. The medical team is considering adjusting her ventilator settings to improve oxygenation while minimizing lung injury. Which of the following strategies is most appropriate for managing Emily's ARDS?
A) Increase tidal volume to 10 mL/kg predicted body weight
B) Implement prone positioning
C) Increase FiO2 to 100%
D) Use high-frequency oscillatory ventilation

Question 56: Sarah, a 45-year-old female, presents to the emergency department with acute lower back pain radiating down her left leg. She reports numbness and tingling in her left foot. Upon examination, you note decreased strength in dorsiflexion of the left foot. Which of the following is the most likely diagnosis?
A) Lumbar spinal stenosis
B) Herniated lumbar disc at L4-L5
C) Sciatica due to piriformis syndrome
D) Sacroiliac joint dysfunction

Question 57: John, a 45-year-old male, was admitted to the ICU following a motor vehicle accident resulting in an acute spinal cord injury at the T6 level. During your assessment, you note that John has bradycardia and hypotension. What is the most appropriate initial intervention to address these symptoms?
A) Administer atropine to manage bradycardia
B) Initiate dopamine infusion for hypotension
C) Elevate the head of the bed to improve circulation
D) Apply a warming blanket to maintain body temperature

Question 58: A 68-year-old male named Mr. Thompson presents to the emergency department with melena, dizziness, and hypotension. He has a history of peptic ulcer disease and is currently taking NSAIDs for chronic arthritis pain. After initial stabilization, what is the most appropriate next step in managing his suspected acute GI hemorrhage?
A) Administer intravenous proton pump inhibitors (PPIs)
B) Perform an urgent endoscopy
C) Initiate blood transfusion
D) Start octreotide infusion

Question 59: In the context of dementia, which neurotransmitter is most commonly associated with memory and cognitive function deficits, often targeted by pharmacological treatments?
A) Dopamine
B) Serotonin
C) Acetylcholine
D) GABA

Question 60: John, a 58-year-old male with a history of type 2 diabetes, presents to the emergency department with confusion, polyuria, and dehydration. His blood glucose level is 620 mg/dL. Which of the following is the most likely diagnosis?

A) Diabetic Ketoacidosis (DKA)
B) Hyperosmolar Hyperglycemic State (HHS)
C) Hypoglycemia
D) Lactic Acidosis

Question 61: In the context of Abdominal Compartment Syndrome (ACS), which of the following is the most reliable method for measuring intra-abdominal pressure (IAP) in critically ill patients?
A) Direct abdominal wall palpation
B) Bladder pressure measurement
C) Gastric tonometry
D) Rectal pressure measurement

Question 62: John, a 62-year-old male with a history of hypertension and diabetes, presents to the emergency department with shortness of breath and fatigue. An echocardiogram reveals an ejection fraction of 35% and significant left ventricular dilation. Which pharmacological intervention is most appropriate to improve his cardiac function?
A) Digoxin
B) Beta-blockers
C) Calcium channel blockers
D) Diuretics

Question 63: John, a 68-year-old patient with a history of heart failure, presents to the emergency department with worsening dyspnea and fatigue. Upon examination, he exhibits jugular venous distention, ascites, and peripheral edema. Which of the following interventions is most appropriate to address his current symptoms?
A) Administer intravenous furosemide
B) Start oral beta-blocker therapy
C) Initiate ACE inhibitor treatment
D) Provide supplemental oxygen therapy

Question 64: A 55-year-old patient named Mr. Johnson, with a history of chronic alcohol use, presents with confusion, ataxia, and ophthalmoplegia. As a critical care nurse, you suspect Wernicke's encephalopathy. Which of the following interventions is most critical to initiate immediately?
A) Administer intravenous thiamine before glucose
B) Provide high-dose intravenous glucose
C) Initiate benzodiazepine therapy
D) Start intravenous hydration with normal saline

Question 65: In managing a critically ill patient experiencing severe agitation, which pharmacological intervention is most appropriate to minimize the risk of delirium while effectively controlling symptoms?
A) Lorazepam
B) Haloperidol
C) Dexmedetomidine
D) Midazolam

Question 66: During a blood transfusion, Mr. Thompson, a 68-year-old patient with chronic kidney disease, suddenly develops chills, fever, and back pain. As a critical care nurse, you suspect a transfusion reaction. Which immediate action is most appropriate to take?
A) Stop the transfusion and maintain IV access with normal saline.
B) Administer antihistamines to alleviate symptoms.
C) Continue the transfusion at a slower rate while monitoring vital signs closely.
D) Increase the rate of transfusion to quickly complete the process.

Question 67: In the context of viral encephalitis, which of the following viruses is most commonly associated with severe neurological complications in adults?

A) Cytomegalovirus (CMV)
B) Herpes Simplex Virus Type 1 (HSV-1)
C) Varicella-Zoster Virus (VZV)
D) Epstein-Barr Virus (EBV)

Question 68: In the context of Acute Kidney Injury (AKI), which of the following biomarkers is considered most reliable for early detection and diagnosis, reflecting kidney tubular damage before changes in serum creatinine levels are observed?
A) Serum Creatinine
B) Blood Urea Nitrogen (BUN)
C) Neutrophil Gelatinase-Associated Lipocalin (NGAL)
D) Cystatin C

Question 69: In the context of pleural effusions, which diagnostic procedure is considered the gold standard for differentiating between transudative and exudative effusions?
A) Chest X-ray
B) Pleural biopsy
C) Thoracentesis with Light's criteria analysis
D) CT scan of the chest

Question 70: In the management of cardiogenic shock, which of the following interventions is most critical in improving myocardial contractility and reducing afterload?
A) Administering norepinephrine
B) Initiating intra-aortic balloon pump therapy
C) Providing intravenous fluids aggressively
D) Using beta-blockers

Question 71: John, a 62-year-old male with a history of hypertension and hyperlipidemia, presents to the emergency department with chest pain radiating to his left arm and jaw. His ECG shows ST-segment elevation in leads II, III, and aVF. Which immediate intervention is most appropriate for John to reduce myocardial damage?
A) Administer intravenous nitroglycerin
B) Initiate aspirin therapy
C) Perform percutaneous coronary intervention (PCI)
D) Start beta-blocker therapy

Question 72: Which gait disorder is characterized by a wide-based, unsteady, and staggering walk often associated with cerebellar dysfunction?
A) Spastic gait
B) Ataxic gait
C) Festinating gait
D) Steppage gait

Question 73: A 65-year-old patient named Mr. Johnson is recovering from a lobectomy due to lung cancer. On the second postoperative day, he exhibits signs of respiratory distress and decreased breath sounds on the operated side. As a critical care nurse, what is the most appropriate initial intervention?
A) Administer supplemental oxygen and reassess in 30 minutes.
B) Perform chest physiotherapy to clear secretions.
C) Prepare for possible re-intubation and mechanical ventilation.
D) Assess for a pneumothorax and prepare for chest tube insertion.

Question 74: A 45-year-old patient named John is admitted to the ICU with severe fatigue, hypotension, and hyponatremia. His medical history reveals long-term corticosteroid use for rheumatoid arthritis. The critical care team suspects adrenal insufficiency. Which of the following is the most appropriate initial treatment for John?
A) Intravenous hydrocortisone
B) Oral fludrocortisone
C) Intravenous dexamethasone
D) Oral prednisone

Question 75: In the management of SIADH (Syndrome of Inappropriate Antidiuretic Hormone Secretion), which of the following interventions is most critical in preventing complications related to hyponatremia?
A) Administration of hypertonic saline
B) Fluid restriction
C) Administration of loop diuretics
D) Increasing dietary sodium intake

Question 76: Mr. Johnson, a 65-year-old patient with a history of stroke, is admitted to the critical care unit. He has difficulty swallowing and is at risk for aspiration. As his nurse, you are monitoring him closely. During your assessment, you notice he has developed a new cough after meals and his oxygen saturation has decreased. Which intervention is most appropriate to reduce the risk of aspiration in Mr. Johnson?
A) Elevate the head of the bed to 30 degrees during meals.
B) Provide thickened liquids with meals.
C) Administer prophylactic antibiotics.
D) Encourage Mr. Johnson to use a straw when drinking.

Question 77: A 45-year-old male named John presents to the emergency department with sudden onset of sharp chest pain and shortness of breath. He has a history of chronic obstructive pulmonary disease (COPD) and is a long-term smoker. On examination, you note decreased breath sounds on the right side and hyperresonance on percussion. Which of the following is the most likely diagnosis?
A) Tension pneumothorax
B) Spontaneous pneumothorax
C) Pleural effusion
D) Pulmonary embolism

Question 78: Sarah, a 35-year-old female, was involved in a high-impact car accident and is suspected of having a pelvic fracture. As a critical care nurse, what is the most immediate action to take upon her arrival at the emergency department?
A) Administer intravenous fluids to prevent hypovolemic shock.
B) Perform a pelvic binder application to stabilize the fracture.
C) Conduct a focused assessment with sonography for trauma (FAST).
D) Obtain a CT scan of the pelvis for detailed evaluation.

Question 79: During the postoperative management of a patient who underwent a craniotomy for tumor resection, which of the following interventions is most critical to prevent increased intracranial pressure (ICP)?
A) Administering hypotonic fluids
B) Elevating the head of the bed to 30 degrees
C) Encouraging frequent coughing exercises
D) Maintaining a supine position

Question 80: In the context of thoracic surgery, which of the following is the most critical parameter to monitor immediately post-operatively to prevent respiratory complications?
A) Central venous pressure (CVP)
B) Arterial blood gases (ABG)
C) Chest tube drainage
D) Oxygen saturation (SpO2)

Question 81: Which of the following factors is most

critical in the initial assessment for developing a care plan to prevent pressure injuries in critically ill patients?
A) Nutritional status
B) Mobility level
C) Skin moisture
D) Patient age

Question 82: In the context of traumatic brain injuries, which of the following is most characteristic of an epidural hematoma compared to other types of intracranial hemorrhages?
A) Rapid onset of symptoms following a lucid interval
B) Gradual onset of symptoms over several days
C) Bleeding occurs between the brain and arachnoid membrane
D) Most commonly associated with rotational injuries

Question 83: In the context of PTSD management, which intervention is considered most effective in reducing symptoms by directly addressing traumatic memories and altering associated negative beliefs?
A) Cognitive Processing Therapy (CPT)
B) Eye Movement Desensitization and Reprocessing (EMDR)
C) Prolonged Exposure Therapy (PE)
D) Trauma-Focused Cognitive Behavioral Therapy (TF-CBT)

Question 84: John, a 68-year-old male patient in the ICU, has been diagnosed with hypoactive delirium following a hip surgery. He exhibits confusion, lethargy, and decreased responsiveness. As his critical care nurse, which of the following interventions is most appropriate to address his hypoactive delirium?
A) Increase environmental stimulation by keeping the lights on and playing music.
B) Administer antipsychotic medication to manage symptoms.
C) Encourage family involvement and reorientation strategies.
D) Provide sedative medication to help with restlessness.

Question 85: In the management of a patient with a subarachnoid hemorrhage (SAH) due to an aneurysm, which of the following interventions is most critical in preventing rebleeding during the acute phase?
A) Administration of nimodipine
B) Maintaining systolic blood pressure below 140 mmHg
C) Initiating anticoagulation therapy
D) Early surgical clipping or endovascular coiling

Question 86: A 55-year-old patient named John is admitted to the ICU with acute hepatic failure. His medical history reveals chronic use of acetaminophen for osteoarthritis pain management. Considering the scenario, which of the following interventions is most critical in managing John's condition?
A) Administering N-acetylcysteine (NAC)
B) Initiating hemodialysis
C) Providing high-dose vitamin K
D) Starting corticosteroid therapy

Question 87: In the context of unstable angina, which of the following diagnostic tests is most likely to provide definitive evidence of myocardial ischemia without necrosis?
A) Troponin I level
B) ECG with ST-segment depression
C) Cardiac MRI
D) Stress echocardiography

Question 88: Emily, a 72-year-old patient with a history of recurrent urinary tract infections, presents with confusion, fever, tachycardia, and hypotension. As her critical care nurse, you suspect urosepsis. Which of the following interventions should be prioritized to stabilize Emily's condition?
A) Administer broad-spectrum antibiotics immediately.
B) Initiate aggressive fluid resuscitation.
C) Obtain blood cultures before starting antibiotics.
D) Administer vasopressors to maintain blood pressure.

Question 89: In the context of managing a patient with a subarachnoid hemorrhage (SAH), which of the following interventions is most critical to prevent rebleeding in the acute phase?
A) Administering nimodipine to prevent vasospasm
B) Maintaining systolic blood pressure below 160 mmHg
C) Initiating anticonvulsant therapy to prevent seizures
D) Providing hypertonic saline to manage cerebral edema

Question 90: John, a 65-year-old male with a history of smoking and recurrent respiratory infections, presents with a persistent productive cough and dyspnea. His sputum culture is negative for bacterial pathogens. Which of the following management strategies is most appropriate for John's chronic bronchitis symptoms?
A) Initiate broad-spectrum antibiotics
B) Prescribe inhaled corticosteroids
C) Recommend smoking cessation and pulmonary rehabilitation
D) Start oral corticosteroids

Question 91: Mrs. Thompson, a 78-year-old patient with a history of osteoporosis and recent hip surgery, is admitted to the critical care unit. She is at high risk for falls due to her musculoskeletal condition and medication regimen. As her nurse, what is the most effective intervention to prevent falls in Mrs. Thompson during her hospital stay?
A) Place a fall risk sign on her door and ensure she wears non-slip socks.
B) Implement hourly rounding to assess her needs and provide assistance.
C) Educate her about using the call light before attempting to get out of bed.
D) Keep the bed in the lowest position with side rails up at all times.

Question 92: John, a 58-year-old male with a history of hypertension and hyperlipidemia, presents to the emergency department with chest pain that started at rest and has persisted for over 20 minutes. An ECG shows ST-segment depression, and his troponin levels are normal. Which initial management step is most appropriate for John in the context of unstable angina?
A) Administer sublingual nitroglycerin
B) Initiate intravenous heparin
C) Administer high-dose statin therapy
D) Perform immediate coronary angiography

Question 93: In the context of rhabdomyolysis, which of the following laboratory findings is most indicative of severe muscle injury and requires immediate clinical intervention?
A) Elevated creatine kinase (CK) levels
B) Increased serum potassium levels
C) Decreased serum calcium levels
D) Elevated lactate dehydrogenase (LDH) levels

Question 94: In the context of muscular dystrophy, which of the following genetic mutations is most commonly associated with Duchenne Muscular Dystrophy (DMD)?
A) Mutations in the SMN1 gene
B) Mutations in the DMD gene
C) Mutations in the COL6A1 gene

D) Mutations in the LMNA gene

Question 95: In the management of Immune Thrombocytopenic Purpura (ITP), which of the following treatments is most appropriate for a patient with severe thrombocytopenia and active bleeding?
A) Intravenous Immunoglobulin (IVIG)
B) Low-dose aspirin
C) Splenectomy
D) Platelet transfusion

Question 96: In the management of acute spinal cord injury, which of the following interventions is most critical in preventing secondary injury during the initial phase of treatment?
A) Administration of high-dose corticosteroids
B) Maintenance of mean arterial pressure (MAP) above 85 mmHg
C) Immediate surgical decompression
D) Use of hypothermia therapy

Question 97: Sarah, a 68-year-old patient with a history of hypertension and hyperlipidemia, presents with transient ischemic attacks (TIAs). Imaging reveals significant carotid artery stenosis. As her critical care nurse, which of the following interventions should be prioritized to reduce her risk of stroke?
A) Initiate dual antiplatelet therapy with aspirin and clopidogrel.
B) Recommend carotid endarterectomy for symptomatic stenosis.
C) Increase antihypertensive medication to lower blood pressure aggressively.
D) Start high-dose statin therapy immediately.

Question 98: In the context of pelvic fractures, which of the following is the most critical initial management step to prevent hemodynamic instability in a patient with suspected pelvic fracture?
A) Immediate surgical intervention
B) Application of a pelvic binder
C) Administration of intravenous fluids
D) Full body CT scan

Question 99: A 68-year-old diabetic patient, Mr. Thompson, is admitted to the ICU with severe dehydration and renal insufficiency. During your assessment, you notice the early signs of a pressure injury on his sacral region. Considering his medical history and current condition, which intervention would be most effective in preventing the progression of this pressure injury?
A) Increase protein intake to promote tissue repair.
B) Implement a repositioning schedule every two hours.
C) Apply a hydrocolloid dressing to maintain a moist environment.
D) Utilize an air-fluidized bed to reduce pressure.

Question 100: In the context of critical care management, which of the following hormones is primarily responsible for increasing renal absorption of water without affecting sodium reabsorption?
A) Aldosterone
B) Antidiuretic Hormone (ADH)
C) Atrial Natriuretic Peptide (ANP)
D) Renin

Question 101: John, a 52-year-old diabetic patient, presents with persistent pain and swelling in his right foot. An MRI reveals bone marrow edema suggestive of osteomyelitis. Blood cultures are negative, but wound cultures show growth of Staphylococcus aureus. Considering the clinical presentation and current guidelines, what is the most appropriate initial treatment for John's condition?
A) Oral ciprofloxacin
B) Intravenous vancomycin
C) Oral clindamycin
D) Intravenous ceftriaxone

Question 102: A 55-year-old patient named Mr. Johnson presents with a non-healing ulcer on his lower leg. He has a history of diabetes mellitus and peripheral artery disease. During assessment, you notice the ulcer has a pale base, minimal exudate, and is located on the lateral aspect of the ankle. Based on this scenario, which type of ulcer is most likely affecting Mr. Johnson?
A) Venous stasis ulcer
B) Diabetic neuropathic ulcer
C) Arterial insufficiency ulcer
D) Pressure ulcer

Question 103: In critically ill patients with acute kidney injury (AKI), which of the following is the most effective strategy to prevent contrast-induced nephropathy (CIN) during diagnostic imaging procedures?
A) Administration of N-acetylcysteine prior to the procedure
B) Use of low-osmolar contrast media
C) Adequate hydration with isotonic saline before and after the procedure
D) Use of sodium bicarbonate infusion

Question 104: A 55-year-old patient named John presents with persistent headaches, nausea, and occasional seizures. An MRI reveals a space-occupying lesion in the frontal lobe. Considering the location and symptoms, what is the most likely type of brain tumor affecting John?
A) Meningioma
B) Glioblastoma multiforme
C) Oligodendroglioma
D) Astrocytoma

Question 105: John, a 65-year-old male with a history of lung cancer, presents to the emergency department with shortness of breath and chest discomfort. On examination, he has muffled heart sounds and distended neck veins. An echocardiogram reveals a large pericardial effusion. Which of the following is the most appropriate immediate management for this patient?
A) Administer diuretics to reduce fluid overload
B) Perform pericardiocentesis to relieve cardiac tamponade
C) Initiate corticosteroid therapy to reduce inflammation
D) Start intravenous fluids to maintain blood pressure

Question 106: Which of the following factors is most likely to exacerbate asthma symptoms in patients with a history of allergic rhinitis?
A) Cold air exposure
B) Exercise
C) Exposure to pollen
D) Emotional stress

Question 107: In the context of gastrointestinal bleeding, which of the following interventions is most critical to perform first in a hemodynamically unstable patient?
A) Administering proton pump inhibitors intravenously
B) Initiating intravenous fluid resuscitation
C) Performing an urgent endoscopy
D) Administering blood transfusions

Question 108: In the context of gastrointestinal resections, which of the following surgical approaches is most likely to be recommended for a patient with familial adenomatous polyposis to prevent colorectal

cancer?
A) Partial colectomy
B) Total proctocolectomy with ileal pouch-anal anastomosis (IPAA)
C) Segmental resection
D) Subtotal colectomy

Question 109: Mr. Johnson, a 68-year-old male, has just undergone a right pneumonectomy due to non-small cell lung cancer. As a critical care nurse, you are monitoring his respiratory status in the immediate postoperative period. Which of the following findings would be most concerning and require immediate intervention?
A) Decreased breath sounds on the right side
B) Tracheal deviation to the left
C) Oxygen saturation of 92% on room air
D) Mild subcutaneous emphysema around the incision site

Question 110: Which of the following complications is most directly associated with prolonged immobility in critically ill patients, particularly affecting musculoskeletal function?
A) Pressure ulcers
B) Deep vein thrombosis (DVT)
C) Muscle atrophy
D) Urinary tract infections (UTIs)

Question 111: A 45-year-old patient named John presents to the emergency department with severe respiratory distress following a motor vehicle accident. Imaging reveals a tracheal perforation. As the critical care nurse, what is the most appropriate initial intervention to stabilize John's condition?
A) Administer high-flow oxygen therapy via non-rebreather mask
B) Prepare for immediate surgical intervention
C) Initiate mechanical ventilation with positive end-expiratory pressure (PEEP)
D) Perform needle decompression of the thorax

Question 112: In the management of a patient with a fractured rib, which intervention is most critical to prevent complications associated with impaired ventilation?
A) Administering high-flow oxygen therapy
B) Encouraging deep breathing exercises
C) Applying a thoracic binder for support
D) Initiating opioid analgesics for pain relief

Question 113: John, a 58-year-old male with a history of hypertension, presents to the emergency department with exertional dyspnea and palpitations. An echocardiogram reveals asymmetric septal hypertrophy. Which of the following interventions is most appropriate for managing his condition and preventing sudden cardiac death?
A) Implantable cardioverter-defibrillator (ICD) placement
B) Beta-blocker therapy
C) Alcohol septal ablation
D) Dual-chamber pacemaker implantation

Question 114: A 68-year-old patient named Mr. Johnson presents to the emergency department with a high fever, productive cough, and shortness of breath. His medical history includes chronic obstructive pulmonary disease (COPD). After initial assessment and chest X-ray, which finding would most strongly suggest a bacterial cause for his acute respiratory infection?
A) Bilateral interstitial infiltrates
B) Consolidation in the right lower lobe
C) Hyperinflated lung fields
D) Diffuse alveolar damage

Question 115: In the management of a traumatic hemothorax, which intervention is most critical to prevent complications associated with retained blood in the pleural space?
A) Immediate needle decompression
B) Chest tube insertion with continuous suction
C) Administration of broad-spectrum antibiotics
D) High-flow oxygen therapy

Question 116: A 75-year-old patient in the ICU develops acute delirium. Which of the following interventions is most effective in managing delirium in this patient, according to current best practices?
A) Administering low-dose antipsychotics
B) Implementing a structured reorientation program
C) Increasing sedative medications at night
D) Using physical restraints to prevent harm

Question 117: In assessing a patient for potential abuse or neglect, which of the following clinical signs is most indicative of physical abuse in the context of musculoskeletal injury?
A) Spiral fractures in non-ambulatory infants
B) Greenstick fractures in toddlers
C) Simple bruises on extremities
D) Hairline fractures in adolescents

Question 118: In patients with myasthenia gravis, which of the following is the most effective initial treatment to improve muscle strength by enhancing neuromuscular transmission?
A) Corticosteroids
B) Plasmapheresis
C) Acetylcholinesterase inhibitors
D) Intravenous immunoglobulin (IVIG)

Question 119: A 55-year-old patient named John presents with symptoms of dyspnea, fatigue, and jugular venous distension. An echocardiogram reveals normal left ventricular size but significantly reduced ventricular filling due to increased myocardial stiffness. Which of the following is the most likely diagnosis for John's condition?
A) Hypertrophic Cardiomyopathy
B) Restrictive Cardiomyopathy
C) Dilated Cardiomyopathy
D) Constrictive Pericarditis

Question 120: Sarah, a 58-year-old female with a history of hypertension and coronary artery disease, is admitted to the ICU with complaints of palpitations and dizziness. Her ECG shows an irregularly irregular rhythm without distinct P waves, consistent with atrial fibrillation. Which of the following is the most appropriate initial treatment to control her heart rate?
A) Amiodarone
B) Digoxin
C) Metoprolol
D) Diltiazem

Question 121: A 45-year-old patient named John is admitted to the ICU with severe thrombocytopenia. His platelet count is critically low, and he presents with petechiae and mucosal bleeding. After reviewing his medical history, you note that he recently started a new medication for atrial fibrillation. Which of the following medications is most likely responsible for John's thrombocytopenia?
A) Warfarin
B) Heparin
C) Digoxin
D) Amiodarone

Question 122: In the context of viral encephalitis, which of the following viruses is most commonly associated with severe neurological damage in adults?
A) Varicella-zoster virus (VZV)
B) Epstein-Barr virus (EBV)
C) Herpes simplex virus type 1 (HSV-1)
D) Cytomegalovirus (CMV)

Question 123: Mrs. Thompson, a 68-year-old patient in the ICU, has been displaying hypoactive delirium post-operatively. As her critical care nurse, you are tasked with identifying the most appropriate intervention to manage her condition. Which of the following actions should you prioritize?
A) Initiate a low-dose antipsychotic medication.
B) Reorient the patient frequently and ensure a calm environment.
C) Increase sensory stimulation to improve alertness.
D) Administer benzodiazepines to reduce anxiety.

Question 124: Sarah, a 68-year-old diabetic patient, presents with a non-healing ulcer on her right foot. Despite appropriate wound care and antibiotic therapy, the ulcer shows minimal improvement. Which of the following interventions is most likely to enhance wound healing in this patient?
A) Increase protein intake to support tissue repair
B) Optimize blood glucose levels to improve circulation
C) Apply hyperbaric oxygen therapy to enhance oxygenation
D) Use topical antimicrobial agents to reduce bacterial load

Question 125: John, a 56-year-old male with a history of liver cirrhosis, presents to the emergency department with confusion, disorientation, and asterixis. His family reports recent dietary indiscretions. Which of the following is the most likely initial treatment to manage his condition?
A) Intravenous thiamine
B) Lactulose administration
C) High-protein diet
D) Intravenous glucose

ANSWER WITH DETAILED EXPLANATION SET [4]

Question 1: Correct Answer: A) Check the pedal pulse on the affected leg.
Rationale: Checking the pedal pulse is crucial as it directly indicates blood flow through the bypass graft, helping assess its patency. While measuring ABI (Option B) provides information about blood flow, it's less immediate and practical post-surgery. Capillary refill time (Option C) offers indirect evidence but isn't as definitive as palpating pulses. Monitoring skin color and temperature (Option D) can suggest perfusion issues but isn't specific for graft patency assessment. Thus, checking the pedal pulse offers immediate and direct evidence of successful revascularization post-fem-pop bypass.

Question 2: Correct Answer: B) Low serum iron and high total iron-binding capacity (TIBC)
Rationale: Iron deficiency anemia is characterized by low serum iron and high TIBC due to increased transferrin levels, reflecting the body's attempt to capture more iron. Option A is incorrect because elevated serum ferritin usually indicates adequate or excess iron stores. Option C is incorrect as high MCV is associated with macrocytic anemias like vitamin B12 deficiency. Option D is incorrect since an increased reticulocyte count suggests a response to anemia but does not specify the type, and it is typically seen in hemolytic anemias or after treatment initiation.

Question 3: Correct Answer: B) Initiate aggressive intravenous fluid resuscitation
Rationale: In acute pancreatitis, early aggressive IV fluid resuscitation is crucial to prevent hypovolemia and maintain organ perfusion. Option A (antibiotics) is not routinely recommended unless infection is suspected. Option C (nasogastric suction) may be used for severe vomiting but isn't an initial step. Option D (parenteral nutrition) is considered if oral intake is not possible for prolonged periods but not immediately necessary. Fluid resuscitation addresses the immediate risk of hypovolemic shock, making it the correct choice.

Question 4: Correct Answer: B) Lorazepam
Rationale: Lorazepam is preferred for initial treatment of status epilepticus because of its rapid onset and efficacy. Phenytoin (A) is used for longer-term control but takes longer to act. Levetiracetam (C) is effective for seizure control but not typically first-line in acute settings. Valproic Acid (D) is useful for various seizure types but lacks the rapid action required for status epilepticus. The choice of Lorazepam aligns with guidelines emphasizing quick seizure termination, crucial in preventing neurological damage.

Question 5: Correct Answer: C) Noradrenergic system
Rationale: The noradrenergic system is primarily implicated in PTSD, especially concerning hyperarousal symptoms. This is due to its role in stress response and arousal regulation, often leading to heightened vigilance and anxiety. While the serotonergic system (Option B) influences mood and anxiety, it is not as directly linked to hyperarousal as the noradrenergic system. The dopaminergic system (Option A) relates more to reward and motivation processes, whereas the GABAergic system (Option D) is associated with inhibitory control but not specifically with PTSD's hyperarousal symptoms.

Question 6: Correct Answer: B) Open reduction and internal fixation (ORIF) with a dynamic hip screw is commonly used for unstable intertrochanteric fractures.
Rationale: Option B is correct because ORIF with a dynamic hip screw provides stability and allows for early mobilization in unstable intertrochanteric fractures, aligning with contemporary surgical practices. Option A is incorrect as closed reduction and casting are not adequate for these fractures due to instability risks. Option C is incorrect as external fixation is not standard due to complications like pin site infections. Option D is incorrect because total hip arthroplasty is reserved for specific cases, such as severe joint damage, not typically young patients with these fracture types.

Question 7: Correct Answer: D) Abdominal distension with absent bowel sounds
Rationale: Abdominal distension with absent bowel sounds suggests paralytic ileus and potential perforation due to transmural necrosis, necessitating urgent surgery. Option A indicates peritoneal irritation but not specifically necrosis. Option B suggests partial obstruction or non-transmural ischemia, while Option C may indicate obstruction but not necessarily necrosis. The absence of bowel sounds in conjunction with distension highlights severe ischemic damage, distinguishing it from other conditions that might present with similar symptoms but less critical implications.

Question 8: Correct Answer: B) Implementing a structured reorientation program
Rationale: Implementing a structured reorientation program is effective for managing hypoactive delirium, as it helps maintain cognitive engagement without excessive sedation. Benzodiazepines (A) can worsen delirium. Increasing environmental stimuli (C) may overwhelm patients, exacerbating symptoms. Antipsychotics (D), while sometimes used, are not first-line due to potential side effects. Reorientation addresses cognitive deficits directly and is supported by evidence-based practice for improving outcomes in hypoactive delirium cases.

Question 9: Correct Answer: B) Perform needle decompression
Rationale: Needle decompression is crucial for tension pneumothorax, as it rapidly alleviates pressure and restores normal intrathoracic dynamics. Option A, administering oxygen, helps in reabsorption but does not immediately relieve pressure. Option C, corticosteroids, are ineffective for mechanical issues like pneumothorax. Option D, antibiotics, are irrelevant unless infection is present. Needle decompression directly addresses the life-threatening nature of a tension pneumothorax by releasing trapped air, making it the most appropriate immediate intervention compared to other supportive or non-specific treatments.

Question 10: Correct Answer: A) Administering Mannitol

Rationale: Mannitol is an osmotic diuretic that effectively reduces ICP by drawing fluid out of brain tissue and into the bloodstream. While hypertonic saline (B) can also reduce ICP, it primarily works by increasing serum osmolality rather than direct diuresis. Elevating the head (C) aids venous drainage but does not utilize osmotic mechanisms. Controlled hyperventilation (D) reduces ICP by causing vasoconstriction via decreased CO2 levels but lacks diuretic action. Thus, Mannitol directly addresses ICP reduction through osmotic diuresis, distinguishing it from other options.

Question 11: Correct Answer: B) Maintaining normothermia during the perioperative period
Rationale: Maintaining normothermia during the perioperative period is crucial for preventing SSIs, as hypothermia can impair immune function and wound healing. While prophylactic antibiotics (A) are important, their timing is critical and usually recommended within one hour before incision. Antiseptic solutions (C) are essential but not as impactful alone without temperature control. Occlusive dressings (D) may protect wounds but do not directly prevent infections like maintaining body temperature does. Normothermia supports optimal physiological conditions, reducing infection risk effectively compared to other options.

Question 12: Correct Answer: B) Increased pulmonary capillary wedge pressure
Rationale: Increased pulmonary capillary wedge pressure (PCWP) is a direct indicator of left ventricular dysfunction because it reflects elevated pressures in the left atrium and pulmonary circulation due to impaired left ventricular ejection. Option A, elevated right atrial pressure, typically indicates right-sided heart issues. Option C, decreased cardiac output, can result from various conditions, not specifically left ventricular dysfunction. Option D, elevated systemic vascular resistance, often relates to afterload issues rather than direct ventricular performance. PCWP directly correlates with left-sided heart function, making it the most specific indicator in this context.

Question 13: Correct Answer: A) Hyperkalemia
Rationale: Hyperkalemia is the most critical electrolyte imbalance in TLS due to its potential to cause life-threatening cardiac arrhythmias. While hypocalcemia, hyperphosphatemia, and hyperuricemia are also associated with TLS, they do not pose an immediate risk of cardiac complications like hyperkalemia. Hypocalcemia can exacerbate cardiac issues but typically results from phosphate imbalances. Hyperphosphatemia primarily affects calcium levels, while hyperuricemia leads to renal complications. Prompt correction of hyperkalemia is essential to prevent cardiac arrest, making it the primary concern in acute TLS management.

Question 14: Correct Answer: A) Administering antihypertensive medication to maintain systolic blood pressure below 160 mmHg
Rationale: Controlling blood pressure is critical in acute ICH management to prevent rebleeding and further neurological damage. Option A is correct as it aligns with guidelines recommending maintaining systolic BP below 160 mmHg. Option B is incorrect because anticoagulation increases bleeding risk. Option C may be necessary but isn't always immediate unless there's significant mass effect. Option D is incorrect; corticosteroids are not routinely recommended for ICH-related edema as they don't improve outcomes and may cause harm.

Question 15: Correct Answer: C) Perform decompressive laparotomy.
Rationale: The correct answer is C) Perform decompressive laparotomy. In cases of Abdominal Compartment Syndrome (ACS), surgical intervention is often necessary to relieve pressure and restore organ perfusion. Option A, increasing fluids, could exacerbate ACS by raising intra-abdominal pressure further. Option B, administering diuretics, may not effectively reduce compartment pressures or address the underlying cause. Option D, elevating the head of the bed, does not directly reduce intra-abdominal pressure and might worsen respiratory mechanics in this context. Therefore, immediate surgical intervention is crucial for ACS management.

Question 16: Correct Answer: B) Alveolar epithelial cell injury and fibroblast proliferation
Rationale: The progressive decline in lung function in pulmonary fibrosis is mainly due to alveolar epithelial cell injury and subsequent fibroblast proliferation, leading to excessive collagen deposition and scarring. Option A is incorrect as excessive mucus production is more associated with obstructive lung diseases like chronic bronchitis. Option C, bronchial smooth muscle hypertrophy, relates to asthma. Option D, pulmonary vasoconstriction, is typically seen in pulmonary hypertension. The correct option focuses on the fibrotic process central to pulmonary fibrosis, distinguishing it from other respiratory pathologies.

Question 17: Correct Answer: A) Consider Alex's cognitive function and decision-making capacity.
Rationale: Cognitive function and decision-making capacity are crucial in assessing risk-taking behavior, as they directly impact a patient's ability to make informed choices. While peer pressure (B) and understanding consequences (D) are relevant, they are secondary to cognitive assessment in clinical judgment. Past medical history (C) provides context but doesn't address current decision-making ability. Therefore, evaluating cognitive function is essential for determining if Alex can make safe decisions about his health and discharge timing.

Question 18: Correct Answer: A) Bowel obstruction
Rationale: Bowel obstruction is the most frequent complication of abdominal adhesions, as they can cause narrowing or blockage of the intestines. While perforation (B) and intra-abdominal abscesses (C) are possible, they occur less commonly than obstructions. Ischemic bowel disease (D), although serious, is not directly linked to adhesions as frequently as obstructions are. Adhesions primarily lead to mechanical issues like obstruction rather than vascular complications like ischemia. This understanding is crucial for clinical judgment in managing post-surgical patients.

Question 19: Correct Answer: B) Decreased platelet count
Rationale: In DIC, decreased platelet count is a key indicator due to excessive consumption of platelets in widespread clotting. Option A is incorrect as fibrinogen levels typically decrease in DIC. Option C is incorrect since hemoglobin levels are not directly affected by DIC. Option D is incorrect because PT usually prolongs due to clotting factor consumption. The correct option, B, reflects the consumptive coagulopathy characteristic of DIC, distinguishing it from other hematological disorders where platelet count may not be as significantly impacted.

Question 20: Correct Answer: B) Assessing pupillary response to light
Rationale: Assessing pupillary response to light is critical as it directly indicates increased intracranial pressure (ICP), which can lead to herniation if not monitored. While hypertension (Option A) and altered respiratory patterns (Option C) can also indicate ICP changes, they are less specific compared to pupillary changes. Infection signs

(Option D) are important but not directly related to immediate ICP complications. Pupillary assessment provides direct insight into cranial nerve function and potential brain swelling, making it the most crucial evaluation in this scenario.

Question 21: Correct Answer: B) Suppressed Thyroid-Stimulating Hormone (TSH) level
Rationale: The most definitive laboratory test for diagnosing hyperthyroidism, particularly in a thyroid storm, is a suppressed TSH level. In hyperthyroidism, excess thyroid hormones lead to negative feedback on the pituitary gland, suppressing TSH production. While elevated Free T4 and increased Total T3 levels (options A and C) are indicative of hyperthyroidism, they do not definitively diagnose it as they can be influenced by other factors. Option D, elevated Reverse T3, is not typically used in diagnosing hyperthyroidism and is more related to non-thyroidal illness syndrome.

Question 22: Correct Answer: C) Initiating intravenous fluid resuscitation
Rationale: The most critical initial treatment in DKA is initiating intravenous fluid resuscitation to restore intravascular volume and improve renal perfusion. Option A, administering insulin, is crucial but follows fluid replacement to avoid hypoperfusion-related complications. Option B, providing oral glucose, is incorrect as hyperglycemia is present. Option D, administering sodium bicarbonate, is reserved for severe acidosis (pH <7.0), not typically first-line. Fluid resuscitation corrects dehydration and helps reduce hyperglycemia by improving kidney function, thus making it the most appropriate initial intervention in this scenario.

Question 23: Correct Answer: B) Decreased serum calcium levels
Rationale: Decreased serum calcium levels are indicative of severe acute pancreatitis and are associated with poor prognosis due to fat necrosis binding calcium. While elevated amylase (A) and lipase (C) are markers of pancreatitis, they do not directly correlate with severity. Increased bilirubin (D) might suggest biliary obstruction but is not specific for pancreatitis severity. Recognizing hypocalcemia's role in severity assessment is crucial for clinical judgment in gastrointestinal critical care.

Question 24: Correct Answer: A) Administration of lactulose
Rationale: Lactulose is a non-absorbable disaccharide that reduces ammonia production by promoting its excretion through conversion to lactic acid, lowering colonic pH, and enhancing ammonia trapping. While dietary protein restriction (B) can decrease ammonia precursors, it is less effective alone. Neomycin (C), an antibiotic, reduces intestinal bacteria but is secondary to lactulose in efficacy. Branched-chain amino acids (D) are nutritional supplements that support muscle metabolism but do not directly reduce ammonia levels. Thus, lactulose's direct impact on ammonia excretion makes it the most effective intervention.

Question 25: Correct Answer: C) Administer intramuscular vitamin B12 injections and a low-residue diet.
Rationale: Intramuscular vitamin B12 injections are essential due to malabsorption in Crohn's disease, as oral supplements may not be absorbed effectively. A low-residue diet helps reduce bowel symptoms. Option A is incorrect because oral B12 may not be absorbed. Option B is inappropriate initially without assessing other interventions. Option D could exacerbate symptoms by increasing bowel activity. Thus, C is the most suitable intervention based on Emily's condition and current clinical guidelines for managing malabsorption in Crohn's disease.

Question 26: Correct Answer: A) Anastomotic leak
Rationale: Anastomotic leak is the most critical complication following an esophagectomy due to its potential for rapid deterioration and sepsis. While chylothorax (B) and recurrent laryngeal nerve injury (C) are significant, they typically present later and are less immediately life-threatening. Pulmonary embolism (D), although severe, is less directly associated with esophageal surgery compared to anastomotic issues. Monitoring for signs such as fever, tachycardia, and chest pain is essential for early detection of leaks, making it a priority in postoperative care.

Question 27: Correct Answer: B) Severe Combined Immunodeficiency (SCID)
Rationale: Severe Combined Immunodeficiency (SCID) is characterized by defects in both humoral and cell-mediated immunity due to genetic mutations affecting T-cell development. This distinguishes SCID from Chronic Granulomatous Disease (A), which involves defective phagocyte function, Common Variable Immunodeficiency (C), which primarily affects antibody production, and Selective IgA Deficiency (D), which involves low levels of IgA but normal T-cell function. The key difference lies in SCID's impact on T-cells, crucial for both arms of adaptive immunity, unlike the more specific deficiencies seen in other options.

Question 28: Correct Answer: A) Monitoring for signs of fat embolism syndrome
Rationale: In the context of femur fractures, fat embolism syndrome (FES) is a critical concern due to fat globules potentially entering the bloodstream post-injury, leading to respiratory distress and neurological symptoms. While hydration (Option B), immobilization (Option C), and compartment syndrome assessment (Option D) are important, FES poses an immediate life-threatening risk, necessitating vigilant monitoring. Option B is less immediate than FES concerns; Option C is routine but not as urgent; Option D is relevant but less common in closed femur fractures compared to FES.

Question 29: Correct Answer: A) Acetaminophen
Rationale: Acetaminophen is the most common cause of drug-induced hepatic failure, particularly in patients with pre-existing liver conditions. It is metabolized in the liver, and excessive doses can lead to toxic metabolites causing liver damage. Ibuprofen and aspirin, though associated with gastrointestinal issues and renal effects, are less likely to cause hepatic failure. Metformin primarily affects glucose metabolism and lactic acidosis risk but not directly linked to hepatic coma. Thus, acetaminophen's hepatotoxic potential makes it the correct answer compared to others focused on different organ systems or effects.

Question 30: Correct Answer: B) Discontinue heparin and initiate argatroban.
Rationale: The correct action for suspected HIT is to discontinue all forms of heparin and start a non-heparin anticoagulant like argatroban. Option A is incorrect because warfarin can worsen thrombosis in acute HIT due to its initial procoagulant effect. Option C is inappropriate as continuing heparin can exacerbate HIT. Option D is misleading since low molecular weight heparins can also trigger HIT. Thus, initiating argatroban effectively addresses the risk of further thrombosis without exacerbating HIT.

Question 31: Correct Answer: D) Insert a chest tube on the affected side.
Rationale: In cases of hemothorax, especially post-

trauma, inserting a chest tube is crucial to evacuate blood from the pleural space and re-expand the lung. Option A, while supportive, does not address the underlying issue. Option B is typically used for tension pneumothorax, not hemothorax. Option C stabilizes hemodynamics but does not resolve pleural space fluid accumulation. Therefore, chest tube insertion directly addresses both respiratory distress and circulatory compromise by removing accumulated blood and allowing lung re-expansion.

Question 32: Correct Answer: C) Video-assisted thoracoscopic surgery (VATS)
Rationale: Video-assisted thoracoscopic surgery (VATS) is often preferred for managing empyema as it allows direct visualization and debridement of the pleural space, facilitating effective drainage and resolution. While intravenous antibiotics (Option A) are crucial for treating infection, they do not address loculated fluid. Thoracentesis (Option B) may temporarily relieve symptoms but is less effective for complex or organized empyema. Chest tube placement (Option D) aids in drainage but may not be sufficient alone for more advanced cases, where VATS provides superior outcomes through comprehensive clearance.

Question 33: Correct Answer: A) Administration of intravenous thrombolytics
Rationale: Intravenous thrombolytics, such as tissue plasminogen activator (tPA), are critical for dissolving clots and restoring blood flow if administered within 3-4.5 hours after symptom onset. While aspirin and anticoagulants help prevent further clots, they do not address acute clot dissolution. Blood pressure control is essential but secondary to immediate clot resolution in acute management. The timely use of thrombolytics directly targets the embolic blockage, reducing ischemic damage more effectively than the other options when considering immediate intervention strategies.

Question 34: Correct Answer: D) Genetic Testing
Rationale: Genetic testing is the most definitive method for diagnosing muscular dystrophy, as it identifies specific gene mutations responsible for the condition. While serum CK levels (Option A) and EMG (Option B) can indicate muscle damage and dysfunction, they are not specific to muscular dystrophy. Muscle biopsy (Option C) can show characteristic changes but may not pinpoint the exact type of muscular dystrophy without genetic confirmation. Genetic testing directly identifies mutations, providing a precise diagnosis essential for targeted management strategies.

Question 35: Correct Answer: C) Computed tomography angiography (CTA)
Rationale: CTA is the preferred diagnostic test for suspected aortic rupture due to its rapid acquisition time, high sensitivity, and ability to provide detailed images of the aorta. While TTE can assess some aspects of the heart and proximal aorta, it lacks detail for distal segments. A chest X-ray may show indirect signs but is not definitive. MRI offers excellent detail but is less accessible in emergencies due to longer acquisition times. Therefore, CTA is crucial for quick confirmation and management planning in suspected aortic rupture cases.

Question 36: Correct Answer: C) Elevation of the head of the bed to 30 degrees
Rationale: Elevating the head of the bed to 30 degrees optimizes venous drainage and reduces ICP, a key measure in managing traumatic brain injury. While hyperventilation (A) can lower ICP by reducing CO2 and cerebral blood flow, it may risk ischemia. Mannitol (B), an osmotic diuretic, decreases ICP but is not always first-line due to potential side effects. Mild hypothermia (D) may reduce metabolic demand but lacks immediate impact on ICP compared to head elevation. Thus, option C is most directly effective and safest for initial ICP reduction.

Question 37: Correct Answer: D) Cerebral angiography
Rationale: Cerebral angiography is considered the gold standard for confirming brain death as it directly visualizes the absence of cerebral blood flow. While EEG (Option A) assesses electrical activity, it does not confirm blood flow absence. Transcranial Doppler ultrasound (Option B) can detect reduced or absent flow but is less definitive than angiography. The apnea test (Option C) evaluates respiratory drive in response to CO2 buildup but does not assess cerebral circulation. Thus, cerebral angiography provides the most conclusive evidence by directly showing no blood reaching the brain.

Question 38: Correct Answer: B) Administration of antihypertensive medication to control blood pressure
Rationale: The most critical initial step in managing ICH is controlling elevated blood pressure, as it can exacerbate bleeding and worsen outcomes. Antihypertensive medications are prioritized to stabilize the patient's condition. While surgical evacuation (A) may be necessary, it depends on hematoma size and location. Anticoagulant therapy (C) is contraindicated as it can increase bleeding risk. Hyperventilation (D) is not a first-line treatment for ICH; its use is reserved for acute ICP reduction in certain cases. Thus, option B addresses immediate stabilization by mitigating further hemorrhage risk.

Question 39: Correct Answer: A) Administering intravenous fluids to maintain hemodynamic stability
Rationale: Administering intravenous fluids is crucial in the early management of severe acute pancreatitis to address hypovolemia and maintain hemodynamic stability. While early enteral nutrition (B) is important, it is secondary to stabilizing vital signs. Prophylactic antibiotics (C) are not routinely recommended unless there's evidence of infection. Analgesics (D) are essential for comfort but do not address the immediate life-threatening issues like fluid resuscitation does. Therefore, option A is prioritized based on contemporary guidelines focusing on initial stabilization in severe cases.

Question 40: Correct Answer: B) Dilated Cardiomyopathy
Rationale: The correct answer is B) Dilated Cardiomyopathy, characterized by ventricular dilation and systolic dysfunction, leading to reduced ejection fraction. Option A (Hypertrophic Cardiomyopathy) typically involves thickened heart muscle without dilation. Option C (Restrictive Cardiomyopathy) features normal-sized ventricles but impaired filling. Option D (Arrhythmogenic Right Ventricular Cardiomyopathy) primarily affects the right ventricle and involves fibrofatty replacement of myocardium. John's presentation aligns with dilated cardiomyopathy due to the combination of ventricular dilation and systolic dysfunction observed in his echocardiogram.

Question 41: Correct Answer: C) Control blood pressure aggressively
Rationale: Controlling blood pressure aggressively is critical in managing hemorrhagic stroke to prevent rebleeding and limit hematoma expansion. While mannitol (A) may reduce intracranial pressure, it does not address the underlying cause. Nimodipine (B) is used for subarachnoid hemorrhage to prevent vasospasm but is not immediately relevant here. Anticoagulation (D) is contraindicated as it can worsen bleeding. The correct approach focuses on stabilizing hemodynamics to

minimize further neurological compromise.
Question 42: Correct Answer: A) Administer nimodipine
Rationale: Nimodipine is crucial in managing subarachnoid hemorrhage due to its ability to prevent cerebral vasospasm, a common complication that can lead to ischemic injury. Option B (mannitol) is used for reducing intracranial pressure but not specific for vasospasm prevention. Option C (anticoagulation therapy) is contraindicated as it could exacerbate bleeding. Option D (lumbar puncture) is inappropriate after diagnosis by CT and could worsen herniation risk if increased intracranial pressure exists. Thus, nimodipine's role in preventing vasospasm makes it the correct choice.
Question 43: Correct Answer: A) Increase dietary protein intake.
Rationale: Increasing dietary protein intake is crucial for wound healing as proteins provide essential amino acids necessary for tissue repair and regeneration. Option B (applying heat packs) could exacerbate inflammation. Option C (increasing fluid intake) supports hydration but does not directly enhance healing. Option D (prophylactic antibiotics) may prevent infection but does not address the underlying need for nutrients critical in wound repair. Thus, option A is most aligned with promoting healing through nutritional support in a diabetic patient.
Question 44: Correct Answer: B) Initiate aggressive intravenous hydration
Rationale: Initiating aggressive intravenous hydration is crucial in managing Tumor Lysis Syndrome as it helps dilute serum electrolytes and supports renal excretion of uric acid and other metabolites. Option A (calcium gluconate) addresses hyperkalemia but does not prevent TLS progression. Option C (allopurinol) reduces uric acid production but is not immediate. Option D (renal replacement therapy) is for severe cases when conservative measures fail. Hydration directly addresses the root cause by enhancing renal clearance, thus preventing complications associated with TLS.
Question 45: Correct Answer: C) Use verbal de-escalation techniques and maintain a calm environment.
Rationale: Verbal de-escalation and maintaining a calm environment are primary interventions for managing aggression, as they address underlying anxiety without escalating the situation. Option A, physical restraint, may increase agitation and is a last resort. Option B, administering sedatives, should follow non-pharmacological methods unless immediate risk exists. Option D, increasing stimuli, can exacerbate aggression by overwhelming the patient. Thus, option C aligns with contemporary practices prioritizing non-invasive strategies in behavioral management.
Question 46: Correct Answer: C) Optimize fluid resuscitation to maintain hemodynamic stability.
Rationale: Optimizing fluid resuscitation is crucial in maintaining perfusion and preventing further renal damage in AKI, especially post-hemorrhage. Diuretics (A) may worsen hypovolemia. CRRT (B) is indicated for severe cases but not first-line here. Protein restriction (D) addresses uremia but doesn't address acute hemodynamics. Thus, ensuring adequate fluid balance directly supports renal perfusion and function, making option C the most appropriate intervention in this scenario.
Question 47: Correct Answer: B) Administration of corticosteroids
Rationale: Corticosteroids are administered to reduce cerebral edema associated with space-occupying lesions, providing rapid symptomatic relief. While immediate surgical resection (A) may be necessary, it is not the first step. Chemotherapy (C) is not an initial treatment for acute symptoms. Observation (D) is inappropriate given the severity of symptoms and midline shift. Corticosteroids effectively manage increased intracranial pressure temporarily, allowing time for further diagnostic and therapeutic planning, distinguishing it from other options that do not address acute symptom relief directly.
Question 48: Correct Answer: D) Botulinum toxin
Rationale: Botulinum toxin is frequently used in CP to target specific muscle groups, reducing spasticity and improving mobility. While Baclofen (A) is also used, it affects the central nervous system more broadly and may cause sedation. Diazepam (B) can reduce spasticity but has significant sedative effects. Dantrolene (C) works peripherally on muscles but is less effective in targeted spasticity management compared to botulinum toxin. The targeted action of botulinum toxin makes it preferable for localized treatment in CP, aligning with contemporary therapeutic strategies.
Question 49: Correct Answer: C) Initiating non-invasive positive pressure ventilation (NIPPV)
Rationale: Initiating NIPPV is critical as it reduces preload and afterload while improving oxygenation, addressing both respiratory distress and hemodynamic compromise. While A) furosemide aids in fluid removal, its effect is not immediate. B) Supplemental oxygen improves hypoxemia but does not address the underlying mechanical issues. D) Nitroglycerin can reduce preload but may not be sufficient alone in severe cases. NIPPV provides immediate respiratory support and hemodynamic stabilization, crucial in acute pulmonary edema management.
Question 50: Correct Answer: D) Monitoring intracranial pressure and initiating mannitol therapy if needed
Rationale: The most critical initial intervention in fulminant hepatitis is monitoring intracranial pressure and administering mannitol to manage cerebral edema. While A), B), and C) are relevant, they do not directly address acute cerebral edema management. Glucose administration (A) helps prevent hypoglycemia, lactulose (B) reduces ammonia but is more preventive, and fluid restriction (C) prevents hyponatremia but does not directly manage existing cerebral edema. Mannitol directly reduces intracranial pressure, addressing the immediate threat of brain herniation in fulminant hepatitis.
Question 51: Correct Answer: B) Streptococcus pneumoniae
Rationale: Streptococcus pneumoniae is the leading cause of community-acquired pneumonia (CAP) in adults, necessitating its inclusion in empirical antibiotic regimens. While Mycoplasma pneumoniae and Haemophilus influenzae are significant pathogens, they are less prevalent than Streptococcus pneumoniae. Legionella pneumophila, though important, is typically associated with specific risk factors and environmental exposures. The choice of antibiotics often targets Streptococcus pneumoniae due to its frequency and potential severity. Understanding the epidemiology and common pathogens aids in effective clinical decision-making and appropriate treatment selection.
Question 52: Correct Answer: A) Administer intravenous heparin immediately.
Rationale: Administering intravenous heparin is crucial to prevent thrombus propagation and further ischemia in acute peripheral vascular insufficiency. Option B (elevating the limb) can worsen ischemia by reducing perfusion pressure. Option C (warm compress) may increase metabolic demand and exacerbate tissue damage. Option D (fluid resuscitation) does not directly

address the clot causing ischemia. Heparin acts quickly to inhibit clot formation, aligning with contemporary practice guidelines for managing acute arterial occlusion, making it the most appropriate immediate intervention in this scenario.

Question 53: Correct Answer: B) Haloperidol
Rationale: Haloperidol is the preferred choice for immediate control of hyperactive delirium symptoms due to its rapid onset and efficacy in reducing agitation. Unlike lorazepam (A), which can worsen delirium by causing sedation, haloperidol directly addresses psychotic symptoms without significant sedation. Quetiapine (C) and risperidone (D) are atypical antipsychotics used for longer-term management but lack the immediate action required in acute settings. The selection of haloperidol is based on its established use in critical care for acute delirium control, making it superior for urgent symptom management.

Question 54: Correct Answer: B) Initiate mechanical ventilation with positive end-expiratory pressure (PEEP)
Rationale: The correct answer is B) Initiate mechanical ventilation with PEEP. Lung contusions can lead to alveolar instability and impaired gas exchange. PEEP helps maintain alveolar recruitment and improve oxygenation. Option A, high-flow oxygen, may not be sufficient alone for severe contusions. Option C, bronchoscopy, is not indicated unless there's airway obstruction or foreign body suspicion. Option D, prophylactic antibiotics, are not routinely recommended without signs of infection. Therefore, initiating mechanical ventilation with PEEP is the most effective initial management step in this scenario.

Question 55: Correct Answer: B) Implement prone positioning
Rationale: Prone positioning improves oxygenation in ARDS by enhancing ventilation-perfusion matching and reducing lung stress. Option A (increasing tidal volume) risks volutrauma; Option C (increasing FiO2) can cause oxygen toxicity; Option D (high-frequency oscillatory ventilation) lacks evidence of superiority over conventional methods. Prone positioning, supported by recent studies, optimizes gas exchange without exacerbating lung injury, making it the preferred strategy in this scenario.

Question 56: Correct Answer: B) Herniated lumbar disc at L4-L5
Rationale: The symptoms of acute lower back pain with radiation down the leg and weakness in dorsiflexion suggest a herniated disc at L4-L5, compressing the L5 nerve root. Option A, lumbar spinal stenosis, typically presents with bilateral symptoms and worsens with walking. Option C, piriformis syndrome, causes sciatic-like symptoms but without specific motor weakness like dorsiflexion loss. Option D, sacroiliac joint dysfunction, often causes localized pain without radicular symptoms or significant motor deficits. Hence, B is the most accurate diagnosis based on Sarah's presentation.

Question 57: Correct Answer: A) Administer atropine to manage bradycardia
Rationale: Atropine is indicated to treat bradycardia associated with neurogenic shock following acute spinal cord injury. Bradycardia results from unopposed vagal tone due to sympathetic nervous system disruption. While dopamine (Option B) can address hypotension, it does not directly target bradycardia. Elevating the head (Option C) may worsen hypotension by reducing venous return. A warming blanket (Option D) addresses hypothermia but not cardiovascular instability. Therefore, Option A is correct as it directly targets the underlying cause of John's symptoms in this scenario.

Question 58: Correct Answer: B) Perform an urgent endoscopy
Rationale: The correct answer is B) Perform an urgent endoscopy. In cases of suspected acute GI hemorrhage, particularly with a history of peptic ulcer disease, early endoscopy is crucial for diagnosis and potential therapeutic intervention. Option A (Administer IV PPIs) is important but typically follows diagnostic confirmation. Option C (Initiate blood transfusion) may be necessary based on hemoglobin levels but does not address the source of bleeding. Option D (Start octreotide infusion) is more relevant for variceal bleeding rather than peptic ulcers. Early endoscopy allows direct visualization and treatment, making it the priority.

Question 59: Correct Answer: C) Acetylcholine
Rationale: Acetylcholine is crucial for memory and cognitive functions, and its deficiency is linked to Alzheimer's disease, a common form of dementia. Pharmacological treatments often aim to increase acetylcholine levels to improve symptoms. Dopamine (A) and serotonin (B) are more related to mood disorders, while GABA (D) primarily affects inhibitory neurotransmission. Though dopamine can influence cognition, it is not the primary target in dementia treatment. Understanding these differences helps in identifying acetylcholine as the key neurotransmitter involved in dementia-related cognitive deficits.

Question 60: Correct Answer: B) Hyperosmolar Hyperglycemic State (HHS)
Rationale: HHS is characterized by extremely high blood glucose levels (>600 mg/dL), significant dehydration, and altered mental status without ketoacidosis. Unlike DKA (Option A), which presents with ketones in urine and acidosis, HHS typically occurs in type 2 diabetes and lacks significant acidosis. Hypoglycemia (Option C) would present with low blood glucose, not high. Lactic acidosis (Option D) involves elevated lactate levels and metabolic acidosis, not primarily hyperglycemia. The absence of ketones and extreme hyperglycemia points to HHS as the correct diagnosis.

Question 61: Correct Answer: B) Bladder pressure measurement
Rationale: Bladder pressure measurement is considered the gold standard for assessing intra-abdominal pressure due to its accuracy and minimal invasiveness. Direct abdominal wall palpation (A) is subjective and unreliable. Gastric tonometry (C) measures gastric mucosal CO2, not IAP. Rectal pressure measurement (D) is not standard for IAP assessment. The bladder method involves inserting a catheter into the bladder and measuring pressure, reflecting true intra-abdominal conditions, making it superior to other methods in clinical practice.

Question 62: Correct Answer: B) Beta-blockers
Rationale: Beta-blockers are recommended for dilated cardiomyopathy to improve cardiac function by reducing heart rate and myocardial oxygen demand, thus enhancing ejection fraction. Digoxin (A) can help with symptoms but doesn't improve survival. Calcium channel blockers (C) are not typically used due to negative inotropic effects. Diuretics (D) manage symptoms but don't directly enhance cardiac function or ejection fraction like beta-blockers. Beta-blockers are supported by contemporary research for improving outcomes in dilated cardiomyopathy patients.

Question 63: Correct Answer: A) Administer intravenous furosemide
Rationale: Administering intravenous furosemide is the

most appropriate intervention for John's acute symptoms of fluid overload, as it effectively reduces volume overload by promoting diuresis. While beta-blockers (B) and ACE inhibitors (C) are essential in chronic heart failure management for their long-term benefits on cardiac remodeling and mortality reduction, they do not provide immediate relief of fluid retention symptoms. Supplemental oxygen (D) may assist with hypoxia but does not address the underlying fluid overload causing John's symptoms. Therefore, diuretics are prioritized in acute decompensated heart failure scenarios.

Question 64: Correct Answer: A) Administer intravenous thiamine before glucose
Rationale: Administering intravenous thiamine before glucose is crucial in preventing further neurological damage in Wernicke's encephalopathy. Thiamine deficiency can be exacerbated by glucose administration, worsening symptoms. Option B (high-dose glucose) without prior thiamine can precipitate acute encephalopathy. Option C (benzodiazepines) addresses alcohol withdrawal but not the root cause here. Option D (hydration) does not address the immediate risk of neurological deterioration due to thiamine deficiency. Thus, prioritizing thiamine administration aligns with contemporary research and recognized treatment protocols for this condition.

Question 65: Correct Answer: C) Dexmedetomidine
Rationale: Dexmedetomidine is favored for managing agitation in critically ill patients as it provides sedation without significant respiratory depression and has a lower risk of causing delirium compared to benzodiazepines like Lorazepam (A) and Midazolam (D). While Haloperidol (B) is used for delirium, it does not have sedative properties. Dexmedetomidine acts on alpha-2 adrenergic receptors, offering sedation and analgesia with minimal cognitive impairment, making it superior in minimizing delirium risk compared to the other options.

Question 66: Correct Answer: A) Stop the transfusion and maintain IV access with normal saline.
Rationale: The correct action is to stop the transfusion immediately and maintain IV access with normal saline to prevent further reaction and ensure venous access for potential treatments. Option B is incorrect as antihistamines are not first-line in acute reactions. Option C is inappropriate because continuing the transfusion could worsen the reaction. Option D is dangerous as increasing the rate could exacerbate symptoms and lead to severe complications. This approach aligns with contemporary guidelines on managing suspected transfusion reactions effectively.

Question 67: Correct Answer: B) Herpes Simplex Virus Type 1 (HSV-1)
Rationale: HSV-1 is the most common cause of severe viral encephalitis in adults, leading to significant neurological complications. While CMV, VZV, and EBV can cause encephalitis, they are less frequently associated with severe cases in immunocompetent adults. CMV typically affects immunocompromised individuals; VZV can cause encephalitis post-varicella or zoster infection but is less common. EBV is primarily linked to infectious mononucleosis with rare neurological involvement. The high incidence and severity of HSV-1 encephalitis make it the primary concern among these options.

Question 68: Correct Answer: C) Neutrophil Gelatinase-Associated Lipocalin (NGAL)
Rationale: NGAL is a sensitive biomarker for early detection of AKI, indicating tubular injury before serum creatinine levels rise. Unlike serum creatinine and BUN, which reflect kidney function and can lag behind actual damage, NGAL rises rapidly in response to tubular injury. Cystatin C is useful for estimating glomerular filtration rate but not as specific for early tubular damage. This makes NGAL superior for early diagnosis in AKI, providing clinicians with a timely intervention window compared to other markers that may delay detection.

Question 69: Correct Answer: C) Thoracentesis with Light's criteria analysis
Rationale: Thoracentesis with Light's criteria analysis is the gold standard for differentiating transudative from exudative pleural effusions. It involves analyzing pleural fluid protein and lactate dehydrogenase levels. Chest X-rays (Option A) can detect effusions but cannot differentiate types. Pleural biopsy (Option B) helps diagnose specific conditions like malignancy but is not primarily used for distinguishing effusion types. A CT scan (Option D) provides detailed imaging but lacks biochemical differentiation capability. Thus, thoracentesis with Light's criteria remains essential for accurate diagnosis.

Question 70: Correct Answer: B) Initiating intra-aortic balloon pump therapy
Rationale: Initiating intra-aortic balloon pump (IABP) therapy is crucial as it enhances myocardial perfusion and decreases afterload, improving cardiac output. While norepinephrine (Option A) increases blood pressure, it can elevate afterload, worsening cardiac workload. Aggressive fluid administration (Option C) may exacerbate pulmonary congestion in cardiogenic shock. Beta-blockers (Option D) reduce myocardial oxygen demand but are not suitable during acute decompensation. IABP specifically addresses both contractility and afterload issues, making it the optimal intervention for immediate hemodynamic support in cardiogenic shock.

Question 71: Correct Answer: C) Perform percutaneous coronary intervention (PCI)
Rationale: PCI is the most effective immediate intervention to restore blood flow in ST-elevation myocardial infarction (STEMI), minimizing myocardial damage. While aspirin (B) is critical for antiplatelet effects, it does not directly restore perfusion. Intravenous nitroglycerin (A) helps reduce chest pain but is not definitive treatment. Beta-blockers (D) are beneficial post-stabilization but not immediately crucial in acute STEMI management. PCI directly targets the occlusion, making it superior in urgent scenarios like John's.

Question 72: Correct Answer: B) Ataxic gait
Rationale: Ataxic gait is a wide-based, unsteady, and staggering walk commonly linked to cerebellar dysfunction. The cerebellum is crucial for coordination and balance, which are impaired in ataxia. Spastic gait (A) involves stiff movements due to upper motor neuron lesions. Festinating gait (C) is seen in Parkinson's disease, characterized by short, accelerating steps. Steppage gait (D) results from foot drop due to peripheral nerve damage. The key difference lies in the underlying neurological cause; ataxic gait specifically relates to cerebellar issues.

Question 73: Correct Answer: D) Assess for a pneumothorax and prepare for chest tube insertion.
Rationale: In post-lobectomy patients, pneumothorax is a common complication leading to respiratory distress and decreased breath sounds. Immediate assessment and preparation for chest tube insertion can relieve symptoms by re-expanding the lung. Option A delays necessary intervention, risking further deterioration. Option B is inappropriate without ruling out pneumothorax as it may

worsen the condition. Option C is premature without addressing the underlying issue of potential pneumothorax first. Recognizing these subtle differences is crucial in critical care nursing, aligning with contemporary research on postoperative thoracic surgery complications.

Question 74: Correct Answer: A) Intravenous hydrocortisone
Rationale: Intravenous hydrocortisone is the initial treatment of choice for suspected adrenal insufficiency, especially in acute settings, due to its glucocorticoid and mineralocorticoid effects. Oral fludrocortisone (B) is used for long-term management but not acute treatment. Intravenous dexamethasone (C), while a glucocorticoid, lacks mineralocorticoid activity, making it less suitable initially. Oral prednisone (D) is inappropriate in an acute crisis due to delayed onset and oral route limitations. Hydrocortisone's dual action makes it ideal for addressing both glucocorticoid and mineralocorticoid deficiencies rapidly.

Question 75: Correct Answer: B) Fluid restriction
Rationale: Fluid restriction is the cornerstone in managing SIADH to prevent further dilutional hyponatremia. While hypertonic saline (A) can be used in severe cases, it risks rapid sodium correction. Loop diuretics (C) may aid in excreting free water but are not first-line due to potential electrolyte imbalances. Increasing dietary sodium (D) does not address the underlying issue of water retention. Therefore, fluid restriction remains the most effective initial intervention to control serum sodium levels and prevent neurological complications associated with hyponatremia.

Question 76: Correct Answer: B) Provide thickened liquids with meals.
Rationale: Providing thickened liquids (Option B) reduces the risk of aspiration by slowing down the swallowing process, allowing better coordination and reducing penetration into the airway. Elevating the head of the bed (Option A) helps but isn't as effective alone without dietary modifications. Prophylactic antibiotics (Option C) do not prevent aspiration; they treat infections post-aspiration. Using a straw (Option D) can increase aspiration risk by directing liquid quickly to the pharynx, challenging those with dysphagia. Thus, Option B directly addresses Mr. Johnson's swallowing difficulties, making it most appropriate.

Question 77: Correct Answer: B) Spontaneous pneumothorax
Rationale: Spontaneous pneumothorax is common in patients with COPD due to bleb rupture. Decreased breath sounds and hyperresonance suggest air in the pleural space. Tension pneumothorax (A) involves hemodynamic instability, which isn't present here. Pleural effusion (C) would show dullness, not hyperresonance. Pulmonary embolism (D) typically presents with normal breath sounds or crackles, not decreased breath sounds and hyperresonance. The scenario aligns with spontaneous pneumothorax given John's risk factors and clinical presentation.

Question 78: Correct Answer: B) Perform a pelvic binder application to stabilize the fracture.
Rationale: Applying a pelvic binder is crucial as it stabilizes the fracture and reduces hemorrhage risk, which is vital in acute management. While intravenous fluids (Option A) are essential for preventing shock, immediate stabilization takes precedence. A FAST exam (Option C) helps identify internal bleeding but does not directly address fracture stabilization. A CT scan (Option D) provides detailed imaging but delays immediate intervention. Thus, Option B is prioritized for its direct impact on reducing morbidity and mortality in pelvic fractures.

Question 79: Correct Answer: B) Elevating the head of the bed to 30 degrees
Rationale: Elevating the head of the bed to 30 degrees is crucial in preventing increased ICP by promoting venous drainage from the brain. Hypotonic fluids (Option A) can exacerbate cerebral edema, increasing ICP. Frequent coughing (Option C) raises ICP due to increased intrathoracic pressure. A supine position (Option D) may impede venous outflow, elevating ICP. Thus, Option B is correct as it effectively balances cerebral perfusion and venous return, minimizing ICP risks post-craniotomy.

Question 80: Correct Answer: D) Oxygen saturation (SpO2)
Rationale: Monitoring oxygen saturation (SpO2) is crucial post-thoracic surgery as it provides immediate feedback on the patient's respiratory status and gas exchange efficiency, helping to detect hypoxemia early. While ABG analysis (Option B) offers comprehensive data, it is not continuously available. Chest tube drainage (Option C) is important for detecting bleeding or pneumothorax but doesn't directly assess oxygenation. Central venous pressure (Option A) monitors fluid status but is less relevant for immediate respiratory assessment. SpO2 allows continuous, non-invasive monitoring, crucial for timely intervention in respiratory complications.

Question 81: Correct Answer: B) Mobility level
Rationale: Mobility level is crucial as immobility significantly increases pressure injury risk due to prolonged pressure on skin. While nutritional status (A), skin moisture (C), and patient age (D) are important, they are secondary in initial assessment. Nutritional deficits can worsen skin integrity, moisture can lead to maceration, and age affects skin resilience, but without addressing mobility, these factors alone cannot prevent pressure injuries effectively. Prioritizing mobility allows for targeted interventions like repositioning and support surfaces to mitigate risk.

Question 82: Correct Answer: A) Rapid onset of symptoms following a lucid interval
Rationale: An epidural hematoma typically presents with a rapid onset of symptoms after an initial lucid interval due to arterial bleeding, usually from the middle meningeal artery. This differentiates it from subdural hematomas (Option B), which have a gradual symptom onset due to venous bleeding. Option C describes subdural hematomas, where bleeding occurs between the dura mater and arachnoid membrane. Option D is more characteristic of diffuse axonal injury rather than epidural hematoma. Understanding these distinctions is crucial for accurate diagnosis and treatment in critical care settings.

Question 83: Correct Answer: B) Eye Movement Desensitization and Reprocessing (EMDR)
Rationale: EMDR is recognized for its unique approach involving bilateral stimulation to process traumatic memories and modify negative beliefs, shown to be highly effective in PTSD treatment. While CPT, PE, and TF-CBT are also evidence-based therapies targeting PTSD symptoms, EMDR's distinctive mechanism of action makes it particularly potent. CPT focuses on cognitive restructuring, PE emphasizes repeated exposure to trauma cues, and TF-CBT combines trauma-sensitive interventions with cognitive-behavioral techniques. EMDR's specific efficacy in altering memory processing distinguishes it as the correct answer.

Question 84: Correct Answer: C) Encourage family

involvement and reorientation strategies.
Rationale: Encouraging family involvement and using reorientation strategies (C) are key interventions for managing hypoactive delirium, as they help anchor the patient in reality without exacerbating symptoms. Option A could worsen confusion by overstimulating the patient. Option B might be considered but is not first-line due to potential side effects. Option D is inappropriate as sedation can worsen hypoactivity. Therefore, option C is correct because it addresses the underlying cognitive issues while promoting a supportive environment for recovery.
Question 85: Correct Answer: D) Early surgical clipping or endovascular coiling
Rationale: Early surgical clipping or endovascular coiling is crucial to prevent rebleeding in aneurysmal SAH. While nimodipine (Option A) reduces vasospasm risk, it does not prevent rebleeding. Maintaining systolic blood pressure (Option B) is important but secondary to securing the aneurysm. Anticoagulation therapy (Option C) increases bleeding risk and is contraindicated. Therefore, securing the aneurysm through clipping or coiling directly addresses and prevents rebleeding by isolating the aneurysm from cerebral circulation, making Option D the most critical intervention.
Question 86: Correct Answer: A) Administering N-acetylcysteine (NAC)
Rationale: N-acetylcysteine (NAC) is the antidote for acetaminophen overdose, crucial for preventing liver damage by replenishing glutathione stores. Hemodialysis (Option B) is not typically first-line for acetaminophen toxicity. High-dose vitamin K (Option C) is used for coagulopathy due to vitamin K deficiency, not acetaminophen-induced liver failure. Corticosteroids (Option D) are not indicated in this context and may worsen liver function. NAC's role in detoxifying harmful metabolites makes it the most critical intervention, distinguishing it from other treatments aimed at different mechanisms or conditions.
Question 87: Correct Answer: B) ECG with ST-segment depression
Rationale: An ECG with ST-segment depression is indicative of myocardial ischemia, a hallmark of unstable angina. Unlike troponin I, which indicates myocardial necrosis, ST-segment changes occur due to ischemia without cell death. Cardiac MRI can show structural changes but is not typically used acutely. Stress echocardiography assesses function under stress but isn't definitive in acute settings. Thus, while all options assess cardiac health, only ECG changes directly indicate ischemia specific to unstable angina.
Question 88: Correct Answer: B) Initiate aggressive fluid resuscitation.
Rationale: Fluid resuscitation is crucial in stabilizing patients with urosepsis to address hypoperfusion and maintain organ function. While administering antibiotics (Option A) is essential, fluids take precedence to support circulation. Blood cultures (Option C) should be obtained but not delay fluid therapy. Vasopressors (Option D) are used if hypotension persists despite adequate fluid resuscitation. The priority is to restore hemodynamic stability through fluids before other interventions.
Question 89: Correct Answer: B) Maintaining systolic blood pressure below 160 mmHg
Rationale: Maintaining systolic blood pressure below 160 mmHg is crucial to prevent rebleeding in SAH. Elevated blood pressure increases the risk of rebleeding, a major cause of mortality. While nimodipine (A) prevents vasospasm, it doesn't directly address rebleeding.

Anticonvulsants (C) are important but not primarily for rebleeding prevention. Hypertonic saline (D) manages cerebral edema but doesn't directly impact rebleeding risk. Thus, controlling blood pressure is paramount, aligning with contemporary guidelines and research on SAH management.
Question 90: Correct Answer: C) Recommend smoking cessation and pulmonary rehabilitation
Rationale: The primary management for chronic bronchitis involves addressing underlying causes, such as smoking cessation, which reduces inflammation and progression. Pulmonary rehabilitation improves lung function and quality of life. Option A (broad-spectrum antibiotics) is incorrect due to the absence of bacterial infection. Option B (inhaled corticosteroids) may help with inflammation but are not first-line without asthma symptoms. Option D (oral corticosteroids) are reserved for acute exacerbations, not chronic management. Thus, option C directly targets the cause and optimizes long-term outcomes in chronic bronchitis.
Question 91: Correct Answer: B) Implement hourly rounding to assess her needs and provide assistance.
Rationale: Hourly rounding (Option B) effectively prevents falls by proactively addressing patient needs, reducing their likelihood of attempting risky movements alone. While non-slip socks and signage (Option A) are helpful, they don't actively engage or monitor the patient. Educating on call light use (Option C) is important but doesn't guarantee compliance or understanding, especially if cognitive impairments are present. Keeping side rails up (Option D) can pose additional risks, such as entrapment or climbing over them, which might increase fall risk rather than reduce it. Hence, proactive engagement through hourly rounding is most effective.
Question 92: Correct Answer: A) Administer sublingual nitroglycerin
Rationale: Sublingual nitroglycerin is the first-line treatment for relieving chest pain in unstable angina due to its vasodilatory effects, improving coronary blood flow. While intravenous heparin (Option B) is crucial for anticoagulation, it follows initial symptom relief. High-dose statins (Option C) are important long-term but not immediate interventions. Immediate coronary angiography (Option D) is reserved for high-risk patients or those not responding to medical therapy. Therefore, sublingual nitroglycerin is prioritized initially for rapid symptom relief.
Question 93: Correct Answer: A) Elevated creatine kinase (CK) levels
Rationale: Elevated creatine kinase (CK) levels are a hallmark of rhabdomyolysis, reflecting severe muscle injury. While increased serum potassium (B) can occur due to cell lysis and cause cardiac issues, CK elevation directly indicates muscle breakdown severity. Decreased serum calcium (C) may result from calcium binding to damaged muscle, but it's less specific than CK for diagnosing rhabdomyolysis. Elevated LDH (D) is non-specific and can indicate various tissue injuries. Therefore, CK is the primary marker for assessing the extent of muscle damage in rhabdomyolysis.
Question 94: Correct Answer: B) Mutations in the DMD gene
Rationale: Duchenne Muscular Dystrophy (DMD) is primarily caused by mutations in the DMD gene, which encodes for dystrophin, a protein crucial for muscle fiber integrity. The SMN1 gene mutation is related to spinal muscular atrophy, not DMD. COL6A1 mutations are linked to collagen VI-related myopathies, and LMNA mutations are associated with Emery-Dreifuss muscular

dystrophy.

Question 95: Correct Answer: A) Intravenous Immunoglobulin (IVIG)
Rationale: Intravenous Immunoglobulin (IVIG) is the preferred treatment for severe thrombocytopenia with active bleeding in ITP, as it rapidly increases platelet counts. Option B, low-dose aspirin, is contraindicated due to increased bleeding risk. Option C, splenectomy, is considered in chronic cases but not suitable for acute management. Option D, platelet transfusion, provides only temporary relief as autoantibodies destroy transfused platelets. Thus, IVIG remains the most effective immediate treatment option in this scenario.

Question 96: Correct Answer: B) Maintenance of mean arterial pressure (MAP) above 85 mmHg
Rationale: Maintaining MAP above 85 mmHg is crucial to ensure adequate spinal cord perfusion, reducing the risk of secondary injury. While high-dose corticosteroids (Option A) were historically used, their benefits are controversial and not universally recommended. Immediate surgical decompression (Option C) is vital for certain cases but not universally applicable. Hypothermia therapy (Option D) is experimental and lacks sufficient evidence for routine use. Therefore, ensuring proper perfusion through MAP management remains the most consistent strategy supported by contemporary research for preventing further damage in acute spinal cord injury.

Question 97: Correct Answer: B) Recommend carotid endarterectomy for symptomatic stenosis.
Rationale: Carotid endarterectomy is recommended for patients with significant symptomatic carotid artery stenosis to prevent stroke. Option A is less effective alone without addressing the stenosis surgically. Option C might help long-term but isn't immediate intervention. Option D reduces cholesterol but does not directly address mechanical obstruction. Carotid endarterectomy directly removes the plaque causing the stenosis, thereby reducing stroke risk significantly, aligning with current guidelines for symptomatic patients with significant stenosis.

Question 98: Correct Answer: B) Application of a pelvic binder
Rationale: The application of a pelvic binder is crucial for stabilizing the pelvis and reducing bleeding by compressing the fracture site, which helps prevent hemodynamic instability. While intravenous fluids (Option C) are important for resuscitation, they do not address bleeding directly. Immediate surgical intervention (Option A) might be necessary later but is not the first step. A full body CT scan (Option D) is essential for diagnosis but does not stabilize the patient initially. The binder's role in mechanical stabilization makes it the priority in acute management.

Question 99: Correct Answer: D) Utilize an air-fluidized bed to reduce pressure.
Rationale: Utilizing an air-fluidized bed (Option D) is most effective for reducing pressure on vulnerable areas like the sacral region, especially in patients with compromised skin integrity due to diabetes and dehydration. While increasing protein intake (Option A) supports tissue repair, it does not directly alleviate pressure. Repositioning (Option B) is essential but less effective than specialized beds in high-risk cases. Hydrocolloid dressings (Option C) maintain moisture but do not relieve pressure. The air-fluidized bed addresses both pressure reduction and skin protection comprehensively.

Question 100: Correct Answer: B) Antidiuretic Hormone (ADH)
Rationale: Antidiuretic Hormone (ADH), also known as vasopressin, is crucial for water reabsorption in the kidneys, specifically acting on the collecting ducts to increase water permeability and absorption without altering sodium reabsorption. Aldosterone (Option A) increases both sodium and water reabsorption. Atrial Natriuretic Peptide (Option C) promotes sodium and water excretion. Renin (Option D) initiates a cascade that indirectly affects sodium balance but not directly similar to ADH. Understanding these distinctions is essential for managing fluid balance in critical care settings.

Question 101: Correct Answer: B) Intravenous vancomycin
Rationale: The most appropriate initial treatment for suspected osteomyelitis caused by Staphylococcus aureus, particularly in a diabetic patient, is intravenous vancomycin due to its efficacy against MRSA. Option A, oral ciprofloxacin, is less effective against MRSA. Option C, oral clindamycin, is not the first-line therapy for severe infections like osteomyelitis. Option D, intravenous ceftriaxone, lacks adequate MRSA coverage. Vancomycin's broad coverage against resistant strains makes it the preferred choice in this scenario, aligning with contemporary guidelines for managing osteomyelitis in diabetic patients.

Question 102: Correct Answer: C) Arterial insufficiency ulcer
Rationale: The characteristics described—pale base, minimal exudate, and location on the lateral ankle—are indicative of an arterial insufficiency ulcer, common in patients with peripheral artery disease. Venous stasis ulcers typically have more exudate and occur on the medial malleolus. Diabetic neuropathic ulcers are usually found on weight-bearing areas like the plantar surface of the foot. Pressure ulcers develop over bony prominences due to prolonged pressure. Understanding these distinctions helps in accurate diagnosis and treatment planning for integumentary complications in critical care settings.

Question 103: Correct Answer: C) Adequate hydration with isotonic saline before and after the procedure
Rationale: Adequate hydration with isotonic saline is the most effective strategy to prevent CIN, as it dilutes nephrotoxic agents and maintains renal perfusion. While N-acetylcysteine (A) and sodium bicarbonate (D) have been used, evidence supporting their efficacy is less robust. Low-osmolar contrast media (B) reduces risk but does not replace hydration's effectiveness. Hydration directly addresses intravascular volume status, crucial in preventing AKI. Therefore, despite other options having some theoretical benefits, isotonic saline hydration remains the cornerstone intervention according to current guidelines and research findings.

Question 104: Correct Answer: B) Glioblastoma multiforme
Rationale: Glioblastoma multiforme is the most common and aggressive primary brain tumor in adults, often presenting with symptoms like headaches, nausea, and seizures due to its rapid growth and mass effect. While meningiomas are common, they typically cause symptoms through compression rather than invasion. Oligodendrogliomas can present similarly but are less aggressive. Astrocytomas can occur in the frontal lobe but vary greatly in severity. The rapid symptom progression and frontal lobe location make glioblastoma multiforme the most likely diagnosis for John's case.

Question 105: Correct Answer: B) Perform pericardiocentesis to relieve cardiac tamponade
Rationale: In the context of pericardial effusion with signs of cardiac tamponade (muffled heart sounds, distended

neck veins), immediate pericardiocentesis (Option B) is critical to relieve pressure on the heart. Diuretics (Option A) are not effective for tamponade; they may worsen hypotension. Corticosteroids (Option C) are used for inflammatory causes but do not address acute tamponade. Intravenous fluids (Option D) can temporarily support blood pressure but do not resolve tamponade. Thus, Option B is essential for immediate relief and stabilization in this scenario.

Question 106: Correct Answer: C) Exposure to pollen
Rationale: Exposure to pollen is a common trigger for asthma exacerbations, especially in individuals with allergic rhinitis, due to its role as an allergen that can provoke both upper and lower respiratory tract responses. While cold air and exercise can induce bronchoconstriction, they are not directly linked to allergic pathways like pollen. Emotional stress may affect asthma indirectly through behavioral or physiological changes but lacks the direct allergenic effect of pollen. Understanding these distinctions helps in managing and preventing asthma attacks effectively.

Question 107: Correct Answer: B) Initiating intravenous fluid resuscitation
Rationale: Initiating intravenous fluid resuscitation is crucial for stabilizing hemodynamically unstable patients with gastrointestinal bleeding. It addresses hypovolemia and maintains perfusion to vital organs. While administering proton pump inhibitors (Option A) reduces acid secretion, it does not immediately stabilize hemodynamics. Urgent endoscopy (Option C) is diagnostic and therapeutic but secondary to initial stabilization. Blood transfusions (Option D) are essential but typically follow fluid resuscitation to address volume deficits. Therefore, Option B is prioritized based on immediate physiological needs and aligns with contemporary clinical guidelines.

Question 108: Correct Answer: B) Total proctocolectomy with ileal pouch-anal anastomosis (IPAA)
Rationale: Total proctocolectomy with IPAA is the preferred approach for familial adenomatous polyposis due to the high risk of colorectal cancer. This method removes the entire colon and rectum, significantly reducing cancer risk. Partial colectomy and segmental resection leave portions of the colon intact, increasing cancer risk. Subtotal colectomy removes most but not all of the colon, still posing a cancer threat. The IPAA creates a new pathway for waste elimination while preserving continence, making it superior in preventing cancer progression in these patients.

Question 109: Correct Answer: B) Tracheal deviation to the left
Rationale: Tracheal deviation to the left after a right pneumonectomy suggests mediastinal shift, which can compromise cardiovascular function and requires immediate intervention. A) Decreased breath sounds on the right are expected post-pneumonectomy. C) Oxygen saturation of 92% is slightly low but not immediately alarming in this context. D) Mild subcutaneous emphysema can occur postoperatively but is not as urgent as tracheal deviation. The key difference is that option B indicates a potentially life-threatening situation requiring prompt action, unlike the other options which represent less critical postoperative findings.

Question 110: Correct Answer: C) Muscle atrophy
Rationale: Muscle atrophy is a direct consequence of prolonged immobility, leading to decreased muscle mass and strength due to lack of use. While pressure ulcers (A), DVT (B), and UTIs (D) are complications associated with immobility, they are not directly related to musculoskeletal function. Pressure ulcers result from sustained pressure on the skin, DVT from venous stasis, and UTIs from urinary stasis. Muscle atrophy uniquely impacts the musculoskeletal system by reducing muscle tissue, emphasizing the need for early mobilization in critical care settings.

Question 111: Correct Answer: A) Administer high-flow oxygen therapy via non-rebreather mask
Rationale: Administering high-flow oxygen is crucial to improve oxygenation and stabilize the patient initially. Surgical intervention (B) is necessary but not immediate; preparation takes time. Mechanical ventilation with PEEP (C) may worsen the perforation by increasing airway pressure. Needle decompression (D) addresses tension pneumothorax, not tracheal perforation. The priority is to ensure adequate oxygen delivery while preparing for further interventions, making option A the most appropriate initial step.

Question 112: Correct Answer: B) Encouraging deep breathing exercises
Rationale: Encouraging deep breathing exercises is crucial in preventing atelectasis and pneumonia, common complications due to impaired ventilation from rib fractures. While high-flow oxygen (A) can address hypoxemia, it doesn't improve lung expansion. Thoracic binders (C) may restrict breathing, worsening ventilation. Opioid analgesics (D), although necessary for pain management, can suppress respiratory drive. Therefore, deep breathing exercises directly enhance alveolar ventilation and lung expansion, making them the most effective intervention in this context.

Question 113: Correct Answer: A) Implantable cardioverter-defibrillator (ICD) placement
Rationale: ICD placement is crucial for preventing sudden cardiac death in patients with hypertrophic cardiomyopathy at high risk. While beta-blockers (B) manage symptoms by reducing heart rate and contractility, they do not prevent sudden death. Alcohol septal ablation (C) reduces obstruction but is not primarily for sudden death prevention. Dual-chamber pacemakers (D) are generally used for rhythm management, not sudden death prevention. The ICD is specifically indicated in patients with significant risk factors, such as previous cardiac arrest or family history of sudden cardiac death, aligning with contemporary guidelines.

Question 114: Correct Answer: B) Consolidation in the right lower lobe
Rationale: Consolidation in the right lower lobe strongly suggests a bacterial pneumonia, often seen in acute respiratory infections caused by bacteria like Streptococcus pneumoniae. Option A, bilateral interstitial infiltrates, typically indicates viral infections or atypical pneumonia. Option C, hyperinflated lung fields, is associated with COPD exacerbations rather than bacterial infections. Option D, diffuse alveolar damage, is more indicative of acute respiratory distress syndrome (ARDS). Thus, consolidation aligns best with bacterial infection given Mr. Johnson's symptoms and history.

Question 115: Correct Answer: B) Chest tube insertion with continuous suction
Rationale: Chest tube insertion with continuous suction is crucial to effectively evacuate blood from the pleural space, preventing complications such as fibrothorax and infection. Needle decompression (A) is primarily for tension pneumothorax, not hemothorax. Antibiotics (C) are supportive but do not address blood evacuation. High-flow oxygen (D) improves oxygenation but does not resolve the underlying issue of retained blood. The primary goal is to remove blood efficiently, making chest

tube insertion with suction the correct choice.

Question 116: Correct Answer: B) Implementing a structured reorientation program

Rationale: Implementing a structured reorientation program is most effective for managing delirium by promoting cognitive engagement and reducing confusion. Option A, administering antipsychotics, can be helpful but is not the first-line treatment due to potential side effects. Increasing sedatives (Option C) may worsen delirium by increasing sedation and confusion. Physical restraints (Option D) can increase agitation and risk of injury. Thus, reorientation programs address the root causes of delirium without the adverse effects associated with pharmacological or physical interventions.

Question 117: Correct Answer: A) Spiral fractures in non-ambulatory infants

Rationale: Spiral fractures in non-ambulatory infants are highly suggestive of physical abuse due to the twisting mechanism required, which is inconsistent with typical accidental injuries in this age group. Greenstick fractures (Option B) and simple bruises (Option C) may occur from normal play or accidental falls. Hairline fractures (Option D) can result from sports activities in adolescents. The key distinction lies in the developmental capabilities and typical injury patterns for each age group, making spiral fractures a red flag for abuse.

Question 118: Correct Answer: C) Acetylcholinesterase inhibitors

Rationale: Acetylcholinesterase inhibitors, such as pyridostigmine, are the first-line treatment for myasthenia gravis as they increase acetylcholine availability at neuromuscular junctions, improving muscle strength. Corticosteroids (Option A) are used for long-term immune suppression but not as initial treatment. Plasmapheresis (Option B) and IVIG (Option D) are reserved for acute exacerbations or pre-surgical preparation. These options are closely related but differ in their immediate application and mechanism of action, making Option C the most suitable initial choice.

Question 119: Correct Answer: B) Restrictive Cardiomyopathy

Rationale: Restrictive cardiomyopathy is characterized by normal ventricular size but impaired filling due to myocardial stiffness, aligning with John's symptoms and echocardiogram results. Hypertrophic cardiomyopathy (A) involves thickened ventricular walls, while dilated cardiomyopathy (C) features enlarged ventricles. Constrictive pericarditis (D) can mimic restrictive patterns but typically involves pericardial thickening or calcification. The key difference is that restrictive cardiomyopathy directly affects myocardial compliance without significant changes in ventricular wall thickness or size, unlike the other options.

Question 120: Correct Answer: C) Metoprolol

Rationale: Metoprolol is often preferred for initial rate control in atrial fibrillation due to its effectiveness in reducing ventricular response by blocking beta-adrenergic receptors. While amiodarone (A) can be used for rhythm control, it's not first-line for rate control. Digoxin (B) is less effective during exertion and not typically first choice. Diltiazem (D), a calcium channel blocker, is also effective but may be less preferred in patients with concurrent heart failure or hypotension compared to beta-blockers like metoprolol.

Question 121: Correct Answer: B) Heparin

Rationale: Heparin-induced thrombocytopenia (HIT) is a well-documented adverse effect where the immune system forms antibodies against platelet factor 4-heparin complexes, leading to platelet destruction. Warfarin (A) typically affects coagulation factors rather than platelets directly. Digoxin (C), used for heart rate control, does not commonly cause thrombocytopenia. Amiodarone (D), while having multiple side effects, is not known to cause significant thrombocytopenia like heparin. Therefore, heparin is the most likely cause of John's condition based on his recent medication history and symptoms.

Question 122: Correct Answer: C) Herpes simplex virus type 1 (HSV-1)

Rationale: Herpes simplex virus type 1 (HSV-1) is the most common cause of severe viral encephalitis in adults, leading to significant neurological damage if untreated. While VZV and EBV can cause neurological complications, they are less frequently associated with acute encephalitis compared to HSV-1. CMV primarily affects immunocompromised individuals rather than the general adult population. The key difference lies in HSV-1's neurotropism and prevalence as a causative agent of encephalitis, making it the primary concern for severe neurological outcomes in adults.

Question 123: Correct Answer: B) Reorient the patient frequently and ensure a calm environment.

Rationale: The primary intervention for hypoactive delirium is non-pharmacological, focusing on reorientation and a calm environment (Option B). Antipsychotics (Option A) are used cautiously due to side effects. Increasing sensory stimulation (Option C) may worsen confusion. Benzodiazepines (Option D) can exacerbate delirium, especially in elderly patients. Therefore, frequent reorientation and maintaining a calm setting are essential to manage hypoactive delirium effectively, aligning with contemporary research emphasizing non-drug interventions as first-line management.

Question 124: Correct Answer: B) Optimize blood glucose levels to improve circulation

Rationale: Optimizing blood glucose levels is crucial for diabetic patients as hyperglycemia impairs wound healing by affecting circulation and immune response. While increased protein intake (A) supports tissue repair, it does not address underlying circulatory issues. Hyperbaric oxygen therapy (C) can enhance healing but is less effective if glycemic control is poor. Topical antimicrobials (D) help reduce bacterial load but do not directly address impaired healing due to poor circulation and high blood glucose. Thus, maintaining optimal blood glucose is paramount for effective wound healing in diabetic patients like Sarah.

Question 125: Correct Answer: B) Lactulose administration

Rationale: Lactulose is the correct treatment for hepatic encephalopathy, as it reduces ammonia levels by promoting its excretion. Option A (Intravenous thiamine) is used for Wernicke's encephalopathy, not hepatic. Option C (High-protein diet) could worsen hepatic encephalopathy due to increased ammonia production. Option D (Intravenous glucose) does not address ammonia accumulation directly. The key difference lies in targeting ammonia reduction specifically, which lactulose effectively achieves by acidifying the colon and trapping ammonia for excretion.